Claude Brown

MANCHILD IN THE PROMISED LAND

With a New Introduction by Nathan McCall

A Touchstone Book
Published by Simon & Schuster
New York   London   Toronto   Sydney   New Delhi

Touchstone
A Division of Simon & Schuster, Inc.
1230 Avenue of the Americas
New York, NY 10020

All the names in this book—with the exception of public figures, judges, staff members at the Wiltwyck School for Boys, Mr. Alfred A. Cohen, the Reverend William M. James, Mr. Louis Howard, and the author—are entirely fictitious, and any resemblance to the names of living persons is wholly coincidental.

This Touchstone trade paperback edition January 2012

TOUCHSTONE and colophon are registered trademarks of Simon & Schuster, Inc.

For information about special discounts for bulk purchases,
please contact Simon & Schuster Special Sales at
1-866-506-1949 or business@simonandschuster.com.

The Simon & Schuster Speakers Bureau can bring authors to your live event. For more information or to book an event contact the Simon & Schuster Speakers Bureau at 1-866-248-3049 or visit our website at www.simonspeakers.com.

Designed by Jacquelynne Hudson

Manufactured in the United States of America

13 15 17 19 20 18 16 14

Library of Congress Control Number: 2011937817

ISBN 978-1-4516-2667-4
ISBN 978-1-4516-3157-9 (pbk)
ISBN 978-1-4516-2617-9 (ebook)

To the late Eleanor Roosevelt,
who founded the Wiltwyck School for Boys,
and to the Wiltwyck School, which is still finding Claude Browns

Introduction
By Nathan McCall

Claude Brown's *Manchild in the Promised Land* has the power to transform lives. I don't recall when I was first introduced to the book—by the time I ran across it I was well into my adult years—and I have been unable to shake the feeling that it was not soon enough. Lord knows there were plenty of times growing up when I could have benefited from having read that book. Claude Brown's account was stunningly real to me. As much as a book can actually be an experience, the story carried me back to the streets.

Brown's rowdy journey from puberty to adulthood was surprisingly similar to my own wild escapades which came years after he terrorized New York City streets. Like him, my stormy passage began with juvenile scrapes with the law and eventually escalated into street fights, drug deals, and gunplay. It all drew to a screeching halt years later when, at age twenty, a botched armed robbery landed me in jail. I emerged from prison and went through a makeover of sorts, which eventually led me to pen my own autobiography, Makes Me Wanna Holler.

At its core, Manchild is a tale about youthful rebellion and the thrashing search for self. It is an account of Brown's thorny voyage, wrapped in a whole slew of urban exploits.

Indeed, "Sonny," as Brown was known growing up, was a hard-core delinquent in his day. He hung with guys called Turk and Butch and Kid. They ran the streets of Harlem, plunging into mischief and petty crime. Brown played hooky as often as he showed up for classes, and he graduated through the ranks of reform schools like most kids get grade promotions. He dashed from one adventure to another at such breakneck speed that his exasperated mother wondered aloud: "Boy, why you so damn bad?"

I could relate to so many of Brown's challenges, especially to his ultimate struggle to escape the hood and build a productive life for himself. The book left me wondering: What if I had encountered Manchild before going through my own destructive stretch? Would I have continued in that direction or altered paths?

Of course, that is impossible to know. I do know this, though: In *Manchild*, Brown not only got it down, he got it right. Rarely does somebody as thoroughly addicted to the streets as Brown get in a position to write about it. Hell, few people survive intact, let alone publish chronicles that illuminate the harrowing experiences for the rest of the world.

That's why, even now, some five decades after its 1965 publication, the book still delivers with the force of a slug to the gut. That's why Brown's raucous memoir remains one of the seminal accounts of black life in urban America.

Anyone who has read *Manchild* can appreciate its remarkable staying power. What makes this story so engrossing is the authentic voice that does the telling. Brown narrated the tale with unflinching candor in the gritty street lingo of his day. And he blended two elements that, when artfully applied, often make for an effective literary pairing: tragedy and humor.

Without stooping to sermonizing or psychobabble, the book offers blunt, incisive commentary on our society. While turning the pages, one cannot help but wonder: What does it say about America that Brown and his buddies were conditioned from the get-go for the tragic consequences of low expectations? And how do we account for the chilling casualness with which Claude Brown resigned himself to a life of crime and imprisonment?

Throughout the book, such weighty issues come nestled in a breezy narrative that is laugh-out-loud funny. Readers will howl while following Brown into his first clumsy romance with a girl called Sugar. He was crazy for Sugar, but she was too "ugly" to date in public.

And then there was Brown's annual reform school visit to the home of— get this—Eleanor Roosevelt, who was deeply committed to social causes. After pondering why he'd not seen roaches in her big house, Brown concluded the sneaky bugs would likely come out of hiding after he and the rest of Eleanor's guests were gone.

Humor aside, *Manchild* is much more than an entertaining yarn about an extremely wayward child. This is a sociological work in its own right.

Manchild provides a glimpse into the plight of generations of black families that fled the suffocating rural South in the 1940s, '50s, and '60s. They migrated North, only to find that the concrete "Promised Land" was merely a different, more densely populated hell.

The sojourn that landed Brown's family in New York is reminiscent of the crossings of many ethnic migrations. Yet *Manchild* demonstrated that the African-American version of that rite was a uniquely dicey undertaking. It was loaded with racial land mines that often exploded, leaving dark travelers' lives shattered.

Claude Brown survived. He had every reason to crumble under the weight of the limited options history handed him—and there were times in this riveting tale when it seemed he might just yield to violence or drugs or madness and self-destruct. Yet, against enormous odds he claimed his life as his own and had one helluva ball. After a trip to law school, he ultimately devoted himself to social activism on behalf of at-risk youth.

I met Claude Brown some years ago in Washington, D.C. I had just published *Makes Me Wanna Holler* and was traveling the promotion circuit. Brown and I were brought to BET to do a joint interview.

Brown was jovial and very generous with advice. "You're gonna meet a lot of people and get invited to a lot of parties," he predicted. "Don't let too many people buy you drinks."

That was classic "Sonny," trying to pull my coat.

On some level, I'd expected the cocky dude who'd fondly alluded to "short-pants days" to pimp through the doorway, sidle, up and slap me five. But here, before me, was an older man. Potbellied and gray, Brown had earned his street creds nearly a generation before my time. The images *Manchild* evoked were so powerful and clearly drawn that Brown the youngblood, the fastliving cat who gave as much as he got, had remained frozen in my mind.

That's what great books do: They arrest the imagination and leave it suspended, sometimes indefinitely.

People old enough to actually remember the America of *Manchild* often use the book as a reference point. For many blacks the book authenticated their particular reality, which was largely overlooked in the broader world. In the 1950s and '60s, when Martin Luther King and others commanded the nation's attention by marching in the streets, there were a whole lot of disengaged Claude Browns, invisible black folk, *hanging* in the streets.

Readers too young to have experienced the period will nevertheless recognize universal elements in *Manchild* that ring strikingly familiar. Like few writers then or since, Brown captured the essence of what it means to confront a world run by adults who either don't know, or seem to have forgotten, just how tough it is to manage the business of growing up.

In this, the twenty-first century, so often cited brightly as the age of

Obama, it would be tempting to assume that Brown's story merely recalls days long gone by. It is a testament to *Manchild's* raw, commanding narrative that when read today the story remains startlingly relevant. It still shouts with the urgency of now.

Ultimately, *Manchild* sounds a piercing alarm about the isolation felt by blacks stuffed into the nation's city centers. Since the times "Sonny" raced through Harlem, raising hell, so much for African-Americans has changed and so much has remained the same.

Preface

I want to talk about the first Northern urban generation of Negroes. I want to talk about the experiences of a misplaced generation, of a misplaced people in an extremely complex, confused society. This is a story of their searching, their dreams, their sorrows, their small and futile rebellions, and their endless battle to establish their own place in America's greatest metropolis—and in America itself.

The characters are sons and daughters of former Southern sharecroppers. These were the poorest people of the South, who poured into New York City during the decade following the Great Depression. These migrants were told that unlimited opportunities for prosperity existed in New York and that there was no "color problem" there. They were told that Negroes lived in houses with bathrooms, electricity, running water, and indoor toilets. To them, this was the "promised land" that Mammy had been singing about in the cotton fields for many years.

Going to New York was good-bye to the cotton fields, good-bye to "Massa Charlie," good-bye to the chain gang, and, most of all, good-bye to those sunup-to-sundown working hours. One no longer had to wait to get to heaven to lay his burden down; burdens could be laid down in New York.

So, they came, from all parts of the South, like all the black chillun o' God following the sound of Gabriel's horn on that long-overdue Judgment Day. The Georgians came as soon as they were able to pick train fare off the peach trees. They came from South Carolina where the cotton stalks were bare. The North Carolinians came with tobacco tar beneath their fingernails.

They felt as the Pilgrims must have felt when they were coming to America. But these descendants of Ham must have been twice as happy as the Pilgrims, because they had been catching twice the hell. Even while planning the trip, they sang spirituals as "Jesus Take My Hand" and "I'm on My Way" and chanted, "Hallelujah, I'm on my way to the promised land!"

It seems that Cousin Willie, in his lying haste, had neglected to tell the folks down home about one of the most important aspects of the promised land: it was a slum ghetto. There was a tremendous difference in the way life was lived up North. There were too many people full of hate and bitterness crowded into a dirty, stinky, uncared-for closet-size section of a great city.

Before the soreness of the cotton fields had left Mama's back, her knees were getting sore from scrubbing "Goldberg's" floor. Nevertheless, she was better off; she had gone from the fire into the frying pan.

The children of these disillusioned colored pioneers inherited the total lot of their parents—the disappointments, the anger. To add to their misery, they had little hope of deliverance. For where does one run to when he's already in the promised land?

1

"**Run!**"

Where?

Oh, hell! Let's get out of here!

"Turk! Turk! I'm shot!"

I could hear Turk's voice calling from a far distance, telling me not to go into the fish-and-chips joint. I heard, but I didn't understand. The only thing I knew was that I was going to die.

I ran. There was a bullet in me trying to take my life, all thirteen years of it.

I climbed up on the bar yelling, "Walsh, I'm shot. I'm shot." I could feel the blood running down my leg. Walsh, the fellow who operated the fish-and-chips joint, pushed me off the bar and onto the floor. I couldn't move now, but I was still completely conscious.

Walsh was saying, "Git outta here, kid. I ain't got no time to play."

A woman was screaming, mumbling something about the Lord, and saying, "Somebody done shot that poor child."

Mama ran in. She jumped up and down, screaming like a crazy woman. I began to think about dying. The worst part of dying was thinking about the things and the people that I'd never see again. As I lay there trying to imagine what being dead was like, the policeman who had been trying to control Mama gave up and bent over me. He asked who had shot me. Before I could answer, he was asking me if I could hear him. I told him that I didn't know who had shot me and would he please tell Mama to stop jumping up and down. Every time Mama came down on that shabby floor, the bullet lodged in my stomach felt like a hot poker.

Another policeman had come in and was struggling to keep the crowd outside. I could see Turk in the front of the crowd. Before the cops came, he asked me if I was going to tell them that he was with me. I never answered. I looked at him and wondered if he saw who shot me. Then his question began to ring in my head: "Sonny, you gonna tell 'em I was with you?" I was bleeding on a dirty floor in a fish-and-chips joint, and Turk was standing there in the doorway hoping that I would die before I could tell the cops that he was with me. Not once did Turk ask me how I felt.

Hell, yeah, I thought, I'm gonna tell 'em.

It seemed like hours had passed before the ambulance finally arrived. Mama wanted to go to the hospital with me, but the ambulance attendant said she was too excited. On the way to Harlem Hospital, the cop who was riding with us asked Dad what he had to say. His answer was typical: "I told him about hanging out with those bad-ass boys." The cop was a little surprised. This must be a rookie, I thought.

The next day, Mama was at my bedside telling me that she had prayed and the Lord had told her that I was going to live. Mama said that many of my friends wanted to donate some blood for me, but the hospital would not accept it from narcotics users.

This was one of the worst situations I had ever been in. There was a tube in my nose that went all the way to the pit of my stomach. I was being fed intravenously, and there was a drain in my side. Everybody came to visit me, mainly out of curiosity. The girls were all anxious to know where I had gotten shot. They had heard all kinds of tales about where the bullet struck. The bolder ones wouldn't even bother to ask: they just snatched the cover off me and looked for themselves. In a few days, the word got around that I was in one piece.

On my fourth day in the hospital, I was awakened by a male nurse at about 3 A.M. When he said hello in a very ladyish voice, I thought that he had come to the wrong bed by mistake. After identifying himself, he told me that he had helped Dr. Freeman save my life. The next thing he said, which I didn't understand, had something to do with the hours he had put in working that day. He went on mumbling something about how tired he was and ended up asking me to rub his back. I had already told him that I was grateful to him for helping the doctor save my life. While I rubbed his back above the beltline, he kept pushing my hand down and saying, "Lower, like you are really grateful to me." I told him that I was sleepy from the needle a nurse had given me. He asked me to pat his behind. After I had done this, he left.

The next day when the fellows came to visit me, I told them about my early-morning visitor. Dunny said he would like to meet him. Tito joked about being able to get a dose of clap in the hospital. The guy with the tired back never showed up again, so the fellows never got a chance to meet him. Some of them were disappointed.

After I had been in the hospital for about a week, I was visited by another character. I had noticed a woman visiting one of the patients on the far side of the ward. She was around fifty-five years old, short and fat, and she was wearing old-lady shoes. While I wondered who this woman was, she started across the room in my direction. After she had introduced herself, she told me that she was visiting her son. Her son had been stabbed in the chest with an ice pick by his wife. She said that his left lung had been punctured, but he was doing fine now, and that Jesus was so-o-o good.

Her name was Mrs. Ganey, and she lived on 145th Street. She said my getting shot when I did "was the work of the Lord." My gang had been stealing sheets and bedspreads off clotheslines for months before I had gotten shot. I asked this godly woman why she thought it was the work of the Lord or Jesus or whoever. She began in a sermonlike tone, saying, "Son, people was gitting tired-a y'all stealing all dey sheets and spreads." She said that on the night that I had gotten shot, she baited her clothesline with two brand-new bedspreads, turned out all the lights in the apartment, and sat at the kitchen window waiting for us to show.

She waited with a double-barreled shotgun.

The godly woman said that most of our victims thought that we were winos or dope fiends and that most of them had vowed to kill us. At the end of the sermon, the godly woman said, "Thank the Lord I didn't shoot nobody's child." When the godly woman had finally departed, I thought, Thank the Lord for taking her away from my bed.

Later on that night, I was feeling a lot of pain and couldn't get to sleep. A nurse who had heard me moaning and groaning came over and gave me a shot of morphine. Less than twenty minutes later, I was deep into a nightmare.

I was back in the fish-and-chips joint, lying on the floor dying. Only, now I was in more pain than before, and there were dozens of Mamas around me jumping up and screaming. I could feel myself dying in a rising pool of blood. The higher the blood rose the more I died.

I dreamt about the boy who Rock and big Stoop had thrown off that roof on 149th Street. None of us had stayed around to see him hit the ground, but I just knew that he died in a pool of blood too. I wished that he would stop screaming, and I wished that Mama would stop screaming. I wished they would let me die quietly.

As the screams began to die out—Mama's and the boy's—I began to think about the dilapidated old tenement building that I lived in, the one that still had the words "pussy" and "fuck you" on the walls where I had scribbled them years ago. The one where the super, Mr. Lawson, caught my little brother writing some more. Dad said he was going to kill Pimp for writing on that wall, and the way he was beating Pimp with that ironing cord, I thought he would. Mama was crying, I was crying, and Pimp had been crying for a long time. Mama said that he was too young to be beaten like that. She ran out of the house and came back with a cop, who stopped Dad from beating Pimp.

I told Pimp not to cry any more, just to wait until I got big: I was going to kill Dad, and he could help me if he wanted to.

This was the building where Mr. Lawson had killed a man for peeing in the hall. I remembered being afraid to go downstairs the morning after Mr. Lawson had busted that man's head open with a baseball bat. I could still see blood all over the hall. This was the building where somebody was always shooting out the windows in the hall. They were usually shooting at Johnny D., and they usually missed. This was the building that I loved more than anyplace else in the world. The thought that I would never see this building again scared the hell out of me.

I dreamt about waking up in the middle of the night seven years before and thinking that the Germans or the Japs had come and that the loud noises I heard were bombs falling. Running into Mama's room, I squeezed in between her and Dad at the front window. Thinking that we were watching an air raid, I asked Dad where the sirens were and why the street lights were on. He said, "This ain't no air raid—just a whole lotta niggers gone fool. And git the hell back in that bed!" I went back to bed, but I couldn't go to sleep. The loud screams in the street and the crashing sound of falling plate-glass windows kept me awake for hours. While I listened to the noise, I imagined bombs falling and people running through the streets screaming. I could see mothers running with babies in their arms, grown men running over women and children to save their own lives, and the Japs stabbing babies with bayonets, just like in the movies. I thought, Boy, I sure wish I was out there. I bet the Stinky brothers are out there. Danny and Butch are probably out there having all the fun in the world.

The next day, as I was running out of the house without underwear or socks on, I could hear Mama yelling, "Boy, come back here and put a hat or something on your head!" When I reached the stoop, I was knocked back into the hall by a big man carrying a ham under his coat. While I looked up at him, wondering what was going on, he reached down with one hand and snatched me up, still holding the ham under his coat with his other hand. He stood me up against a wall and ran into the hall with his ham. Before I had a chance to move, other men came running through the hall carrying cases of whiskey, sacks of flour, and cartons of cigarettes. Just as I unglued myself from the wall and started out the door for the second time, I was bowled over again. This time by a cop with a gun in his hand. He never stopped, but after he had gone a couple of yards into the hall, I heard him say, "Look out, kid." On the third try, I got out of the building. But I wasn't sure that this was my street. None of the stores had any windows left, and glass was everywhere. It seemed that all the cops in the world were on 145th Street and Eighth Avenue that day. The cops were telling everybody to move on, and everybody was talking about the riot. I went over to a cop and asked him what a riot was. He told me to go on home. The next cop I asked told me that a riot was what had happened the night before. Putting two and two together I decided that a riot was "a whole lotta niggers gone fool."

I went around the corner to Butch's house. After I convinced him that I was alone, he opened the door. He said that Kid and Danny were in the kitchen. I saw Kid sitting on the floor with his hand stuck way down in a gallon jar of pickled pigs' ears. Danny was cooking some bacon at the stove, and Butch was busy hiding stuff. It looked as though these guys had stolen a whole grocery store. While I joined the feast, they took turns telling me about the riot. Danny and Kid hadn't gone home the night before; they were out following the crowds and looting.

My only regret was that I had missed the excitement. I said, "Why don't we have another riot tonight? Then Butch and me can get in it."

Danny said that there were too many cops around to have a riot now. Butch said that they had eaten up all the bread and that he was going to steal some more. I asked if I could come along with him, and he said that I could if I promised to do nothing but watch. I promised, but we both knew that I was lying.

When we got to the street, Butch said he wanted to go across the street and look at the pawnshop. I tagged along. Like many of the stores where the rioters had been, the pawnshop had been set afire. The firemen had torn down a sidewall getting at the fire. So Butch and I just walked in where the wall used to be. Everything I picked up was broken or burned or both. My feet kept sinking into the wet furs that had been burned and drenched. The whole place smelled of smoke and was as dirty as a Harlem gutter on a rainy day. The cop out front yelled to us to get out of there. He only had to say it once.

After stopping by the seafood joint and stealing some shrimp and oysters, we went to what was left of Mr. Gordon's grocery store. Butch just walked in, picked up a loaf of bread, and walked out. He told me to come on, but I ignored him and went into the grocery store instead. I picked up two loaves of bread and walked out. When I got outside, a cop looked at me, and I ran into a building and through the backyard to Butch's house. Running through the backyard, I lost all the oysters that I had; when I reached Butch's house, I had only two loaves of bread and two shrimp in my pocket.

Danny, who was doing most of the cooking, went into the street to steal something to drink. Danny, Butch, and Kid were ten years old, four years older than I. Butch was busy making sandwiches on the floor, and Kid was trying to slice up a loaf of bologna. I had never eaten shrimp, but nobody seemed to care, because they refused to cook it for me. I told Butch that I was going to cook it myself. He said that there was no more lard in the house and that I would need some grease.

I looked around the house until I came up with some Vaseline hair pomade. I put the shrimp in the frying pan with the hair grease, waited until they had gotten black and were smoking, then took them out and made a sandwich. A few years later, I found out that shrimp were supposed to be shelled before cooking. I ate half of the sandwich and hated shrimp for years afterward.

The soft hand tapping on my face to wake me up was Jackie's. She and Della had been to a New Year's Eve party. Jackie wanted to come by the hospital and kiss me at midnight. This was the only time in my life that I ever admitted being glad to see Jackie. I asked them about the party, hoping that they would stay and talk to me for a while. I was afraid that if I went back to sleep, I would have another bad dream.

The next thing I knew, a nurse was waking me up for breakfast. I didn't recall saying good night to Jackie and Della, so I must have fallen asleep while they were talking to me. I thought about Sugar, how nice she was, and how she was a real friend. I knew she wanted to be my girl friend, and I liked her a lot. But what would everybody say if I had a buck-toothed girl friend. I remembered Knoxie asking me how I kissed her. That question led to the first fight I'd had with Knoxie in years. No, I couldn't let Sugar be my girl. It was hard enough having her as a friend.

The next day, I asked the nurse why she hadn't changed my bed linen, and she said because they were evicting me. I had been in the hospital for eleven days, but I wasn't ready to go home. I left the hospital on January 2 and went to a convalescent home in Valhalla, New York. After I had been there for three weeks, the activity director took me aside and told me that I was going to New York City to see a judge and that I might be coming back. The following morning, I left to see that judge, but I never got back to Valhalla.

I stood there before Judge Pankin looking solemn and lying like a professional. I thought that he looked too nice to be a judge. A half hour after I had walked into the courtroom, Judge Pankin was telling me that he was sending me to the New York State Training School for Boys. The judge said that he thought I was a chronic liar and that he hoped I would be a better boy when I came out. I asked him if he wanted me to thank him. Mama stopped crying just long enough to say, "Hush your mouth, boy."

Mama tried to change the judge's mind by telling him that I had already been to Wiltwyck School for Boys for two and a half years. And before that, I had been ordered out of the state for at least one year. She said that I had been away from my family too much; that was why I was always getting into trouble.

The judge told Mama that he knew what he was doing and that one day she would be grateful to him for doing it.

I had been sent away before, but this was the first time I was ever afraid to go. When Mama came up to the detention room in Children's Court, I tried to act as though I wasn't afraid. After I told her that Warwick and where I was going were one and the same, Mama began to cry, and so did I.

Most of the guys I knew had been to Warwick and were too old to go back. I knew that there were many guys up there I had mistreated. The Stinky brothers were up there. They thought that I was one of the guys who had pulled a train on their sister in the park the summer before. Bumpy from 144th Street was up there. I had shot him in the leg with a zip gun in a rumble only a few months earlier. There were many guys up there I used to bully on the streets and at Wiltwyck, guys I had sold tea leaves to as pot.

There were rival gang members up there who just hated my name. All of these guys were waiting for me to show. The word was out that I couldn't fight any more—that I had slowed down since I was shot and that a good punch to the stomach would put my name in the undertaker's book.

When I got to the Youth House, I tried to find out who was up at Warwick that I might know. Nobody knew any of the names I asked about. I knew that if I went up to Warwick in my condition, I'd never live to get out. I had a reputation for being a rugged little guy. This meant that I would have at least a half-dozen fights in the first week of my stay up there.

It seemed the best thing for me to do was to cop out on the nut. For the next two nights, I woke up screaming and banging on the walls. On the third day, I was sent to Bellevue for observation. This meant that I wouldn't be going to Warwick for at least twenty-eight days.

While I was in Bellevue, the fellows would come down and pass notes to me through the doors. Tito and Turk said they would get bagged and sent to Warwick by the time I got there. They were both bagged a week later for smoking pot in front of the police station. They were both sent to Bellevue. Two weeks after they showed, I went home. The judge still wanted to send me to Warwick, but Warwick had a full house, so he sent me home for two weeks.

The day before I went back to court, I ran into Turk, who had just gotten out of Bellevue. Tito had been sent to Warwick, but Turk had gotten a walk because his sheet wasn't too bad. I told him I would probably be sent to Warwick the next day. Turk said he had run into Bucky in Bellevue. He told me that he and Tito had voted Bucky out of the clique. I told him that I wasn't going for it because Bucky was my man from short-pants days. Turk said he liked him too, but what else could he do after Bucky had let a white boy beat him in the nutbox? When I heard this, there was nothing I could do but agree with Turk. Bucky had to go. That kind of news spread fast, and who wanted to be in a clique with a stud who let a paddy boy beat him?

The next day, I went to the Youth House to wait for Friday and the trip to Warwick. As I lay in bed that night trying to think of a way out, I began to feel sorry for myself. I began to blame Danny, Butch, and Kid for my present fate. I told myself that I wouldn't be going to Warwick if they hadn't taught me how to steal, play hookey, make homemades, and stuff like that. But then

I thought, Aw, hell, it wasn't their fault—as a matter of fact, it was a whole lotta fun.

I remembered sitting on the stoop with Danny, years before, when a girl came up and started yelling at him. She said that her mother didn't want her brother to hang out with Danny any more, because Danny had taught her brother how to play hookey. When the girl had gone down the street, I asked Danny what hookey was. He said it was a game he would teach me as soon as I started going to school.

Danny was a man of his word. He was my next-door neighbor, and he rang my doorbell about 7:30 A.M. on the second day of school. Mama thanked him for volunteering to take me to school. Danny said he would have taught me to play hookey the day before, but he knew that Mama would have to take me to school on the first day. As we headed toward the backyard to hide our books, Danny began to explain the great game of hookey. It sounded like lots of fun to me. Instead of going to school, we would go all over the city stealing, sneak into a movie, or go up on a roof and throw bottles down into the street. Danny suggested that we start the day off by waiting for Mr. Gordon to put out his vegetables; we could steal some sweet potatoes and cook them in the backyard. I was sorry I hadn't started school sooner, because hookey sure was a lot of fun.

Before I began going to school, I was always in the streets with Danny, Kid, and Butch. Sometimes, without saying a word, they would all start to run like hell, and a white man was always chasing them. One morning as I entered the backyard where all the hookey players went to draw up an activity schedule for the day, Butch told me that Danny and Kid had been caught by Mr. Sands the day before. He went on to warn me about Mr. Sands, saying Mr. Sands was that white man who was always chasing somebody and that I should try to remember what he looked like and always be on the lookout for him. He also warned me not to try to outrun Mr. Sands, "because that cat is fast." Butch said, "When you see him, head for a backyard or a roof. He won't follow you there."

During the next three months, I stayed out of school twenty-one days. Dad was beating the hell out of me for playing hookey, and it was no fun being in the street in the winter, so I started going to school regularly. But when spring rolled around, hookey became my favorite game again. Mr. Sands was known to many parents in the neighborhood as the truant officer. He never caught me in the street, but he came by my house many mornings to escort me to class. This was one way of getting me to school, but he never found a way to keep me there. The moment my teacher took her eyes off me, I was back on the street. Every time Dad got a card from Mr. Sands, I got bruises and welts from Dad. The beatings had only a temporary effect on me. Each time, the beatings got worse; and each time, I promised never to play hookey again. One time I kept that promise for three whole weeks.

The older guys had been doing something called "catting" for years. That catting was staying away from home all night was all I knew about the term. Every time I asked one of the fellows to teach me how to cat, I was told I wasn't old enough. As time went on, I learned that guys catted when they were afraid to go home and that they slept everywhere but in comfortable places. The usual places for catting were subway trains, cellars, unlocked cars, under a friend's bed, and in vacant newsstands.

One afternoon when I was eight years old, I came home after a busy day of running from the police, truant officer, and storekeepers. The first thing I did was to look in the mailbox. This had become a habit with me even though I couldn't read. I was looking for a card, a yellow card. That yellow card meant that I would walk into the house and Dad would be waiting for me with his razor strop. He would usually be eating and would pause just long enough to say to me, "Nigger, you got a ass whippin' comin'." My sisters, Carole and Margie, would cry almost as much as I would while Dad was beating me, but this never stopped him. After each beating I got, Carole, who was two years older than I, would beg me to stop playing hookey. There were a few times when I thought I would stop just to keep her and Margie, my younger sister, from crying so much. I decided to threaten Carole and Margie instead, but this didn't help. I continued to play hookey, and they continued to cry on the days that the yellow card got home before I did.

Generally, I would break open the mailbox, take out the card, and throw it away. Whenever I did this, I'd have to break open two or three other mailboxes and throw away the contents, just to make it look good.

This particular afternoon, I saw a yellow card, but I couldn't find anything to break into the box with. Having some matches in my pockets, I decided to burn the card in the box and not bother to break the box open. After I had used all the matches, the card was not completely burned. I stood there getting more frightened by the moment. In a little while, Dad would be coming home; and when he looked in the mailbox, anywhere would be safer than home for me.

This was going to be my first try at catting out. I went looking for somebody to cat with me. My crime partner, Buddy, whom I had played hookey with that day, was busily engaged in a friendly rock fight when I found him in Colonial Park. When I suggested that we go up on the hill and steal some newspapers, Buddy lost interest in the rock fight.

We stole papers from newsstands and sold them on the subway trains until nearly 1 A.M. That was when the third cop woke us and put us off the train with the usual threat. They would always promise to beat us over the head with a billy and lock us up. Looking back, I think the cops took their own threats more seriously than we did. The third cop put us off the Independent Subway at Fifty-ninth Street and Columbus Circle. I wasn't afraid of the cops, but I didn't go back into the subway—the next cop might have taken me home.

In 1945, there was an Automat where we came out of the subway. About five slices of pie later, Buddy and I left the Automat in search of a place to stay the night. In the center of the Circle, there were some old lifeboats that the Navy had put on display.

Buddy and I slept in the boat for two nights. On the third day, Buddy was caught ringing a cash register in a five-and-dime store. He was sent to Children's Center, and I spent the third night in the boat alone. On the fourth night, I met a duty-conscious cop, who took me home. That ended my first catting adventure.

Dad beat me for three consecutive days for telling what he called "that dumb damn lie about sleeping in a boat on Fifty-ninth Street." On the fourth day, I think he went to check my story out for himself. Anyhow, the beatings stopped for a while, and he never mentioned the boat again.

Before long, I was catting regularly, staying away from home for weeks at a time. Sometimes the cops would pick me up and take me to a Children's Center. The Centers were located all over the city. At some time in my childhood, I must have spent at least one night in all of them except the one on Staten Island.

The procedure was that a policeman would take me to the Center in the borough where he had picked me up. The Center would assign someone to see that I got a bath and was put to bed. The following day, my parents would be notified as to where I was and asked to come and claim me. Dad was always in favor of leaving me where I was and saying good riddance. But Mama always made the trip. Although Mama never failed to come for me, she seldom found me there when she arrived. I had no trouble getting out of Children's Centers, so I seldom stayed for more than a couple of days.

When I was finally brought home—sometimes after weeks of catting—

Mama would hide my clothes or my shoes. This would mean that I couldn't get out of the house if I should take a notion to do so. Anyway, that's how Mama had it figured. The truth of the matter is that these measures only made getting out of the house more difficult for me. I would have to wait until one of the fellows came around to see me. After hearing my plight, he would go out and round up some of the gang, and they would steal some clothes and shoes for me. When they had the clothes and shoes, one of them would come to the house and let me know. About ten minutes later, I would put on my sister's dress, climb down the back fire escape, and meet the gang with the clothes.

If something was too small or too large, I would go and steal the right size. This could only be done if the item that didn't fit was not the shoes. If the shoes were too small or large, I would have trouble running in them and probably get caught. So I would wait around in the backyard while someone stole me a pair.

Mama soon realized that hiding my clothes would not keep me in the house. The next thing she tried was threatening to send me away until I was twenty-one. This was only frightening to me at the moment of hearing it. Ever so often, either Dad or Mama would sit down and have a heart-to-heart talk with me. These talks were very moving. I always promised to mend my bad ways. I was always sincere and usually kept the promise for about a week. During these weeks, I went to school every day and kept my stealing at a minimum. By the beginning of the second week, I had reverted back to my wicked ways, and Mama would have to start praying all over again.

The neighborhood prophets began making prophecies about my life-span. They all had me dead, buried, and forgotten before my twenty-first birthday. These predictions were based on false tales of policemen shooting at me, on truthful tales of my falling off a trolley car into the midst of oncoming automobile traffic while hitching a ride, and also on my uncontrollable urge to steal. There was much justification for these prophecies. By the time I was nine years old, I had been hit by a bus, thrown into the Harlem River (intentionally), hit by a car, severely beaten with a chain. And I had set the house afire.

While Dad was still trying to beat me into a permanent conversion, Mama was certain that somebody had worked roots on me. She was writing to all her relatives in the South for solutions, but they were only able to say, "That boy musta been born with the devil in him." Some of them advised Mama to send me down there, because New York was no place to raise a child. Dad thought this was a good idea, and he tried to sell it to Mama. But Mama wasn't about to split up her family. She said I would stay in New York, devil or no devil. So I stayed in New York, enjoying every crazy minute.

Mama's favorite question was, "Boy, why you so bad?" I tried many times to explain to Mama that I wasn't "so bad." I tried to make her understand that it was trying to be good that generally got me into trouble. I remember telling her that I played hookey to avoid getting into trouble in school. It seemed that whenever I went to school, I got into a fight with the teacher. The teacher would take me to the principal's office. After I had fought with the principal, I would be sent home and not allowed back in school without one of my parents. So to avoid all that trouble, I just didn't go to school. When I stole things, it was only to save the family money and avoid arguments or scoldings whenever I asked for money.

Mama seemed silly to me. She was bothered because most of the parents in the neighborhood didn't allow their children to play with me. What she didn't know was that I never wanted to play with them. My friends were all daring like me, tough like me, dirty like me, ragged like me, cursed like me, and had a great love for trouble like me. We took pride in being able to hitch rides on trolleys, buses, taxicabs and in knowing how to steal and fight. We knew that we were the only kids in the neighborhood who usually had more than ten dollars in their pockets. There were other people who knew this too, and that was often a problem for us. Somebody was always trying to shake us down or rob us. This was usually done by the older hustlers in the neighborhood or by storekeepers or cops. At other times, older fellows would shake us down, con us, or Murphy us out of our loot. We accepted this as the ways of life. Everybody was stealing from everybody else. And sometimes we would shake down newsboys and shoeshine boys. So we really had no complaints coming. Although none of my sidekicks was over twelve years of age, we didn't think of ourselves as kids. The other kids my age were thought of as kids by me. I felt that since I knew more about life than they did, I had the right to regard them as kids.

In the fall of 1945, I was expelled from school for the first time. By the time February rolled around, I had been expelled from three other schools in Harlem. In February, Mama sent me downtown to live with Grandpapa on Eldridge Street. Papa enrolled me in a public school on Forsythe and Stanton Streets. It was cold that winter, and I usually went to school to be warm.

For weeks, everybody thought things were going along fine. The first day I didn't come home from school, Papa ignored it, thinking that I had gone uptown. But the next day, Mama received a card from Bellevue Hospital's psychiatric division informing her that I was undergoing psychiatric observation and that she was allowed to visit me on Wednesdays and Sundays. My grandfather knew nothing about any of this, so when Mama (his oldest daughter) came to him wanting to know what her son was doing in Bellevue, Papa asked, "How did he get there?" They both came over to Bellevue believing I had gone crazy. Dad didn't bother to come, because, as he put it, "That's where he shoulda been years ago." I was glad Dad didn't come, because he might not have believed that I was falsely accused of trying to push a boy in school out of a five-story window. Mama had already heard my teacher's version of the window incident, and now I was trying to explain my side of the story. My teacher had told her that I persuaded a boy to look out of the window to see an accident that hadn't taken place. Because of the window's wide ledge, I was holding his legs while he leaned out of the window. The boy started screaming and calling for help. When he got down out of the window, the boy said that I had been trying to push him out of the window. Just because we had fought the day before and I was the only one who saw the accident, I ended up in the nutbox.

I don't think my story completely convinced Mama or Papa, but they gave me the benefit of the doubt. Mama told me that I would have to stay in the hospital for a few weeks. Her eyes were filled with tears when she said good-bye, and I tried to look sad too, but I was actually happy. I thought about how nice it was going to be away from Dad. Also, there were a few of my friends there, and we were sure to find something to get into. I had already had a couple of fights and won, so this was going to be a real ball.

I had lots of fun in the nutbox and learned a lot of new tricks, just as I thought. I didn't know it at the time, but many of the boys I met in Bellevue would also be with me at Wiltwyck and Warwick years later. Some of those I had bullied in the nutbox would try to turn the tables later on in life. Some would succeed.

There were a few things around to steal. There were plenty of guys to fight with and lots of adults to annoy. The one drawback that the nutbox had was school and teachers. But I found the nutbox to be such a nice place that I was sad when Mama came to take me home.

When I returned home, I was told that my former school had refused to readmit me. This was the best news I had heard since I started going to school. I thought that I had finally gotten out of going to school. But two weeks later, I was enrolled in another school in Harlem.

Within two months from the time I had left Bellevue, I found myself in Manhattan's Children Court for the first time. The reason was that I had been thrown out of two more schools, and there weren't any more in Manhattan that would accept me. The judge told Mama that if I was still in New York State when the fall semester began, he would send me someplace where I would be made to go to school. After Mama had promised the judge that I would not be in New York when September rolled around, we went home.

This was the first time that Mama had been in court, and she was pretty angry about the whole thing. All the way uptown on the bus, Mama kept telling me that I should be ashamed of myself for making her come down to that court and face those white people. Every ten or twelve blocks, Mama would stop preaching just long enough to look at me and say, "Child, maybe that head doctor was right about you," or, "Boy, why you so damn bad?" She didn't understand what the psychiatrist was talking about when he was telling her about my emotional problems. Since she couldn't understand the terms he was using, Mama thought he was trying to tell her in a nice way that I was crazy. Of course, she didn't believe him. "That ole big-nose, thick-eyeglasses white man, he looked kinda crazy his own self," she said. No, she didn't believe him, whatever it was that he had said—but sometimes she wondered if that man might have been right.

When we got back uptown, Mrs. Rogers, who lived next door to us, came over to find out how things had gone in court. Mrs. Rogers, Danny's mother, had made many trips to Manhattan's Children Court. Now she had come to sympathize with Mama. Mrs. Rogers—who was also a jackleg preacher (she did not have a church)—called everybody "child," "brother," or "sister." What a person was called by Mrs. Rogers depended on whether or not he was "saved." To be saved meant to live for the Lord. Mrs. Rogers was saved, and so was her husband; she couldn't understand why all her children had not yet been "hit by spirit."

Mrs. Rogers, a big, burly woman about fifteen years older than Mama, always called Mama "child." I can remember her saying to Mama when we came home from court that day, "Child, ain't that Lexington Avenue bus the slowest thing in this whole city?" I always found Mrs. Rogers' visits hard to take. She was a very nice meddlesome old woman, but too godly to have around constantly. Poor Danny, he had to live with it. Mrs. Rogers had told Mama that Danny was so bad because his behavior was the Lord's way of testing her faith. Dad called Mrs. Rogers the "preacher woman." He believed that Mrs. Rogers was going against the Lord's Word and that this was the reason for her son's behavior. He had often said that "the Lord never told no woman to go out and preach the Gospel to nobody." Dad said that if the Lord had wanted a woman to preach, he would have chosen a woman to be one of his apostles.

On this day, Mrs. Rogers' advice was no different from the other times. After Mama had told Mrs. Rogers about what had happened in court, Mrs. Rogers began her usual sermon, saying, "Child, you just gotta pray, you just gotta pray and trust in the Lord." I always left the house at this point, because our house would be used as a practice pulpit for the next two or three hours.

As I ran down the stairs, I tried to imagine what was going on in the house. In a little while, Mrs. Rogers would be patting her foot real fast, and she would start talking real loud, clapping her hands, shaking her head, and every other word would be "Jesus" or "Lord." I wondered why Mrs. Rogers never got tired of talking about the Lord. Before Mrs. Rogers finished her private sermon, she would have Mama talking about the Lord and patting her feet. By the time Mrs. Rogers was ready to leave, she would have Mama promising to come to a church where she was preaching next Sunday. Mama would promise, and Mrs. Rogers would start telling her how good it is to be saved, to walk with Jesus, and to let God into your soul. Even though Mama knew Dad wasn't going to let her go to a sanctified church with that "jackleg preacher woman," she still promised to go. Dad always said, "All those sanctified people is just a bunch of old hypocrites, and none of 'em ain't a bit more saved than nobody else."

Mrs. Rogers never talked about saving Dad. She said, "That man got the devil in him," and I believed it. As a matter of fact, I had suspected something like that long before Mrs. Rogers did.

We had all been to Mrs. Rogers' Sunday sermon once. All of us except Dad. She was preaching that time in what looked like a church-apartment to me and a church-store to Carole. I think most of the people there were relatives of Mrs. Rogers. All of her family was there except for Danny; he had escaped on the way to church. June, one of Mrs. Rogers' daughters, was playing an old, out-of-tune upright piano. Another one of Danny's sisters was banging two cymbals together and mumbling something about Jesus. She seemed to be in a trance. Mr. Rogers was shaking a tambourine and singing about Jesus with a faraway look in his eyes. Mrs. Rogers, who was dressed in a white robe, got up and started preaching. After Mrs. Rogers had been preaching for about fifteen minutes, an old lady got up and started screaming and shouting, "Help me, Lord Jesus!" She was still throwing her arms up and shouting for Jesus to help her when a younger woman jumped up and hollered, "Precious Lord Jesus, save me!" Mrs. Rogers' voice was getting louder all the time.

For two hours, she preached—and for two hours, people were getting up, shouting, jumping up and down, calling to Jesus for help and salvation, and falling out exhausted. Some of these "Holy Rollers," as Dad called them, would fall to the floor and start trembling rapidly; some of them even began to slobber on themselves. When I asked Mama what was wrong with those people and what they were doing on the floor, she told me that the "spirit" had hit them. When Carole heard this, she began to cry and wanted to get out of there before the spirit hit us. Mrs. Rogers had gone over to a man who was rolling on the floor, slobbering on himself, and babbling as if he were talking to the Lord. She held the man's hand very tight and told him repeatedly to walk with the Lord and not to fear Jesus. She was saying to the man, "Brother, say, 'Yes, Jesus; yes, Jesus.'" After a while, the man calmed down, and Mrs. Rogers said he had been saved.

Carole and Margie were frightened by these strange goings-on. I had been fascinated until now. But now this spirit thing had Mama jumping up and shouting. I joined Carole and Margie in a crying chorus, and the three of us started pulling on Mama. After Mama had jumped, clapped her hands, and had her say about Jesus, she fell back in her chair, tired and sweating. One of Mrs. Rogers' blood sisters had started fanning Mama. Carole, Margie, and I had stopped crying, but we were still scared, because we didn't know if Mama was all right or not.

In the makeshift pulpit, Mrs. Rogers was looking real pleased with herself, probably thinking that she had saved a lot of people. I think Mrs. Rogers judged her sermon by the number of people who were hit by the spirit and fell down during her sermon. She cautioned the people who were saved about "backslidin'" and told them about how happy they were going to be with Jesus in their lives. She also asked some of the old saved souls to "testify." After three or four saved souls had told about what a good friend Jesus had been to them, Mrs. Rogers began her third request for money. The ushers, who were also relatives of Mrs. Rogers, passed a china bowl down each row. Carole and Margie dropped the nickel that Mama had given to each of them in the bowl, then they turned and looked at me. Although that was the first time we had ever been to church together, they would have been surprised if I had put my nickel in the bowl. I didn't surprise them that day.

While Carole and Margie were busy telling Mama about me not putting my nickel in the bowl, I was pulling a chair from the aisle behind us. All the chairs in the place were kitchen chairs, and they weren't all the same size. Before I could get the chair into our aisle, a big fat shiny dark-skinned woman with a man's voice said, "Boy, leave dat chair 'lone." I was frightened by the heavy, commanding voice, but not as much as I was after I looked up and saw that great big old woman giving me the evil eye. My first thought was that she was a witch or a hag, whatever that was. I knew she couldn't be the boogeyman; not in church. But the longer I looked, the more I doubted her being anything other than the boogeyman. About thirty seconds later, when I had gotten my voice back, I meekly said, "Dat ain't your chair." The next thing I heard was the sound of Mama's hand falling heavily across my mouth. As I started crying, I heard Mama say, "What I tole you about sassin' ole people?" While I went on crying, Mama was telling me about the dangers of talking back to old people. I remember her saying, "If one of these ole people put the bad mouth on you, maybe you'll be satisfied."

For years afterward, the mention of church always reminded me of the day that we went to hear Mrs. Rogers preach. To me, a church was a church-apartment where somebody lined up a lot of kitchen chairs in a few rows, a preacher did a lot of shouting about the Lord, people jumped up and down until they got knocked down by the spirit, and Mrs. Rogers put bowls of money on a kitchen table and kept pointing to it and asking for more. It was a place where I had to stand up until I couldn't stand any more and then had to sit down on hard wooden chairs. The one good thing I got out of going to hear Mrs. Rogers preach was a new threat to use on Carole and Margie. Whenever Carole and Margie would threaten to tell on me, I told them that if they did, the spirit would hit them the way it hit those people in Mrs. Rogers' church-apartment.

Maybe Dad was right when he said Mrs. Rogers was just robbing people in the name of the Lord. Anyway, I felt pretty good about her not getting my nickel.

Even though Dad didn't care for preachers and churches, he had a lot of religion in his own way. Most of the time, his religion didn't show. But on Saturday night, those who didn't see it heard it. Sometimes Dad would get religious on Friday nights too. But Saturday night was a must. Because it always took liquor to start Dad to singing spirituals and talking about the Lord, I thought for years that this lordly feeling was something in a bottle of whiskey. To me, it was like castor oil or black draught. You drink it and the next thing you know, you're doing things.

I was introduced to religion on Saturday night. I don't recall just when, but as far back as I can remember, Saturday night was the Lord's night in our house. Whenever Dad was able to make it home on his own two feet, he would bring a recording of a spiritual, a plate of pigs' feet and potato salad from the corner delicatessen or a plate of fish-and-chips from the wine joint around the corner, and whatever was left of his last bottle of religion. He usually got home about three o'clock in the morning, and the moment he hit the block I could hear him singing (or yelling) the record he had. By the time he got upstairs, everybody in the building knew the song and hated it. Before Dad was in the house, I could hear him calling me.

By the time he finished unlocking and relocking the door at least six times, kicking on it, cursing out the lock and the neighbors who had tried to quiet him down, I was up and had already turned on the phonograph. On her way to the door, Mama would say, "Boy, turn that thing off and git back in that bed." While Mama told Dad how disgusting he was, I would be busily picking out the pigs' feet or fish-and-chips with the least amount of hot sauce on them. When Mama had gotten tired of competing with Dad's singing, she went back to bed. As Dad gave me the record—usually by Sister Rosetta Tharpe, the Dixie Hummingbirds, or the Four Blind Boys—he would tell me how somebody I had never heard of sang it in the cotton fields or at somebody's wedding or funeral "down home." After listening to the record at least a dozen times, Dad would turn the phonograph off, and we would sing the song a few times. Before dawn started sneaking through the windows, Dad and I had gone through his entire repertoire of spirituals. By daybreak, we were both drunk and had fallen on the floor, and we stayed there until we awoke later in the day.

When Dad awoke on Sunday, it was usually around eleven or twelve o'clock. If he had half a bottle of religion around, we would continue our Sunday singing. If there was less than half a bottle around, Dad would just ignore Mama's protests and take me with him to a King Kong joint. I recall one of their Sunday morning arguments.

Mama said, "Ain't no six-year-old child got no business drinking that King Kong."

Dad said, "I was drinking it when I was five, and I'm still here working hard and steady five and six days a week."

The King Kong joint was usually in a basement apartment and operated by a friend of Dad's or a relative. Dad knew where most of the joints in the neighborhood were, and many times we had to go from one to another for what seemed like hours. Sometimes the cops would get there before we did, and at other times the stuff hadn't finished cooking. But eventually, we would find a bottle and enough drunks to make a quartet and would sing some spirituals.

Saturdays and Sundays were the only days that Dad mentioned the words "God" and "Lord." But on these days, he made up for the rest of the week. He was very serious about the spirituals and the Lord on weekends. To his way of thinking, this was a private kind of religion all his own. Nobody understood except him and the Lord, but that was enough understanding for him. It had to be right, because his daddy had lived that way.

Grandpa had made the "best goddamn corn liquor" in Sumter County, according to Dad. Dad promised me, every time he got drunk, that he would teach me how to make good corn liquor. He often said that he was making corn liquor long before he even knew how to plow, and he couldn't remember not knowing how to plow. Dad claimed that there were no baby-nursing bottles in the South when he was coming up. He said that when a baby cut his first tooth, "his papa would take him off the titty and put him on the corn-liquor jug." I never learned how to make good corn liquor, but I learn quite a few good lies about drinking and making it.

Whiskey was one of my best friends. I talked to whiskey bottles all the time. That is, all the time I was by myself or with Toto, Bucky, or Bulldog. These were the times when I knew I wouldn't have to explain anything to anybody. These guys knew what I was saying to the whiskey bottle and what it meant to me even though I never told them. We would fight almost every day and call each other dumb, but to me they were some real smart guys. The smartest thing about them was that you never had to explain anything to them for them to know it. They just knew it anyway. I had whiskey, and they probably had a good friend like that too, a friend who could tell you if it was okay to go home. The only time I could go home after being away for a few days would be on a Friday or Saturday night. On these nights, Dad would have a bottle of whiskey and wouldn't be so mad, so he wouldn't beat me too badly. Some Friday and Saturday nights he didn't have any whiskey, and I got a real bad beating. Whenever that happened, I would curse those whiskey bottles that had told me it was okay to go home. The next chance I got, I would break every whiskey bottle I could find. Most of the time, the whiskey bottles were on my side, and I wouldn't go home. That round brown bottle had more than religion in it. It must have had the Lord in it. I never saw him in it, but I know he was there.

When I reached the street that day after my first time in court, school wasn't out yet. I knew the guys wouldn't be in the backyard at that time of day. They were probably on the hill or downtown stealing. I thought: I bet I missed a whole day of fun. I ain't goin' back to no damn court no more. They make you wait all day on those hard benches, and you gotta ride all day to get there and ride all day to get back. No, I'm just not goin' to that fuckin' court no more.

I was anxious to find somebody to tell about my day in court. I went up to the park, but there was no one there. So I jumped on the back of a trolley car and hitched it up to 161st Street and Amsterdam Avenue. There was a five-and-dime store up there that was a favorite spot of ours for ringing cash registers. I stopped in there, rang the cash register, and decided to go to a movie. Even though I had forty dollars now, I was going to sneak in. All I had was four tens, and I knew better than to take any one of them out in Harlem. Somebody would try to shortchange me or shake me down. Sneaking in the Roosevelt Theatre was the only thing to do.

I wouldn't have taken all tens, but to ring the cash register without anybody seeing me, I had to stoop down below the counter and reach up to the cash register. I would push down real slow on one key and hold the drawer with my other hand, letting it come out as quiet as I could. When I got the drawer out far enough to get my hand in it, I would let the key up real slowly, grab a handful of bills from three slots, and push the drawer back in. Not having anyone to lay chickie for me, I had to do it quicker than most of the time. So I just took the first bills I got my hands on.

Butch had taught me how to ring cash registers. He must have told it to me a hundred million times and had me tell it back to him just as many times before I tried it. The first cash register I ever rang was in a drugstore on Broadway. There was one man at a long counter. Butch had picked this spot out for me because it was so easy and I hadn't done it before. Butch told me to wait until he did something to make the man come down to the far end of the counter. I watched Butch from inside the telephone booth.

He walked up the aisle until he got to the candy display, then he stumbled forward, knocking over the candy and chewing gum display. The man came running out from behind the counter. As he came out, I came out of the telephone booth, went behind the counter, and within a matter of seconds was at the other end of the aisle helping Butch and the counterman pick up the stuff. Butch would pick it up and drop it again until he saw me coming. After we had picked up everything, the man thanked us and went back to his duties, and I walked out with his money.

Butch had warned me many times to never ring a cash register when there was nobody around to keep the person on the counter busy. But sometimes when I needed some money and there was no one around, I would go and do it alone. When I told Butch what I had done, he would tell me that I was dumb and would probably end up in jail before I was ten. His putting me down didn't stop me from ringing cash registers alone. It just stopped me from telling him about it.

Butch was pretty serious about stealing. That's probably why he was so good at it. I had a lot of respect for him and his ability to steal. I once had hopes of getting to be as good a thief as Butch, but every time I got good at something, he would teach me something else. After a while, I realized that I could never get to be as good as Butch—he knew too much. But I would still be the second-best thief in the neighborhood.

The first thing I did when I got into the show that day was to yell out, "Forty thieves!" to see if any of my friends in the gang were there. That afternoon I got a loud "Yo!" from one of the front rows. It was Bucky. He hadn't been to school that day and had sneaked into the show about one o'clock. He had already seen the movie, but it was good, so he was seeing it over. "Goldie was in here a little while ago, but he hadn't been home for the past few nights, so he had to go and steal something to eat," he said. Bucky told me that he hadn't seen any of the other fellows all day. They must have been downtown stealing.

Bucky was about my age, had curly hair, was always dirty, like most of us, and had buck teeth. Of all the dirty kids on the block, Bucky was the dirtiest. He had just moved to our neighborhood around the first of the year.

Bucky had lots of sisters and brothers, and his mother was still having more sisters and brothers for him. He also had some sisters and brothers who, he said, lived with their aunts. These I had never seen. Bucky didn't have a father, and his mother was on relief. All the kids in Bucky's family knew when the relief check came. On that day, they would all follow Miss Jamie around until she cashed it. Then they would beg her to buy some food before she started drinking up the money. Every month when check day rolled around, Bucky and his brothers and sisters would always be arguing with their mother. Miss Jamie was forever telling them to wait someplace until she cashed the check, that she would come back and buy some food. But they all knew that if they ever let her out of their sight with that check, they wouldn't see her for days. When she did show up, she would tell them how she got robbed or how her pocket was picked or how she lost the money. So she would spend half of the day trying to duck the kids, and they would stick with her. If there was only one kid around, or even two, she could easily get away. She would usually go into a bar, where she knew the kids couldn't follow her, and she would leave the bar by another exit. When the kids got wise to this, one of them would start looking for the other exit as soon as she entered the bar. But even then, she could get away if there was only one at the exit she used. She would give him fifty cents as a bribe and jump into a cab.

Bucky was the only guy I knew who could stay out all night and not be missed. Sometimes he would go out and stay for days and still get home before his mother. Sometimes Bucky would go home and there would be nobody there. The lady next door always had the low-down. The usual reason for the house being empty was that the welfare investigator had come by and had taken all the kids to the Children's Shelter. Whenever this happened while Bucky was away from home, he would go to the police station and tell them what had happened. After the policemen had gotten to know Bucky and were familiar with his home situation, he only had to walk in and they would send him to the Shelter without asking him anything. The Shelter was a second home to Bucky. He liked it more than his first home. At the Shelter, he always got three meals a day, and three meals beats none any way you look at it. Whenever I missed Bucky from around the block, I had a pretty good idea where he was, but he would always say that he was staying with his aunt in Brooklyn. That aunt was the great mystery in Bucky's life.

When Bucky moved into the neighborhood, I sort of adopted him. He had his first fight in the neighborhood with me, and since he was pretty good with his hands, we became friends after three fights. I used to take him home with me and feed him. After a while Bucky got to know what time we usually ate supper, and if he didn't see me on the street, he would come to my house looking for me. If I wasn't in, he would ask if he could come in and wait for me. He knew that somebody would offer him something to eat if he was there at suppertime. Dad started complaining about Bucky coming up to the house for supper every night. So Mama would tell Bucky to go downstairs and look for me if I wasn't there when he came by. When I brought him home with me, sometimes the family would slip into the kitchen one at a time to eat without his knowing it, or they would try to wait until he left. Bucky would never leave as long as he thought that we had not eaten supper. When Bucky was finally gone, Dad would start telling me how stupid I was and threatening to give my supper to Bucky the next time I brought him home with me. Dad said that Bucky had a roguish look about him and that he didn't trust him. Some of the fellows didn't like him either. They said he looked too pitiful.

That day after we saw the show, I went up to Bucky's house to show him a homemade that I had found a week before. I didn't have any bullets for it yet, but that wasn't important—I knew somebody I could steal them from. As I walked through the door—which was always open because the lock had been broken and Miss Jamie never bothered to have it fixed—I saw Bucky on the floor with his arm around his little sister's throat. He was choking her. Meanwhile, his big sister was bopping him on the head with a broom handle and they were all screaming. After I had watched the three-way fight for a minute or less, I started toward Dixie to grab the broom. Before I could get close enough to grab the broom handle, everything stopped. For a whole second, everything was real quiet. Dixie threw down the broom and started crying. Debbie was already crying, but I couldn't hear her because Bucky was still choking her. He let her go and started cursing. When Debbie got up, I saw what she and Dixie were crying over and what Bucky was cursing about. The three of them had been fighting over one egg, and the egg was broken in the scuffle.

Bucky had run out of the house cursing, and I was standing where he had left me. Dixie and Debbie were facing me on the other side of the room. They were staring at the broken egg on the floor, and their crying was getting louder all the time. I was staring at them and wondering why they were making so much fuss over one broken egg. They sure looked funny standing there with their mouths wide open and tears rolling down their dirty faces and into their mouths. I began to laugh and mimic them. Dixie threw the broom at me and missed. Knowing what they were going to do as soon as I left, I decided to get even with Dixie for throwing the broom at me. Before either of them realized what I was doing, I had stepped on the egg and was smearing it all over the floor. Debbie began to cry louder, and Dixie was all over me, scratching, biting, and hitting me with what seemed like ten hands. Without thinking, I started swinging. I didn't stop swinging until I heard Dixie crying again. She went over to what was left of that old ragged couch they had in the living room, threw herself down on it, and went on crying into the cushions. I went over and touched her on the shoulder and told her I was sorry. She only raised her head enough to scream as loud as she could and tell me to let her alone. I told her to wait there while I went to steal her some eggs. She yelled that she didn't want any eggs and that when her older brother got out of jail, she was going to get him to kick my ass.

Less than ten minutes after I had left Dixie crying on the couch, I walked in the house with a dozen eggs and a loaf of bread. Dixie was sitting up on the couch now. Her eyes were red, but she wasn't crying; her face still had tearstains on it, and her mouth was stuck out as if she were mad at somebody. Not saying anything, I walked over to her and offered her the eggs and the loaf of bread. I was standing in front of her holding out the eggs and bread. She just sat there staring at me as if she didn't believe it or as if she wondered how I had come by these things. Seeing that she needed a little encouragement, I pushed the eggs and bread against her chest saying, "Here, take it." She took them and started walking slowly toward the kitchen. It seemed as though she still didn't believe it was really happening, that if she should make a fast or sudden move, the eggs and bread would be gone. She carried the food to the kitchen like somebody carrying a large basin of water that was filled to the brim. When I heard Dixie moving about in the kitchen, I went in, feeling that everything was all right now and that she knew I hadn't played a joke on her.

Dixie was running some water into a small pot. She asked me if I wanted a boiled egg. I told her that I liked my eggs scrambled. She said the only grease in the house was some fish grease and if she scrambled the eggs in it, they would taste like fish. After she had put six eggs on the stove to boil, Dixie said she was sorry for scratching me and didn't mean what she had said about telling her brother to beat me up when he came home. I told her that I was sorry for laughing at her and that I hadn't meant to hit her so hard. I asked her if she wanted to make friends, and she said all right. We shook hands and started talking about the things we disliked in each other.

Claude Brown

She said I just thought I was too bad and was always messing with somebody. I told her that she was all right, but she should stop licking the snot off
her lip when her nose was running. Also, I thought she looked crazy always
pulling her bloomers up through her skirt.

While Dixie and I were testing out our new friendship, Debbie had
come in and sat down. She just sat quietly and kept watching the pot. When
Dixie got up and went over to the stove to turn the fire off beneath the pot,
Debbie's eyes followed her. Dixie started cutting up eggs to make sandwiches, but I told her to just give me an egg and some salt. She made two
sandwiches, one for herself and one for Debbie.

After the second round of eggs, Dixie sent Debbie downstairs to play.
When Debbie had gone into the street, Dixie asked me if I wanted to play
house, and I said okay. We got up from the milk crates that we had been sitting on in the kitchen. There were no chairs there. In fact, the only chair in
the house was the one in the front room by the window. There had to be
a chair in that spot. When Miss Jamie had money, she played numbers and
waited all day long to hear what the first figure was. Mr. Bob, the number
man, would come by and signal up to the window to let her know what
each figure was as it came out. When he gave the signal, Miss Jamie would
either say something about the Lord and send one of the kids down for her
money or say, "Oh-h-h, shit!" and send somebody down with some money
to put on another figure . . . if she had any more money.

By the time Dixie and I reached the front room, we were old friends. She
took off her bloomers without giving it a thought. She didn't want to lie
down on the bed because it was wet from her little brothers sleeping there
the night before. It didn't even bother her that her drawers were dirty and
ragged. They looked as if she had been wearing them for months, but still
she didn't ask me to turn around or close my eyes while she took them off.
This meant we were real good friends now.

As I was leaving, I told Dixie that I would bring her something nice
when I came back. She tried to get me to say what it was, and when she had
failed at this, she said she didn't believe me anyway. But I knew she did and
that she would be waiting for me to come back.

After she had finished telling me what a liar I was, I slapped her playfully
and ran down the stairs. When I reached the street, I looked up and down
the avenue for Bucky, but he wasn't around. So, I decided to wait in front of
his house and let him find me.

Mr. Mitchell, the man who owned the fruit store next to Bucky's house, was afraid to go to the back of the store after seeing me sitting on the running board of a car in front of his store. Mr. Mitchell was a West Indian, and I didn't like him. I didn't like any West Indians. They couldn't talk, they were stingy, and most of them were as mean as could be. I like Butch, but I didn't believe that he was really a West Indian.

Mr. Mitchell was looking at me as if he thought I would jump up at any time and run away with his whole store. But I just sat there and looked right back at him. I thought about Mr. Mitchell and Mr. Lawson. Mr. Mitchell didn't seem to be a West Indian all the time, and he wasn't mean like Mr. Lawson. Mr. Lawson, who was the super of our house, was the meanest man on the Avenue. He was said to have killed half a dozen men. Dad had killed a man too, but that was for saying something nasty to Mama. I would have killed that bastard too. I think anybody would have killed him. Killing all those people wasn't what made Mr. Lawson mean. He was mean because he was a West Indian.

As I was sitting there on the running board of that car, I heard a voice that had always been pleasing to my ear as long as I could remember. It was little Pimp saying, "Sonny, Mama want you." Pimp was my favorite person in the whole family. Maybe that was because he was my only brother. Or maybe it was just because. Whenever I stayed away from home for days I missed him, and sometimes I would even go to the house of the lady who kept him, Margie, and Carole while Mama was working. I missed Margie and Carole too, but not as much as I missed Pimp. He was my brother, and that was different. I would always bring him something that I had stolen, like a cap gun or a water pistol. I was waiting for Pimp to grow up; then we could have a lot of fun together. Right now, all I could do was tell him about all the fun I was having outrunning the police, stealing everything I wanted, and sleeping in a different place every night. Man, I couldn't wait to teach him these things. That little nigger sure was lucky to have me for a brother. I threw my arm around Pimp and started choking him playfully as we started toward the house to see what Mama wanted me for.

When we got to the door, I stopped and told Pimp to be quiet. It was a habit of mine by now to listen at the door before going in. Whenever I heard a strange voice, I usually made a detour. But this day I was going in in spite of the strange voice. I knew it was safe even though it was strange, because it was a lady's voice. That meant that it couldn't be the cops or a truant officer, and I hadn't stolen anything from a lady that day, so it had to be just a visitor.

Mama was sitting in the living room on the studio cot drinking beer, and a light-skinned pretty lady was sitting in the big chair across from Mama, drinking beer too. I walked into the middle of the living room and stopped, staring at the lady who shouted out, "Is this Sonny Boy?"

When Mama answered, "Yeah, that's Sonny Boy," this woman just reached up and grabbed me with both hands, saying, "Boy, come here and kiss your aunt."

Before I could defend myself, she was smothering me to death between two gigantic breasts. I was let up for some air, but before I had taken two breaths, the lady was washing my face with sloppy kisses that stank from beer. I was getting mad and thinking that maybe I'd better tell her I didn't go for all that baby shit and that I didn't mean to have any more of it, aunt or no aunt. But when my long-lost aunt regained her senses and let me out of her bear hug, I wasn't mad any more. I had realized that this was just another one of those old crazy-acting, funny-dressing, no-talking people from down South. As I stood on the other side of the room looking at her, I was wondering if all the people down South were crazy like that. I knew one thing—I had never seen anybody from down there who looked or acted as if they had some sense. Damn, that was one place I never wanted to go to. It was probably eating corn bread and biscuits all the time that made those people act like that.

Mama started telling Aunt Bea how Pimp got his name, because Aunt Bea had said, "That sho don't sound like nothin' to be callin' no child." When Mama started getting labor pains while she was carrying Pimp, there was nobody around to get an ambulance but Minnie, the neighborhood prostitute. Minnie called an ambulance, but it was a long time coming, and Mama's pains were getting worse. Minnie got scared and ran out and got a cab and took Mama to the hospital.

All the way to the hospital, Minnie kept saying, "It better be a girl, 'cause I'm spending my last dollar on this cab, and I never gave a man no money in my life." Minnie was real proud to tell people that she had never had a pimp and would never give a nigger a dime. Well, when Mama came out of the operating room, Minnie was still out there with her fingers crossed and praying for it to be a girl. Minnie left the hospital cursing, but not before she had become a godmother and had named her godson Pimp. Mama told Minnie that she was sorry but that it must have been the Lord's will.

Minnie said, "That's all right, 'cause the cab fare was only seventy cents. And, anyway, he's such a cute little nigger, maybe he was born to be a pimp, and maybe it was in the cards for me to be the first one to spend some money on him." Minnie began teasing Mama about Pimp's complexion, saying, "Girl, you know you ain't got no business with no baby that light; it looks like it's a white baby. . . . I know one thing—that baby better start looking colored before your husband see him." Mama said all her children were born looking almost white. And that Carole was even lighter than that when she was born, but, that by the time she was five years old, she was the cutest little plump, dimple-cheeked black gal on Eighth Avenue. This was probably because my grandfather is more white than he is colored.

After Mama finished telling Aunt Bea how Pimp got his name, she started telling me and Pimp that Aunt Bea had a real nice farm down South. When she had told us all there was to tell about that real nice farm, Mama asked us if we wanted to go home with Aunt Bea when she left in a couple of weeks. Pimp said no because he knew that was what Mama wanted to hear. I said I wanted to go right away, because I had just heard about all those watermelon patches down South.

"In a couple of weeks, all you chillun goin' home with your Aunt Bea for the rest of the summer," Mama said.

I asked if I could have the beer bottle that was nearly empty. After I turned it up to my mouth and finished emptying it, I asked Pimp if he wanted to go to the show. We went into the kitchen to collect some more bottles to cash them in for show fare.

We could hear Mama and Aunt Bea talking in the living room. Mama was telling Aunt Bea how bad I was and that sometimes she thought I had the devil in me. Aunt Bea said that was probably true "'cause his granddaddy and his great-granddaddy on his daddy's side both had it." Next Aunt Bea was telling Mama how my great-grandfather, Perry Brown, had tied his wife to a tree and beat her with a branch until his arm got tired. Then she told Mama about what my grandfather, Mr. Son Brown, did to a jackleg preacher from Silver when he caught him stealing liquor from his still down in the Black Swamp. She said Grandpa circled around that old jackleg preacher and started shooting over his head with a shotgun and made the preacher run smack into a bear trap that he had set for whoever was stealing his liquor. After that the jackleg preacher only had one foot, and everybody said Mr. Son Brown shouldn't have done that to the preacher just for taking a little bit of whiskey.

I thought, Yeah, I guess there is a whole lotta devil in the Brown family and especially in Dad, 'cause he sure is mean.

Then I heard Aunt Bea ask Mama a familiar-sounding question: "Do you think somebody done work some roots on the po child?"

Mama said, "Lord, I sho hope nobody ain't work no roots on my child." Mama was quiet for a while, then she said, "They got some West Indian people around here who is evil enough to do anything to anybody, and they always 'fixing' somebody. I always tell that boy to stop playin' and fightin' with those West Indian chillun, but he just won't listen. Who knows? Maybe he done did sumpin to one-a those kids and they people found out about it and worked some roots on him. Anything might happen to that little nigger, 'cause he so damn bad. Lord, I ain't never seen a child in my life that bad. I know one thing—if I don't git that boy outta New York soon, my hair gonna be gray before I get thirty years old. Sumpin gotta be wrong with the boy, 'cause nobody in my family steal and lie the way he do, and none-a his daddy people ain't never been no rogues and liars like he is. I don't know who he coulda took all that roguishness at.

"Seem like nobody can't make him understand. I talk to him, I yell at him, I whip his ass, but it don't do no good. His daddy preach to him, he yell at him, he beat him so bad sometimes, I gotta run in the kitchen and git that big knife at him to stop him from killin' that boy. You think that might break him outta those devilish ways he got? Child, that scamp'll look Jesus dead in the eye when he standin' on a mountain of Bibles and swear to God in heaven he ain't gon do it no more. The next day, or even the next minute, that little lyin' Negro done gone and did it again—and got a mouthful-a lies when he git caught.

"And talk about sumpin mannish! I had to go to school with him one mornin' to see his teacher. I got the postcard on a Friday, and all that weekend I was askin' him what the teacher wanted to see me about, and all that weekend he was swearin' to some Gods and Jesuses I ain't never heard of before that he didn't know why in the world his teacher wanted to see me, unless somebody was tellin' lies on him again. And I told him, I said, 'Mind, now, my little slick nigger, you know I know you, and a lotta those lies people was tellin' on you was as true as what Christ told his disciples. Now, don't you let me go to that school and find out these lies they tellin' on you now got as much Gospel in 'em as those other lies had. 'Cause if I do, so help me, boy, I'm gonna take down your pants right there in that classroom and beat your ass until the Lord stop me.' He still kept sayin' he didn't do nothin' and had the nerve to poke out his lips and git mad at me for always blamin' him for sumpin he ain't did. You know that little scamp had me huggin' and kissin' him and apologizin' for what I said to him?

"So, Monday mornin' rolled around, and I went to school with him. I had to watch him close, had hold his hand from the minute he got up that mornin', 'cause I could tell by the look in his eye that if I took my eye offa him, that would be the last time I'd see him for the whole week. When I got to the school and talked to the teacher, I came to find out this Negro done took some little high-yaller girl in the closet one day when the teacher went outta the room. After he done gone and got mannish with this little yaller girl, he's gonna go and throw the little girl's drawers out the window. I almost killed that nigger in that classroom. As hard as people gotta work to get they kids clothes, he gon take somebody's drawers and throw 'em out the window. I bet you a fat man he never throwed nobody else clothes out no window. Ain't nothin' I kin do 'bout that high-yaller-woman weakness he got, 'cause he take that at his daddy. But I sho am glad they ain't got no little white girls in these schools in Harlem, 'cause my poor child woulda done been lynched, right up here in New York.

"They had him down there in one of those crazy wards in Bellevue Hospital, but they let him come home, so I guess it ain't nothin' wrong with his head. I think one-a dem doctors did think Sonny Boy was a little crazy though, 'cause he kept talkin' to me with all those big words, like he didn't want me to know what he was tellin' me. I don' know, maybe he didn' say Sonny Boy was crazy. It mighta been that he just don' know how to talk to regular people. You know, mosta those white doctors don' know how to talk to colored people anyway.

"Some of his teachers even said he was smart in doing his schoolwork and when he wasn't botherin' nobody. The trouble is that he's always botherin' somebody. He had one teacher, a little Jew-lady teacher, she was just as sweet as she could be. And she liked Sonny Boy and was always tryin' to be nice to him. She use to buy his lunch for him when he went lyin' to her about bein' hungry, after he done spend his lunch money on some ole foolishness. Well, one day she caught him lookin' up her dress, and she smacked him. Do you know that crazy boy hit her back? Yeah, I mean punch her dead in her face and made the poor lady cry. When I heard about it, I beat him for what seem like days, and I was scared to tell his daddy 'bout it, 'cause I know Cecil woulda killed him for doin' sumpin as crazy as that. And when I finished beating him, I told that nigger if I ever heard of him hitting or even talkin' back to that nice little Jew-lady again, I was gonna break his natural-born ass. Well, they throwed him outta that school right after that, so I guess he didn't git a chance to do that again.

"Yeah, sumpin is sho wrong with that boy, but I don't think he's crazy or nothin' like that, 'cause he got a whole lotta sense when it comes to gittin' in trouble. And when I stop to think about it, I don't believe nobody worked no roots on him, 'cause he got too much devil in him to be tricked by them root workers. But what coulda happen is that he went someplace and sassed some old person, and that old person put the bad mouth on him. Yeah, more'n likely that's what happened to him, 'cause he always sassing old people. I beat him and keep tellin' him not to talk back to people with gray hair, but that little devilish nigger got a head on him like rock. Lord, I don' know what to do with that boy. I just hope Pimp don't never git that bad."

When I got tired of hearing how bad I was and about the roots and the bad mouth, I took Pimp to the show. On the way to the show, Pimp asked me to tell him about roots. I didn't want to tell him that I didn't know, because he thought I knew everything, almost as much as God. So I started telling him things about roots and root workers based on the tales I had heard Mama tell about somebody working roots on somebody else "down home." I said, "Only people down South work roots, because you can't git roots around here." Pimp wanted to know what was wrong with the roots in the park. "Those ain't the right kinda roots," I said. "You have to git roots that grow down South. All kinda roots grow down there—money roots, love roots, good-luck roots, bad-luck roots, killin' roots, sick-makin' roots, and lotta other kinda roots."

"Sonny, do you know how to work roots?"

"Yeah, man, I can work some kinda roots, but some roots I'm not so sure about."

"Sonny, who teached you how to work roots?"

"Nobody. I just know 'cause I heard so much about it."

"Sonny, did you ever work any roots on anybody?"

"No, man, not yet."

"When you gonna work some on somebody?"

"When somebody who I can't beat make me real mad, that's when I'm gonna work some roots on somebody."

"You gonna work some roots on Daddy, Sonny?"

"No, man, he's too evil; you can't work roots on real evil people."

"Carole said God gon strike Daddy dead if he don't stop being so mean to us."

"Uh-uh, Pimp, I don't think God gon mess with Dad. 'Cause he woulda did it when Dad cut Miss Bertha husband throat that time or one-a those times when he beat me wit that ironing cord or that time when he cussed out the preacher. No, man, I don' think God gon mess wit Dad."

"Sonny, you think God is scared-a Daddy?"

"Man, I don' know. I know one thing—all the stuff he been doin' ain't nobody but the police been botherin' him."

"Maybe God gonna put the police on Daddy, huh, Sonny?"

"Yeah, man, maybe."

"Sonny, Margie said they got snakes down South and they bite people and the people die when the snakes bite 'em. Is that true, Sonny?"

"Yeah, it's true, but they don't bite everybody. They didn' bite Dad, and they didn' bite Mama, and I know a whole lotta people they didn' bite."

"Sonny, is the boogeyman down South too?"

"Man, how many times I done told you it ain't no boogeyman?"

"But Margie keep on sayin' it is."

"The next time she say it, punch huh in huh mout' real hard and she won't say it no more."

"Mama said the boogeyman comes around at night wit a big burlap sack and gits all bad kids and put in that burlap sack and nobody don't see 'em no more."

"Man, Mama's just try'n'-a scare you. You know it ain't no boogeyman, 'cause I told you so. You 'member all those times Mama and everybody use to say the boogeyman was gonna git me if I didn't stop bein' so bad? Well, I didn't git no gooder; I even got badder than I was then. Ain't no boogeyman got me yet. That's 'cause it ain't no boogeyman. Every place anybody even told me the boogeyman was, I went there and looked for him, but he ain't never been in none-a dem places. The next time somebody tell you the boogeyman is someplace, git you a big stick and go see him. If I'm around, come and get me and I'll show you it ain't no boogeyman."

"You ever been down South, Sonny?"

"Uh-uh not yet, but I know it ain't no boogeyman down there."

"They got crackers down there, ain't they, Sonny?"

"Yeah, Mama said they got crackers down South."

"Sonny, what is crackers? They ain't the kinda crackers you buy in the candy store, is they?"

"No, the crackers down South is white people, real mean white people."

"Is Mr. Goldman a cracker, Sonny?"

"No, he's a Jew."

"But he's white and look real mean."

"I know that, but some white people is crackers and some-a dem is Jews, and Mr. Goldman is a Jew. You see, Pimp, white people is all mean and stingy. If one-a dem is more stingy than he is mean, he's a Jew; and if he is more mean than he is stingy, then he's a cracker."

"But, Sonny, how kin you tell 'em?"

"That's easy. Just ask me. I'll tell you what they is."

"Sonny, I ain't goin' down South."

"Why ain'tcha?"

" 'Cause they got snakes down dere, they got roots down dere, and they got crackers too. Uh-uh, I ain't goin' down dere. You goin', Sonny?"

"Yeah, I'm goin'."

"Why?"

" 'Cause that judge said I better go."

Two weeks later, I was on my way down South for a summer vacation that lasted a year.

2

A year later, we were passing a farm in North Carolina. Mama was showing Pimp some goats from the train window. I was glad that she had brought Pimp down with her. I think I had missed him more than I had anybody else in the family. But Mama and Pimp had been down South for about a week before we got on the train this morning to go home, and I was tired of playing with Pimp and answering all those questions.

I wondered if Dad had missed me. I knew he hadn't. I knew what he would say to me when I got back. As usual, he would have a hard time, stumbling over words and repeating himself at least five times to say nothing more than, "Be good or I'm'a kill you." I hated that more than anything else. When Dad tried to talk to me, it never worked out. It would always end up with him hitting me, not because of what I had done but because it came easier to him than talking. Most of the time, I didn't mind. It was easier for me than trying to listen to all that stupid shit he was telling me with a serious face. Sometimes I would bullshit him by looking serious and saying something to make him think he was saying something real smart. I had a special way of bullshitting everybody I knew, and that was how I bullshitted Dad. But most of the time, he would be too mad to be bullshitted, and he would end up pounding on me anyway. I didn't really care, because I was just waiting and wondering—waiting till I got big enough to kick his ass and wondering if he would want to talk then. I could just see him trying real hard to talk and me not listening to anything, just kicking his ass time after time.

It was going be good to get back to New York and see Danny and Butch and Kid. I thought that Carole and Margie would be glad to see me, and I had missed them too. But I hadn't missed anybody as much as I'd missed Grace, except maybe Pimp. Grace was the prettiest girl I had ever met, and we were in love, or something like that.

When Grace first came into my class in P.S. 90, Mrs. Newton introduced her to the rest of the second graders as a "nice little girl in a pretty new dress" and told her how we were all glad to have her. Grace never lifted her eyes from the floor while Mrs. Newton introduced her. She looked like she was scared or shy; it was hard to tell which. Anyway, she didn't look pretty then.

I used to bother all the girls in the class. Most of them I had beaten up at least once. I didn't like girls much and used to get a lot of fun out of beating them up and chasing them home after school. I chased Grace home one day, but I didn't beat her up. I pulled on her, grabbed her around the neck, and ran with her hat. After a while, I stopped chasing other girls home and only chased Grace home.

One day when Grace didn't come to school, Rosalind, one of the girls I used to chase and beat up, asked me why I didn't chase her home any more. I told her that she wasn't as pretty as Grace and not to mess with me any more, because I wasn't going to chase her, but I would punch her in her mouth when I got a chance. Rosalind started saying that Grace looked funny with that brace on her teeth. I punched her in her mouth, and she ran home crying and promised to get her big sister on me. That was the first time I had thought about the brace on Grace's teeth. I had seen it, but I just never thought about it. When I thought about Grace, I thought about her long hair with the Shirley Temple curls and the freckles on her face that used to look funny. They sure didn't look funny any more. Anybody who laughed at them had better be able to beat me. Grace was the first girl I ever saw with freckles, and I liked her, freckles and all.

Grace was the only person I didn't have a way to bullshit. Everybody else I knew, I had a special way, everybody. Grace was the first girl I wanted to play with, and I wanted to play with her all the time. She was the first girl I knew who was nice to look at all day long and whose face I could see even when I wasn't looking at her. Mama's name was the first name that made me happy when I heard it. Grace was the second name to make me happy at the sound of it, and it made me happier than Mama's name sometimes.

In Mrs. Newton's second-grade class, the kids had to rest for one hour each day, and there were cots in the class for them to lie down on. One day, when I found my cot next to Grace's, she asked me which girl I liked best in the whole class. Even though I knew the question would come one way or another at some time or another, that was the happiest question I had ever been asked, and all I could answer was, "You." I prayed she would give me the same answer when I asked her who was her favorite boy in the whole class. We both gave the right answer, and I told everybody I knew that Grace was the prettiest girl in the world, and some of them I told it to over and over again.

I sure wanted to see Grace again and find out if she still liked me. I sure was sorry for not doing it to Grace when I had the chance that day up on the roof. I knew she wanted me to. She wanted me to do it to her real bad. And I would have too, if it wasn't for her little sister wanting me to do it to her too and not giving me a chance to get Grace by herself.

The year I had spent down South didn't look so bad from the train going to New York. I could even remember some good things about it that I didn't even know before. I had some fun down there. I didn't even hate Grandpa any more. Maybe I never did really hate him except for that time when he made me stay in the woods and saw down a tree when I was freezing. Or when he got the gun at me that time when he caught me playing house with Reverend Green's daughter. He told me he was going to kill me for being such a nasty damn scamp that nobody could bring their daughter around without me taking them under the house. He would have killed me that day if I hadn't run in the woods and stayed until that damn old owl scared the hell out of me. I know he would have shot me, because he had the devil in him. I had heard of a lot of people having the devil in them, but I never saw anybody who had it in them for sure until I met Grandpa.

The people down South said that somebody had put the bad mouth on Grandpa or had worked roots on him because he was so evil and that was why his whole right side was stiff. Grandma said God had put his hand on Grandpa as a warning for him to change his evil ways, but it seemed that the only thing that changed about Grandpa was that he was only half as able to do the evil he used to do. He sure was an evil man.

The time I hated him most and shouldn't have was that "hog-killing" time when I hit the hog on the head with the ax. The hog didn't die. Grandpa said, "Boy, you ain't shit." I wanted to hit him in the head with that ax, but I was scared of what would happen if he didn't die. On the train, I started hating that damn hog for not dying. Grandpa was still evil as hell, but he was all right with me now.

I learned some things down South too. I learned how to talk to a mule and plow a straight row in the sweet-potato patch. I even learned how to say "yas'm" and "yas suh." And Grandma told me what peckerwoods were and taught me not to call white potatoes white potatoes, "because they ain't white potaters, they is ice potaters." But I don't think I really learned those things—I think I just made believe I learned them. As soon as I got on that train going back to New York, I knew white potatoes were white potatoes, and I knew I had said "yas suh" and "yas'm" for the last time. And Grandpa told me some of the best-sounding lies I'd ever heard. At first, the only way I could tell they were lies was to keep watching Grandma when he started telling me things: when he was lying, Grandma would be peeking at him over her glasses in a certain way. After a while, I could tell when he was lying, because he would always start scratching his head when he started lying. I guess that's what made me pretty good at lying when I went back to New York. I learned to tell when Grandpa was lying, and I learned to lie to him so well that he only hit me with that oak stick of his two times for lying. That oak stick was real hard, so my lies had to be good.

I learned a lot about the church songs Dad and I used to sing. Grandpa didn't go to church any more, but he knew all about the songs and who sang them at what funeral. The best songs were sung at the funerals for the "bad niggers." I learned that a bad nigger was a nigger who "didn't take no shit from nobody" and that even the "crackers" didn't mess with him. Because a bad nigger raised so much hell in life, people couldn't just put him in the ground and forget him. I met an old man who used to be a bad nigger; he had one eye and one hand, and he looked just like what people said he used to be, a bad nigger.

One time I went to a funeral for a bad nigger. A lot of people were there, and most of them had heard about him but were seeing him for the first time. I guess they were scared to see him while he was still alive—and still bad. He was a real black man with big purple lips, and he had some ashy-looking powder on his face. They said he was a real big man, but he was lying down when I saw him. And they said he was so mean, he looked like the devil; but his eyes were closed when I saw him, and he just looked dead to me. At his funeral, a lot of ladies cried, and the preacher talked about him real loud for a long time. Before the preacher started talking, somebody sang "Before This Time Another Year" and "Got on My Traveling Shoes." When the preacher finished talking about him, they took the casket outside and put it down in the ground. I had seen people do that before, but I didn't think they would do it this time. It just didn't seem like the right way to treat a bad nigger, unless being dead made him not so bad any more.

Sometimes Grandpa used to hum some of the church songs when he was sitting in his rocking chair out on the porch patting his foot and watching the sun go down behind Mr. Hayward's tobacco barn. He would close his eyes and just start humming away. Maybe he was thinking about a funeral where he sang a song real good for somebody. Or maybe he was thinking about a funeral that didn't happen yet, a funeral where he wouldn't hear the songs, wouldn't know who was singing them, and wouldn't hear the preacher talking . . . talking about him . . . real loud. Maybe he was thinking about who would sing his favorite song for him and hoping that Mr. Charlie Jackson would live long enough to do the singing for him.

I couldn't understand why they sang nothing but those sad old church songs. They sure seemed to be some dumb country people to me. They didn't know any boogie songs or jump songs—they didn't even know any good blues songs. Nobody had a record player, and nobody had records. All the songs they sang, they'd been singing for years and years.

Somebody would sing real good at Grandpa's funeral, and a lot of people would be there. It would have to be a big funeral, because Grandpa was a real bad and evil nigger when he was a young man. He had the devil in him, and everybody knew it, even people who didn't know him. When Grandma took me to town or to church, people would come up to me and stare at me for a while, then ask, "Boy, is Mr. Son Brown yo' granddaddy?" And after a while, I knew why they were looking at me so hard; they were trying to see if I had the devil in me too.

For a long time, I used to be scared of Grandpa. He used to go walking in the woods in the evening, and when I asked Grandma where Grandpa was always going, she said he was hunting the devil. I only asked one time. I started to follow him once, but I got scared and changed my mind.

People used to say I was going to be just like Grandpa, since I had the devil in me too. I never paid attention to what people said about being like Grandpa until one day. That day, my cousin McKinley Wilson and me were out in the yard seeing who could pick up the biggest and heaviest sack of corn. While I was straining to pick up a sack, I heard Grandma scream and felt a stinging feeling on my neck that made me drop the sack, jump up and down, and grab my neck. When I turned around to see what had happened to me, I saw Grandma standing there with a switch in her hand. She was screaming and hollering a whole lot of things at me, but all I could make out was that she was going to kill me if I ever did that again. I didn't know what to think except that maybe she was going crazy. She had never said anything when I messed with the wasps' nests and got stung and cried and kept on messing with them. I couldn't understand why she had hit me, and Grandma didn't talk much. I knew she had mistreated me, and I had to do something about it, so I started walking, walking back to New York.

When Grandma caught up with me on the highway, she had a bigger switch, and she was real mad. After she finished beating me for running away, she said she had hit me because she didn't want me to be walking like Grandpa. I asked her if Grandpa had gotten his stroke from lifting corn.

She said, "It wasn' no stroke that makes Grandpa walk the way he do. The stroke just stiffened up his right side. But you see the way he gotta swing his left leg way out every time he take a step?"

I said, "Yeah, I seen him do that."

Grandma said that Grandpa walked that way because he was toting corn one day. I didn't understand, but I kept on listening. Then Grandma started telling me about the things I saw Grandpa cut out of the pig to keep the bacon from getting rank when they killed the pig. And she told me that right above the things that make the bacon rank are the chitterlings and that chitterlings press against a thin window in pigs and boys and men. I never knew I had chitterlings in me until that day. Grandma said if somebody lifted something too heavy for him, the chitterlings would press right through that window and the man would have a hard time walking and doing a lot of other things for the rest of his life. She said one time Grandpa was in the woods making liquor, and his dog started barking. Grandpa picked up his still and started running with it. The still was too heavy—the window broke, and now Grandpa had to walk real slow. She was saying that she didn't mean to hit me. She just didn't want me to break my window.

We walked back home up the highway. Grandma had her arm around my shoulder, and I had my arm around her waist. That was the only time I ever touched Grandma—and the only time I recall wanting her to touch me and liking her touch. When I saw the house coming at us up the road, I was kind of sad. I looked at Grandma's wrinkled face and liked it. I knew I had fallen in love with that mean old wrinkled lady who, I used to think, had a mouth like a monkey. I had fallen in love with a mean old lady because she hit me across the neck for trying to lift a sack of corn.

Down South seemed like a dream when I was on the train going back to New York. I saw a lot of things down South that I never saw in my whole life before, and most of them I didn't ever want to see again. I saw a great big old burly black man hit a pig in the head with the back of an ax. The pig screamed, oink-oinked a few times, lay down, and started kicking and bleeding . . . and died. When he was real little, I used to chase him, catch him, pick him up, and play catch with him. He was a greedy old pig, but I used to like him. One day when it was real cold, I ate a piece of that pig, and I still liked him.

One day I saw Grandma kill a rattlesnake with a hoe. She chopped the snake's head off in the front yard, and I sat on the porch and watched the snake's body keep wiggling till it was nighttime. And I saw an old brown hound dog named Old Joe eat a rat one day, right out in the front yard. He caught the rat in the woodpile and started tearing him open. Old Joe was eating everything in the rat. He ate something that looked like the yellow part in an egg, and I didn't eat eggs for a long time after that.

I saw a lady rat have a lot of little baby rats on a pile of tobacco leaves. She had to be a lady, because my first-grade teacher told a girl that ladies don't cry about little things, and the rat had eleven little hairless pink rats, and she didn't even squeak about it.

I made a gun down South out of a piece of wood, some tape, a piece of tire-tube rubber, a nail, some wire, a piece of pipe, and a piece of door hinge. And I saw nothing but blood where my right thumbnail used to be after I shot it for the first time. The nail grew back, little by little. I saw a lot of people who had roots worked on them, but I never saw anybody getting roots worked on them.

Down South sure was a crazy place, and it was good to be going back to New York.

The smell of the Eighth Avenue Subway was all I needed to make me know that I was really in New York and that I would not be hearing that old red rooster crowing out in the chicken house.

The train ride uptown was the longest train ride I ever took. As the train came to each station, I remembered something about that station. I remembered shaking down the two white shoeshine boys at the Forty-second Street station. And I remembered that time the cops saw me beating in a gum machine at the Fifty-ninth Street station and I had to run across the subway tracks in front of a train. I sure was fast. I must have done something at Seventy-second Street, but I couldn't remember it, and that bothered me. I remembered the way that lady screamed when I snatched her pocket-

41

book at Eighty-first Street. She screamed so loud that it scared me. She acted like somebody was killing her. A lot of people started chasing me, and the woman kept on screaming. I got scareder and dropped the pocketbook. I got away, but I should have kept that pocketbook. The way that lady was screaming, she must have had a lot of money in it.

At every stop, I wanted to get off the train and yell that I was back. I wanted everybody to know that I was back and that it was, like Goldie used to say, "goddamn good" to be back.

When I came out of the subway at 145th Street and St. Nicholas Avenue, I thought there had never been a luckier person in the world than me. I wanted to grab the sidewalk and hug it tight. I wanted to run away from Mama and Pimp, run and jump on the back of the trolley car going up the hill. The trolley cars had changed. Somebody went and painted them orange and green; they used to be red and yellow.

It was Sunday morning. Kids were coming from church with their mothers and fathers, and some people were sick and vomiting on the street. Most of the people were dressed up, and vomit was all over the street near the beer gardens. There was a lot of blood near the beer gardens and all over the sidewalk on Eighth Avenue. This was a real Sunday morning—a lot of blood and vomit everywhere and people all dressed up and going to church. Some of them were all dressed up and sleeping on the sidewalk or sleeping on building stoops. It was all real good to see again, real good. There were the ladies going to church in white dresses and trying real hard not to look at the men standing on the corners cussing and saying fresh things to them— but trying real hard to listen to what the men were saying without looking as if they were hearing it. That man who was all dressed up and sleeping on the sidewalk propped up against the newspaper stand with a smile on his face sure looked happy. I was so happy to see them, to see it, to see it all, to see Harlem again.

As I came to our stoop, people started calling me and running up to me asking stupid questions. Was I a good boy now? How did I like down South? I would have said something smart or cursed them out, but I was so happy to see everybody, I just smiled, laughed, and said yeah to everything. Everything would have been good and happy if only I didn't have to see Dad in a little while. A lot of times I used to wish that Dad would die and that Mr. Sam would marry Mama and be our father. Mr. Sam used to like Mama, and he was real nice. He believed everything I told him. Dad was real mean, and he didn't believe anything I told him. But Dad told Mr. Sam that if he ever came across our threshold again, he was going to kick him in his ass. Mr. Sam must have believed Dad, because he didn't come back any more.

The hallway looked smaller, but it was still the same, the way it was supposed to be looking on Sunday morning. Somebody had gotten cut the night before, and blood was still in the hall. And somebody had pissed on the stairs, and it was still there, just like it should have been. Whoever pissed on that radiator sure was lucky Mr. Lawson hadn't caught him, because the super might have hit him in the head with his baseball bat and busted his head open, like he did to that other man that time. On the landing just before ours, somebody had vomited. Pimp stepped in it and started to cuss, but he remembered that he was with Mama. That sure seemed funny—I didn't know Pimp knew how to cuss. I started thinking that there might be a lot of things that I didn't know about him now, and that scared me, so I stopped thinking about it.

When we walked into the house, everybody was sleeping. I started feeling sorry for Carole and Margie for being home with nobody but Dad for a whole week. I sure felt sorry for them. I wanted to run into their rooms and wake them up. I knew they would be real glad to see me, and I wondered what they looked like now. But I had to go through Dad's room to get to theirs. Dad was still in bed, but he was awake.

We just stared at each other for a long time. I knew he was wondering what to say, and I was wondering what to say back to him when he finally did find something to say. I said hello, and Dad asked me if I liked it down South and if I was going to be a good boy now. I stood up way over on the other side of the room, answered him real fast, and waited for the next question to come. We talked for a long time about nothing, and I knew that Dad was the same and that I still didn't like him. Carole came out of her room and screamed when she saw me. Her scream woke up Margie, and she ran in shouting my name. But then both of them saw that Dad was talking to me, so they stood over on the far side of the room smiling and waving at me. I hated Dad more than ever before now, hated him because Carole and Margie were over there and I was over here and we all had to stay where we were till he finished talking about nothing. I wanted to touch Carole and Margie and push them and grab them and hit them. I had really missed them while I was down South, and I was still missing them now while Dad just kept on talking.

I wanted to kick Dad in his ass for all the times he had beaten Carole and Margie while I was away. And I knew he had beaten them, especially Margie, because she wasn't scared of him. Maybe he had even beaten Carole too sometimes. Margie forgot about Dad talking, or maybe she knew he wasn't saying anything. Anyway, while Dad was still talking to me, Margie ran up to me and jumped up on me, threw her arms around my neck, and just kept screaming. Dad didn't say anything, and I think he was thankful to Margie for getting him out of that talking that he had to do. After he stopped talking, the only thing I remembered hearing him say was, "It looks like you growed a little bit." And I wondered what he was thinking when he said that. He was probably thinking that soon he wouldn't be able to hit me any more.

Carole and Margie started showing me the scars on their legs, knees, and arms that they had gotten from falling down or being pushed down by somebody they wanted me to beat up for them. I told them all about down South and the things that happened down there. Margie was the same as she used to be, and Carole was almost the same. For a while I couldn't figure out what was different about her, but when she started laughing, I saw it. I thought, Carole has titties on her chest. Oh, shit, real titties. I asked her when and where did she get them and asked her to show them to me, but she wouldn't. She said she couldn't because she wasn't supposed to. I got mad at her and started to feel sad because we weren't as good friends as we used to be. I was real sorry I had stayed down South so long now. . . . Something happened and I didn't know about it.

That was the first time I had ever been away from Harlem for more than a month or two, and to me New York was Harlem. New York sure seemed changed. Even the people didn't look the same. Some people were smaller than they used to be, and some people were bigger. A lot of people weren't living on Eighth Avenue any more, and some people who weren't living there before were living there now. Some of the stores weren't there any more, and some of the ones still there had new owners and looked different from before. Some of the old cops were gone, but it looked like they had more than before. Some of the cops got killed for messing with people, and some of them got killed just for trying to be bad. It seemed like a whole lot of people had gotten killed or just died.

I didn't know what to do. Danny had moved away, and Kid and Butch were in Warwick. I could see that it wasn't as easy to steal things as it used to be. Most of the white people up on the hill had moved away, and colored people owned the stores now. And it was hard to steal from the colored store owners, because they could run fast and were always watching you. I started looking for somebody to hang out with and was real glad to see Bucky. Bucky was hanging out with a boy named Bulldog and a boy named Knoxie. Bulldog was a nice guy. He was real dumb and would do anything I told him to do. Knoxie thought he was bad and liked to try to boss people around. The first day I met Knoxie, we got into a fight and kept fighting for a long time. One day I beat Knoxie two times. After that, Knoxie and I got to be real good friends, even better friends than Bucky and I. I started taking Knoxie downtown and to Brooklyn with me and showing him how to steal different things and how to shake down newspaper boys and stay out all night. Knoxie taught me how to dance. He taught me how to do a dance called the Applejack and a dance called the Bop. I told Knoxie what had happened to me down South with the homemade gun, and he taught me how to make a zip gun. They didn't have zip guns before I went down South.

I liked Knoxie because he had a lot of heart; he would do almost anything. We started a gang, and I was president and Knoxie was war counselor. Knoxie was a good war counselor because he started a lot of fights. Everywhere we went, Knoxie would find a gang to start a fight with. Some of the guys in our gang were scared to go out of our turf and rumble because they didn't know the backyards and the roofs in other turfs. Knoxie was always ready to go anywhere to fight—and was ready to fight anybody who didn't want to go with him. So I kept the gang together by fighting Knoxie every other week when he started picking on somebody. The other guys used to say that Knoxie didn't care where he went to fight because he didn't have a mother. Bugsy said Knoxie didn't cry when he got stabbed in the face because he didn't have a mother to feel sorry for him. Knoxie said he did have a mother and was always taking somebody home to show them his mother, but she was never home. It got to a point where a guy who was losing an argument with Knoxie would ask Knoxie if he wanted to come home with him to see his mother. Knoxie would start swinging, and some guys would start laughing. After a while, Knoxie stopped arguing with everybody. Then one day Leroy asked Knoxie if he could borrow his zip gun to take to school and shoot a teacher. Knoxie said no, and the argument led to Knoxie's mother. When Leroy asked if he wanted to come home with him to see his mother, Knoxie said, "Who would want to see that old nasty, dirty, stinkin' bitch but the iceman?" That was the last time I recall anybody talking about the mother Knoxie didn't have.

Grace was in Carole's class, and I gave Carole a note asking Grace to be my girl friend. Grace said yes, and we were in love again. I got the feeling that Carole didn't like Grace, because every time I asked her if she thought Grace was the prettiest girl in her class, she seemed to get mad. Carole kept telling me about a girl in her class who liked me and whose name was Sugar. I kept telling Carole that I didn't know Sugar, didn't want to know Sugar, and didn't want to hear any more about Sugar. One day Carole brought Sugar home for lunch with her. Sugar had buckteeth and a big mouth. I thought she was the ugliest girl I'd ever met, and I told her what I thought. I beat up Sugar the first day I met her and every day after that for a long time.

I found out that Sugar would bring candy and pickles to class and give them to Carole, so Carole liked her and wanted me to like her too. After I got used to Sugar being ugly and having buckteeth, I didn't mind her always hanging around, and I stopped beating her up. Sugar started coming around on the weekends, and she always had money and wanted to take me to the show. Sometimes I would go with Sugar, and sometimes I would just take her money and go with somebody else. Most of the time I would take Sugar's money, then find Bucky and take him to the show. Sugar used to cry, but I don't think she really minded it too much, because she knew she was ugly and had to have something to give people if she wanted them to like her. I never could get rid of Sugar. She would follow me around all day long and would keep trying to give me things, and when I didn't take them, she would start looking real pitiful and say she didn't want me to have it anyway. The only way I could be nice to Sugar was to take everything she had, so I started being real nice to her.

One day I got into a fight with J.J. and didn't know why. J.J. was saying it would be all right for somebody to have a girl friend like Sugar if he didn't mind not kissing her, because her teeth would be in the way for kissing. He said that every time somebody wanted to kiss Sugar, he would have to let her know way ahead of time so she could start closing her mouth or whatever she did to get her teeth out of the way. That was the last thing I heard before I found my fist in J.J.'s face. After that, everybody started saying that I liked Sugar—at least everybody who could beat me or who thought they could beat me. After that, I told Sugar to stay away from me and showed her I wasn't playing by not taking anything from her any more.

Sugar could fight pretty good for a girl, so when she told Grace to stay away from me, Grace did. Then I got mad at Sugar and had to see her again. She knew I would. I told Sugar that if she ever bothered Grace again, I was going to beat her ass black and blue. She said, "No you ain't." But I did. Then we bought some pomegranates and went to the park and talked about why I liked Grace. Sugar said she couldn't see why I liked Grace so much, since Grace was a scaredy-cat and messed around with all the boys on their block. After a while Sugar asked me if I had ever done it to Grace. I told her that it was none of her business. Then she said I probably did, since all the other boys on the block had. I asked her how she knew about it, and she said it was none of my business, so we stopped talking about Grace.

I told Sugar that I liked her a little bit and that we could be friends, but she would have to stay out of my personal life. (I had heard a man say that in a picture at the Odeon about three weeks before. And I had been waiting for three weeks to say it to somebody. I liked the way it sounded when I said it. It sounded better than when the man said it in the movies.) Sugar said that was all right because she only liked me a little bit too. I told her I liked her like a sister and it wasn't the kind of liking where you wanted to kiss somebody or do it to them. Sugar laughed and said that was just because I was young and didn't know what was good yet. I laughed too and told her she was just as young as I was if she was that old. Sugar said she was almost thirteen and that she knew I was only ten or maybe ten and a half. I told her I didn't believe she was twelve years old, but I knew she must have been, because she was in Carole's class in school, and Carole was almost thirteen. That made me feel kind of bad. It seemed that all the girls I knew were older than I was. Most of the guys I knew, too. I didn't mind the guys being older, but it seemed as if I should have been older than the girls, at least some of them. But I told myself that was all right; I was getting older, and one day I would be older than everybody. All I had to do was wait. When Sugar and I left the park, we were good friends, and she was happy about it. In fact, we were both kind of happy about it.

Sugar started coming around every day again. Sometimes on Saturdays she would come around real early in the morning before I got out of bed and would try to slip in bed beside me without waking me up. Most of the time I would wake up before she could get all the way in and would push her out on the floor and call for Mama. Mama would never answer. She had the same nickname as Sugar, and she liked Sugar. Anything Sugar did was all right.

Mama used to say that Grace looked like an old woman with that wire and gold in her mouth and that when I grew up, I was going to marry Sugar. Mama always knew that she would hit a number one day for a lot of money or would win a sweepstakes. She was going to buy a white house with a red top down South for me and Sugar. I would always say, "No, Mama, me and Grace." And Mama would always say, "All right, you mark my words."

One day a few months after I got back from the South, I didn't feel like staying in school, so I went looking for somebody to play hookey with. Bulldog and Toto were in the same class; and as always, Bulldog was sleeping. Toto came out and went back to get Bulldog. This took some time, because their teacher knew they were hookey partners and wouldn't let them out of the class together. So Bulldog had to get the pass, since he couldn't run so fast. We waited for Toto in the backyard across the street from the school. When he came, we all went downtown looking for something to steal. We didn't steal too much that day, so we kept on looking after it got dark. Late that night, we found a good store to break into. It was at Broadway and 147th Street. There were a lot of radios and clocks and electric irons and stuff like that. And the store had a transom that didn't seem to have a burglar alarm on it.

Since Bulldog was slow at running and doing most things, he stayed outside and we passed the stuff out to him. When I had started filling up the third shopping bag, Toto called me to the window. He was still passing the stuff out to Bulldog. Bulldog had fallen asleep, but he was still taking the stuff that Toto was passing to him. He was taking it and passing it to two big white cops behind him.

I thought the cops would take us to the Children's Center on 104th Street. Instead, they took us to a place I had heard about but had never been to before, a place called the Youth House way down on East Twelfth Street.

I remember the day I went to the Youth House because it was four days before Carole's birthday party. Carole was going to be thirteen years old the next Sunday. Everybody was going to be at Carole's party. Well, almost everybody, because I wasn't going to be there now, unless we had a real softhearted judge. Bulldog wouldn't be there either, and he would miss it; he really liked to eat, especially cake and ice cream and stuff like that. Toto couldn't come anyway. We had been in trouble a lot of times before, and Mama wouldn't let him come to our house. She said he was too roguish. Mama said that of all the little rogues I hung out with, Toto was the most roguish-looking one. One time Mama was telling Dad about Toto, and Dad said, "All them little rogues he hangs out wit look like they'll steal anything that ain't nailed down." And Mama said, "Well, Toto is the one who looks like he'll steal the nails and all." But that was all right, because Toto's mother didn't let him hang out with me either, and she probably said the same thing about me.

When we went to court the next day, we didn't get a softhearted judge; we got a mean old colored lady named Judge Bolin. I had seen her picture on a magazine cover one time, that colored magazine that Jackie Robinson, Joe Louis, and Pigmeat use to have their pictures in sometimes. That lady judge looked meaner than she did on the magazine cover. She had a hard-to-hear voice, but you could hear it—everybody in the courtroom was real quiet when she said something. She had a face on her that looked like the hardest thing in the world to do with it would have been to smile. I wondered what would happen if somebody in the courtroom said something funny and she tried to smile at it. I thought that her face would probably crack up from the strain. But that wasn't going to happen anyway, because everybody in the place seemed to be scared of her. It almost made me scared of her. I started to get scared of her too until I saw what was going on. This lady judge was just like the mean old queens I had seen in sword-fighting pictures at the Odeon. She was bullying everybody in that courtroom with a low voice, even the men, who seemed like a bunch of turkeys, scared of a woman.

Whenever she wanted to show the people there how bad she was, instead of hitting somebody or yelling at them she just looked at them or talked even softer. When she started talking softer, she was bullying everybody in the queen's courtroom. I thought, It's like she's sayin', "Goddamit, you peasants better shut up and listen to me, 'cause I'm gonna ask you what I said, and everybody who don't know is gonna git his head chopped off!" So the softer she talked, the quieter everybody was and the harder they listened, because their heads depended on it. When she looked at somebody, his head went on the hatchet man's list, and there was nothing he could do but wait for the man with the black hood over his face to come and get him.

I wondered what would happen if I yelled out, "Ain't nobody scared-a you, you ole bitch!" I had never called a lady a bitch, but I called a big girl a bitch one time and ran real fast. I thought that if I didn't act scared, the mean queen would get real mad and would probably send me to that place called Sing Sing. So I did the best thing—stayed real quiet and acted as if I were scared of her too. I thought, This lady judge couldn't have a husband like Dad and be as mean as she is, 'cause Dad would beat her ass. Or would he? Maybe this lady is too mean for anybody to beat, even Dad.

From the minute I laid eyes on the mean queen, I knew she wasn't going to send me home, and she didn't. She gave me another day to come back to court and sent me back to the Youth House. Toto was sent there too, but Bulldog had to go to the Children's Center.

Before we left the court, Mama said, "That judge said you don't come back to court before January 5. Boy, do you know that's next year? You wasn't home for last Christmas, and you won't be home for this one either. And you won't be home for Carole's birthday party next Sunday. It's just November 14, and you only been back in New York three months and four days. Boy, sometimes I git the feelin' you ain't gon never stay home no more."

I told Mama that I didn't care so much about not being home and that if Bulldog had stayed awake, I would have brought Carole the biggest and best birthday present she'd ever had. All Mama did was look at me with tears in her eyes, and I knew she was thinking, Lord, what's the matter with my child?

When the bus was all loaded and ready to take us back to the Youth House, one of the boys in the seat behind me tapped me on the shoulder and said, "Hey, shorty, ain't that your mother standin' on the court stoop?"

"Yeah."

He said, "Man, she's cryin'."

I said, "So what?" as if I didn't care. But I cared; I had to care: that was the first time I had seen Mama crying like that. She was just standing there by herself, not moving, not making a sound, as if she didn't even know it was cold out there. The sun was shining, but it was cold and there was ice on the ground. The tears just kept rolling down Mama's face as the bus started to pull away from the curb. I had to care. Those tears shining on Mama's face were falling for me. When the bus started down the street, I wanted to run back and say something to Mama. I didn't know what. I thought, Maybe I woulda said, "Mama, I didn' mean what I said, 'cause I really do care." No, I wouldn'a said that. I woulda said, "Mama, button up your coat. It's cold out here." Yeah, that's what I forgot to say to Mama.

There was something good about being in the Youth House. It made me feel big, as if I had outgrown the Children's Center. That was for kids. For one thing, you couldn't get out of the Youth House. The windows had iron gates on them, and the doors were always locked. But after a while, I didn't want to go anyway. Being in the Youth House was much better than being down South. In the Youth House, they showed movies twice a week, and you could play pool, basketball, checkers, go swimming, fight, and do a lot of other things. The Youth House was clean too. It wasn't as clean as the Center, but it was cleaner than most of the places I had been to. What I didn't like about the Youth House was that I had to clean my room every other day. Then they gave me a roommate I could beat, and I stopped cleaning it and started learning how to do what Danny used to call "git by."

Once I learned how to get by, the Youth House became one of the nicest places I had ever been. I really liked it there. I became a member of the Council on my floor. Toto was a member too, and we both were getting by real good. The people in the Youth House trusted the Council members more than they did the rest of the boys. So Toto and I could steal a lot of things and nobody would even think we did it. Sometimes when we took something and thought somebody might find out, we would bully some punky guy and make him say that he did it. And if things really got bad, like everybody on the floor losing play privileges for a while, we would take whatever we stole and put it in somebody else's room. Then when the searching started, either me or Toto would find it, and the person whose room we found it in would get in trouble. As time went on, the floor supervisor started getting wise to us, but this didn't mean that we had to stop. We just had to find a new way to do what we wanted to do, and we always found one. I was getting by real good, and I didn't care if I never left the Youth House.

I was learning to shoot pool real good. Before I came to the Youth House, I never had a chance to learn. I wasn't big enough to go in the poolroom on 145th Street. Mama came to visit me every Saturday or Sunday, so it was just like being out on the street, only better, because I could do everything I wanted to do—steal, fight, curse, play, and nobody could take me and put me anywhere. I was already in the only place they could put me. I had found a way to get away with everything I wanted to do. When I got out, I was going to tell Knoxie and Bucky and everybody what a good time you could have in the Youth House. And I was going to find Danny and tell him that I had found out how to do all the things we wanted to do and get away with it. The only thing you had to do was go to the Youth House first, then you didn't have to worry about anything after that.

Around Christmas time, Toto started saying that I was changing and that he wasn't going to hang out with me any more when we got out of the Youth House. He said that I was bullying everybody and that sooner or later somebody was going to kick my ass. So I got mad and kicked his. Before that time, I had never been in a fight with Toto; but I always knew I could beat him, and he knew it too, so there was nothing for us to fight about. We wouldn't have had that fight if I hadn't said something about his mother. He had to fight after that, because a guy who won't fight when somebody talks about his mother is the worst kind of punk.

Toto was right in what he said. I guess that's why I got mad. Just about everybody on the third floor of the Youth House was scared of me, and I liked it. This was the first time I had ever been anyplace where nearly everybody was scared of me, and before I knew anything, I was liking it. And I didn't care what anybody said or how right what they were saying was. I was having more fun than I'd ever had in my whole life. I knew I was doing things to people that I never would have done out on the street, but I didn't care. It didn't make sense to be in the Youth House if you were only going to do the things you did out on the street.

One Sunday, Mama and Dad came to visit me, and while we was sitting in the visiting room talking, a boy came over to us with his mother, pointed at me, and said, "He's the one who's always hittin' on me." I jumped up, swung at him, and missed, and while Dad was holding me, I called him a lying faggot. Dad slapped me in the mouth. It didn't hurt much, but I got mad and I cried. I wanted to kill him for hitting me in front of all those people—and in front of some of the guys I was bullying too.

I said to myself, That's all right, 'cause when I git big enough to kill him, I'll jis have one more thing to kill him for. So I stopped crying. Dad was going to make me kill him. Sometimes I was only going to kick his ass real good when I got big, but then he would do something like that, and I would start planning to kill him again.

Mama was looking scared about something, and she said, "Boy, where you heard that word at?"

I knew what word she was talking about, but still I said, "What word?"

Mama said, "That word you called that little white boy; that's what word."

"Oh, you mean 'liar'?"

Dad slapped me and promised to beat my ass right there in that visiting room if I kept on playing dumb. So I told Mama that everybody called him that.

"Do everybody know what it means?" Mama asked me.

I thought I saw a way out with this question. So I said, "Yeah, it means he can't fight and lets everybody pick on him. That's what it means."

Dad said, "Oh," and started to say something else, but Mama beat him to it, like most of the time.

"What does everybody pick on him for?"

I said, " 'Cause he won't fight, that's why. Anyway, I don't pick on him. He was lyin' when he said that."

Mama said, "Look, nigger, you know that boy didn't bring his mother over here and point you out just to tell lies on you." Mama looked over me and started talking to Dad.

After Dad had slapped me, Mama went over and talked to the other boy's mother. Mama came back and told Dad that the white lady had said that her son was a meek boy and wasn't "aggressive or somethin' another like that." Mama couldn't understand white people too well anyway, and when they used those big words she couldn't understand them at all.

Mama could understand Jewish people pretty well because she had worked for them for years. That's how she could tell if a white person was Jewish or not, I guess, by whether or not she could understand them.

Dad said, "Maybe the little boy is got girlish ways, and if he is, ain't nothin' nobody can do about it, especially if he won't fight."

Tears started sneaking down Mama's face. The first tear stopped for a little while on the rough spot on her cheek, then it went on down and stopped between her lips, and her lipstick started shining. I didn't watch it any more. Dad got up and went over on the other side of Mama and put his arm around her. I reached into the bag of fruit that Mama and Dad had brought me, took out a pear, and started eating it; I liked pears. Dad started telling Mama that it wasn't so bad, since I was only ten years old; and, anyway, it wasn't as if I was the one who couldn't fight. I had a feeling that Dad was only going to make Mama cry louder and more, because he never knew what to say to her.

And that was just what happened. Mama started crying more and saying, "He'll be eleven years old soon, and he gittin' into that shit already."

Dad said, "Can't nothin' real bad happen before he gits thirteen or fourteen."

"Lord knows I want that boy to be around some girls when he git that age."

And Dad said, "No, Sugar, he'll be home then if he ever learn to stay outta trouble."

Mama just kept on crying, and Dad couldn't do anything about it. I could have told Dad what to say to make Mama stop crying. I could even have told him something to tell her to make her smile. It would have been a lie, but it would have made Mama feel real good. But I didn't say anything. It wasn't my place to say anything. And Dad kept on holding her and saying stupid things to her and Mama kept on crying and I kept on eating the pear.

I didn't know it then, but at the Youth House I met a lot of guys I was going to see again and live with again in a lot of places, white guys, Spanish guys, colored guys, all kinds of guys. The Youth House had more guys in it than Bellevue did, and it didn't have any girls. Some of the guys in the Youth House were a little crazy, but it was only when somebody made them mad, not that real crazy kind of crazy or the all-the-time kind of crazy like the guys in Bellevue. Most of the guys in the Youth House were all right; some of them just couldn't fight. But even the ones who couldn't fight were going to be with me again in other places and for more time than in the Youth House. Some of the guys I didn't like there I was going to like someplace else, and some other time we were going to be friends and fight for each other.

On January 5, Toto and I went to court, and when the mean queen said she was going to place me in some kind of school for boys, it didn't bother me. I don't know why, but I just didn't care. Then she said she was going to send me home for a while first, till they had room for me. She was talking to Mama, and I could hear her, but I couldn't understand what the mean queen was saying. I knew it wasn't anything bad—Mama didn't look like she was about to cry like she did when the queen sent me to the Youth House. I kept watching Mama, and Mama kept looking up at the queen from the bottom of her eyes and nodding her head faster and faster to let the queen know that she understood her. It seemed like Mama was trying to make that mean lady judge stop talking and let us leave before the queen changed her mind and sent me back to the Youth House.

Mrs. Jones, Toto's mother, was standing right next to Toto and me. And Toto was watching her and trying to look pitiful, just like I was. Mama and Mrs. Jones sure did look crazy with their heads going up and down faster and faster as they peeped up at the mean queen from the bottom of their eyes and tried to look as if they knew what she was saying to them. All I knew was that I was supposed to look sorry for what I had done. Toto knew this too, so we were both looking real sorry while our mothers nodded their heads. All the time, I was wishing that I had gotten caught with somebody else, because Toto was too good at looking pitiful. He was so good that he even made me feel sorry for him. After a while, I stopped trying to look sorry and just tried to look like Toto. I sure was glad that Bulldog wasn't there, because he could look more pitiful than anybody I knew without even trying. When he started looking pitiful, he might have made the mean queen think that Toto and I were laughing. Mama said that they had sent Bulldog to Bellevue from the Children's Center and that he was still there.

All the head nodding stopped, and Mama and Mrs. Jones were thanking the mean queen. On the way home, we walked over to Lexington Avenue, and Mama bought me a hot dog and a glass of soda. It was kind of good being outside in the street again. Mrs. Jones bought a hot dog for Toto too, and then Mama and Mrs. Jones started telling us that we were in a lot of trouble and that we were going to be sent away to a school for bad boys until we were twenty-one. Mama asked me if I was ever going to be good or if I was just planning to spend my whole life in jail, die in the electric chair, or let somebody kill me for stealing something.

I was glad to be with Mama, and I wanted to be nice to her because she had tried so hard to get the mean queen to send me home. So I told Mama the truth. I told her that I didn't know what was going to happen and that there was nothing I could do about it anyway.

Mama got mad and said, "You little dumb nigger, didn' you hear that lady judge say she gonna send you away someplace to a school?" Mama looked down the counter and saw a white man drinking a cup of coffee. Then she looked down at the floor real fast. She wanted to hit me, but she remembered I had just gotten out of the Youth House, and she didn't want to start hitting me already. Mama looked at the floor for a little while, and I knew she was ashamed that the white man had heard her call me a nigger.

Then I said, "Mama, that's nothing, 'cause I don' care, and it ain't none-a his business anyway."

Mama said, "Boy, hurry up and eat that hot dog." The next thing Mama said was something about hoping that I didn't think that lady judge was talking about a real school. Mama said that the judge was sending me to a reform school and that I might get out when I was eighteen if I was real good till that time. Mama asked me again if I understood that. I told her that there was nothing I could do about it now and that maybe I would die before I went, so it didn't make sense for me to worry about it. And I told Mama that Grandpa use to always say that. Mama said that Grandpa was older than me and that Grandpa had never stolen anything from anybody—

or at least he had never gotten caught. I said I never thought that I was older than Grandpa and that I didn't get caught all the time either. Mama got mad, and I kept on eating the hot dog. I liked Mama a whole lot, but there were things that she just couldn't understand, and she wouldn't listen to me when I tried to explain them to her.

When I got back home I promised Dad and Mama that I wasn't going to hang out with Toto any more, and I didn't for two whole days. I even went to school for a week straight without playing hookey once. Then Knoxie started coming by my house early in the morning, and we would go up on the Hill instead of going to school. I just stopped going to school altogether, and nobody seemed to care about it. I had to leave the house every morning so Dad and Mama wouldn't know I wasn't going to school, but nobody sent any absence cards to my house, and the truant officer didn't come around either. I didn't know what was going on, but I liked it, whatever it was. Well, I liked it for a while anyway.

One day when I hadn't been to school in a long time, Mama said, "So you ain't been goin' to school, huh? Okay, have your fun young man, 'cause pretty soon you gonna be someplace where they'll make you go to school."

This was the kind of thing that was supposed to make Dad grab the ironing cord and me at the same time, but Dad didn't do a thing, and I got scared. Not knowing what I was scared of and not knowing that it was too late to "git by," I started going to school almost every day.

Even though I was going to school a whole lot, I still had time to get into trouble with Knoxie, Bucky, and Toto. They all knew I was going to a place called Warwick. All of us had been hearing about Warwick for years. We kind of knew that we would all get there one day. The judge said I was going to a place called Wiltwyck, but Bubba Williams said that there was no place by that name and that the judge just didn't know how to say Warwick. Bubba knew everything. He knew almost as much as God, so I had to be going to Warwick, because Butch and Kid were there, and it made me feel as old as them to be going there too. Toto was mad because he wasn't going. I kept telling him that he was too young, but not to worry, because I would probably still be there when he got old enough. This made him real mad, because we were the same age. But I kept telling him I was older than he was.

Mama said I would have to stay up there till I was twenty-one if I was bad; but if I was real good, I could come home when I was eighteen. When I told Bubba about it, he said I would probably come home when I was fourteen. He thought I was twelve then. So I was telling everybody who didn't know any better that I was going to Warwick for two years. Knoxie was the only one I knew who didn't think it was so great—he thought there wouldn't be anything up there to steal. He kept trying to talk me out of going. I knew that Knoxie was just worrying about losing a stealing and fighting partner. But just to shut him up, I promised to duck out on Mama the day I was supposed to go away. Knoxie said that he would stay home from school and that I could come around his house and stay as long as I wanted to.

I was supposed to go away about a week after my birthday. I was going to be eleven years old, but almost everybody thought I was going to be thirteen, since that's what I told them. I wasn't really lying about my age; I was just tired of not being older than anybody but Bulldog, who wasn't even around any more. I was planning on having a real big birthday and going-away party on the Sunday after my birthday. I had started stealing things for the party and had invited everybody I knew about a month ahead of time.

Bucky was going to miss me a lot while I was away. I was his most important friend. Since food was the most important thing in the world to Bucky, I was always showing him where some food was and how to get it. When I was teaching Bucky how to stay out all night, he use to get hungry all the time and would do dumb things that might have gotten us caught just to get some food. When we would be looking for a store to break into, Bucky always wanted to break into a restaurant, a candy store, or a grocery store. It didn't make sense to break into those kind of stores, because they didn't have anything you could sell for some money. Anyway, if somebody got hungry, he could always go up to 155th Street to the Father Divine place and say "peace" to the people there and get all the food he could eat for just fifteen cents. If you were real quick with your hands, you only had to say "peace" and smile every time the lady looked at you. After I showed Bucky where the peace place was, he hardly ever went home. Sometimes I would see him in the street with a big old turkey leg. Other kids would ask him where he had gotten it, and he would just tell them, "Father gave it to me," meaning Father Divine. Bucky was the only guy I knew who would go strutting down the street with a turkey leg in his hand and a pocketful of biscuits.

I guess everybody had something about them that was kind of crazy when it came to stealing or catting out. When I was on the cat, I knew that I was going to get caught sooner or later, but I just didn't want to get caught before I had stolen a new suit. This was usually the first thing I would steal when I was going to cat out. A new suit would make anybody look respectable, and the cops wouldn't bother you if you looked respectable. Butch had taught me that before I started catting out, and I never forgot it. If I had a new suit on when the cops brought me home, Mama and Dad respected me too. I didn't mind not having money; as long as I had a new suit, it meant the same thing—that I could do okay out in the street. Bubba said that was how you could tell how slick a nigger was—by how well he did in the street. Butch said Mr. Jimmy, the hustler, was the slickest cat on Eighth Avenue. Mr. Jimmy knew how to "git by" in the street so well that he had never had a job since he left Alabama twenty years before. Mr. Jimmy changed cars every year, dressed up with shining shoes every day of the week, always had plenty of money, always had a pretty woman with him, and kept his hair slicked back.

I knew Mr. Jimmy from Dad's Saturday night crap games. He used to be out on the avenue on Sunday morning with an orange crate with a piece of cardboard on it and three nutshells. Mr. Jimmy would hide a little pea under one of the nutshells and bet people that they couldn't find the pea. I used to try to be on Eighth Avenue every Sunday morning just to watch Mr. Jimmy switch those shells around. He had some real quick hands. I watched a lot of people search for that pea, but I never saw anybody find it. That is, anybody but Bubba Williams, and that didn't count, because Bubba was Mr. Jimmy's hustling buddy. Bubba would always find the pea a few times, then he would go to the corner and watch for the cops while other people paid a whole lot of money to look for a pea they couldn't find. Sometimes Mr. Jimmy had three cards out on the avenue, and people would be looking for a card that nobody could find. When I walked up to where Mr. Jimmy was, I would always say hello to him and he would say hello back to me, and it made me feel good, especially if some of my friends were with me. Yes, I guess Mr. Jimmy was the slickest cat on Eighth Avenue, just as Butch said, because nobody ever found that pea or that card, and Mr. Jimmy is still doing good out in the street.

My eleventh birthday—the first birthday party I had ever had—was really something. On the night before the party, I took Knoxie and Bucky down to Delancey Street, where we waited until three o'clock in the morning for a nightclub to close. It was a Roumanian nightclub, but to us it was a Jewish nightclub. It had to be Jewish, because being white and talking funny so nobody could understand you was what made people Jewish. When the

Jewish nightclub closed we went in with three shopping bags. Only a little bit of change was in the cash register, but we ate a lot of turkey and other kinds of funny-tasting meat. When we left the place, the three shopping bags were full of champagne for my birthday party.

It was the best party Eighth Avenue had ever seen. The people came all afternoon and all night. Ages ranged from twelve to thirty-five. Most of the people there didn't know me, and I didn't know them, and nobody cared about not knowing somebody. The word got out about the champagne, and everybody who passed by the house came in to get some champagne and pigs' feet.

After all that foolishness with the cake, I forgot about everybody at the party. Everybody but Sugar. Sugar was one of my best friends now, and I told her so. She had on a pretty white dress; her hair was curled; she looked as if somebody had worked some magic on her. Sugar must have known she looked brand-new, because she didn't act the way she acted most of the time. She didn't laugh—she only smiled; and she didn't talk loud. She seemed to know that it was my party and that she was just a guest. This was the first time I had ever seen Sugar act that way, and I didn't expect her to do it for long. I kept looking at her and waiting for her to do something crazy like come over to me and stick her tongue out at me and start playing. But every time I looked at Sugar, she was still sitting there and still looking brand-new.

I don't know how I got to her in that crowded living room. Sugar never said a word; she just held my hand and followed me quietly from one room to another until we found one with nobody in it. Sugar seemed to know I wanted to say something to her, but she didn't know what. She acted like she was waiting for something to happen and like that something was about to happen. Sugar seemed to know that what I said to her was going be something real good, something I had never told her before. I had that same feeling about it. I didn't know what I was going to say to her, but I knew I wasn't going to tell her that she was ugly like I did most of the time. And I knew that Sugar wasn't going to argue and jump all over me when I got her where I was taking her to. I couldn't understand what had happened to Sugar, but she sure was different. She was still ugly, but there seemed to be so many pretty things about her that pretty girls didn't have.

Me and Sugar stayed in that room for a long time, and when we came out it seemed like the world had changed colors. I still don't know all of what happened to me in that room with Sugar. I knew it wasn't the champagne that did it. For the next two years whenever I was in the city, Sugar and I never had to say anything to each other. We came out of that room with a whole lot of understanding. Sugar could look at me and make me smile or even laugh, and it wasn't because she looked funny either; it was just that sometimes when she looked at me, I felt so good I just had to laugh or at least smile. And I could look at her and make her whole face light up. When we would hit each other, the hit always meant something that both of us understood. Our hitting wasn't like before, when we would hit each other kind of hard. Now we only tapped each other just hard enough to say what we wanted to say.

It was snowing real hard outside. Mama was so nervous, she tied my tie about six times before getting it right. I was all set to go downtown to an office to meet somebody who was going to take me upstate. Mama had locked my shoes in the closet the night before to make sure I didn't get out of the house while she was getting the other kids ready for school. Even though I couldn't get my shoes, Mama made me stay in the front room till we were ready to go. And every chance she got, Mama would come in the front room to check on me. She knew that if I had enough time, I would get my shoes out of that closet somehow. When Mama couldn't come out of the kitchen, she would call to me and ask me what I was doing. Every time she asked, I told her the real truth, that I wasn't doing anything.

It seemed like I had already started serving my time that morning, sitting there all dressed up, with everything on but my shoes and hat, in the room farthest away from the door. I was just sitting there at the window watching all that snow falling and feeling kind of sad. The snow just kept on falling, and I knew it was covering more than just the sidewalk. I knew Knoxie was waiting for me to come to his house, and I knew I wasn't going to make it, but I didn't care. Maybe it was because I knew what I would be doing for the next few days if I went to Knoxie's house. And I was wondering what would happen if I went to that office. Who would I meet there? Would there be something to steal there? Maybe I didn't care about not meeting Knoxie because I knew I couldn't get my shoes out of the closet.

Watching the snow fall made me think about a lot of things. I thought about what Dad had said the night before. He knew he would already have left for work when I got up that morning, so he gave me his good-bye speech the night before. I never used to listen to Dad when he talked to me—I never thought he had anything to say worth listening to—but I always used to make believe I was listening to him. But that night, I didn't even pretend I was thinking about what he said.

Dad started telling me that it would be a long time before I would see the streets of New York City again. And that maybe when I got back, I would appreciate them enough to stop all that goddamn stealing and stay home like somebody with some sense. He talked on and on like that. Then he said something. Dad asked me if I remembered when I used to get up every Sunday morning to go out and watch Mr. Jimmy win money from people who were dumb enough to go hunting for a pea that wasn't there. I told him I remembered. Then he asked me if I knew what a fool was. I said a fool was somebody stupid. Dad said I was right, but there was more to it than that. He said it takes a stupid person to keep looking for something that is never there. Dad told me to go into the kitchen and get a black-eyed pea.

When I came back with the pea, Dad had set up the card table and was sitting at it with three half nutshells in front of him. I gave him the pea, and Dad started switching the shells around the way Mr. Jimmy used to do. It looked like Dad was doing it real slow, and I was sure I knew where the pea was all the time. I never knew Dad could do that trick, and even then I was sure he was doing it too slow. When Dad stopped sliding the nutshells around, he told me to pick up the one I thought the pea was under. We did this ten times. Each time, I was sure the pea was under the shell I picked up. Ten times I picked the wrong shell. After I made that last wrong pick, Dad looked at me and just kept shaking his head for a little while. Then he said, "That's jis what you been doin' all your life, lookin' for a pea that ain't there. And I'm mighty 'fraid that's how you gon end your whole life, lookin' for that pea."

Mama was hollering for me to get ready to go. When I turned away from the window and looked at her, she was handing me my shoes. She didn't look at my eyes; she just kept telling me to hurry up because she had to go to work after she left the office we were going to. I knew by the way Mama was not looking at me that she was going to be crying before I left her that morning.

When we went into the Wiltwyck School office on 125th Street, I still thought I was going to Warwick, so I didn't feel so bad. We had to wait in a little room for a while, then a white lady with a sad-looking face came in. She smiled at me, but her face still looked sad. The white lady with the sad face took Mama into another room. They stayed for a long time. Then the white lady came back into the room where I was. She had her coat on. She told me Mama had said good-bye and took me by the hand. I didn't believe Mama would do that, but she did. She left and didn't even say good-bye. I told myself I didn't care. I said to myself, Fuck it! I don't need nobody anyway. But I kept feeling sad inside, and I kept wishing that white lady would shut the hell up. She told me that her name was Mrs. Grimes and that this was the first time she was going up to Wiltwyck too. Mrs. Grimes was a weird-looking lady. She wasn't old, but she had gray hair and a lumpy face. She looked too sad to be doing so much talking, but she seemed scared to stop talking.

While we were riding the train up to Wiltwyck, I kept thinking about the date on the big calendar in the office. It was March 4. I never used to pay attention to dates before, but I kept thinking about that March 4 and watching the snow fall outside the train window. The train passed a big red-brick wall. I heard Mrs. Grimes say, "That's Sing Sing."

I said, "Wow! The real Sing Sing!" I couldn't wait to get back home and tell everybody on the block I had seen Sing Sing, not in the movies, but the real Sing Sing.

When we finally reached Wiltwyck, where we were welcomed by Mr. Stillman, the resident director, snow was everywhere. It was almost lunchtime. Mrs. Grimes and I went into the lunchroom to eat. The lunchroom was crowded, and some of the boys there looked like they were happy. But they all looked real strange. I looked for Butch and Kid and Goldie, who were all in Warwick too. I didn't see anybody I knew. I asked a man sitting next to me, "Ain't this Warwick?"

He said, "No, this is Wiltwyck."

I was numb for a while; all I could feel was a warm tear starting down my face on its way to my chin.

3

I can't remember going to sleep that first night at Wiltwyck. I only remember lying there in a strange bed, in a strange place, for what seemed like a year-long night. I closed my eyes about a million times, hoping that I would open them and escape from that bad dream. But every time I opened my eyes, it was still there.

By the time daylight began to creep into that big old room that everybody was calling a dormitory, I had already been planning for a good two hours how I was going to get out of Wiltwyck. I couldn't run away, because I didn't know where I was and wouldn't have known which way to run. So the best way to get out was to talk that white man named Mr. Stillman into letting me go home. I decided to find Mr. Stillman as soon as I got up, and I was going to tell him that I had something real important to tell him. While Mr. Stillman was listening to me, I was going to fall down and grab my chest and start breathing real hard, like I was dying. They would probably take me to the hospital and try to find out what was wrong with me, and when they couldn't find anything wrong, they would probably kick me out of the hospital. But then I was going to stop eating, stop talking, and eat some soap powder or a lot of salt and get real sick. When they put me back in the hospital and tried to feed me, I wasn't going to eat, not even if they gave me fried chicken and pear pie. And every time the doctor asked me how I felt, I was going to say, "I wanna go home." That's all I was going to say to anybody, and I wasn't going to eat anything as long as they kept me there.

I knew they would have to send me home. They wouldn't want me to die on them. I was only up there for playing hookey and stealing and stuff like that. I hadn't killed anybody, so they couldn't let me die.

When a real tall, real light-skinned man came into the dormitory, clicked on the lights, and started yelling all over the place, everything was all set in my mind. I was sure I would be back on the streets by the next week.

I was still lying in bed thinking about how I was going to get out of Wiltwyck when a voice boomed, "Let's git one!" right in my ear. Before I could turn my head to look at him, my bed started jumping up and down real fast. The bed stopped jumping all of a sudden, then the bed next to mine started jumping up and down. The light-skinned white-looking man was shaking it and yelling, "Let's git one!" Guys were jumping out of bed and running to the bathroom, so I jumped out of bed and ran to the bathroom too. I asked a guy who was washing next to me how I could see Mr. Stillman. He told me all I had to do was go to his office. After throwing a handful of water on my face, I dashed out the door to find Mr. Stillman's office. Before I could get out of the house, I heard a voice booming out my name. Before I stopped running, I knew it was that tall, light-skinned man. And before I turned around, I knew that I didn't like that man and never would.

When I told him where I was going, he said Mr. Stillman wasn't in his office yet and that I had to make up my bed before I could go to see him. So I went back and made up my bed, then I started out to see Mr. Stillman again. Again I heard the real loud voice of the man that everybody was calling Simms. When I turned around this time, I knew that I would never like anybody named Simms as long as I lived.

The man named Simms told me that Mr. Stillman wasn't going to be in his office until after breakfast and that in the meantime someone would show me what my job in the house was. After I finished my job, which was cleaning the bathroom, and had breakfast, a bell rang. Everybody started heading for the last place I wanted to go—the school building. I started walking away from the crowd, but before I could begin to hope that I was going to get to Mr. Stillman's office, I heard the voice that I had learned to hate in just a few hours. I turned around and faced Simms. At first, I wanted to cry. Here was this big man I hated and couldn't do anything to. If I hit him, he probably would kill me. But I had to do something, because he kept fucking with me. Mr. Simms asked me where I was going. I opened my mouth to tell him, but the thing I heard myself saying—smiling to protect myself—was, "Mr. Simms, are you white or colored?" When I heard what I said, I thought, Lord, please have mercy on me.

After what seemed like a real long time, Mr. Simms smiled, real quick, and said, "C'mon, boy, you have to go to school now. Mr. Stillman will come to your class when he gets here."

I wished I had called him Mr. Red instead of asking him what I did. Not the way white people say red, but the way Dad and colored people his age say it. I should have said, "Whatcha want now, Mr. Re-e-e-d?" I'll bet he wouldn't have smiled then. He might have killed me, but he wouldn't have smiled. But I don't think he would have killed me—he would have lost his job. Then I thought, The next time he messes wit me, I'll call him that. . . . No, I'll call him yaller. Yeah, I'll say, "Whatcha want, Mr. Yaller Man?" If he wasn' so big, I'd call him yaller nigger. But if I did that, he prob'ly would kill me, job or no job.

I kept asking the teacher, who was a real pretty, light-skinned lady, to let me go to see Mr. Stillman. When the teacher got tired of me asking her to let me go, she told me that Mr. Stillman wasn't at the school but that I could see Mr. Upshur, who was Mr. Stillman's assistant. I knew she was lying, but I smiled and asked the teacher to let me go to see Mr. Upshur. The teacher sent one of the guys in the class with me. The guy showed me Mr. Upshur's office and left. I went into the office and asked to see Mr. Stillman. The secretary told me that Mr. Stillman wasn't going to be in all day but that Mr. Upshur would see me as soon as he was free. I sat down and waited for a few minutes, and Mr. Upshur came in. When he said he was Mr. Upshur, I knew he couldn't help me. He was colored. What could he do for anybody?

It seemed that everybody was trying to stop me from seeing Mr. Stillman, but I was going to see him as soon as I got out of school. All I had to do was stop telling people I wanted to see him, then they couldn't stop me.

When I came out of school that first afternoon, Wiltwyck looked different from the way it had looked the day before. The sun was shining. It was real cold, and everything that wasn't moving around was covered with snow and ice. Some of the trees had little sticks stuck in them, with buckets and tin cans hanging on the end of the little sticks. Boys were sledding on a hill near the four houses that everyone lived in. Some were riding two on one sled, some were fighting over one sled, and some were crashing into trees, but everybody seemed to be having a whole lot of fun. The first thing that had caught my eye when I came out of the school building was the trees with the buckets on them. I asked Mr. Cooper, who was the counselor in charge of the sled riding, why the buckets were on the trees. Mr. Cooper told me that they were maple trees and that they were being tapped for the sap to make maple syrup. Mr. Cooper was a real funny-looking man. He was tall, thin, and kind of dark-skinned; not real dark, but a little darker than me. He was scarey-looking at first; he never smiled, and he didn't seem to like anybody. Everybody but me called him Cooper or Coop. Mr.

Cooper wasn't a counselor in the house I was in, and I was glad. I didn't like being around him.

I went over to two guys who were fighting over a sled. When I asked whose sled it was, they both said, "Mine." And when I asked if I could have a ride, both of them said, "After me." A guy named Dunbaker, who was my working partner in cleaning the bathroom, came up to the guys who were fighting over the sled. He told them he would hold the sled while they fought to see who was going to get it. Dunbaker gave me the sled and said that I could have one ride but that if I gave him my beret, I could have the sled for the rest of the winter. The beret didn't mean so much to me, but I had to keep it, at least until I could find out why everybody had been trying to steal it ever since I got there. So I made a deal with Dunbaker to let him wear my beret as long as he let me ride the sled.

When I came down the hill for the third time, Dunbaker came up to me and said he wanted to ride the sled. I knew what Dunbaker wanted before he said anything, but I was busy watching a man talking to Mr. Cooper, farther down the hill. He looked like Mr. Stillman. When I got up off the sled, I saw the man coming toward me. He had the same kind of pipe that Mr. Stillman had been smoking the day before, my first day. And he was wearing the same kind of gray coat. When he got close enough for me to see his eyes, I was sure it was Mr. Stillman.

Mr. Stillman—everybody but me called him Stilly—had tiny red eyes that looked at people in a mean way from way back in his head. He must have had the only pair of eyes in the world like that. The pipe was almost as close to Stilly as his eyes. I never saw him without the pipe. I used to think that the pipe was the thing he cared about most in the world. . . . I watched Stilly coming up the slope. His look never changed. He seemed to be in his own world, just him and his pipe. I had tried to see Mr. Stillman all day. He was going to be my out; he was in charge of everything in this crazy place. He was the one who looked like and acted like he knew the most. And now here he was . . . a pair of eyes and a pipe and a big gray coat.

After asking how I was, the pipe waited a while, then it said, "You wanted to see me?"

I just asked him if he knew where I could get a sled. I was in Wiltwyck, really in it.

Wiltwyck was different from the other places I had been in. Some guys had been there for years, and just about everybody had at least one real good friend or partner. When two or three guys were partners, they would share everything they got hold of—packages from home, food and fruits that their parents brought them on visiting day, things they stole, and stuff like that. It took me a long time to find a real partner, one I would share my loot and secrets with.

I knew K.B. about a year before we became ace boon coons. K.B. was the first cat I locked with up at Wiltwyck. We had three fights before we decided we couldn't beat each other, but it was a year before we got tight.

K.B. was from the Brownsville section of Brooklyn. He was a little cat with a loud mouth, big eyes, and a left hand that nobody ever saw coming at him. And like me, K.B. could beat a lot of big guys. Being so good with his hands didn't stop K.B. from being one of the nicest cats around. He would always rather argue than fight. Maybe this was because K.B. knew he was real good with his hands and was trying to learn how to be good with talk. He was always trying to get me to tell off guys he didn't like. When we first pulled tight, K.B.'s favorite saying was, "Ask Claude." I think Horse broke him out of that habit by asking him if he thought I was his father.

K.B. and I didn't get to be partners the way most of the guys did. We never said anything about being partners and sharing stuff we got. We just pulled tight and started getting in trouble together, stealing things and fighting together. One day after we became aces, we had our first fight in over a year because K.B. stole some canned apricots out of the kitchen and didn't give me any. After that, we shared everything we stole, found, were given, and even the things we bought. Because I could read and knew a lot of words, K.B. thought I was the smartest cat up at Wiltwyck and maybe in the whole world. I never told him any different.

I think K.B. must have been real shy when he came to Wiltwyck, because he used to beg me to tell him about the girls I knew. Late at night when I was sleepy and tired of lying all day and half the night, I would listen to K.B. tell me about Linda. For the six months that my bed was next to K.B.'s, I went to sleep hearing about Linda. After a week of hearing about Linda, I had to meet her just to see if she was as fine as K.B. said she was. K.B. said she was real dark-skinned, had long hair, wore lipstick, had "titties, little ones, but tits just the same," had a pretty face, and was real fresh. K.B. said he had done it to her one time up on the roof, and he used to tell me about it so much and in so many different ways that it had to be a lie.

Most of the time, K.B. couldn't think about anything but girls, and anybody who could tell him a good lie about girls could get him to do things. Sometimes when I wanted K.B. to help me steal something, I would have to promise to tell him about a real pretty, real fresh girl. K.B. was always trying to jerk off, and he said he shot one time; but I didn't see it, so I didn't believe it. But about a year after K.B. and I had moved to Aggrey House, I heard K.B. come tearing down the stairs yelling as loud as he could. It was around one in the morning. He woke up everybody in the first-floor dormitory. I was awake and wondering what was going on, when K.B. came running into the dormitory with his dick in his hand and yelling, "Claude, I did it! I did it!" When he reached my bed and yelled out, "Man, I shot," all the beds in the dormitory started jumping, and everybody crowded around my bed with flashlights before K.B. stopped yelling.

Some guys just said things like "Wow" or "Oh, shit," but Rickets said, "Man, that's the real stuff."

Horse said, "Man, that ain't nothin' but dog water."

K.B. said, "That ain't no dog water, man, 'cause it's slimy."

Horse, who was always talking about facts, said, "Man, that can't be scum, 'cause scum is white."

Knowing that scum was white, most of the guys said that Horse was right and that it was just dog water. I said that dog water was more than he ever made. Horse went heading for the bathroom saying he was going to show me what the real stuff looked like. Everybody followed Horse and watched and cheered him on while he tried for the real stuff. Horse only made dog water, just like K.B., but nobody paid much attention—everybody was trying to jerk off that night. It was a matter of life or death. After what seemed like hours of trying and wearing out my arm, I shot for the first time in my life. A lot of other guys did it for the first time too, but some cats just got tired arms.

After K.B. and I had been tight for a few months, a lot of guys started trying to get tight with us; and before we knew it, we had a gang. Our gang was always robbing the kitchen late at night, gang fighting with Windsor House, or just stealing for the fun of it.

One day in the summer of the year after I came to Wiltwyck, Simms, who had been transferred from Carver House about a year before, came into the house waving a piece of paper, grinning and shouting my name. When he came into the dormitory and saw me sitting on my bed, he ran up to me, stuck the paper in my face, and said, "Read that, Claude Brown." It was a transfer slip for me and K.B. We were going to be moved to Aggrey House, the Big "A," where all the older cats lived and where Simms was a counselor. I didn't like Simms, and I didn't like the idea of going where all those big guys were. Some of them, like Jake Adams and Stumpy Edwards, were real mean cats. I told Simms that I wasn't going to stay in Aggrey House. He just smiled and said, "Don't tell me you're scared, Claude Brown?" I told him I wasn't scared, that I just didn't want to go and wasn't going to stay.

But I really was scared of Simms. I had seen him smack big Jim Cole in the gym one day. Jim Cole was about six feet tall and weighed about 185 pounds. When Simms smacked him, the smack picked Jim up off his feet and slammed him against a wall about ten feet away. Simms was real tall, and he had long arms, big hands, and could move real fast. He would lean toward one side of a cat and hit him when the guy started moving away from him. It wasn't easy to get out of the way if he wanted to hit you. I saw a lot of guys try, but I never saw any of them make it. I had only seen Simms hit one cat who didn't cry. That was Stumpy Edwards. And that was another reason I didn't want to go to Aggrey House—I didn't want to be in the same house with a cat who could be hit by Simms and not only wouldn't cry, but even looked mean.

When I told Simms for the second time that I wasn't going to Aggrey House, he showed me Stilly's name on the transfer slip and said, "Come on, boy, git your things. We're gonna see how much hell you can raise over in my house."

I ran to the linen room to get our counselor, Claiborne, and said to him, "Mr. Claiborne, Simms is here wit a piece-a paper, but I ain't goin' nowhere."

Simms was right behind me. He handed Claiborne the paper. Clay read the paper and kept looking at it for a while. Then he raised his head, looked at me for a while, smiled sadly, and said, "Claude, get your ace. You gotta go."

Simms was still smiling when K.B. came running in, yelling like he always did. For once, Claiborne didn't bother to tell K.B. not to make so much noise. He just kept looking for some socks for us. K.B. looked at me as if to say, "Is it true?"

Before he could say anything, I said, "Man, I ain't goin'."

K.B. said, "Claiborne, do I have to go?"

Clay turned around. His face was trying to smile when he said, "That's what Mr. Stillman said."

Everything was real quiet in the linen room . . . and real sad too. The only one who wasn't sad was Simms. He was smiling and gloating. I had become the main problem at Wiltwyck, and Simms had been telling me for nearly a year that I would be a different boy if I were in his house. Now he was going to get a chance to prove it.

Claiborne was a strict counselor, but I had gotten used to him. I liked him even though he was always telling me he didn't trust me and always thought I had a hand in everything that went on. The moment he heard something had been stolen, he would come looking for me. But that was all right, because I was usually the one who had stolen it or had told somebody else to steal it or had stolen it from whoever had stolen it first.

Claiborne liked K.B. more than he liked anybody else in Carver House. One day K.B. made a bet with Jody that the next time Claiborne messed with him, he was going to punch Claiborne in the mouth. Jody took the bet, but he wasn't the only one who thought K.B. was lying. We all did. I hoped K.B. was lying, for his own sake. Claiborne was mean and didn't play. On the same day that K.B. made the bet with Jody, Claiborne came into the dormitory and told K.B. to get into his bed and be quiet. K.B. started talking louder than before. Claiborne walked over to K.B. and reached for him. True to his word, K.B. punched Claiborne right smack in the mouth. Claiborne was more shocked than anybody else. This kind of thing just didn't happen to Claiborne, and he didn't know how to take it. Claiborne couldn't hit K.B., since K.B. was just a kid; but he grabbed K.B.'s hand and started twisting it, and K.B. started yelling for Nick, our other counselor, to help him before Claiborne broke his arm. But Claiborne wasn't crazy. For the next two weeks, K.B. was Claiborne's yardbird. He had to go everywhere Claiborne went from morning till night. He even had to ask Claiborne when he wanted to go to the bathroom. When the other guys were playing ball or sledding or ice skating, K.B. would be there, but he had to stay with Claiborne and just watch. The one good thing about it was that everybody knew why K.B. was Clay's yardbird, and it gave him a bigger reputation as a bad cat. After that, Claiborne and K.B. became real good friends. At least the friendship was as good as it could get between counselors and boys.

The day K.B. and I were supposed to go to Aggrey House, I kept wishing Nick was around; but Nick was off. I knew Nick would have done something, because that's the way he was.

I thought Nick was an ugly cat the first time I saw him. But before long, Nick was the most beautiful cat up at Wiltwyck. He came in the door of Carver House one afternoon during the daily rest period. This was a time when everybody had to go and lie on his bed for about two hours. We used this time to bullshit and lie mostly, but sometimes somebody would really go to sleep. Nobody was sleeping when Nick walked into Carver House for the first time. He kind of leaned over when he walked, and he had a big bounce. It was hard to tell if Nick was young or old or young and old. When I first noticed him, K.B. and Jody were talking to him, feeling him out. He was standing just inside the dormitory doorway. I had heard him say, "Hi, fellas." But looking at him, it was hard for me to believe he had said that.

Nick was looking real serious while he was talking to K.B. and Jody. He was a funny-looking guy. He had real sad eyes that kept trying to smile at every cat who came up to him to ask if he was the new counselor and to size him up. His teeth all seemed to be rotten and stuck out too far. Looking at his face, I thought his hair should have had a lot of gray in it, but it was a rough black all over. I liked the way Nick looked—kind of cautious, as if he knew he was in our turf and had to be cool till we got to like him. I started to yell out to the guys on the other side of the room to stop fucking with that man and tell him where Claiborne's room was. But before I could say it, Nick was bouncing up the stairs like he knew where he was going, and K.B. and Jody were arguing about whether or not he was a nice guy. Before long, somebody in the dorm said that he was nicer than Claiborne, and nobody argued about that.

In a couple of months, Nick was running Carver House. We were all part of his gang. He would never help us rob the kitchen and stuff like that, but he used to take us on hikes around Farmer Greene's apple orchard and look the other way sometimes. He was more like one of the guys because he liked a lot of the things we liked. He would play the dozens, have rock fights, and curse us out. But I think we liked Nick mostly because he was fair to everybody. Nick never liked to see anybody getting bullied, but he was always ready to see a fair fight. I liked the way Nick was always lying to us. Everybody knew he was lying most of the time, but we didn't care, because he used to tell such good lies. Nick was a real big cat, even bigger than Simms, and he was from Texas; and some of the lies he used to tell were bigger than him and Texas.

Nick was much better to have as a counselor than Simms. Nick didn't get excited real quick the way Simms did, and Nick had sense. I wasn't so sure about Simms. I was always getting into fights with Nick, since I knew I wouldn't lose too bad. When Nick hit me, I would just hit him back and keep swinging. But somehow I just couldn't see myself taking Simms on and living afterwards.

Within six months after I had moved into Aggrey House, most of the guys who had been in Carver House with me had been transferred to Aggrey. I had my old gang from Carver and some bigger cats who were already in Aggrey when I got there. I was raising twice the hell that I had raised in Carver House, and Simms wasn't smiling now. Some of the counselors were starting to say that nothing could be done with me and that I should be sent to Warwick. But there was a new man, Papanek, in charge of everything at Wiltwyck, and he didn't feel that I should be sent to Warwick or anyplace like that. Papanek had the last word on everything about Wiltwyck. Even Stilly had to listen to him, like it or not. At first, most of the cats up at Wiltwyck thought Papanek was kind of crazy. And I think some of the counselors felt that way too. But Papanek wasn't anything like crazy. He was probably the smartest and the deepest cat I had ever met. Before long, we all found out that Papanek was the best thing that had ever happened to Wiltwyck and maybe one of the best things that could ever happen to any boy who got into trouble and was lucky enough to meet him.

I remember the first day Papanek came to Wiltwyck. Everybody was told to come to the auditorium that afternoon. For a long time, we had heard rumors about getting a new director, and it seemed that this was the day. The counselors usually had a lot of trouble getting guys to go to the auditorium for anything other than a movie. But the day Papanek showed, it was different. Everybody, boys and counselors, was real anxious to see what this cat looked like, if he knew anything, if he was big or small, mean or kind, colored or white, young or old. We wanted to know what kind of changes were in store for us . . . for Wiltwyck. Every boy and every counselor knew that the man we were going to meet that afternoon would be the one to handle all our troubles at Wiltwyck for a long time to come. Just the thought of a cat being able to do that was enough to make us really wonder about him. Some of us wanted to know mainly if he was as mean as the outgoing director. All I ever knew about that cat was that he was mean as hell, and I think that's all a lot of cats ever knew about him. He looked like one of those mean old preachers who would think nothing of killing somebody in the name of the Lord. I hated to be around the cat. He never smiled, and he was too quick to take off his belt and beat your ass.

After Stilly told us that the new director was going to introduce himself to us and say a few words, most of us were still looking for the cat when he started talking. I remember Papanek saying, "My name is Ernst Papanek." I just watched him. He wasn't tall or short, and he was real straight, with a bald head and a kindly face. He didn't look real bold, but he seemed to have a whole lot of confidence, as if he knew he could handle Wiltwyck. Like everybody else, I was more interested in him than in what he was talking about. To me, he just didn't look like the kind of cat who could handle Wiltwyck. The poor guy looked like somebody even the counselors could run over. After a while, Papanek stopped talking and asked if there were any questions. After the first question, it seemed that Papanek was talking with everybody, not to us.

As we left the auditorium after hearing Papanek tell us who he was, where he was from, and what he wanted to do at Wiltwyck, I had the feeling that the rule of the staff was over. It was a good feeling. I knew that the boys were going to run Wiltwyck now. And I was going to be the one in charge. I was going to be the director of Wiltwyck, thanks to that poor old nice Mr. Papanek.

I tried to joke about Papanek's accent with K.B. and Horse, but they seemed to be kind of lost. Tito said, "Man, he sure can't talk." J.J. said something about how shiny Papanek's bald head was. A few guys tried to laugh, but I could tell they were faking. Some of the counselors were trying to make fun of Papanek, but they were faking it too. I couldn't understand this. I started talking to everybody about the new director, counselors and boys; everybody was lying and trying to hide it, but I could tell that they liked him and thought he was a nice guy. I got kind of scared of this guy Papanek. He had come to Wiltwyck and talked for a little while. And in that little while, with just talk, he had won every living ass in the place—just took over everything with a few words that we couldn't even understand too well. No, I didn't like this cat. He was slick . . . real slick. Papanek was so slick that he didn't have to be mean. He could take anyplace right on over in less than a day and never fire a shot. I had never met anybody that slick before. He scared me a little bit, but I had to get to know this cat and find out just how smart he was.

I went looking for Papanek. I had to talk to him and find out about him. I saw him coming out of the dining room, talking with a couple of kids. He had his arm around their shoulders, and a lot of guys were crowding around him and walking with him. I wondered if he thought he was

Jesus or some fucking body like that. Papanek stopped and started answering questions asked by some of the cats crowding around him. He was leaning forward with his neck stuck out and his hands folded behind his back. I used to be afraid of people who kept their hands behind their backs, because I once had a teacher who used to slap me right after she put her hands behind her back.

When I came up to Papanek and his crowd, I just stood on the outside and listened for a while. I don't know if I was scared or just wanted to get a better idea of what I was up against before I declared war. Floyd Saks was telling Papanek about all his ills and troubles. Papanek was listening, but he seemed to know that Floyd was a little crazy and just liked to fuck with people by talking a lot of nonsense for a long time. Papanek knew Floyd had him, but he didn't seem to know how to get away. He kept looking over the crowd and all around him, as if hoping to see somebody who would call him and save him from Floyd. Every time Papanek would look away, Floyd would call his name and make him pay attention to what he was saying, crazy though it was. I think too many people were trying to pick Papanek's pocket at the same time, so nobody was getting anything. But it didn't really matter, because they would have just given whatever they took back to him. They liked this cat.

I didn't say anything to Papanek that first day, but after he took over, we were warring until I went home for good. After I got to know Papanek, I found out how to really bother him; but I had to keep finding new ways, because the cat was slicker than anybody else at Wiltwyck. It was hard to bother him the same way twice. Papanek brought a whole new way of doing things to Wiltwyck. He made a rule that boys were not to be beaten or even slapped by counselors any more. I expected Stilly to leave the day that Papanek passed that rule, but he didn't. He stayed on for nearly a year. Then I guess he just couldn't take it any more.

Papanek might have been a little crazy, but he meant all the crazy things he said to the boys and counselors. This was one of the things that made Papanek so hard to fight. I could never catch him in a lie, and he would never hit anybody. And as time went by, nobody could make him mad. At least he never showed it. He would look real sad sometimes, but he wouldn't get mad. But you could always tell when he got excited, because his accent would get stronger but his words would be real clear. I had never met anybody before who never got mad, and I had never met anybody who was always telling the truth like Papanek. But that's the way he was. If you asked him the hard

Wiltwyck questions like, "When am I going home?" or, "Why are you keeping me here so long?" and Papanek couldn't tell you, he wouldn't lie about it. He would tell you something that left you knowing no more than before you asked him the question, but you would feel kind of satisfied about it. Sometimes he would have you talking about something else altogether different from what you asked him, and most of the time you would never know it. He was smarter than social workers, that was for sure, because he knew how to answer the hard questions without lying. So nobody could ever be mad at him for lying to them. And even though cats up at Wiltwyck lied a whole lot, like me, we didn't like grown-ups to lie to us about important things like the hard questions. Sometimes I used to get real tired of all that damn truth Papanek was telling, but I couldn't get mad at him for it.

For the next year or more, I tried to make life real sad for Papanek. This became harder and harder as time went by, because I grew to like him more and more, just like everybody else.

A few months after I moved into Aggrey House, a lady moved in. She was a white lady with white hair. She was kind of old, but her hair wasn't white because she was old, and it wasn't dyed white. It looked like it was supposed to be white and always had been. I was standing with some other guys around the quadrangle post at the end of the walk leading to Aggrey House on the afternoon the lady moved in. It was a hard thing to understand, a lady moving into Aggrey House. At first we thought that she was going to be living there but not working there. Some of the guys were helping her take her stuff up to the third floor, where most of the counselors lived. This lady had a real hard-looking face, and she smoked a cigarette without putting her hands on it and talked while she was smoking. I had never seen a white lady do that before.

K.B. was pulling on me to come with him and get a dime. The lady was giving out dimes to all the guys who had helped her take her things upstairs. K.B. hadn't carried a thing upstairs, but he said the lady didn't know who had. He said he had gotten one dime, gone in the house through the back way, come to the front, gone up to the lady with his hand out, and had gotten another dime. He was all set to go for a third one, but he wanted me to come with him because this was too good to miss.

K.B. said, for about the third time, "C'mon, Claudie."

I said, "Man, I'll bet she smokes a lotta cigarettes."

K.B. said that she talked funny and must be from another country.

Horse said, "Man, they must be crazy puttin' her in here wit us."

Jake Adams said, "Why, Horse? What you gonna do to her?"

Somebody said they should have put her in Robeson House with the little guys. But it looked as though she was going to be a counselor in Aggrey House. All the cats were betting that she wouldn't stay more than two weeks. But I wasn't so quick to bet. I had never seen a lady who smoked cigarettes like this lady. She looked like she knew something.

The lady who lived in Aggrey House was Mrs. Meitner. She was from Germany and sounded like it. Mrs. Meitner once had a big house in Germany, and her family use to grow a lot of grapes and make a lot of wine. I guess she was kind of rich. When Hitler took over the country, he took Mrs. Meitner's house, put her in a concentration camp, killed her husband and most of her friends. She told me and some more cats about it one day, real fast, smiled, and started talking about something else. That was the only time I ever heard her talk about it.

Mrs. Meitner was not out of place in Aggrey House. The first week she was there, she showed us a lot of judo and won a whole lot of friends. Guys tried to make her leave by walking past the stairs naked when they heard her coming down, but that didn't work either. Mrs. Meitner would just stop whoever it was and make him stand there and talk to her. The cat who was naked would get embarrassed long before she did. After a while, people just stopped messing with Mrs. Meitner and faced the fact that she was there to stay. Little by little, everybody started liking Mrs. Meitner. She was real smart and could do a lot of things. I started liking her more than anybody else at Wiltwyck.

Every day I saw Mrs. Meitner, I liked her more and more. One day we were sitting on the wall near the shrine, just me and Mrs. Meitner, and I asked her how old she was. She wouldn't tell me, not even when I said I was in love with her and wanted to know if she was too old for me. She just smiled and said she was too young for me. I told her I wasn't playing, that I was really in love with her. She told me she had a grown son who was an architect. After she told me that, she looked at me for a long time. I guess I was supposed to say I was sorry or something like that. But I didn't. I told her again that I was in love with her. She kept smiling, just looking at me and smiling. I said, "You think nobody can be in love with you just 'cause you got a grown son who is an architect. . . . Damn, that's crazy." She got up and walked away—didn't say a thing, just walked away.

When it was time to go to bed, I hadn't seen Mrs. Meitner for a couple of hours, and I started looking for her to find out if she was mad at me. Her door wasn't locked, but I knocked on it so she would say something and so I could tell by the way her voice sounded if she was mad or not. She was sitting in a chair facing the window when I came in, and she didn't turn around for a long time; but I was sure that she knew it was me when she heard the knock on the door. It seemed like she came to life when she turned around. She looked at me and said, "Yes?"—in a real lively sort of way. I said I was sorry if I had said the wrong thing, that I had meant to tell it to her in another way but that it just hadn't come out the way I wanted it to. Mrs. Meitner got up from the straw rocking chair and walked over to me. She didn't look at me yet; she just reached behind me and closed the door. Then she told me to go over and sit in the rocking chair.

The sun was going down, and what was left of it was shining through the window; that was the only light in the room, just a little bit of sunlight. Mrs. Meitner was wearing slacks when I came into the room. She went behind a screen and came out in a housecoat. She sat down on the far end of the couch. I turned the chair around to face her when she asked me if I wanted a cigarette. I said no thanks. Even though I was surprised when she offered me the cigarette, I said no thanks real calm. She had offered it to me in a real calm voice. That's how I knew she meant it. If I had said yes, I know she would have given me the cigarette, even though the boys at Wiltwyck were not allowed to smoke.

Mrs. Meitner just sat there looking at me for a while . . . looking at me and smoking on her strong cigarettes. I knew they were strong—I had stolen one and smoked it once. I didn't think she knew about that, but maybe she did. Maybe that's why she offered me the cigarette.

After a while, I said, "Well, are you?"

She said, "Am I what?"

"Are you mad at me?"

She got up and said, "Of course not. Why should I be?" She walked over to the hot plate in the corner, poured two cups of coffee, and gave one to me. Then she went back to the couch, sat down, crossed her legs, and started drinking the coffee.

I took a sip of coffee, mostly because I thought I was supposed to. Mrs. Meitner's housecoat was kind of open near the top, and I could see part of her breasts. The part I saw was kind of wrinkled, and at first it sort of scared me. I started thinking she must be real, real old. After a while, I told myself that it didn't matter—and I meant it. When I asked her what her house in Germany looked like, she smiled and said it was odd that I should ask about it, because she had just been thinking about it. I could tell she wasn't lying. She had her real smile on, her happy smile. Whenever somebody said something that made her happy, Mrs. Meitner would smile real big, and her eyes would light up and seem to get deeper and fill up with happiness. She smiled for real.

I smiled now too. Everything I had said before asking about the house didn't matter. I kept looking at her happy face as she reached under the small table near the couch and pulled out a picture album. She brought it over to where I was sitting and put it in my lap and started telling me about her house and turning the pages at the same time. I kept watching her eyes and her face and she looked like a little girl, a very pretty, happy little girl. I was sorry I didn't know her when she was about my age, because I knew she must have been real pretty . . . and happy.

Before I looked at the album, I told her that if a picture of her husband was in it, I didn't want to see it. I didn't tell her, but I hated her husband and thought it was good that the Germans had killed him. All I knew about him was that he used to be her husband and was the father of her architect, and that was enough to hate him for. He might have been a real nice guy, but I still hated him for being her husband. And I hated myself for not being her husband and for being so young.

She put her arm around my shoulder, and we turned the pages together. I smiled at and liked the pictures that seemed to make her happy. But the more pictures we looked at, the more I hated myself for not being older and bigger than I was. And I hated myself for never having been to all the places she had been to and for missing out on so much of her life. After listening to the songs from South Pacific and looking at pictures of Mrs. Meitner's life, I felt kind of silly for having said what I did to her. So I said I was sorry and all. She gave me a sort of pat-on-the-head smile, said we were still friends, and shook my hand, and I left.

Lying in my bed thinking about it that night, I felt that I had done something crazy—I had fallen in love with the nicest lady I knew, and for no reason. I decided that I didn't hate Mrs. Meitner's husband, and I wished that the Germans hadn't killed him. But I still wished that I had been married to her for all those years and that her architect was our architect. I just knew her eyes used to have a brighter light and were even deeper then. . . . No, I didn't hate her husband. I couldn't, because he had been part of her happiness. I hated Hitler for not letting her stay happy.

I kept thinking about Mrs. Meitner holding the album real tight . . . just standing there and holding on to the memories of her happy times . . . real tight. If I had seen those pictures before, I don't think I would have said what I did to her earlier that evening. But I knew I liked her a lot and wanted to be her friend more than before. I decided to do something for her. I knew she liked to paint and make costumes, so I, who had never painted before, spent a whole day watching Floyd Saks paint. That night, I kept going over in my mind what I had seen Floyd do that day. The next day, I painted a portrait of Felix the Cat and a wicked sorcerer and gave them to Mrs. Meitner. That was the first time I had ever painted anything, and it was the last time too. Both paintings were so good that nobody but the guys who saw me painting them believed that I had done it. But Mrs. Meitner knew I had painted them, and she liked them. That was all that mattered.

When I went home for a visit from Wiltwyck, it seemed like the whole city had changed. I had forgotten all about roaches until I went back home. I had been to that nice old rich white lady's house up in Hyde Park, which wasn't too far from Wiltwyck. She had a big old house that seemed like a whole lot of houses bunched together. The cats who had been up there before said that she used to invite all the cats from Wiltwyck to her house every year and that everybody used to eat until he got sick or just tired of eating. This lady had a real big house; and the first time I went into it, I couldn't understand why she didn't have any roaches in a house that big. I thought they just might have been hiding all the time I was there, but it wasn't like roaches to hide when there were a lot of people around eating food and stuff. That's why Mama didn't like roaches—they were always coming out and showing off when company came.

I had seen this old rich lady hanging around Wiltwyck a couple of times. I spoke to her the first time I saw her, and she said she was a member of some board or something like that. She started asking me a lot of stupid questions like did I like it up there and things like that. After that, I never had anything to say to her. I knew she was a nice lady, but she seemed to be a little crazy or something, and her voice didn't sound real. It sounded like one of those ladies in the movies. But that was all right, because she wasn't around too much, just once in a while.

I knew that her name was Mrs. Roosevelt and that she used to be married to a cat who was President of the United States. It sure seemed funny to me that the President of the United States would have had time to bother with that crazy-acting old lady. I figured that Dad was right about white people. He would read the paper and say, "White people sure do some damned fool things." I thought that the lady named Mrs. Roosevelt didn't have any roaches in her house because the President used to live there. Roaches didn't want to mess with the President. I said to myself, I bet they come chargin' in here as soon as they find out he's gone. . . . Yeah, they're just waitin' to git the news. Roaches are slick like that.

On that first visit home, the bus from Wiltwyck stopped at Mt. Olivet Baptist Church on 120th Street and Lenox Avenue. A lot of cats' mothers and fathers and sisters and brothers and foster fathers and foster mothers and aunts and uncles had come to meet them. Most of the people who met the bus were smiling or laughing. A few were crying, but they weren't looking sad.

Carole and Sugar came to meet me. I was glad to see Carole, but I was kind of mad at her for bringing Sugar with her. I decided to get out of there in a hurry before anybody else asked me who Sugar was. Mr. Moore, my social worker, had already asked me if Sugar was my sister. I was real quick to say, "No, she ain't nothin'-a mine." Then I introduced him to Carole and told him that Sugar was a friend of Carole's. After that, we left in a hurry.

Sugar was all right, but she was just too ugly to be introduced to anybody as anybody else's anything. Carole had to go and pay the gas and light bill on 125th Street. Sugar and I rode the bus uptown together. We didn't say anything until it was almost time to get off.

Sugar said, "Why didn't you write?"

I said, "For what?"

She didn't say anything else after that, and I was surprised. But Sugar had changed, just like everything else in Harlem. She was still ugly and all that, but she acted kind of different. She didn't say much; she just kept looking at me like she wanted me to say something to her. Sugar had changed a lot. She was growing up. She was nice—and almost as much fun to be with as some of the cats I knew.

It seemed that everybody I used to hang out with before I went to Wiltwyck was in Warwick or someplace like it. Nobody seemed to be out on the street. Knoxie had moved downtown, and everybody was saying that he had turned "good boy" on us. They said the cat stopped stealing and started going to school and stuff like that. At first, I didn't believe that kind of talk about Knoxie. But after everybody kept saying it, I sure wanted to see that cat and find out for myself. I knew I could make him steal something. But I didn't find out on that visit, because I didn't see Knoxie.

After being in the city for a few days, I started visiting some of the guys from Wiltwyck, and they started coming around the house. Dad didn't go for these cats coming around. He even told me to tell "all them little rogues not to come to the house," but I never said anything to anybody. Mama used to treat all the cats real nice. She liked to get into everybody's business, and most of the cats didn't have a home or any relatives. Mama used to be a soft touch for cats who didn't have a mother. And even Dad used to feel sorry for guys who didn't have a mother or father. So after a while, I told everybody I brought to the house to say their mother was dead or their father was dead or that everybody they knew was dead. It seemed that having dead mothers and fathers made anybody look less like a rogue to Dad.

For that whole time, I didn't hang out with any of my old running partners. I just went around with cats from Wiltwyck, but we did the same things. We stole things, hitched bus rides, and looked for any kind of trouble to get into. When the two-week home visit was up, I just didn't care too much. Nobody seemed to care . . . nobody but Sugar, and she didn't matter much. She said I should have spent more time with her. I told her that the next time I came home, I would spend all my time with her. I don't know why I said that, and after saying it, I was kind of sorry I had. I guess I just wanted to tell her something that would stop her from looking so sad. Sugar smiled when I said it; she even looked happy. It made me feel kind of good.

When I got on the bus, I kept playing with Sugar out the window, and when some cats in back of me started teasing me about how ugly my girl was, it didn't seem to matter, not even a little bit. When the bus started pulling away and Sugar was standing on tiptoe for me to kiss her, I wanted to, but I just couldn't. I wanted to—real, real bad—but her buckteeth might have gotten in the way. Sugar ran beside the bus for a while, and her eyes had a kind of begging look in them. She stopped at the corner where the bus turned; her begging eyes had water in them . . . and so did mine.

One time I came home to go to court. When I was about four or five years old, I got hit by a bus on Eighth Avenue. Everybody said I kept hollering for my shoe, even after they got me to the hospital. Every time something happened to me, it seemed that I would always lose one shoe. The bus didn't hurt me, but while I was up at Wiltwyck, Mama and Dad were trying to get some money from the bus company. So I had to come down from Wiltwyck to go to court and see about it. That was the first time I had ever been in court with Dad. All the times I went to court for getting into trouble, Mama always went with me. I sure felt funny going to court with Dad.

Mama never acted biggety in court, but she would bow her head only so low. But as soon as I got up that morning, I could tell that Dad was going to be a real drag. He got up with his hat in his hand and was bowing his head before we even got out of the house. He kept telling me how to act and what not to say. I pretended I was listening to him real hard, hoping he would feel kind of smart and maybe act like somebody with some sense when he got in court. But what I really wanted to tell him was, "Shit, man, I been in court before, so you better watch me and let me pull your coat about how to act in front of that judge and those other white people." But if I had said that, he would have kicked my ass.

I just had a real bad feeling that I was going to get fucked over in that court worse than ever before. This was the first time I was going to court and didn't have to worry about the judge sending me away. I would have felt that I owned the court that day if Dad hadn't acted so goddamn scarey. He kept saying we were going to get a lot of money from the bus company if I said the right things and acted the way he told me to. Dad said we were bound to get a lot of money—we had a good Jewish lawyer from way downtown. But I knew damn well we were going to need a lot more than a good Jewish lawyer that morning.

When we got to court, the lawyer was already there. He spoke to Dad, and Dad yes-sirred him all over the place, kept looking kind of scared, and tried to make the man think he knew what he was talking about. When the lawyer came over to me and said, "Hello, Claude; how are you?" and shook my hand and smiled, I had the feeling that God had been kicked right out of heaven and the meek were lost. And when he started talking to me—not really talking to me, just saying the stupid things that white people say to little colored boys with a smile on their faces, and the little colored boys are supposed to smile too—nothing in the world could have made me believe that cat was on our side. We weren't even people to him, so how the hell was he going to fight our fight? I wanted to ask Dad why he went and got this guy, but I knew why. He thought all Jews were smart. I could have gotten all that shit right out of his head. Anybody could see that this cat wasn't so smart. No, he was just lucky—lucky that the world had dumb niggers like Dad in it.

When we went into the courtroom, the lawyer went up to where the judge was sitting and started talking to him. They seemed to be friends or something. Almost everybody there seemed to be friends—the bus driver, the other lawyer, the people from the bus company. The only ones who didn't seem to be friends with anybody was me and Dad. I wanted to act real tight with Dad and show those people that we didn't need to be friends with them. But Dad was too scared to do anything but sit there with his hat in his hand and say yes sir. I sure hated him for that.

The lawyer told us to sit down "over there" for a while. Dad almost ran to the seat, and I wanted to grab him by his coat, kick him in his ass real hard, and say, "Look here, you simple-actin' nigger, you better try to be cool, 'cause you wit me." But I couldn't do that and go on living, so I just went over and sat down.

While Dad and I were sitting there waiting for something to happen, I kept thinking about the time I saw a big black man take a little pig out of his pen at hog-killing time down South. He took the pig and tied him to a post, patted him on the back a couple of times, then picked up his ax and hit the pig in the head and killed him. The pig died without giving anybody any trouble, and the big black pig killer was happy. In fact, everybody was happy, because we were all friends and part of the family. The only one there who didn't have a friend was the pig.

I had a feeling that something like what happened to the pig was going to happen in the courtroom and that Dad and I had already been patted on the back. I looked at the big, fat-faced judge sitting up there on the bench. He didn't look mean or anything like that, but he didn't look like he was a right-doing cat either. I even wished it was that old evil-looking lady judge who sent me to Wiltwyck sitting up there. She looked mean as hell, but I don't think I would have felt so much like that pig if she had been up there. I knew she wouldn't have been a friend of those lawyers and the people from the bus company. She looked like nobody could be her friend. And that was how it seemed that a judge should be. And she was colored too; maybe we would have been real people to her.

When the lawyer called us up to the bench and the big, fat-faced judge looked at us like it was his first time seeing pigs like these, I had the feeling that this fool in the black gown was all set to kill something before he was sure of what it was. I couldn't understand what the judge and the lawyers were talking about; the words they were using were too big. When I heard the judge say something about a hundred dollars, I grabbed my head and looked at Dad. He was still looking at the judge and nodding his head up and down. He didn't even know that he had been hit in the head with an ax. I bet Mama would have known. The lawyer told Dad something about his fifty dollars, and Dad just kept nodding his head. And I used to think he was a real bad nigger. But not after that. I knew now that he was just a head nodder, and nobody could tell me any different. For a long time after that, I hated to see anybody nod his head. I sure was mad when we left that court-room. I promised myself that when I got big enough, the first time I saw Dad nod his head at any white man, I was going to kick him dead in his ass.

When we got on the subway to go home, Dad told me that if anybody asked me how much money we got, I was to say I didn't know. I knew something like that was going to come. He was going to go uptown and tell everybody we had gotten a thousand dollars or something like that. That was the first time I could remember looking Dad in the eye. I heard myself saying, "I guess we ain't nothin' or nobody, huh, Dad?" He went on talking like he didn't even hear me, and I wasn't listening to what he was saying either. I just wanted to get back to Wiltwyck and steal something and get into a lot of trouble. I never wanted to go back to anyplace so bad in all my life. I wanted to be around K.B. and Horse and Tito and other cats like me. We could all get together up at Wiltwyck, raise a lot of hell, and show people that we weren't pigs and that we couldn't be fucked over but so much. Simms and Claiborne and Nick and Papanek and everybody else up at Wiltwyck knew I was somebody—even when I wasn't getting into trouble. I couldn't wait to get back to where I wasn't a pig.

In the winter after the summer that I moved into Aggrey, I had my old gang from Carver back together, but things were kind of different. Tito was presi-dent, K.B. was vice-president, and I was the war counselor. The gang was made up this way because that was the way I wanted it. Tito felt good being president of something. It was the first time in his life that he had ever been president of anything. And K.B. felt real great about being vice-president. I made Horse the treasurer. Nobody else counted much. No, I couldn't be any more than what I was already, the main cat on the Wiltwyck scene. Most people didn't know it, but when Papanek wasn't at Wiltwyck I ran the place. Every time something happened, Stilly, Simms, or Mrs. Chase or all three of them would come running to me. Mrs. Chase was Stilly's assistant.

That winter, my clique was really raising a lot of hell. We were stealing everything we found, breaking into every place that had a lock on it—just about all of us could pick locks—fighting with other houses, and stomping cats we didn't like. It was mainly J.J. and Stumpy who liked to stomp cats. J.J. liked it because he couldn't beat anybody in a fair fight, and whenever we stomped somebody, all of us stomped him. Stumpy liked to stomp cats because he was a real bully, and it made him feel real good. His eyes used to light up when he did it. J.J. was a real nice guy, and he was one of the best liars up at Wiltwyck, maybe even better than me. J.J. was an orphan, and he had lived in and out of foster homes and places like Wiltwyck all his life. So he really knew how to make people like him, man or woman, white or colored. This made him one of the slickest cats on the Wiltwyck scene. Stumpy was a real nice guy too, but he needed somebody to kick him in his ass every now and then just to let him know how nice he was.

One day that same winter, Simms called everybody into the living room, where we used to have our house meetings. He told us that some girls were coming to Wiltwyck soon from a place called Vassar College and that they were going to teach us things like skiing, music, painting, and stuff like that. Simms said he expected us to treat those chicks better than the guys in the other houses, since we were older than the other guys. He had that "if you don't do right I'm gonna kick your ass" tone in his voice when he told us about the chicks from Vassar, but nobody cared much, because Simms hadn't hit a cat in a long time.

The first day the girls came to Wiltwyck, the cats in Aggrey swarmed all over them. In fact, everybody took to them right away. They were all white and not so hip, but most of them were real fine, so nobody cared about them being white and not being hip. It really wasn't hard to be nice to these chicks, because they were all real sweet. They were some of the nicest girls I had ever met, and some of them knew some things too. You could talk to them, and they could understand things. Every day, they would come to Wiltwyck early in the morning and stay until evening. One day, the girls from Vassar took us to the college for a picnic. It sure was a big place, and I never saw so many pretty girls in one place before in all my life. There must have been about a million bicycles at that place. The girls said we could ride any of the bikes we wanted to, but we had to remember where we got them from and put them back when we finished. We really broke up some bikes that day. I saw Horse bring a bike back in five parts.

J.J. caused a girl to faint. He was coming down this steep hill real fast. There was a brick wall at the bottom, and J.J. couldn't steer too well. When

J.J. hit the wall, he didn't get hurt, but the bike was all smashed up, and J.J. went straight up into the air about fifteen feet. The girl was standing on the bridge, and when she heard the crash, she turned around just in time to see J.J. going up, and she fainted. When they woke her up, the girl said that she fainted because she thought sure the boy would be killed, but Rickets said that seeing a nigger flying through the air on the campus of Vassar College was enough to make any nice, respectable white girl faint. And sometimes Rickets knew what he was talking about.

Cathy, my piano teacher, was a big, fine chick. She was white, but she was from China. Her father was a doctor or something in China, and she was born there and had lived there, but she was still white. She just came over here to go to Vassar College. She didn't speak Chinese or anything. As a matter of fact, she spoke real good English, and she was a sweet person, real big and real fine. Cathy ran over to J.J., who was lying there on the ground playing dead, and kneeled down beside him. She raised his head and put it in her lap and started screaming all over the place for somebody to get a doctor. I knew if she kept that up for long, they would never get J.J. up from there.

J.J. sneaked one eye open, looked up at those big breasts right over in his face, and started snuggling. I wanted to say, "Poor Cathy." She just shouldn't have done that. Somebody should have pulled her coat. I would have, but J.J. was a friend of mine, so I couldn't do that. After a while, she saw this cat opening one eye and getting closer, and I think she felt kind of foolish. So she threw his head off her lap and told him to get up. He laughed and got up. And everybody thought it was pretty funny.

But that wasn't the funniest thing that happened that day. The funniest thing was when we were in the music room and another girl screamed. We turned around to see what it was, and this girl was trying to jump up off a piano stool, because while she was playing the piano, somebody was under there playing with her legs. That was dear old Rickets. That's the way he was.

We had a lot of fun at Vassar College, and the girls were really something wonderful. I never would have thought that white girls could be so nice. Cats could look all up under their dresses and everything, and all they did was laugh.

We got along real fine with the girls until the day J.J. got lost in a snow-storm with the skiing teacher. They had searching parties out for them, lots of searching parties, all day long. But J.J. and the skiing teacher were lost in a blizzard for about four hours. Everybody in the world was wondering where they could be. But nobody found them. After the snowing was over J.J. and the teacher came back, with smiles on their faces. They were happy, and I suppose everybody was happy—that is, everybody but Stilly and the rest of the staff. They were a little peeved. They wondered where in the world a nigger could be in a snowstorm with some pretty little Norwegian skiing teacher. That's not supposed to happen to people from poor Negro backgrounds.

J.J. said he and the teacher had to stop in some barn for four hours to get out of the storm. All the cats up there envied J.J. that day. I kind of wished I had been caught in that storm too, because that teacher sure was something sweet . . . cute accent too.

After a while, I think they found out that it wasn't working. The guys got used to the girls, and they started treating them like mothers and sisters and that sort of thing. These were guys who cursed out mothers and sisters, and when they started treating these chicks like mothers and sisters, they were cursing them out too. One cat, Baldy, even had enough nerve to slap one of those girls. Now, everybody knew that perhaps you could curse them out or scream at them, but they also knew that no niggers were supposed to be slapping any girls from Vassar College. I guess we were supposed to be glad to even be able to say hello to them.

Then there was the Mac thing. Mac used to operate the movie camera for us on Thursday and Sunday nights. One day, while the girls from Vassar were at Wiltwyck, Mac got locked up in the movie booth with that same skiing teacher, and they had a lot of fun, I suppose, because they stayed in there a long time. Everybody started looking for Mac. He was supposed to be getting the cameras ready. They banged on the doors, they did everything, but nobody could find them. When Mac finally came out and they asked him where he'd been, he said, "In the movie booth." Somebody said, "Lawd, it's time to git these girls outta here."

They were all seniors in college, and when graduation time came around, they had to go. I think, in spite of everything, we missed them, and maybe they missed us too. That was the first time we'd ever known any Vassar girls, but I suppose that was the first time they'd ever known any poor little colored boys.

The summer after the girls from Vassar College left was pretty much the same as the other two summers I'd spent up at Wiltwyck. Only now I'd been at Wiltwyck two years, and there was nothing new about the place. We did the same things. In the summer, we played softball, went fishing; we just ran around and acted crazy in general and waited for fall to come around so we could steal the apples out of Farmer Greene's orchard . . . things like that. We went to Mrs. Roosevelt's house in June for the annual picnic and all that sort of nonsense. To me, Wiltwyck now seemed like a babyish sort of place.

They let me go home that summer for a long visit. And it was good. It was a real good visit. I saw people I hadn't seen in a long time. Kid and Butch were out of Warwick; Danny was home on a visit from Warwick the same time I was there. I sure was glad to see all those guys. We had all been home on visits before, but it seemed that we were never in the city at the same time. And now, here we all were. I felt I was getting a part of my life back that I'd been missing for a long time. It sure was good to see these cats and to find out the new things. All the time I was hanging out with those young guys at Wiltwyck, I was beginning to feel young. But now all my old friends were here, the people I felt I was just as old as, and I felt good.

We started hanging out again. I was thirteen, so now it was okay for me to hang out. Nobody squawked. Butch and Danny used to take me to a place called the Lounge, and we'd dance. It was a cellar. It was dark in there, and we used to listen to records by the Orioles. We would dance the Grind, a dance that anybody could do. All you had to do was stand still and move a little bit.

Then I started staying out real late at night. Sometimes I'd come in at two or three o'clock in the morning, but Mama and Dad wouldn't squawk. They started treating me like I was old now, so whenever I was home, I didn't mind being there. But something else happened that summer—something that made things change, that made Harlem change.

When I came home, Kid and Butch and Danny weren't smoking reefers any more. I'd have a smoke, but they were doing other things. And the first thing that Danny told me was that they were using something that they called "horse." I remember Danny saying, "If I ever catch you messin' wit horse, I'll kill you." I had the feeling that he meant it, but it made me curious about horse. It seemed that they were saying this was something I wasn't old enough for. But I wanted to do the same things they were doing; I wanted to be as old as they were. All the older cats were using horse. The younger cats were still smoking reefers, drinking wine, and stuff like that. But I didn't want to be young. I wanted to be old. And the first time Danny spoke to me about it, I knew I was going to get some horse somehow, somewhere—soon.

Horse was a new thing, not only in our neighborhood but in Brooklyn, the Bronx, and everyplace I went, uptown and downtown. It was like horse had just taken over. Everybody was talking about it. All the hip people were using it and snorting it and getting this new high. To know what was going on and to be in on things, you had to do that. And the only way I felt I could come out of Wiltwyck and be up to date, the only way to take up where I had left off and be the same hip guy I was before I went to Wiltwyck, was to get in on the hippest thing, and the hippest thing was horse. It wasn't like the other time I came home and heard that the Orioles were singing at the Apollo and that guys were going around singing in little goups and trying to imitate them. These things had happened before. The first time I came home, it was still the gang fights. If you were in a gang, you were somebody, and you were doing things. The summer before this one, the Grind was the thing that was going on. But things kept changing, and I'd always been able to change with them and keep up with the neighborhood.

When I left New York that summer and went back to Wiltwyck, the thing I still wanted most was horse. I had been smoking reefers and had gotten high a lot of times, but I had the feeling that this horse was something that was out of this world. Back at Wiltwyck, I started telling everybody about horse. I told K.B. about horse; I told Tito about horse; I told Horse about horse. We just had to get some somehow. We knew that it was medicine and that you could get high off it and that it was better than reefers, but that was about all we knew.

For about six months or more, the guys in Aggrey House used to try to get high by taking a cigarette and sticking the teeth of a comb into it. All it did was stink when you smoked it. It didn't really get cats high, but you could make believe if you had enough imagination. Then I think it was Stumpy who came up with putting camera film into a cigarette. We tried this, and a lot of cats got sick, got headaches, and got everything else, but I don't think anybody ever really got high. When we heard about this horse thing, every cat who knew about it wanted to try some. I'd gotten some guys high off reefers when I took them home with me or when they came to visit me. Now we wanted to get some highs off horse.

K.B. had told me that this was something real big in Brownsville too. I wanted to turn him on before he could turn me on. He thought he was as hip as I was and was into as many things as I was, but I knew he wasn't. If he was the first one to come up with some horse, I would feel bad about that, so I really had to get some horse somehow. I wanted to turn K.B. and everybody else on and show them that I really knew how to get high. I started scheming and thinking that maybe we could steal some from the infirmary. But I didn't know what it was. All I knew was that it was medicine, that it was white, and that for a dollar, in the streets, you could get a capsule. But I didn't know what to look for if I went into the infirmary. So for some time, I had a lot of guys stealing all kinds of caps with white powder in them out of the infirmary. We got some of everything but horse.

Cats were getting sick around there from some of the stuff they were snorting in those white caps. We'd always get a guinea pig, and the guinea pig was usually Teddy D. He'd snort just about anything. He was from Harlem, too, and he'd heard a lot about horse. He was ready to try something new because it was time to move on. I think everybody up there had the feeling it was time to move on. It was time to stop smoking reefers and stop drinking wine; it was time to start really getting high. The old guys out on the streets were really getting high. They were snorting this horse, and this horse was making them bend; it was making them itch and nod and talk in heavier voices. It made you sound like a real gangster or like a real old cat. And everybody wanted to sound old.

I heard somebody talking about horse one night, but I didn't know it. It was Mr. Johnson. Mr. Johnson was one of the counselors, and he had heard some of the guys in our house talking about horse. He came in and told us that it was heroin and that heroin could kill you. He said that when he was going to college, he knew a boy who liked to use this horse. He said that they called it "snow" then but that the real name of it was heroin. And this heroin was something that you take a little bit of for a while, and then you would take more and more and more, and soon you have to take so much that you couldn't take anything else. You couldn't eat, you couldn't drink any water, and after a while, guys just dried up and died. And it was so expensive that you had to steal and rob and do a whole lot of other stuff. What Mr. Johnson was telling us about heroin really sounded frightening, but I knew that horse wasn't heroin; I knew that it was something altogether different. But Mr. Johnson sure scared the hell out of me.

The guys I had seen using it, like Butch and Danny and the others, had just started, of course, but it wasn't doing anything bad to them. It wasn't drying them up. They seemed to feel good. That's what really made me want to use it. Those guys seemed to feel like they were flying, like they were way up in the air; they felt a way that they'd never felt before. And to see so many people going around on those streets feeling so good—I just knew I was missing out on something really big. It would be a drag for someone to come up to you and say, "Man, you ever snort any horse?" and you would have to say, "No." Hell, I wanted to be able to say, "Yeah, man."

I'd forgotten about everything but horse when I went back to Wiltwyck, but then something terrible happened. When I came back to Wiltwyck from that visit in 1950, I found out that K.B. was going home. I couldn't believe that. I panicked. I said, "No, man. You must be jokin'."

He said, "No, man, Stilly told me."

I ran to the office. I looked for Papanek. He wasn't around. I found Stilly. I said, "Stilly, I wanna go home. I gotta go home. If they don' let me outta this place, I'm gonna go crazy. I'm gon tear the place down."

"Don't get excited," Stilly said. "Didn't I promise you a year ago that you would be going home before I left?"

"Yeah," I said, but I had never paid too much attention to Stilly.

He said, "Look, I'm leaving here in a couple of months. I won't be here when school starts, and you won't be here either. Do you believe that?"

I said, "Yeah, man, I believe you." I did, but I still wanted to talk to Papanek. I wanted to scream and let everybody know how I felt about still being at that place after two years—two years and about four months. I had to get out of there.

But Papanek wasn't there, and nobody else was there, and after ranting and raving for a little while, I got used to the idea of being there and not having my old sidekick any more. It was okay when K.B. left. We made plans to see each other when I got out. And we kept those plans. K.B. told me to come to Brownsville when I got out and he would have some horse for me—all the horse I wanted.

I believed him. I knew K.B. would try damn hard and would probably succeed. He had a lot of older brothers, and they were hip guys. Most of them knew things. They'd been in the old gangs in Brooklyn—the Nits and the Robins and the Green Avenue Stompers, the real hip gangs. I couldn't wait. I kept dreaming about that horse that was waiting for me when I got out of Wiltwyck.

4

For two weeks I had been counting the days, and it seemed that the nineteenth of August would never come. But one beautiful morning, it finally came around. I didn't feel too sad about leaving Wiltwyck. I kind of thought I would. Maybe it was because I had been there so long, two and a half years.

I remember waving good-bye to everybody, happily, trying hard to smile. I guess I felt a little sad, but I wanted to get to New York and to all the new things that were waiting for me there—the new girls I'd met on visits home, the new highs, the horse that K.B. was going to have for me. I'd be running with Danny and Butch and Kid again, and I'd be doing the same old things, but I'd be doing them better because I was older and bigger and hipper now. I thought, Oh, Lord, Harlem, let me git to you! It was an exciting feeling—going home.

It was exciting being home for the first few days, the first few weeks. Then I don't know what happened, but suddenly it just seemed to be gone. Harlem had changed a lot. Everybody had changed. I had changed too, but in a different way. I was moving away from things. There was no place for me. I felt lonelier in Harlem than I'd felt when I first went to Wiltwyck. I couldn't go back to Wiltwyck—I had been trying to get away from there for years to get back to this. Now it seemed as though "this" wasn't there any more. It really was confusing for a while.

It seemed as though Butch and Danny and Kid weren't doing the things we used to do, and they didn't want to do the things that I wanted to do. All they wanted to do was get high off some horse and nod, go to dances and things like that, and maybe shoot somebody occasionally if they had been messed with. But they said that bebopping was gone, it was out of style, it was for kids. And since I was one of them, I had to say it was for kids too, and I had to put it down.

After a while, I decided I wasn't going to hang out with Butch and Kid any more. I liked hanging out with the guys I had been at Wiltwyck with better. They were all coming around, and these were the guys I felt more like, so I had to be with them. We had to do the same old things, or we had to find our own new things to do. We couldn't gang fight anymore. We were all kind of lost. Nobody knew what to do. All we knew was that we had to find it, whatever it was, and do it together.

When I first came home, I went over to Brooklyn to see K.B. and to get some horse and to see what this beautiful black bitch by the name of Linda looked like. Linda turned out to be everything K.B. had said she was. She was pretty, with long hair and real white teeth. Linda was the darkest girl I had ever seen, even darker than Jackie. But the thing that moved me most was her long hair. I had never seen a girl so dark with hair so long and pretty, not nappy. I wondered what her parents looked like.

But K.B. couldn't get any drugs. His brothers and all the older cats were into horse, but they wouldn't let him mess with it. They wouldn't let him do anything more than smoke reefers, so that was all he had. We'd been smoking pot before, and this was no big thing. After that first time, I didn't go over there much any more. I couldn't see going way over there to Brownsville just to smoke some pot. So I just stayed in Harlem. I knew I'd get some one day.

I didn't know Johnny D. before I went to Wiltwyck, but he was about the hippest cat on Eighth Avenue, the slickest nigger in the neighborhood. Johnny D. lived in the same building I lived in, but on the top floor. I had met him when I came down on visits from Wiltwyck, but I didn't know the cat real good. All I knew was that he lived in the building, and that he was kind of old. He was a man, anyway, twenty-one. His mother seemed too young to have a son as old as he was. I knew his mother had been living in the building for a few years, but I'd never seen him before. It turned out that Johnny D. had been in jail since he was seventeen, and during that time his mother moved into our building. He got out while I was up at Wiltwyck.

My new gang, the cats from Wiltwyck, used to steal a lot of stuff and sell it to Johnny. Johnny did everything. He used to sell all the horse in the neighborhood. In fact, he seemed to have been the one who brought it into the neighborhood. But, then, Johnny was fast and way ahead of everybody else anyway, so he was expected to do all those things. He was a pimp. He had all kinds of chicks hustling for him. He even had a Chinese girl hustling for him, and that was some shit that nobody else in Harlem had ever done. He sold guns. He had chicks sleeping with cats in nice cribs downtown, and while a chick was sleeping with a cat—or while the cat was sleeping after she'd knocked him off—she'd steal his keys and give them to Johnny. Johnny would give them to Butch or Kid or Danny or some of the older thieves in the neighborhood, and they'd go down there and loot the cat's crib. He was into just about everything.

After I'd been out of Wiltwyck for about six weeks, a guy named Dunny and Tito and I stole some cigarettes from a grocery store's warehouse. We had something like a hundred cartons of cigarettes. We took them to Johnny, but he didn't want to give us too much money. Anyway, that's how he put it. He said, "Why don't I give you cats fifty dollars—and some of the best horse you ever tasted in your life?"

Everybody's eyes perked up. This was the first time anybody had ever offered us any horse, and we had been dying and trying so goddamn hard to get some horse, it was almost like a dream coming true. I don't think any of us even heard about the fifty dollars. We just heard the word "horse."

Dunny looked at me, and I looked at Tito, and we all looked at Johnny. We didn't want to seem too anxious. Maybe he would just give us a little bit of horse and take back twenty-five dollars. So I hesitated.

I said, "Man, I don't know."

Johnny said, "That's some good horse, Sonny." And he took up one of the bags and shook it.

I had never seen horse in bags before, and it seemed like a whole lot. All I'd ever seen was caps; that's what everybody was snorting back then. They were buying dollar caps; they'd snort half a cap, get high, and save half a cap for some other time. You could stay messed up all day long. All you did was nod; you didn't want to eat anything, you didn't want to do anything. I wanted some horse so bad I could taste it. I'd been tasting it for months.

So we said, "Okay, okay, man," after we had waited a while, long enough not to seem like we wanted it real bad. We said, "Okay, man, we'll take that."

We went up on the roof, and I picked up a matchbook. Everybody was crowding real close, and I said, "Like, be still, man; you don't want to waste this stuff, 'cause this stuff cost a whole lotta money." We didn't know it at the time, but Johnny had only given us a five-dollar bag. He had said that it was twenty-five dollars worth of horse. We didn't know that much about horse. All we knew was that it was good and that it was expensive. And since we were going to get to snort some, we didn't care anyway. We just wanted to get high off some horse, and here it was.

Tito said, "Give me some first."

Dunny said, "Let me. . . . Look man, let me get that. Man, it's gon spill." And everybody was grabbing.

I said, "Look man, here; here, you cats, just take it, man, and take what you want." This was how I used to always calm these cats down. I'd say, "Here," and walk away, and they'd start acting like some niggers with some sense.

Everybody cooled down then, and they said, "No, you go on, Sonny. You get straight, man. Here, you take some first."

I knew this was what had to come. Everybody looked at me. I scooped a little bit out of the bag into a piece of matchbook cover the way I'd seen Kid do it so many times. He always looked like he'd hit the ceiling and gone right into another world after a snort. I was anxious. I almost wasted it, I was trying so hard. My hands were shaking because I was trying to do it too fast. And when I put it up to my nose, I couldn't believe it was really happening. I almost wanted to break out and laugh for joy, but I held it back, and I snorted.

Something hit me right in the top of the head. It felt like a little spray of pepper on my brain. But I didn't pay too much attention to it just then. I took some more and put it in the other nostril. The other cats were looking; they were real quiet, everything was real quiet.

Dunny grabbed me and said, "Sonny, give me some," and Tito did the same thing. And I just dropped it; I forgot about them. It seemed like I had left them. Everything was getting rosy, beautiful. The sun got brighter in the sky, and the whole day lit up and was twice as bright as it was before. It looked like Tito and Dunny were arguing and scrambling, trying to get some stuff, but they weren't in the same world I was in. I could reach out and touch them, but everything slowed down so much.

Everything was so slo-o-o-w. And then my head started. My head seemed to stretch, and I thought my brain was going to burst. It was like a headache taking place all over the head at once and trying to break its way out. And then it seemed to get hot and hot and hot. And I was so slow; I was trying to grab my head, but I couldn't feel it. I tried to get up, but my legs were like weights. I got scared. I'd never felt this way in my life before. I wanted to fall down on my knees and say, "Oh, Mama, Mama, help me."

I couldn't seem to talk to Tito. I couldn't seem to talk to Dunny. They were right there in front of me, but they seemed to be so far away that I couldn't reach them. I fell down on my knees and crawled over to them. They were down there scrambling for some horse; they seemed to be talking and hollering about horse and horse and horse, and they couldn't hear me. They couldn't feel me. They didn't know if I was here dying or if something had a hold on me.

My guts felt like they were going to come out. Everything was bursting out all at once, and there was nothing I could do. It was my stomach and my brain. My stomach was pulling my brain down into it, and my brain was going to pull my guts out and into my head. And I said, "O Lawd, if you'll just give me one more chance, one more chance, I'll never get high again."

And then it seemed like everything in me all of a sudden just came out, and I vomited. I vomited on Tito, and he didn't even feel it. He didn't even know it. The cats were still getting high. I was so scared. I thought we'd just killed ourselves. I wanted to pray. I wanted to tell these guys to pray. And they were so wrapped up in this thing; they were still snorting and snorting and talking about nodding and nodding. And it seemed like this went on for years. . . . I couldn't talk to them. I tried to touch them, but I couldn't reach them. I was trying to say something. I was trying to yell, and all these cats could do was nod, nod, nod, nod. I was dying, I was dying. I seemed to roll over fifty times, and every time I rolled over, I thought my guts were going to pour out on the floor.

I threw up, and I threw up. It seemed like I threw up a million times. I felt that if I threw up one more time, my stomach was just going to break all open; and still I threw up. I prayed and I prayed and I prayed. After a while, I was too sick to care.

The next thing I knew, Danny had me in his arms, and he was pouring some buttermilk down me, and he was slapping me and calling, "Sonny, Sonny, Sonny—"

I'd heard his voice for a long time, and then I started feeling the slap, and I was wondering, What the hell is he doin' slappin' me? I was never so glad to see anybody in all my life. And I felt maybe it was the work of the Lord, because Danny's mother was a preacher, and it seemed like I had been in hell and he had come and saved me.

After I was wide awake, Danny slapped me again, real hard. I wanted to hit that nigger then—I didn't go for that big brother thing any more. But I knew I couldn't beat him yet—Danny was more than six feet tall—so I just took it. And after he hit me, he held my collar, real tight, and he said, "Sonny, if I ever again, as long as I live, hear about you usin' drugs, I'm gon kill you. I'm gon git my gun, and I'm gon beat you wit it. I'm gon beat you wit my gun in your head, nigger, until you go in the hospital. 'Cause I'd rather see you there than see you on shit."

I didn't know how to take it. But I had a feeling that Danny meant good, that he meant damn good. Or maybe it was just that I was grateful because

I'd almost died, or I thought I'd almost died, and he'd saved me. So I listened. I kind of felt that this was the last time that he was ever going to tell me anything or play that big brother bit with me—and that he knew it. And since it was the last time, maybe it was something to listen to.

I said to Danny, "Look, man, you don't ever, long as you live, have to worry about me messin' wit any more horse as long as I live."

I was sick for about two days after that. I didn't even want a reefer. I didn't want anything, anything, that was like a high. I started drinking some of Dad's liquor after that, but I was scared of those dry highs.

Anyway, that was the big letdown with horse. For a long time, I just looked at other people and wondered how the hell they could go through that. Dunny still liked it. He said it was pretty good. He said he had a real boss feeling. But Tito felt about the same way I did. He said he wasn't going to fuck with any more of that stuff as long as he lived. The horse had turned out to be a real drag.

Although I was tighter with the guys who had been with me at Wiltwyck now, I still was close to Danny and Butch and Kid. I just didn't look up to them as much as I did before I went to Wiltwyck. Now they were just sort of big brothers. I called them whenever I needed them; if I didn't need them, I didn't see them.

One of the reasons was that they weren't the hippest guys around any more. Johnny D. was the hippest cat on the scene now. Even Butch, Danny, and Kid looked up to him. Everybody used to listen when he said something. It made sense to listen—he was doing some of everything, so he must have known what he was talking about. Sometimes we used to sit on the stoop or up on the roof and talk to Johnny or just listen to him talk shit. He sure seemed to know a lot of things. Johnny just about raised a lot of the cats around there, and I guess I was one of them. To me, what he said was truer than the Word of God.

Johnny was always telling us about bitches. To Johnny, every chick was a bitch. Even mothers were bitches. Of course, there were some nice bitches, but they were still bitches. And a man had to be a dog in order to handle a bitch.

Johnny said once, "If a bitch ever tells you she's only got a penny to buy the baby some milk, take it. You take it, 'cause she's gon git some more. Bitches can always git some money." He really knew about bitches.

Cats would say, "I saw your sister today, and she is a fine bitch." Nobody was offended by it. That's just the way things were. It was easy to see all women as bitches.

Johnny used to always be on the verge of getting done in. It was danger-ous to live in our building when that cat was living there. Somebody was always trying to shoot him or stab him or throw him out the window or something. He was shooting at people, and people were shooting at him. But that was all right. He was big time, that's all there was to it. And every-body knew it, so everybody listened to the things he said.

I remember the first time I saw the cat. I think he was still owing some time from Coxsackie, so he was working and looking like a real working-man. But the cat looked slick—he was made for crime and larceny. In spite of the way he looked and all the things he did, Johnny was one of the nicest cats in the neighborhood. He knew how to be nice. He knew it good.

I was kind of scared of Johnny, but I still always wanted to be around when he started talking. Another thing about him was that he was some-body good to have in your corner. Everybody respected him, the whole neighborhood.

He was the first cat I ever saw hit a guy and knock him out with one punch, just like in the movies. You could see that sort of stuff happen in the gyms, but not on the streets. Cats got out on the street and knocked each other down and cut each other up, but nobody just put a cat away clean, with one punch—no talking, knifing, cutting up, or noise making. That cat was really smooth.

When one of Johnny's girls messed up on him—tried to hold back some money or gave somebody some pants and didn't get any money—he sure was hard on them. It was good to be around when that happened. Some-times Johnny would beat their ass and throw them out and not listen to any-thing. He would say, "Git outta my sight, bitch, and don't ever come back." This used to make some of them act like they wanted to go crazy.

I remember Clara. Clara was a redheaded white bitch of Johnny's, and she had a fine body on her. I was even scared to dream about her, she looked so good, but I did. But Johnny had a lot of chicks like that. The reason I remember Clara so well was that she was the first white girl I ever jugged.

Johnny had gotten mad at her one night for not giving him all the money. He beat her ass and had her in there crying. Then he called Harry. Harry lived upstairs on the fourth floor, right under Johnny. So Johnny called to him out of the window and said, "Git the fellas." Harry called everybody he knew in the building and across the backyard. I was one of the first cats up there, and when I got there I saw this chick lying on the bed crying. I thought, Lord, don't tell me he's gon give that away! And I waited and waited to see what he was going to say.

He kept cursing at her and telling her what a stinking, dirty, funky bitch she was. The chick just kept on crying. And then other cats started busting in the doorway.

Johnny snatched her up off the bed and took her out the door and upstairs to the roof. Everybody followed without being told. We all knew what this meant. She must have really made him mad, because he'd beat her ass, and Johnny didn't beat chicks unless they'd done something really bad or made him mad. And Clara was one of his favorite women.

We got up on the roof. She started hollering, "Johnny, please! Johnny, please don't!" He just left her out there with us and walked.

She called Kid and said, "Kid, please. . . . Kid, I thought you were a friend of mine." And cats kept pushing in on her. Before I knew anything, somebody was reaching over me and snatching her clothes off. I think I was about the third one.

It wasn't anything as great as I thought it was going to be. I just didn't enjoy it as much as I thought I would, but, anyway, the dream came true. And I think it probably came true for a lot of other cats that same night too. A lot of people had their first white girl that night, just about everybody in the building. After that, I was pretty sure that white girls weren't anything different. Bitches were bitches.

It was Johnny's policy to never give a bitch a second chance. He could afford to do that—if you have enough of them, you don't have to be giving out second chances. Johnny used to tell us that you have to be creative and new in the bed and do things to chicks they've never had done to them before. That was the only way you were going to stand out with a chick, especially if she was a bitch who'd been around a whole lot and been in bed with a whole lot of niggers. And Johnny used to say that the worse thing in the world any cat could be was horny. A horny cat was lost, he used to say.

I remember one time he told us the lowest thing a man could do was beg a bitch for her body. I had never begged any of them, but I didn't know just how much truth there was in what Johnny was saying. I'd heard begging—and by some cats I really respected too. But I thought that if you were hip enough, like Johnny, you never had to beg. So I listened. I listened to all that stuff he used to tell us about how to pull bitches, how to make them do what you wanted them to do, and how to keep them yours forever.

I used to think, He's makin' it a point to screw all the good-lookin' bitches in the neighborhood. There were few women around the neighborhood that Johnny wanted to jugg and didn't jugg, even if they were married. Johnny was getting to every fine bitch in the neighborhood and proving all the things he said to us. It's easy to believe a guy and listen to what he's saying when you see he's doing all the things he's talking about.

One time Johnny saw me fighting in the street. Donald Gordon, from 146th Street, and I were going to war, long and strong. After it was over, Johnny said, "Come on up on the roof, Sonny, I want to show you some stuff." So I went on up. I had seen him watching me while I was fighting. A whole lot of grown people were around there watching, and I didn't look as good as I wanted to look. It was too long and too hard.

Johnny brought some gloves out of his house, and we played around up on the roof. He said, "Sonny, I thought you knew somethin'. I thought you'd learned somethin' up at that place where you were. Man, how did those cats let you come out on the street not bein' able to use your hands any better than that?"

I'd always thought I could use my hands pretty good as it was.

We put on the gloves, and he said, "Throw up your hands." I hesitated a while. Then Johnny slapped me with a left glove. "C'mon, throw up your hands. I'm not gon hurt you." He smiled, so I threw up my hands.

He slapped at me again with his left, and I kept trying to fan it away with my right hand. He just kept throwing it in there; he had a real fast hand, and he was hitting me in the face. He just kept on, getting faster and faster and faster. I was just getting mad. I couldn't seem to get a good punch on him.

After a while, I started getting excited, and I hit him one time on his chin. He shouted, "Good! Good! Good! That's it, baby; that's it!"

I stopped and looked. I was wondering what was wrong with him and why he'd shouted like that. Then all of a sudden he hit me straight in the face. I was mad. It almost brought tears, but I just went on throwing everything this way and that way. I wasn't even reaching him. It seemed like he was all around me and never in front of me, and yet he was so close. It seemed like he was hitting me ninety times a second. I just couldn't get started. I just got wilder and wilder.

He grabbed me with both hands and held me and said, "You see, Sonny, every time, you stop. Unless you git excited, you don't stay on a cat. It's like if you git in a good punch and you've got a cat goin', you always slow down instead-a keepin' on, as if to say, 'That's one now.' And the only way you gon rally or really press a cat is when you git excited; and when you git excited, you can't do a goddamn thing, man. It's the same way wit a bitch. If you gon pull a bitch, you can' git excited and let her know that you want that pussy so bad you about to go crazy. You gon lose your brains through your dick?" He said, "No. You see, you just never learned to do things without gittin' excited. C'mon, I'm gon show you how not to git excited when you do things."

And Johnny started showing me how not to get excited. He said, "I want you to hit me in the face three times. I'll put my left hand behind my back, and I'm not gonna hit you. I'm not gon touch you. You can hit me as hard as you want."

The first time I hit him, I didn't hit him too hard. And he just looked and smiled. I hit him again and didn't hit him too hard, but it was harder than the first time. And he smiled at that. I said to myself, Yeah, like this is bullshit.

He said, "Go on and hit me as many times as you want," and I kept on hitting him. I hit him kind of hard, and he said, "Damn, man, like cool it." That was enough. He said, "Look, I'm gon hit you in your face. I'm just gon slap you with my hand, and I'm not gon tell you when, and I'm not gon tell you how many times. If you cry, I'm gon walk away, and I'm gon forget about it. And if you get mad, it's like the whole thing is just lost, and we gotta start all over again."

I had to go along with it. He hit me. He hit me in my face ten times, and each time was harder than the time before. He just slapped me on one side, and I didn't even know which hand was going to come. He said, "Remember, don't git excited. Don't git excited." When he slapped me the fifth time, I was ready to cry. But there was no sense in me even thinking about hitting this nigger, because I knew there was nothing in the world, even with God on my side, that could have helped me to kick his ass.

I just held it back and fought it. After hitting me ten times, each time harder than the time before, he stopped. He said, "You mad at me, man?"

"No, man. I'm not mad at you. I think it's a whole lotta bullshit, and if you wanted to hit me in my face, you could-a told me."

He said, "Uh-huh."

So we sat down, and he started telling me things about bitches and things I liked to hear. He took me downstairs and showed me some pictures

I hadn't seen before. It was pretty nice. He asked me if I wanted to get high. I said, "No, I don't want to get high." Then James Fox came in and said that he had his works and that he wanted Johnny to straighten him. Johnny asked me again if I wanted to get high, and I said, "No, man, I don't mess wit no horse no more."

So he said, "All right." He said he had to take care of some business and would see me later, and he asked me if we were still tight.

"Yeah, man, you know we're all right."

"Okay, now, Sonny, if I ever see you out there in the street fightin' a cat again and not pressin' him, not stayin' on him every time you throw a punch, and not showin' this cat wit every punch that you mean to kick his ass, I'm gon take you up on the roof again, and that time I'm gon kick your ass." And he winked at me.

I said, "Yeah, all right, man," and walked.

I had cut Tito and Dunny and Turk and Bucky and all the cats who were hanging out with me into Johnny too. We all used to sell him stuff, and we all liked to listen to Johnny when he talked. All of us would do anything for him, but after a while we wouldn't sell Johnny the stuff we stole, because we knew the cat was taking us. There were other fences around that we could always get a better deal from. So we stopped doing business with Johnny and just listened to him. And he used to tell us a whole lot of things that we didn't know about.

He told us how to steal furs and what to do with them afterward, how to steal silver, and how to go downtown to the places where few Negroes went and steal stuff. Johnny told us how to dress. He'd tell us things about looking like a delivery boy when you went down on Park Avenue to steal something or looking like a working boy when you went down to the garment center to steal things. He knew a lot about stealing and all kinds of crime.

He knew more about bitches than anything else, and I guess that was his main stick, bitches. At that time—when I was listening to Johnny—I wanted to try a lot of the things that he was telling me about bitches on some of the bitches I knew. Some of the things I was just too scared to try. And some of them . . . I didn't know any chicks I'd dare try those on.

There was one good chick. This was Jackie. Jackie was a beautiful black bitch, and she had a body on her that made Hollywood glamour girls look undernourished. And Jackie was only thirteen years old. I remember the first time I went up to her house. I knew her sister, Trixie. She was a skinny little ugly-looking girl when she was in Carole's class in P.S. 90. But Trixie had gotten older, and she'd gotten fresh. She'd started jugging everybody, and just about everybody knew it. She had a reputation as the main young whore on Eighth Avenue.

Dunny was going with Trixie when I first went up to her house. He took me up there. He'd been telling me about her, but I'd never been able to place her as the girl Carole used to bring home for lunch sometimes, because she was real skinny and funny looking then. But it was the same Trixie. And Trixie wasn't so skinny or so funny looking any more. She had a body on her that was far from funny.

Her sister, Jackie, I'd never seen before. I probably would have paid no attention to her a few years earlier. She probably used to be a funny-looking black girl with nappy hair and knock-knees. You wouldn't want to do anything but pull on her hair or punch her in the mouth or something like that. But the first time I saw Jackie, I didn't know how I'd missed it.

Jackie was almost as hip as Trixie was, and she was only thirteen. She started doing things for me; I guess she liked me. A lot of guys used to come up there, but she used to give me stuff and do a lot of crazy things for me and to me; and when I came up to her house, she never talked to other guys. She always wanted to come around me and play; and if I wanted some money to get some reefers or something like that, she would always run out and get it.

Turk used to always be trying to get some pants from Jackie, but Jackie didn't like him too much. She always told him that he couldn't do anything and that he should take some lessons from me about what to do with a girl in bed. That used to make Turk mad, real mad, because Turk was a big cat, and I was a little cat.

Jackie could always get some money from somebody, so I stayed tight with her. I wanted to stay tight with her, so I didn't treat her too bad. I used to go up there, spend the night. Her mother wouldn't say anything. A lot of cats had come up there to spend the night. It was that kind of place.

Jackie was the first girl I tried some of the things with that I'd learned from Johnny. Just about every time this cat told me something new that you could do with a girl, I tried it out on Jackie. And if it could work on Jackie, I knew what it could do to most of the girls around there. Jackie had had a lot of things done to her, and she'd been to bed with a lot of grown men. That's how she got her money. She was a big girl. But I didn't mind that too much, because she was nice. She liked me, and I liked her. We got along. We were more good friends than anything else, and maybe we just jugged because good friends were supposed to do that sort of thing. Anyway, I liked doing it with her, and I guess she liked doing it with me too, because we just kept doing it. She knew a lot of the older prostitutes in the neighborhood, and I suppose they used to teach her things. She knew a whole lot. As a matter of fact, she taught me a whole lot of things. She was the first girl who ever put her tongue in my ear, and I couldn't take that feeling for a long time. It took me about two weeks to get used to it. At first, it seemed kind of dirty for someone to be putting her tongue in your ear, but after a while, it just felt good.

If you were a cat who could come into Jackie's and make one of the sisters just forget about whatever she was doing and give all her attention to you, you were somebody. It made cats who didn't know you wonder about you and who you were. It made the cats from downtown respect you right away. It had a whole lot of advantages, being good friends with Jackie.

I guess she had her advantages too, because I was known everyplace and respected in most. When she went to school and told the other girls that she was my girl, it made her somebody. Most of the people in the neighborhood knew that I'd been in trouble most of my life and that I'd been in what they thought was a reform school. They thought I was a bad cat. People who didn't even know me had heard about me, and they had a whole lot of respect for me. If Jackie could tell people she was my girl, they would respect her too. Everybody but Sugar. She should never have told Sugar. Sugar used to call Jackie the Black Spanish Girl. I think she called her that one time because she had some big earrings on. She got all her friends in school to call Jackie the Black Señorita and to tease her about the way she dressed.

Jackie couldn't dress as well as Sugar because Jackie's mother didn't care about her. Sugar was an only child, although there were a couple of cousins living in the house with her. Her mother cared about her a whole lot, about how she dressed, what she ate, and whether she did well in school. Sugar could afford to look down on Jackie, since Jackie's mother didn't give a damn whether she even went to school. Half the time she was just lying around the house with some guy and didn't know whether the kids were alive or dead, full or starving. She didn't care.

I used to feel sorry for Jackie, and I used to tell Sugar I was going to kick her ass if she kept messing with Jackie. But Sugar didn't believe it. She knew I'd never bother her for Jackie. I guess she would have been real surprised if I had. I would have too, because Sugar had become somebody close to me. I liked her a whole lot. I wasn't talking about love or anything like that to her, and I never would say anything that would give her any ideas that I was in love with her. But if she came around the house, I wouldn't mistreat her. I don't know what it was, but she meant something to me, a whole lot. So I just let her give Jackie a hard time.

I think after a while Jackie just learned to fight. That's the only way she could stop those girls from calling her those names and talking about her. She started dressing. She started letting Trixie buy her clothes. And she started trying to imitate Trixie and look the way she did. When she really put her mind to it, she looked real good. I didn't mind her telling people she was my girl friend.

All this time, we had been just stealing and messing around with Trixie and other bitches who were fast like that. After a while, we met a whole lot of them all over Harlem. Just like that. They wanted to do some of everything.

I stopped seeing Danny, Butch, and Kid and started concentrating on my new friends and the things we were doing. And that went on just fine for a long while, but one day we got busted stealing. We were breaking into an A & P and the cops ran up on us and caught everybody. I ran up on a roof, and that crazy Alley Bush was running in front of everybody and falling down and blocking the staircase so nobody else could get up. A cop was down at the bottom yelling "Stop! Stop! Or I'll shoot!" Niggers were climbing all over one another trying not to be the last one out in case the cop shot. Alley Bush was lying down hollering, "He gon shoot me! He gon shoot me!" Everybody just ran right over the cat and paid him no mind.

I went over the roof and down the staircase two buildings away. At the bottom, I saw the cops, so I ran behind the steps and started pissing, like I had just gone in there to take a leak.

But the white cop said, "C'mon, fella," and snatched me by my shoulder. "C'mon, let's go."

I said, "Man, what's wrong wit you; other people piss in this hallway."

The cop said, "C'mon, don't be a wise guy now."

He took me on out and threw me in one of the cars. They had everybody there—Mac, Bucky, Turk, Tito, and Dunny. In a little while, they brought out Alley Bush and Earl, Bucky's older brother.

They took us all down to the police station, but they let us go that night. We had to go to court the next morning. I remember that night because it was the first time Dad had beat me since I had come home from Wiltwyck. It was the last time he ever beat me without a fight.

This was about the worst time I'd had since I'd been home. Mama came down to get me that night, the same way she used to before I went to Wiltwyck. Everybody else's mother came down to get them. When I got home, Dad was awake in bed, and he started his same old preaching.

That made me mad. It was like I had never gone away and nothing had changed. It seemed like I was right back where I was years before, and it really made me mad to hear him start all that preaching in his old humdrum voice. He knew he was going to kick my ass afterward, so I never could understand why he had to go through all that preaching first.

When he started that preaching, I just looked down and moved around. The next thing I knew, he was on me. But it was different this time. He didn't have a belt or ironing cord or stick or anything. He was hitting me with his fist. I was balled up. He hit me in my head. I had never hit him; I guess I was too scared. But I had never let anybody hit me with his fist without hitting him back, and it was a scarey kind of feeling. Maybe if he hadn't stopped beating me when he did, I would have hit him this time. But he stopped, and when he stopped, we both knew something. We both knew it was the last time. He had beat me with his fist and hadn't killed me. In fact, he hadn't hurt me that much. That had to be the last time.

When we got in court the next morning, we went before a judge. Some people were sitting around on the sides, but there wasn't a jury. We were just standing there in front of this one judge. He said, "Do you boys know you could have hurt yourselves going into that store the way you did? That plate-glass window could have fallen down on you and broken your necks."

The people there just seemed to be visitors; they reminded me of the board at Wiltwyck that would come around and watch sometimes. They were all white people, in their forties, I guess, and they were just watching.

The judge kept talking to us about how we had risked our lives and how we were lucky not to get hurt. He said he was going to give us another chance. We'd expected this; we'd heard that everyplace they could have sent us was all filled up—Warwick and Wiltwyck and Lincoln Hall. We were all under sixteen, all except Earl, and he wasn't there. They had taken him to another court.

After the lecture, when the judge said, "I'm going to give you boys another chance," I don't know why or what happened, but I heard myself say, "Man, you not givin' us another chance. You givin' us the same chance we had before."

All the other cats looked at me like I was crazy or something, as if to say, "Sonny, what you sayin', what you doin'? You tryin' to git us sent somewhere for life?" Nobody really said anything, but this was all in the look, and I felt sorry for what I had said. I felt sorry because the other cats were there too; in a way, I was talking for them, or against them, and these cats wanted to get back on that street scene. I just didn't care too much about being on the streets myself. I guess I was just fed up with it all.

But when the judge looked at me and shook his head, with his eyes looking real sad, I knew he was going to put me and all the rest of the guys back on the street. He said, after shaking his head, "Yes, son, I guess I'm giving you the same chance you had before. But I hope that you won't use it as you did the last time." Then he said, "Mothers and fathers, you can take your sons home now."

Everybody rushed out like they were scared. Parents looked at me as if to say, "Let me git my boy outta here before this little crazy nigger sends everybody someplace." Alley Bush's father grabbed him by the shoulder and almost ran out of the courtroom.

I guess I was about the last one out. I wasn't too anxious to go. I had a feeling that something kind of bad was in store for me out on the streets. Mama was always having feelings. I guess feelings ran in our family, feelings about bad things anyway. Nobody said anything to me about what I had said in the courtroom, but I knew they talked about it among themselves. We kept on hanging out together, mainly because all of us needed one another and didn't have anybody else to hang out with. So we just had to keep on doing the same things. We had to keep on stealing, keep on playing hookey, keep on playing around with Trixie and Jackie and just see what would happen.

I don't think anybody was too happy. It was a bad time. It was a bad time for me because I was sick. I was sick of being at home. I was sick of the new Harlem, the Harlem I didn't know, the Harlem that I couldn't find my place in. When I was at Wiltwyck, I used to tell everybody jokingly—but I halfway believed it—that Harlem was the capital of the world. I remember telling Nick that there was no greater place in all this world than Harlem. We almost got in a fight one time because he started telling me about people in Harlem suffering and that sort of thing. I was hurt when he told me that. I guess Nick knew it was the truth of it all that hurt me.

The Harlem that I had dreamed of and wanted to get back to seemed gone. I didn't know this place. I didn't know what to do here. I was like a stranger. I longed to get back into Wiltwyck. I wanted to get back to Wiltwyck so bad, even though I knew I couldn't. I used to stay in my room and lie on my bed in the dark. Girls would come around, but I didn't want to be bothered with them. Mama used to worry about me. I guess she was scared—she figured I had been with nothing but boys for a long time, maybe too long.

I was thirteen. That had something to do with it. I was going through some kind of change. But I knew that more than anything in the world, I wanted to get back to Wiltwyck. Wiltwyck had become home, and I felt like a butterfly trying to go back into the cocoon.

I started going down to the Wiltwyck office on 125th Street to talk to Mr. Papanek. First I went down there to see my social worker, Mr. Moore, and he wasn't in. I spoke to Papanek. He was a real nice cat. Nobody could hate him, but we'd never been but so tight—not while I was up at Wiltwyck. I was too busy trying to get my own way to see what a nice cat he really was. He wasn't a pushover kind of cat. He was just a nice cat, a nice cat that you had to respect. When most people say "nice," they mean someone you can run over or get your way with, but he wasn't nice that way. The cat was nice in his mind. The way he looked at life and people was beautiful.

It was about this time that I discovered Papanek's secret. It was really very simple. He had the ability to see everybody as they really are—just people, no more and no less. Also he saw children as people, little young people with individuality, not as some separate group of beings called children, dominated by the so-called adult world. Having this ability alone made him a giant at understanding people; being Papanek . . . made him irresistibly likable.

Papanek had a way of making the whole world seem beautiful and making everybody in life seem to be important. And he made life important from the standpoint of the individual. He made life big, but only in relation to people. He made it go over a whole lot of little nonsensical things like color, like handicaps, like looks. The cat was so beautiful, I stopped asking for Mr. Moore when I went down there. I would ask if Papanek was in, and Papanek would sit and talk to me, always smiling, and looking funny at first. He'd always come out with a smile; he'd look at me, and if I looked sad, he wouldn't smile. We'd just sit and talk about things. I remember one time I went to the Wiltwyck office and sat for a while. The receptionist asked me who I was waiting for, and I told her I was waiting to see Papanek. She told me Papanek wasn't in. I felt hurt and kind of mad. I remembered our old rivalry, and I said, "I didn't want to see the cat anyway." But I knew I was lying to myself, and I felt kind of bad that he wasn't there.

I used to think the cat was a little crazy at first, some of the things he said, but it's hard to really see somebody as being crazy when you like them and know that they mean well. After a while, I didn't think he was crazy any more. I thought he was real smart. He knew so much about nearly everything. He was always telling me things. If I came in saying, "I'm not gonna make it; I gotta git outta this place," he knew I wanted to go back to Wiltwyck. But he seemed determined to force me to make it out on the street.

I had finally found somebody who cared. I'd go in there and tell him, "Now, look, I gotta git away. I'm gon run away from home."

And he'd say, "Well, Claude, don't you love your mother?"

I'd say, "Yeah, man, but it's not just me and her at the house, and I gotta stay there wit all-a 'em. Like, my father too, and me and this cat can't make it. He got one more time to kick my ass and we gon go to war, and somebody in that house is gonna die."

Papanek would look sad and really disappointed. He'd say, "That's bad. I don't think you really mean that." And we'd talk about it, talk and talk and talk, until the cat had me saying that I didn't really mean it. He would give me all kinds of plans for getting along with my father, like just saying nice things to him or only talking to him when he wasn't tired. It seemed all right, but Papanek didn't know my father, and that nigger was something that would have been hell for the devil to get along with.

I had to talk to this cat. He was real stable, and everybody else was crazy. Papanek was the only one I knew who seemed to know what was really going on. When Papanek wasn't in the office, it used to really upset me, because I never went to see him unless there was something really bothering me. Most of the time, I never told him what was really bothering me, but we would talk about something. And regardless of what we talked about, it always made me feel better. I usually didn't tell Papanek what was really bothering me; I didn't think he could understand. He had come up in some-place called Austria, and I figured there wasn't a colored person in the whole country. So what could he know about coming up in Harlem?

I was growing up now, and people were going to expect things from me. I would soon be expected to kill a nigger if he mistreated me, like Rock, Bubba Williams, and Dewdrop had.

Everybody knew these cats were killers. Nobody messed with them. If anybody messed with them or their family or friends, they had to kill them. I knew now that I had to keep up with these cats; if I didn't, I would lose my respect in the neighborhood. I had to keep my respect because I had to take care of Pimp and Carole and Margie. I was the big brother in the fam-ily. I couldn't be running and getting somebody after some cat who messed with me.

I knew that I was going to have to get a gun sooner or later and that I was going to have to make my new rep and take my place along with the bad niggers of the community. Johnny D. was always talking stuff about men in Harlem, saying that the only way men could be friends was that each one had to stay off his friend's toe, but that if a friend got on a friend's toe, you had to be able to tell each other about it and go on being friends. If you couldn't do that, you'd have to go to war, and war certainly ends friendship.

It made life seem so hard. Sometimes I just wanted to give it up. There were all kinds of things bothering me. I used to go over Trixie's house, and Trixie would say, "You little jive nigger, I'd screw you to death." And I'd look at her, and all those curves, and I believed it. I really believed it.

The bad nigger thing really had me going. I remember Johnny saying that the only thing in life a bad nigger was scared of was living too long. This just meant that if you were going to be respected in Harlem, you had to be a bad nigger; and if you were going to be a bad nigger, you had to be ready to die. I wasn't ready to do any of that stuff. But I had to. I had to act crazy.

I had to stay straight with the cats I knew because I didn't have anybody else, and I didn't have anyplace else to go, unless I hung out over in Brook-lyn, and in Brooklyn it was the same thing. You had to get into this thing with the whores, and sooner or later you had to use drugs, and sooner or later you had to shoot somebody or do something crazy like that. And I didn't want to. I used to carry a knife, but I knew I couldn't kill anybody with a knife. I couldn't cut . . . the sight of blood used to do something to me. Dad used to carry a knife. Maybe that was why I was so scared of him. Every time I looked at that big scar on his neck where somebody had tried to cut his throat, it scared me. I never wanted a scar like that. But there was no place to go, and it seemed like all life was just closing in on me and squashing me to death.

Sometimes I used to get headaches thinking about it. I used to get sick. I couldn't get up. And sometimes I'd just jump up out of the bed and run out and say, "C'mon, man, let's go steal somethin'!" I'd get Turk, I'd get Tito, I'd get anybody who was around. I'd say, "C'mon, man, let's go pull a score." It seemed like the only way I could get away.

Sometimes I'd just play hookey from school and go down to the Wilt-wyck office and see Papanek. And when he saw that I was feeling kind of bad about something, he used to tell me little stories.

Once I told him, "I don't think I'm gonna stay on the street, Papanek, not for much longer. I don't think I'll see Christmas on the streets."

I knew he really believed me, but he was trying to act like he didn't. He said, acting jovial, "Claude, oh, you're just being too pessimistic about it. If any boy from Wiltwyck can stay on the streets, if any boy is ready to come home and to get along in New York City in the school system and in the society of New York, it's Claude Brown."

He kept looking at me, and I got the feeling all the while that he was trying to see if I believed it and was going to gauge his belief by just how much of it I seemed to be believing. It made me smile at him, and I felt self-conscious about smiling at him, because at one time I'd thought he was funny or crazy, but I didn't feel that way about him any more. I couldn't afford to; he was all I had then.

He was the first person I ever wanted to do anything for. I wanted to stay out there so that Papanek would be right. I wanted to do this for him. I wanted to stay in the streets.

He would tell me things like, "Claude, you're being pessimistic, and this is one way to lose out on anything. Did I ever tell you about two frogs who were sitting up on a milk vat and fell in?"

I said, "No, you never told me."

He went on looking jovial and said, "Well, there were two frogs sitting on a milk vat one time. The frogs fell into the milk vat. It was very deep. They kept swimming and swimming around, and they couldn't get out. They couldn't climb out because they were too far down. One frog said, 'Oh, I can't make it, and I'm going to give up.' And the other frog kept swimming and swimming. His arms became more and more tired, and it was harder and harder and harder for him to swim. Then he couldn't do another stroke. He couldn't throw one more arm into the milk. He kept trying and trying; it seemed as if the milk was getting hard and heavy. He kept trying; he knows that he's going to die, but as long as he's got this little bit of life in him, he's going to keep on swimming. On his last stroke, it seemed as though he had to pull a whole ocean back, but he did it and found himself sitting on top of a vat of butter."

I'll always remember that story.

After that time in court when the judge gave us that same chance all over again, I went home and stayed in the streets for a while, but I always had a feeling that something was going to happen. I knew that it was just going to be a little while till something happened and I wouldn't be here any longer.

One day, Mama came in the house. She'd had one of her feelings; she was always having them. She came running into the house when she came home from work this day, and she was hollering, "Sonny Boy, Sonny Boy!"

I came out of my room and said, "Yeah, Mama, what?"

She was breathing hard. She said, "Oh, I had one-a those feelin's. My eye was jumpin'."

I said, "Yeah, Mama you always havin' some kinda feelin's."

She said, "I'm glad you here. Everything must be all right. Where's the other children?"

She always figured that if anything had happened to anybody, it would be me. Since I was in the house, everything must have been all right. After a while, she settled down, and we stopped talking about her feelings, then somebody came upstairs and told her she had hit the number.

We just forgot all about her feelings. I forgot about her feelings. Mama forgot about her feelings. Everybody did. She started concentrating on the number. This was the first time she'd had a hit in a long time. They bought some liquor. Mama and Dad started drinking; everybody started making a lot of noise and playing records.

I was just tired. I didn't want to be around it. I didn't feel as though it was really happening to me. I didn't feel like I really belonged there, so I just jumped up and ran out of the house.

First I went up to Trixie's house, but none of my fellows was there. Jackie was there, and she wanted to play, but I couldn't stand to be around her sometimes, and this was one of those times. I could have seen her all that day, because I didn't go to school, but instead of seeing her, I just stayed home and masturbated. I didn't want to be bothered with her. After not finding any of the cats up there, I decided to go up to Bucky's house to see if anybody was up there.

When I got up there, I saw Bucky and Turk sitting around the table playing cards. Earl was playing with them. Mac, Bucky's brother, had come in right after me. Turk asked Mac if he could play some records. Mac said the record player was broken and was in the shop. Mac's younger brother, Phew, came out and said, "No, it ain't. It ain't in the shop. My mama pawned it." We all had a little laugh and went on talking.

I kept walking around the room, and Earl said, "Why don't you sit down, Sonny?"

I said, "Like, fuck you," and this sort of thing, and we started arguing.

After a while, Earl wanted to show us how to play a card game called Strip Me. Nobody was interested in it, mainly because we knew that Earl liked guys. I wasn't interested in it, and Turk wasn't interested in it. I guess he didn't want to play with his brothers, so that was that.

After a while I said, "Come on, Turk, let's go git some sheets, git some money, and buy some reefers."

Turk said, "All right." He was always ready to pull any score.

Bucky got up then and said, "Can't I come, man?"

I said, "Sure, of course you can come, man. Why you wanna act like that?" He'd been acting kind of funny lately, as if I didn't want him coming around any more. I guess he was feeling that me and Turk were getting tight, that Turk was taking his place with me as being my best friend. Turk, Bucky, and I went down to the backyard to steal some sheets and some bedspreads. We could sell them for about three or four dollars and buy a bag of reefer. We'd roll up and get high and then go do something crazy—probably go spend the night up at Trixie's house playing with her and her sister.

When we went in the backyard and got some spreads, and we sent Bucky to sell them to one of our customers, Turk and I went to get some more spreads. Turk tied a rock to the end of a rope and threw the rock up over the spreads to pull them down. Sometimes you could pull the whole line down that way. We were standing in a lighted alleyway; it was like being under a spotlight. Turk had already thrown the rock up about six times, and the rock kept coming down and hitting the ground. Somebody had to hear it sooner or later.

I said, "Turk, look, let me throw it, man, 'cause I know how to do this. I'm good." I told him that I had done some shot-putting up at Wiltwyck.

But he kept saying, "One more time, Sonny. Just let me git one more chance. I know I'll make it this time."

I said, "Okay, man, this is the last time. 'Cause if you don't make it this time, I'm gon take it and I'm gon show you how to git the spread down."

He started winding up the rope to throw it, but then he stopped all of a sudden and said, "Foot it, Sonny! Foot it!"

I said, "Like, what's wrong, man?"

He said, "Run!"

I wasn't the kind of guy who ran from just anything; I was going to know who or what I was running from. So I stood there for a while. Turk started running. Then I heard a shot, one shot. Blam! Then I saw some fire from a gun, and I started running. When I got about midway on the stairs leading up from the backyard, it seemed to just dawn on me. I said, "Oh, shit, somebody's shootin' at us." I kept on running. Then, after I had gotten out of the backyard, I don't know what happened but suddenly I knew I was shot. I didn't feel any blood right away; I didn't feel any pain; I didn't feel anything. All I felt was that I was slowing down. It was like something had a hold on me, and I knew it was a bullet.

I was scared. Turk started yelling, "Don't run! Don't run in there!" I didn't pay any attention to him. My mind was gone. I ran into this fish-and-chips joint, and I told Walsh I was going to die. I said, "Fuck it; like, this is it." This was the only way I was going to get out of Harlem. I just lay down there on the floor when Walsh pushed me off the counter. I said, "Well, this is it." I almost felt good until Mama came and started all that jumping. When Pimp came in and stood there in the doorway with tears in his eyes, I wanted to cry. I wanted to say, "O Lord, give me one more year; just give me one more year to git Pimp ready, 'cause he still needs me."

After I had copped out on the nut and the court sent me back to Youth House, Mr. Moore, my social worker from Wiltwyck, came to see me. He said he was sorry Wiltwyck couldn't take me back. The judge had asked them if I could go back to Wiltwyck, and Mr. Moore asked him if it would be all right for me to step outside. They put me outside while he answered, and I had a feeling that he'd said that they didn't want me up at Wiltwyck or that I'd raise too much hell there, so I was really mad at this cat.

He sat and talked about how he had really expected me to stay on the street for a long time. I wanted to say, "Look man, you can't let me go up to

Warwick. Like, I'm scared. I ain't got no business up there. I been messin' up on the street. I been messin' with people, and I been bullyin' cats. Like, I did some pretty mean things in those gang fights. I'd rather die now than go up there, because those cats will kill me."

But Mr. Moore just wasn't the kind of cat you could tell anything like that to. He was a real nice guy, the meaningless sort of nice guy—a nice guy who couldn't do anything for anybody.

So I said, "Yeah, well, that's all right, because I didn't want to go back to Wiltwyck anyway."

He looked down when I said that, and we both didn't say anything for a while, because we both knew it was a lie. It seemed like a long time before he said, "Well, do you want me to say anything to anybody up at Wiltwyck for you?"

I said, "Yeah, just tell 'em all I said good-bye."

I went back up to my room, and I thought, Oh, Lord, what am I gonna do? What am I gonna do up at Warwick? There was no way out. I'd already gone to the nutbox and back, and all I could do now was go and face whatever was waiting for me up at Warwick.

That night, I couldn't go to sleep. I just kept thinking about it. The day before, Mama had been there and told me that Sugar had been around the house and was sorry that she couldn't see me. She'd given Mama a note to give me, but I didn't even want to read the thing. I said, "Mama, don't give me no note! Don't you understand I'm goin' to Warwick! Don't you know that niggers are waitin' for me up there to kill me!"

She kept saying, "Ain't nobody gon hurt you, 'cause they got guards up there."

And I looked at her and said, "Oh, Lord, this dumb-assed woman! Why do I have to be bothered wit her today?" I wanted to say, "Mama, look, go home. That's all I want you to do. Just leave. All I want you to do is just leave me alone. And don't cry for me and don't start prayin' for me and don't git no feelin's about me or nothin'. Just leave me alone!"

Mama just sat there quietly for a while. Then she said, "Jackie wanted to see you too, that little black nappy-headed girl down Eighth Avenue there."

I said, "Yeah, I'm gonna miss Jackie."

She said, "I always knew you didn't have no sense. I just can't understand why you like those old nasty-behind girls who don't wear no drawers and don't like a nice sweet girl like Sugar."

"Yeah, yeah, yeah. Look, Mama, you don't know as much about Sugar and her sweetness as I know. So don't tell me anything. You don't know that much about Jackie either. I guess you figure because she's real dark-skin and her hair's nappy, she don't wear drawers."

She said, "No, I don't figure that. I ain't got nothin' against dark-skin girls. I ain't never been color struck, and I never try to let none-a my chillun be color struck."

"Now, look, Mama, how can you go talkin' about the girl . . ."

She said, "Yeah, that's one-a the reasons you're here . . . because you won't listen to nobody. Boy, I don't know why your head's so hard."

"No, I ain't gon listen to nobody who don't know what they talkin' about, and you don't know nothin' about that girl. So how you gon be sayin' all that stuff you talkin'?"

Mama said, "Look, I know the girl don't wear no drawers!"

"Mama, how you know she don't wear no drawers? Just because she dark-skin and her hair's nappy?"

She said, "No, that's not the reason. I know she don't wear no drawers, 'cause if she ever wore drawers her dress wouldn't be stuck up in her behind all the time."

I said, "Oh, Mama, please, please, why you always talkin' about somebody and always goin' on crazy like this? Why did you have to come here anyway?"

When I said that, things got real quiet. After a while, I said, "I'm sorry, Mama, I'm sorry."

When you went to Warwick, you had to spend time in a reception center. They didn't put you with the other cats right away. They gave you all kinds of tests. You saw a psychologist. You got shots for smallpox, diphtheria, and anything else that you might catch. Then they showed you the procedures.

You learned how to get your clothes. You learned how to clean up the cottage that they were going to assign you. You learned most of the ropes that you could learn before you got into a cottage. But you never really learned the ropes until you got with the cats who were up there and really knew the whole thing. The people who trained you tried to show you how to get along in the cottage and get out in a hurry. But nobody ever made it. I never heard of anybody coming out the way they showed you to at Warwick.

The reception center was a different setup altogether. You were kind of isolated. Usually there were only about twenty-eight boys in a reception center at the same time. While I was there for my two weeks, any time they took us out they would have some runners with us, some of the older cats from the D section. The cottages were divided into alphabetical sections— A1, A2, and on down to D1, D2, D3, D4—and in the D section they had the older and the bigger cats.

One of the runners was a guy who lived in Brooklyn, but who used to live in Harlem. We were in the Youth House together before I went to Wiltwyck. It was good to see a familiar face. I remembered his name was Bishop. I knew he didn't remember me, so I didn't try to make him recall.

Bishop came in and said, "Man, who is Claude Brown?" Everybody stood aside. We were outside doing our exercises, and there was nobody there but him and another cat from the D group to watch us. I guess they all figured he was going to job me. Nobody said anything, but cats started moving away from me. I got kind of scared too. Bishop was a big cat. He wasn't so tall, not much taller than I was, but he was stocky, and I remembered him from the Youth House. People didn't mess with him. He was real good with his hands. They said he had knocked a few cats out.

I stepped forward. He said, "Man, you Claude Brown?"

"Yeah, man, like, I'm the one."

He said, "A whole lotta cats up here have got it in for you, man."

"Yeah, I guess so."

He said, "It looks like I know you from somewhere."

"Yeah, man, we were in the Youth House together, about four years ago."

"Are you the little cat who I told to punch Bullock in his mouth that time and you did?"

I said, "Yeah, man, like, I'm the one."

He said, "Damn, man, like, if you got the heart that you had back in the Youth House in those days, like, you gotta make it. You just go out there when those niggers start comin' down on you—you just run out there as soon as somebody call your name and say, 'Who is Claude Brown?' Like, you say, 'I am,' and run up and hit the biggest nigger first. Hit him first, and hit him as hard as you can."

I said, "Yeah," and I was listening. I was listening hard, but Bishop didn't know that I wasn't sure I could fight. I didn't know what would happen if I got punched in the stomach. I didn't know if I should hit anybody first or just try to stay away.

After I thought about it, it sounded like some damn good advice, because I knew they were going to kick my ass anyway. I knew it. I'd heard about the copper knives that the cats made in the sheet-metal shop. I could almost feel it. I knew somebody was going to try to knife me. I wouldn't mind getting shot again so much, but I was scared of knives. I didn't mind getting stomped. That shit was nothing new. I'd had my ass kicked good a lot of times, and I'd been hit in the head by just about everything. I'd even been thrown out of a window. Just about everything had been done to me but stabbing. I guess it was always that scar on Dad's neck that made me fear getting stabbed so much.

I made up my mind. When they came down on me, I was just going to hit the biggest cat and pray.

Warwick seemed to be a real nice place. April had something to do with it. It was a nice time of the year to be in the country. The place looked like it was maybe a farm or a summer resort.

I didn't get tight with anybody in the reception center. Mumbles and Charlie Tucker and the cats I had known in the nutbox started pulling away after they heard that a whole lot of bad cats were waiting to get me. They'd talk. They'd say, "Hi, man," and, "How you doin?" but they wouldn't hang out.

The funny thing was that this Italian cat, Minetti, seemed determined to get tight with me. Every time smoking session came around after the meals, he'd come and sit down and want to talk to me. He would tell me about his girl. He would tell me about "that no-good, fuckin' Joe." Just about everything that came out of Minetti's mouth was "fuckin'" or "mother-fucker." He was a funny sort of guy. It was almost like watching somebody out of a comic book, and he used to talk with that funny kind of talk, like Louie, the iceman.

I couldn't seem to stop this guy from getting tight. A lot of times I would catch myself and try to pull away from this cat. I thought, I know I can't be tight with this paddy boy when I get outta here; I'm gon have to find me some strong cats to get tight with, cats with reps. I knew that Minetti wasn't going to be any help. But if it hadn't been for him, I wouldn't have had anybody to talk to. Out of all the cats I knew at the reception center, he was the only one who wasn't scared that there were a whole lot of niggers waiting to get next to my head when I came out. So it just had to be that way. Everybody threw us together.

Sometimes this cat used to make me forget that I'd been shot only three or four months before. We'd start messing around, just joking and clowning. But somebody was always coming up and screaming on him. Minetti was good with his hands, so cats would say, "Man, why don' you stop messin' with so-and-so?" They'd try to talk up a whole lot of ill feeling against him. I usually stayed out of it. I wasn't in too good fighting shape, at least I didn't think so. I just didn't know.

But one day Minetti started arguing with a boy named Freddie Bemar. Freddie was a loudmouthed guy. He was harmless, but he was a loudmouth. He was always messing with people, but everybody knew he couldn't do anything with his hands, so most people paid no attention to him. But this day, Minetti and I were sitting and talking at a table in the recreation room at the reception center. Freddie came in and started screaming at Minetti and saying, "Man, you took my cigarettes off the table."

Minetti just joked it off and started screaming at him playfully. Freddie came over and snatched a cigarette out of Minetti's mouth. When he did that, Minetti was kind of frozen. He didn't know what to do. He said, "Like, Freddie, what you doin', man? What's it all about? What's the matter?" This is the way he used to talk, with just a tiny bit of an Italian accent. When he got excited, he used to go real fast, and you couldn't understand whether he was saying "What's the matter?" or "What's-a what's-a what's-a?"

Nobody understood Minetti as well as I did. It seemed as though he was going to cry in a minute, as though he wanted to say, "Well, Freddie, I don't bother you, and I wouldn't want to bother you; so, like, why, why would you come over here and snatch my cigarette outta my mouth like that and make me look bad?"

I started rising and I started feeling scared. I could almost feel a punch in the stomach already. But I saw all these cats crowding around Minetti, and I didn't dig it, because there were no other paddy boys in there with any heart, and this cat was all right with me. I wasn't going to see him stand alone, so I got up.

Before I realized what I was doing, I said, "Minetti, don't explain yourself to that mother-fucker. Just go on and git your cigarette. That's all. Just go on and git your cigarette and tell that nigger not to do it no more 'cause you ain't playin' with him. That's all you gotta do."

Tucker looked at me and said, "Brown, damn, man, you shouldn't have said that."

It was real wrong to call somebody a nigger in front of a paddy boy. That's the way they felt. It made me feel a little bit bad myself. This sort of cooled everything down. But saying "nigger" wasn't the main thing to me. The main thing was that these cats were trying to fuck over this paddy boy. And this paddy boy was more man than any of those cats there. I didn't care. Between us there was no nigger thing. There was no white, no color thing. To me, he was a beautiful cat; and if you dug people and if people had something that was beautiful about them, they were raceless. And that was the only fucking thing that mattered.

I told those cats, "Don't try to tell me how to carry myself. I been through twice the shit all you niggers been through. And as far as I'm concerned, that paddy boy is twice the nigger any of you cats might think you are or might ever try to be."

After that, nobody ever said anything to me about it.

5

I came out of the reception center on a Friday afternoon. They put me in cottage C2. There were mostly Puerto Rican fellows in there, a few Negroes, and a sprinkling of white cats. The cottage parents were Puerto Rican. I remember it well.

When they were bringing us all up the walk of the cottage area, a lot of cats started bowing their heads and saying, "Bye, Brown," in a whisper, as if they thought I was going to my funeral or something.

Minetti went to cottage A3. But he didn't stay there long, because he kept fucking up, right and left.

When I got into my cottage, there was nobody in there looking for me. There was nobody in there I knew. But I made out and I sat and I waited. A lot of cats in there had heard about me, and they'd heard that cats were out to get me, so they stayed away.

Warwick was a funny kind of place. It was a jail in disguise. The windows in the cottage and in most of the buildings were divided into very small sections, and they had steel dividers that were painted to look like wood. The panes between the dividers were only about six square inches, and the windows were usually down from the top and up from the bottom. It would look like a normal house to anybody from the outside. But if any of the cats had tried to push a window up more from the bottom or pull it down more from the top, they would have found out that it had slats on the side, long wooden slats that wouldn't allow the window to go up or down any more than a couple of inches farther.

It was a pretty place. They had people walking around and looking like they were free, but you had to have a pass to go anywhere; and if you were gone too long, they had somebody out looking for you. They had what they called "area men," and the area men were like detectives up at Warwick. Anytime something happened—if something had been stolen or if someone had gotten stabbed—these were the cats who came around and investigated and found out who had done it. They were usually big cats, strong-arm boys. And they usually found out what it was they wanted to know.

The area men would come for you if you were gone from a place too long, and they would bring runners. Runners were like trustees. They would run after guys in the woods if they ran away, and they'd bring them back. The runners usually came from cottage A4 or one in the D group, where most of the big cats were. A4 was a crazy cottage. They had the nuts in there; they had the rapists, murderers, and perverts in there. These were the most brutal cats up there, and everybody knew it. A lot of times when people ran away, if they saw these cats behind them, they would stop, because they knew they didn't have much chance of getting away. And if they gave the A4 guys a hard time, they'd catch hell when they were caught.

To someone passing by, Warwick looked just like a boy's camp. But everybody was under guard, all the time, and everybody had a job to do. You worked in the bakery or in an office or on the work gangs, and so on. Work gangs were a lot like chain gangs, minus the chains. In the summer, work gangs just busted rock and threw sledgehammers and picked onions and stuff like that. In the winter, the work gangs shoveled coal and shoveled snow. If you were a decent guy or if you could be trusted, you could get a job in one of the offices or in one of the buildings. That's where most of the younger guys worked if they weren't hell raisers. Most of the older guys were runners. They'd take people back from offices, take them around whenever they had to go see their sponsors or social workers. That sort of business. Everybody had a place to fit into, so it seemed.

On Monday, I went out, and they told me I was going to be assigned to a job working in the halls with some woman named Mrs. Washington. She was an elderly lady, about fifty-five, I guess, and she had a gang of boys who used to mop the halls and sweep up in the detail building. Next thing I know I'm down on my knees scrubbing away when I hear something funny. I look up and all these cats are standing about ten feet away. One rugged-looking cat had on a cap and a ragged vest, and he said, "Man, is your name Claude Brown?" I didn't say anything, so he said, "Punk, don't you hear me talkin' to you?" I still didn't say anything. He and all the other cats kept coming closer.

Quick as a flash, this cat was in my collar. He said, "Git up, little punk!"

I said, "I'm gon give you two seconds, man, to git a hold-a yourself and git your hand outta my collar."

All these other cats moved back; I guess they figured it was time for action.

He said, "You gon what?"

Before I could answer, another voice came from in back of the crowd, and the voice said, "I'll give you one second to git your hand outta his collar, or I'm gon bust your mother-fuckin' ass."

The rugged guy let my collar go and turned around real quick.

I recognized the voice. I couldn't see anybody, but I recognized the voice. It was the most beautiful voice I'd ever heard in all my life. It was K.B.

K.B. pushed his way on through the crowd. This first guy was a Spanish cat named Black Joe. I hadn't done anything to him or any of his relatives, but he'd heard a lot of guys were out to get me, so he was going to be the first one and make a rep on me. K.B. came to the front of the crowd, snatched him, pushed him up against the wall, and told him to throw up his hands. He wouldn't throw up his hands, so K.B. gutted him and dropped him.

Then he turned around and faced the crowd. Everybody was looking. The next thing I knew, cats started moving away. K.B. said, "Look, don't nobody move. Don't a nigger move, 'cause I got somethin' to say, and I want all-a y'all—I want every livin' ass here—to hear it, because if you don't, you liable to make the same mistake Black Joe made, and you'll end up right down there wit him. Look, this is my main nigger, my number one nigger, and anybody who fucks wit him, it's just as well as if they'd came and fucked wit me. If you got anything to say to him, against him, or about him, say it to me, because when you fuck wit him, you fuckin' wit me."

Everybody looked and said, "Yeah, man." They started mumbling to themselves. One cat said, "Damn, K.B., I thought this cat was from Harlem, man; like, we didn't know he was tight wit you."

He said, "There're a whole lotta things you cats don't know. But, like, if you fuck wit him, you gon find out all you need to know in a hurry." So everybody moved on.

Then a big cat with one arm came up to me and said, "Hey, Claude, how you doin'?" I didn't know who he was, not for a while anyway. He said, "You don't remember me, huh?"

K.B. knew him, so he smiled at me, and he said, "You don't remember this cat, Claude? You don't remember Gus Jackson?"

Then I recognized him, but the cat had gotten twice as big as he was when he was at Wiltwyck. Gus was one of my first partners when I was at Wiltwyck. He was a big cat, and I used to bully him when I first went up there. But then he started fighting, and we got tight and became partners. Gus had lost one of his arms bebopping in Brooklyn. It didn't matter too much, because all the cats up at Warwick had a whole lot of respect for him. They had more respect for him than they did for the average half-dozen cats up there with two arms. I was so glad to see them; I was so glad to see K.B. and Gus. When I saw them, I relaxed. I felt right at home. I wasn't scared of anything any more. I had a feeling that it wouldn't be long before I'd be running things up there.

After this, I met a lot of cats I'd known at Wiltwyck, in Youth House, in the streets; cats from Brooklyn, cats K.B. had cut me into; and cats I had only seen passing by. But it seemed there were more people up here waiting to get to know me, who'd heard about me and wanted to know me even before I got there, than there were enemies looking to do me in. There were so many people in my corner and people I had been tight with at some time or other, nobody would fuck with me. So I just took my time. I suppose I was the first guy in a long time, or maybe in the history of Warwick, to come up there and stay for four months without getting in a fight. That was probably a record.

One of the first guys I met up at Warwick was a guy I'd read about in the paper. Just about everybody had read about him, I suppose. He had been blamed for shooting somebody in the Polo Grounds in the summer of 1950. It was a jive tip, but there were a whole lot of cats up there on humbles. He was a damn nice guy, but they had him in A4, the crazy cottage. Just about all the guys under sixteen who were up there for murder were in A4.

This guy was on Mrs. Washington's gang with me, and he was telling me one day how they sent him up there on a humble. He said when this guy had gotten shot in the Polo Grounds, they started looking in all the houses on Edgecombe Avenue, and that's where he lived. They started looking for guns and stuff. They had a house-to-house search for guns. And they found a .22 rifle in his house. The man had been shot with a .45, but they blamed it on him.

He turned out to be a real nice cat. It was a funny thing, but all the cats I met up there and all the cats I knew on the streets who had been accused of murder or who had actually killed somebody always seemed to be the nicest cats.

After I'd gotten out of reception, Minetti and I started palling around, and we got tight. A lot of guys used to say, "Oh, man, like stay away from that cat. You know, like, those paddy boys, they all for themselves," and that sort of thing. But I liked him a lot. He was one of the first cats I'd gotten close to up there. In the reception center, if it hadn't been for this paddy boy, I would have been alone. So I didn't give a damn what anybody said.

After a while, Minetti was moved into A4, the crazy cottage. He kept breezing and getting caught and brought back into the detail building. He would have to wait outside the office sometimes. I was usually out there cleaning the halls when they brought him back.

One afternoon, they brought Minetti in, and I was talking to him. He sat on a bench outside the detail office and waited for an area man to come and take him someplace. I asked him what had happened, how he'd gotten caught. He told me he'd stolen a car and it conked out on him. He was running through the woods, and then Skylo, one of the area men, saw him. The cats from A4 ran him down and caught him.

I said that was weak stuff and went on down the hall, mopping. Then I saw some guys coming up to him. I paid it no attention, but he got up, and I heard his voice raised. I turned around. Some cats had him up in a corner and were punching him. There were three of them, and they were runners from A4. It sounded like they were kicking his ass for giving them such a hard time catching him. I thought that was crazy. If a guy is running away, the reason he's running away is to get away, and why should he stop just because somebody is coming for him?

He started going down, and they started kicking him. I knew that in a little while they were going to stomp him. So I ran up there with the mop in my hand. I guess I just didn't do too much thinking. The first thing I knew, I was lashing into those cats with that mop handle, and everybody was hollering and going on. We were raising hell out there in that hall. Skylo, the area man, came out, and he said, "What are you doing, Brown? What's wrong with you?"

Then Mrs. Washington came down the hall, all excited, hollering, "Good God, what is going on here?"

So I told them that the cats had been jumping on this one boy and that I was trying to help him.

Skylo looked at me, and he said, "He's a friend of yours, isn't he?"

"Yeah, in a way."

"Well, take some advice from me, Brown. You stay away from him, because this guy is heading for trouble, and he's not gonna be around here long, and I wouldn't want to see you get yourself into any trouble on account of him."

I pretended to appreciate his advice, then I walked away. But the main thing was that I'd gotten those cats off Minetti. At the same time, I had made them enemies of mine. But that was all right, because I didn't like those cats anyway. I thought they were all jive. The way I saw it, those niggers weren't so crazy. They were just acting like they were crazy. And they'd only act like that with cats who didn't know any better. Now I knew that if I was to breeze and they came after me, one of us would get hurt—me or whoever it was. But I just couldn't get too scared of them. I'd seen cats like that just about all my life.

There were a lot of real hip young criminals at Warwick. It wasn't like Wiltwyck. For one thing, Wiltwyck only had about a hundred guys, and Warwick had five hundred. And Warwick had guys from all over New York City. They had cats from Brooklyn, the Bronx, Manhattan, Queens, and Richmond—everywhere. There were even cats from small towns upstate and from suburban areas of New York City. And Warwick had real criminals. Nobody at Wiltwyck was there for murder, and they didn't have any cats up there who knew how to steal a car without the keys. But it seemed like just about everybody at Warwick not only knew how to pick locks but knew how to cross wires in cars and get them started without keys. Just about everybody knew how to pick pockets and roll reefers, and a lot of cats knew how to cut drugs. They knew how much sugar to put with heroin to make a cap or a bag. There was so much to learn.

You learned something new from everybody you met. It seemed like just about all the Puerto Rican guys were up there for using drugs. They had a lot of colored cats up there for using drugs, but most of them were jive. Most of these guys were just using drugs to be down and to have a rep as a junkie. You could tell that these cats were jive by the way they went around saying, "Yeah, man, do you shoot stuff?" and all this sort of nonsense, as though they were bragging about it. They would start talking about how much stuff they used a day. I'd look at them and say, "Yeah, like, that's real nice," but they could never make me feel bad or anything, because all I had to do was say my name was

Claude Brown. I didn't have to use drugs. I already had a reputation. I'd been other places. I knew people from here, I knew people from there.

Cats had heard about me when I was in Brooklyn gang fighting with K.B. and the Robins. And when I got shot, it was something that everybody seemed to respect me for. I'd only gotten shot with a .32, but the word was out that I'd gotten shot in the stomach with a .38. Cats didn't believe it. They'd come up to me and say, "Man, did you really git shot with a .38?" and I'd either joke it off or act like they were being silly. I'd say, "Shit, people have gotten shot with .45's, so what?" They would go away marveling.

When we were in the dormitory getting ready to take a shower, the cool guys would say, "Hey, Brown, could I see your scar?" or they would just say, "Man, is that your scar?" I'd say, "Yeah, that's it." If they were hip cats, they might just say something like, "Yeah, man, those bullets can really fuck you up." And I'd say something like, "Yeah, but you can keep gittin' up behind 'em."

Cats used to come up and offer me ins on reefers or horse or anything I wanted. I had two or three flunkies after I'd been there for a month. It was no sweat for me; I was ready to stay there for a long time and live real good. I knew how to get along there. I'd had a place waiting for me long before I came. If I'd known that Warwick was going to be as good as it turned out to be, I would never have been so afraid. As a matter of fact, I might have gotten there a whole lot sooner.

At Warwick, it all depended on you when you went home for a visit. The first time, you had to stay there twelve weeks before you could go home. After that, you could go home for a three-day visit, from Friday to Monday, every eight weeks. That's if you didn't lose any days for fucking up or fighting. This was pretty good, because some people were always going home, and they would see your fellows and bring messages back, and your fellows were always coming up every Friday. A new batch of guys would come up and drugs would come up. When you came back from a weekend home visit, you were searched everywhere. They'd even search in the crack of your ass. You had to go to the doctor and let him look for a dose of clap. But cats would always manage to bring back at least a cap of horse or at least one reefer. Everybody could always manage to smuggle in a little bit of something.

By the time Dunny came up to Warwick, I had a place for him. I was there and ready, sitting pretty. I'd already established myself and was waiting for some of the fellows to come up. I'd been up there about eight weeks when Dunny came. He told me Turk was in the Youth House. They'd gotten busted robbing a hardware store on 145th Street, and for some reason—I guess because he had a worse record than Turk—they sent Dunny right on up, but Turk was still in the Youth House waiting to go to court.

When Dunny came up, I saw him passing by the reception crowd, and I stopped and said something to him before Mr. Jenkins, the cat in charge, told me to go on. Dunny said, "Damn, Sonny, we gon live up here, man; like we gon really run the place!" And I sort of had the feeling it was true, because Dunny was a crazy cat, and he had a whole lot of heart. But I wanted to get a chance to pull his coat about the place called the Annex.

The cats who had a little bit of sense but who were just general fuck-ups were sent to the Annex. At the Annex, you didn't get any visits home, and you could only have a visitor once a month. At Warwick, you could have a visitor every Sunday, if your folks wanted to come and see you. Not too many people actually came up there every Sunday, though. At the Annex, you had to do two years. For all that time, you weren't going to be back on the street, see any girls, go to the places you liked to go, or do the things you liked to do. They said the work was harder too.

Up at Warwick, the cats had never really served any time before. They might have been someplace like Wiltwyck, where you went home only every six months, but they could go home for a visit or could go someplace eventually. In places like Warwick, you find a lot of guys who never had any home to go to, so they didn't mind. One place was just as good as another. For them, Warwick was just one more place until the next stop, which would probably be Coxsackie or Elmira or someplace like that. But to the average cat who hadn't ever served any time, the thought of going to the Annex was something frightening. I hadn't served any time, and I wasn't about to serve any time. I wanted to get back on the streets.

My folks didn't come up too much. Dad would never come any place to see me, and Mama couldn't come often because she didn't have that much money. Dad wouldn't give her any money to come up and see me. The way he felt about it was, "Shit, he got his damn self in that trouble, so let him worry about it himself."

We all came out of Warwick better criminals. Other guys were better for the things that I could teach them, and I was better for the things that they could teach me. Before I went to Warwick, I used to be real slow at rolling reefers and at dummying reefers, but when I came back from Warwick, I was a real pro at that, and I knew how to boost weak pot with embalming fluid. I even knew how to cut drugs, I had it told to me so many times, I learned a lot of things at Warwick. The good thing about Warwick was that when you went home on visits, you could do stuff, go back up to Warwick, and kind of hide out. If the cops were looking for you in the city, you'd be at Warwick.

One of the most interesting things I learned was about faggots. Before I went to Warwick, I used to look down on faggots like they were something dirty. But while I was up there, I met some faggots who were pretty nice guys. We didn't play around or anything like that, but I didn't look down on them any more.

These guys were young cats my age. It was the first time I'd been around guys who weren't afraid of being faggots. They were faggots because they wanted to be. Some cats were rape artists because they wanted to be, some cats were flunkies, some cats were thieves, and some cats were junkies. These guys were faggots because they wanted to be. And some of the faggots up there were pretty good with their hands. As a matter of fact, some of them were so good with their hands, they had the man they wanted just because he couldn't beat them.

At Warwick, there was even a cottage just for faggots. If a cat came up there acting girlish, they'd put him right in there. They had a lot of guys in there—Puerto Ricans, white, colored, everything—young cats, sixteen and under, who had made up their minds that they liked guys, and that's all there was to it.

When I first came up there, I had to go to school for half a day. They put me in a class, and there was a faggot in the class. The cat was about a year older than I was, a real nice-looking guy. As a matter of fact, he was so handsome, I guess it would have been hard for him not to be a faggot. He said that he just liked guys, and that's why he was a faggot. This was the first faggot I had ever talked to, except for Earl, Bucky's brother. His name was Baxter.

He used to give me things and offer me cigarettes. These were things you weren't supposed to have outside of the cottages—cigarettes and candies, stuff like that. One day, I had to talk to him. I said, "Like, look, man, I been talkin' to you, and we been all right, and I like you, but I don't want you givin' me things, 'cause that could be misunderstood. And I suppose sooner or later, you'd be wantin' me to give you somethin' or do somethin' for you, and it's, like, that's just not my way, man. Like, the way I hear it, cats who mess around wit faggots usually come out with claps or somethin' like that sooner or later."

He looked at me and laughed and said, "No, I don't want anything from you, Brown. I know how you are, but there aren't many guys around here who think they are down who would . . . you know, who I could talk to and who would treat me like I'm somebody or somethin'. It's like, I just like you, and I know we couldn't have anything goin' in that love vein, but, well, I just like you."

I said, "Yeah, well, I like you too, man. And as long as we both understand how things are, there's no reason why we can't go on bein' friends. But, like, it's gotta be friends like this, man, everybody understandin' where he is."

The cats up there I really disliked as a group weren't the faggots but the guys who were afraid somebody might think they were. Warwick made everybody very conscious of his masculinity, and there were a lot of cute guys up there, guys who were real handsome. They were so handsome that if they weren't good with their hands, somebody was liable to try to make a girl out of them. So these guys used to be brutal, dirty. They used to do a whole lot of wicked stuff to cats. They would stab somebody in a minute or hit a cat in his head with something while he was sleeping, all that kind of stuff, because they were afraid guys would think they weren't mean.

At Warwick, I got my introduction to jazz. Most of the older cats from Brooklyn and Harlem knew something about jazz, and even though I still liked to listen to rock 'n' roll and the singing by groups like the Clovers, since I was swinging with the older cats and had to be in with them, I had to listen to jazz. At first, if cats were talking about Charlie Parker and then said Yardbird, I didn't know what they were talking about. I was only fourteen at the time, and I just wasn't that interested in jazz. I'd never heard about these things before.

Gus Jackson used to start talking about it all the time in class, and I'd talk with him as if I knew something about it. I'd heard a little bit of stuff about Charlie Parker, and I'd read some stuff, so one day when he asked me if I wanted to borrow some of his Bird records, I said, "Yeah, man." Since I was playing this part, I had to. Gus gave me a whole album of 78's by Bird called *Charlie Parker with Strings*.

I took the things to the cottage and kept them for about a week before I played them. Gus kept asking me for them, and I figured that he was going to ask me something about them, so I knew I had to listen to them at least one time.

One day, I was going to my cottage, and I met K.B. He had some pot and gave me a couple of joints. I went to my cottage, got high, and started listening to these records. It seemed like something real different. It was something crazy . . . the music, it was the most beautiful sound I'd heard in all my life. I must have played "Summertime" over about twenty times.

I tried to buy that album from Gus, but it was Gus's favorite, and he wouldn't part with it. But the cat was really moved. Since I liked it, it made him feel good. He lent it to me for another week. After that, I asked him to lend it to me for one more week. Gus was really moved by the whole thing, so he let me keep it for one more week. Gus never got it back. Skylo, the area man, hit Gus soon afterward, and Gus hit him back, knocked him out. By the time I heard about it, Gus was already in the Annex doing two years.

That was how I got my first Charlie Parker album. For a year, I didn't like any of the jazz artists but Charlie Parker, and I still liked the singing groups, the Orioles and the Clovers, these people. But little by little, I started liking other people. I remember that a year later, "Moody's Mood for Love" by King Pleasure came out. I really liked that. I guess I was growing away from that rock 'n' roll thing and getting closer to jazz. So I found jazz at Warwick too, among all the other things.

On my first visit home, I met the Albees. The Albees were crazy-acting people who were always having family fights on Eighth Avenue. There were two girls and three boys in the family. I'd never seen them before. I think they'd just come up from Georgia somewhere, and they acted like it.

I had a fight with Tony Albee, who was about my age, and we started a rivalry. Every time I came home, we'd have this little feud. Pimp would tell him, "I'm gon git my brother to kick your ass," if Tony or his younger brother would mess with Pimp. This became a regular thing. It meant that there was always something to come back to in those streets.

Mama told me that Jackie had asked her if she could come up to see me, and she told her, "Hell, no." Mama said that's what she told her, but Carole said Mama had really cursed her out. I told Mama she didn't have any right to be looking down on this girl just because she was dirty sometimes and because she was dark-skinned. Mama said that Jackie didn't have any business asking to come up to see somebody as sloppy as she looked.

When I came out, I found out that Jackie wasn't looking so sloppy any more. As a matter of fact, she dressed real nice, but Mama still didn't like her.

Mama said she was still just a dirty little neighborhood whore, even if she had learned how to dress.

When I came home, that was one of the first places I went, to see Jackie. It made Mama mad, but it was my life. I was older now. I had grown a lot at Warwick, so I think Mama and Dad didn't think I was a little boy any more. And they didn't try too hard to keep me under their control. If I went out and stayed at Jackie's house all night, it was all right. Whatever I did was all right.

Sugar came around to my house that first time I came home from Warwick. Carole must have told her I was home. Sugar was getting kind of nice looking. Her teeth still weren't straight, but she was getting a shape. I asked her why she hadn't come to see me in the hospital when I had gotten shot. I'd never thought about it before, but when I saw her I said, "You were one-a the first people I expected to see." She told me that she didn't know anything about it until after I had come out. We stayed in the hallway and talked for a long time, a real long time. Then she left, and I went up to see Jackie.

After the first time I came home, Sugar just stopped coming around. She didn't want to see me any more. I forgot about her for a long while.

After about eight months at Warwick, they told me that I'd be going home in about a month. When K.B. heard about it, he panicked. He said, "I want to go home too, man. These people better let me outta here."

"Look, K.B., I been tellin' you ever since I came here, if you want to git outta this place, you got to stop fuckin' up. It's, like, you gotta stop all that beboppin' and you gotta stop all that fuckin' up with the area men, like, just goin' around tryin' to be bad. You can do that shit with the cats around here, but if you start screamin' on the area men like that, you can't possibly win, man. Because these are the cats who can keep you up here all your life if they want to."

"Look, Claude, you don't understand. I'm from Brooklyn. There's a whole lotta stuff goin' on up here that I can't stay out of. You know, like, when my fellas, the Robins or the Stompers, go to war, it's, like, I've got to git into it too, because cats gon be lookin' for me to kick my ass or stab me or some kinda shit like that even if I don't come right out and declare war, because they know, like, I'm in this clique, man. Just about everybody who comes up here from Brooklyn, they know who's in what gang."

I said, "Yeah, man, but that's not the main thing. The main thing is to stop screamin' on the area men. You can go and have your rumbles and shit if you want, but you know if you stab anybody and they find out about it, you're through. The only way you gon make it outta here is to cool it. Didn't I tell you I wasn't gon stay up here a year when I came? And now I'm walkin', right? So it must be somethin' to it."

K.B. said, "Yeah, Claude, it's, like, yeah, man, I should-a listened to you, 'cause I know you usually know what you're talkin' about. I'm gon change my whole way-a actin' up here. And I'm gon be gittin' outta here soon. I'm gon be gittin' outta here in about three months now, just you watch."

I left Warwick after staying up there for about nine months and three weeks. I came home and went to the High School of Commerce, down around Broadway and Sixty-fifth Street.

I didn't go for school too much. The cats there were really dressing, and I didn't have any money. The only way I could make some money was by not going to school. If I told Dad I needed about four or five pair of pants and some nice shirts, he would start talking all that nonsense again about, "I didn't have my first pair-a long pants till I was out workin'." That shit didn't make any sense, not to me. He had been living down on a farm, and this was New York City. People looked crazy going around in New York City with one pair of pants, but this was the way he saw it, and this was the way he talked. I think the nigger used to talk this nonsense because he didn't want to get up off any money to buy me some clothes. So I just said, "Fuck it, I'll buy my own."

The only way I could buy my own was by selling pot when I went to school. And I'd take some loaded craps down there, some bones, and I would beat the paddy boys out of all their money. They were the only ones who were dumb enough to shoot craps with bones.

After a while, I just got tired. I never went to any of the classes, and if I did go to one, I didn't know anything. I felt kind of dumb, so I stopped going there. The only time I went to school was when I wanted to make some money. I'd go there and stay a couple of hours. Maybe I'd take Turk with me. Turk would sell some pot, and I'd shoot some craps, and when we got enough money, we'd go uptown. We'd go to 114th Street, to Tito's house, and we'd party up there. His mother was never home; nobody was there. Nobody cared about him. There were always a lot of girls, and we'd have some pot and some liquor; we'd smoke and we'd jugg some of the old funky girls down there. It was fun. It was something to do. But after a while, I found myself getting tired of the school thing, getting tired of the Harlem thing.

Dad found out what I was doing and said, "The boy ain't no good; he ain't never been no good, and he ain't never gonna be no good." He told me not to come back in the house, so I thought, Fuck it, I don't want to come back in the house no more anyway.

I was only about fifteen, and I couldn't get a job. I couldn't do anything. I didn't like the idea of not being able to get a place and having to stay out on the street. So I just got fed up one day and went back to Warwick. I went down to the Youth House where the bus used to pick up all the boys going to Warwick every Friday. I just told the bus driver and the other cat that was on the bus that my name was Claude Brown, that I had stayed down from Warwick, and that they were looking for me. They said, "Hop on." So I just hopped on and went up to Warwick.

When I got to Warwick, everybody was glad to see me. It was like coming home, a great reunion. I had only been home for about four months, and most of the cats I'd left at Warwick were still there, so there was a place for me.

During my first stay at Warwick, I had been transferred from C2 cottage into B1. They said that I started a riot between the colored cats and the Puerto Ricans. Well, I didn't start it. Maybe I kept it going a little bit, but I didn't start it. They had a big investigation. The assistant superintendent told me that if my name "got associated with this sort of thing again," there was a good chance that I'd get into a lot of trouble, so I'd better cool it. I told him I felt that the Puerto Ricans were getting better treatment than I did, and I told the other cats this, and after a while, everybody could see it.

When I came back to Warwick the second time, they put me back in B1. I stayed there for about three months and went home in September. Warwick was crowded then, and it was easy to get out when the place was crowded, because there were a whole lot of cats in the Youth House waiting to come up there and they had to make room for them. I told them that I was going down South, and I got Mama to tell them the same thing, so they let me out. When they did that, I was back on the streets for a couple of months. I didn't have any intention of going down South; that was one place I never wanted to go any more. I was back on the streets doing the same things I had done before.

K.B. had gotten out about a month before I did, and he went back to Brooklyn and started dabbling in horse. As a matter of fact, he was selling horse, and he wanted to know if I wanted to sell some. He had a connection for me. I told him I didn't want to be messing around with any horse because I didn't care for junkies. If you were dealing horse, junkies were always around you, and junkies were some treacherous cats. I'd known junkies who had robbed their mothers and fathers and pawned everything in the house. They just couldn't be trusted, and I didn't want them around me. I just didn't want anything to do with them.

K.B. just stopped offering, but he started using the stuff. This was one way of putting down bebopping. When you were on horse, you didn't have time for it. And in Brooklyn, a lot of cats were using horse to get away from bebopping. It gave them an out, a reason for not doing it, and a reason that was acceptable. Nobody would say that you were scared or anything like that; they would just say that you were a junkie, and everybody knew that junkies didn't go around bebopping.

So when K.B. started messing with horse, I stopped going to Brooklyn, and I didn't see him any more. I just stayed in Harlem. Alley Bush and Dunny and Turk and Tito and Bucky and Mac were all back on the streets, and we were all hanging out together.

One night in December of 1952, I was sitting at home at about seven o'clock in the evening, when I heard a knock on the door. It sounded just like the police knock, and I knew that knock pretty well by now. So I stopped with the cards and just listened.

I heard a white voice ask, "Is Claude Brown here?" I just went in my room and got my coat. I knew I hadn't done anything, and I figured I'd just have to go down to the police station and see about something and I'd be right back. But I'd forgotten about what had happened the day before. Alley Bush and Bucky and another cat from downtown had broken into somebody's house and stolen some silverware and furs. They brought it uptown for me to off it to a fence for them. I did it and forgot about it.

Mama said, "Yeah, he's here," and I came to the door with my coat on.

One of the white detectives asked me if I knew Alley Bush and Bucky, and I said, "Yeah, I know 'em."

He said, "You want to come with us?"

I just walked out of the door, and Mama kept asking, "What's he done; what's he done?"

They just said, "Well, we don't know yet." And they told her where they were taking me.

I went to the police station and found out what had happened. Then I knew I wasn't going to be coming home that night, and I knew I wasn't going to be there for Christmas. It seemed that one of the furs was a cheap piece that wasn't any good; but Alley Bush, who was kind of stupid and did a lot of stupid things, went around in the same neighborhood trying to sell this piece of junk. I had told him to throw it away. Instead of throwing it away, he tried to sell it, and he got busted—and he mouthed on everybody he knew. He didn't know the fence or he would have mouthed on him too.

The police told me I could get off if I would tell them who the fence was and if they could get the stuff back. I told them that I didn't know, that it was the first time I'd ever seen the guy. They never found out who it was. And a few days before Christmas, I was on my way back up to Warwick, for the third and last time. I was fifteen, and that was the only thing that saved me. Alley Bush was sent to Elmira, but Bucky, the luckiest cat I ever knew, got out of it somehow or other. A couple of weeks later, Tito got busted with a gun, and he was sent to Woodburn. Just about everybody was gone off the streets.

About a week after Christmas, I was sitting in the cottage that they'd put me in, C3. Al Cohen came in. Mr. Cohen was the superintendent of Warwick, and I had known him before, but only slightly, just to say hello to. I didn't think he really knew me. He used to call me Smiley, since I was always smiling. This time he said, "Hi, Smiley, what are you doin' here?" He looked sort of surprised, because he knew I had gone home.

I just looked up and said, "Hello, Mr. Cohen. Like, I just didn't make it, you know? I had some trouble."

He didn't say anything else. He just left.

I still had my rep at Warwick. Before I left the second time, I was running B1 cottage; I had become the "main man." The cottage parents and the area men thought I was real nice. I knew how to operate up there. I had an extortion game going, but it was a thing that the cats went along with because I didn't allow anybody to bully anybody and that sort of thing. Since I didn't get many visitors from home, I made other guys pay protection fees to me when they received visits or packages from home. I just ran the place, and I kept it quiet. I didn't have to bully anybody—cats knew that I knew how to hit a guy and knock out a tooth or something like that, so I seldom had to hit a cat. My reputation for hurting cats was indisputable. I could run any cottage that I'd been in with an iron hand.

After a few weeks, they told me that my work assignment would be Mr. Cohen's house. One of the nice things about that was that I got to know Mrs. Cohen. She was the nicest lady I'd ever met. She was a real person. I didn't get to know Mr. Cohen too well. I'd see the cat, and he'd talk. I'd see him in the morning when I first came in, before he left, and I'd see him in the afternoon if he came home for lunch. But I didn't really know him. I only got to know Mrs. Cohen, the cook, and the chauffeur.

Mrs. Cohen was always telling me that I could be somebody, that I could go to school and do anything I wanted to, because I had a good head on my shoulders. I thought she was a nice person, but I didn't think she was really seeing me as I was. She'd go on and on, and I'd say, "Yeah, uh-huh, yeah, Mrs. Cohen." I didn't believe it. She would get real excited about it and would start telling me about the great future that lay ahead for me. She tried to get me interested in it, but I couldn't tell her how I really felt about it. Even though I was in the third term, I knew I wasn't going to finish high school. I didn't even know anybody who had finished high school. Cats around my way just didn't do that. It wasn't for me; it was for some other people, that high-school business.

She said that I could even go to college if I wanted to. She was nice, but she didn't know what was happening. I couldn't tell her that all cats like me ever did was smoke reefers and steal and fight and maybe eventually get killed. I couldn't tell her that I wasn't going anyplace but to jail or someplace like it. She'd say all these nice things, and I'd try to treat her nice and pretend I believed what she was saying. I couldn't have made her understand that this stuff was impossible for me. Cats who went to college, these were the boys who were in school and playing ball and reading and stuff like that when cats like me were smoking pot and having gang fights and running around with little funky girls. Those other cats were the kind who went to school. Cats like me, they didn't do anything but go to jail.

One time she got Mr. Cohen to talk to me about staying at Warwick, going to high school in the town there until I finished, and then going back to New York after I had gotten my high-school diploma. He just suggested it. He tried to show me that it wasn't being forced on me. I said, "Yeah, Mr. Cohen; like, that's nice," but I think he understood that I wasn't interested in this stuff. He wasn't really going to try too hard, because if I wasn't interested, there was nothing he could do.

All I wanted to do was get back to Harlem. I wanted to get back to Jackie and pot and the streets and stealing. This was my way of life. I couldn't take it for too long when I was there, but this was all I knew. There was nothing else. I wouldn't have known how to stay at Warwick and go to school. I didn't tell him that. When he asked me about staying and going to school, I just said, "Yeah, that would be nice." He saw that I wasn't what you could call excited about it.

One day, Mrs. Cohen gave me a book. It was an autobiography of some woman by the name of Mary McLeod Bethune. When she gave it to me, she said, "Here's something you might like to read." Before that, I had just read pocketbooks. I'd stopped reading comic books, but I was reading the trashy pocketbooks, stuff like *Duke, The Golden Spike*, that kind of nonsense.

I just took it and said, "Yeah, uh-huh." I saw the title on it, but I didn't know who the woman was. I just took it because Mrs. Cohen had given it to me. I said, "Yeah, I'll read it," and I read it because I figured she might ask about it, and I'd have to know something. It wasn't too bad. I felt that I knew something; I knew who Mary McLeod Bethune was, and I figured I probably knew as much about her as anybody else who knew anything about her, after reading a book about her whole life. Anyway, I felt a little smart afterward.

Then Mrs. Cohen gave me other books, usually about people, outstanding people. She gave me a book on Jackie Robinson and on Sugar Ray Robinson. She gave me a book on Einstein and a book on Albert Schweitzer. I read all these books, and I liked them. After a while, I started asking her for books, and I started reading more and more and liking it more and more.

After reading about a lot of these people, I started getting ideas about life. I couldn't talk to the cats in the cottage about the people in the books I was reading. I could talk to them about Jackie Robinson and Sugar Ray Robinson, but everybody knew about them, and there was nothing new to say. But this Einstein was a cat who really seemed to know how to live. He didn't seem to care what people thought about him. Nobody could come up to him and say, "Look, man, like, you're jive," or "You're not down," or any stuff like that. He seemed to be living all by himself; he'd found a way to do what he wanted to in life and just make everybody accept it. He reminded me a lot of Papanek, somebody who seemed to have a whole lot of control over life and knew what he was going to do and what he wasn't going to do. The cat seemed to really know how to handle these things.

Then I read a book by Albert Schweitzer. He was another fascinating cat. The man knew so much. I really started wanting to know things. I wanted to know things, and I wanted to do things. It made me start thinking about what might happen if I got out of Warwick and didn't go back to Harlem. But I couldn't really see myself not going back to Harlem. I couldn't see myself going anyplace else, because if I didn't go to Harlem, where would I have gone? That was the only place I ever knew.

I kept reading, and I kept enjoying it. Most of the time, I used to just sit around in the cottage reading. I didn't bother with people, and nobody bothered me. This was a way to be in Warwick and not to be there at the same time. I could get lost in a book. Cats would come up and say, "Brown, what you readin'?" and I'd just say, "Man, git the fuck on away from me, and don't bother me."

July 12, 1953, I went home for good. There was hardly anybody else out. Just about all the people I used to swing with were in jail. They were in Coxsackie, Woodburn, Elmira, those places. The only ones who were left on the street were Bucky and Turk. Tito was in Woodburn, Alley Bush was in Elmira, Dunny was in Woodburn, and Mac was in Coxsackie.

I felt a little bad after I left, because I knew that the Cohens would find out sooner or later that I wasn't the angel that they thought I was. Actually, I would have had to be like a faggot or something to be the nice boy that Mrs. Cohen thought I was. I think Mr. Cohen knew all the time that although I acted nice in the house and did my work, I still had to raise a little bit of hell down at that cottage and keep my reputation or I wouldn't have been able to stay there as his houseboy. Those cats would have had me stealing cigarettes for them and all kinds of shit like that. I just had to be good with my hands, and I had to let some people know it sometimes.

I guess Mrs. Cohen learned to live with it if she found out. It didn't matter too much, because I was back on the Harlem scene now. I was sixteen years old, and I knew that I'd never be going back to Warwick. The next stop was Coxsackie, Woodburn, or Elmira. I came back on the street and got ready for it. I started dealing pot. I had all kinds of contacts from Warwick.

Butch, Danny, and Kid were all strung out. They were junkies all the way. They had long habits. Kid had just come out of the Army. Danny had been out all the time. Butch had gone into the Army to try to get away from his habit, but they had found the needle marks and had thrown him out. Now they were all out there, and they were just junkies. I used to feel sorry for them, especially Danny, because he had tried so hard to keep me off the stuff.

I was hanging out with just Turk from the old crowd. A guy I hadn't known before but had heard about was on the scene. This was Reno, another of Bucky and Mac's brothers. Reno was slick. He was about twenty-one, and he'd just come out of Woodburn when I came out of Warwick for the last time.

He used to kid me about being a better hustler than I was and said he would show me how to make twice the money. He'd heard about me, and we were sort of friends already when we first met. He told me, "If you gon be a hustler, you gon have to learn all the hustlin' tricks." I agreed with him.

When I first came out, I had to get a job in the garment district, because I was on parole, and I had to keep that job for a while to show my parole officer that I was doing good. I kept the job, and I kept dealing pot. I had the best pot in town. Word got around; after a while, I was making a lot of money. I used to always have about two hundred dollars on me. I started buying hundred-dollar suits and thirty-five-dollar shoes and five-dollar ties and dressing real good.

A whole lot of cats in the neighborhood started admiring me, and they wanted to get tight with me; but to me, even though these guys were my age, they were the younger boys. These were good boys who had been in the house for a long time. They were just coming out, and I didn't feel as though they were ready for me, so I couldn't hang out with anybody but Turk.

Turk was a nice cat, but he was slow. He didn't want to make any money, or he didn't know how. He just wasn't down enough. He had come out of the house kind of late, and the older hustlers didn't know him from way back like they knew me. Nobody would do business with him, so he couldn't really get started. I used to give him some money once in a while, but he couldn't really get started in the hustling life. So I just started hanging out with Reno. Reno had said he was going to show me all the hustling tricks.

After a few months, I quit my first job and just dealt pot. I decided I was going to be a hustler. We were going to start from way back, from all the old hustling tricks, and come up to the modern-day stuff. About three months after I'd been out of Warwick, I was going downtown with Reno to learn how to play the Murphy.

6

I had heard about jostling and the Murphy for a long time, but I didn't really know what it was all about. All I knew for sure was that cats like Reno would go downtown and look for country cats and out-of-towners in Times Square who looked like they didn't know what was happening, and they would run down a story to them about selling them some cunt from some of the finest bitches they ever saw. There were many different ways to play the Murphy, but this was the way cats around my way played it.

Reno briefed me on our way downtown for my first Murphy lesson. He told me that the reason he liked the Murphy so much was that he could make a lot of money in a short period of time. When you're dealing pot, you have to stand around and wait for people to come, so you can sell only so many joints a day. But with the Murphy, if you made one good hit, you came up with maybe two or three hundred dollars for just a few minutes' work.

He told me, "Remember, you got to keep your story straight, and you got to keep a friendly atmosphere with these cats," and he said they would probably be paddy boys. He told me not to be too hip with them. He said to use slang words like "guys" and "a piece-a meat" when talking about girls and to offer them some chewing gum and take out some cigarettes. You had to act suave, because you had to convince these guys that you were a pimp.

After about three tries that night, and about four hundred dollars later, I knew the Murphy. I went down the next week a couple of times on my own. You just had to keep watching for the Man. He was always looking for cats who were down there jostling. They'd have paddy boys down there jostling too, and these cats were smooth. A lot of times, they would pull your coat if they saw the Man pinning you. The paddy boy'd just pass by you and say, "Watch it, baby, the Man is on the next corner," or "The Man is pinning you from across the street."

After a while, you got to know all the jostlers down there, the jostlers, the whores, and everybody who was hustling in the Times Square area. It was a nice way to make some quick money. But I still had my big pot customers, and they were still coming to me. I had the market on the good pot uptown sewed up; I didn't want to blow that. So the only time I'd go downtown and play the Murphy was when I was really up tight, when I needed two or three hundred dollars in a hurry. I could do that in a couple of hours if it was a good night. The best night was usually on the first of the month or near the last of the month, when the soldiers got paid. They used to tell soldiers about watching out for the Murphy boys when they went to town, but there were farmers everywhere who wouldn't listen, who were dreaming.

After a couple of weeks, I was an old pro. I could tell somebody who needed money, "You wait here, and I'll be back uptown in about two hours." I'd tell them I was going to have two hundred dollars when I came back, and I would. All I had to do was walk down the street and see somebody who was looking up at the building like he was fascinated with New York. I'd walk past him, not even stop, and say, "Soldier, you interested in some nice young girls?" The cat's eyes would usually light up, and he'd say, "What? What'd you say?"

I'd keep walking, and he'd usually follow. Then I'd start walking slow, and he would start walking with me, and I'd tell him all kinds of things: "It's nice young girls, colored, white, Chinese, anything you want. They're built fine, nice shapes; they got titties that don't sag down . . . they set right up. Like, they don't even need a brassiere on." I'd really build it up. Then I'd tell him that it would only cost him twenty-five dollars for an hour.

You could push a guy a little bit and say, "Look, fellow, I'm out takin' care-a business and I don't have but so much time. So if you want to git some-a the best pussy in New York, you let me know. If you don't, don't hold me up, don't take all night wit it."

He would ask me things like, "Where is it?" and "How far is it?" I'd tell him that it was at a house and not far from there by cab. Most of the time, he would be taken in by your friendly air, by your offering him a cigarette or some gum. When you were in the cab, you got him to put some money in an envelope and wait for it, as if you were supposed to check his money before he went into the house because the girls might take it from him.

If he didn't go for this, there were a lot of other ways to get his money. If he looked too hip for that, you'd stop at a store and call up a real number. You'd get some chick to talk to you, any chick. You would stop in the middle of the conversation and ask a trick who was watching you, "Look, man, do you want a drink or something while you up there?" Then you'd take the phone and say, "He don't want any drinks. He's gonna have somethin' sent up." You'd carry on a conversation, then you'd ask him again, "Say, fellow, did you want to stay one hour or two hours?"

Most of the time, the chicks you were talking to would be saying, "You crazy?" or screaming or maybe she had already hung up. But he knew you had dialed a phone number and were talking to somebody. After that, even if the chick had hung up, you'd say into the phone, "Look, I'm gonna send this cat over in about ten minutes." You'd end the conversation and go out and talk to him. You'd send him up to a hotel room after he'd given you the money. Sometimes you'd just give him a key and tell him he could go on up to the hotel. Then you'd just come on out. A lot of times, you'd steal a hotel key beforehand and send him up to that room. It didn't matter, because you wouldn't be down there when he came back.

These were just a few tricks of the hustling trade. I thought I became pretty good at it after a while, but during the middle of the month it wasn't as good. Pot was the thing that you could make money on all the time, so I wasn't going to stop dealing pot and depend mainly on the Murphy. I didn't have that much faith in it. Around the first of the month, it was a sure thing; but you could stay down in Times Square all night in the middle of the month and were lucky if you came out with fifty dollars. When it rained and when there was snow on the ground, it was bad for business. But nothing could stop the pot business. Cats were smoking pot all the time. I decided to concentrate on that.

Reno and I pulled tight. We became good friends after I decided I wasn't going to make a career out of jostling. He started teaching me a whole lot of stuff, most of the stuff he knew, I guess. He taught me how to con. He was a good con man, one of the best I'd ever met. He started teaching me how to con cats out of goods, how to shake down prostitutes by pretending you were the law. He showed me the trick in three-card mollie. I used to always think that the trick was to keep your eye on the card. But Reno showed me that I couldn't possibly beat three-card mollie, nor could anybody else, because the card was never there. You had to palm the card. I couldn't do it because my hands were too small. But I was still fascinated, and I felt real slick once I had learned about it and about the pea that was never there either. I remembered that Dad had said that. Knowing all this, I felt I was real slick and ready for street life.

Reno was a pretty hip cat. He'd been in jail for about four years. When horse came on the scene and became a big thing, Reno wasn't on the outside, but cats kept coming up to Woodburn for using horse or for getting busted trying to get some money for horse. He'd met a lot of junkies when he was up there, and he was scared of horse when he came out. But he would snort a little cocaine.

One Saturday night, Reno came uptown. He said he needed some money. So I give him a half a bill, fifty dollars. He told me he'd be back in about an hour and would have something that would give us a ball.

I admired the cat a whole lot, and I respected him. He knew just about all the shit there was to know out in the street. This cat really knew how to live out in the street. I guess he had to, because his mother, Miss Jamie, had never cared about any of the kids. The only way they were going to make it was to learn how to live out in the street, and this cat had mastered it at an early age. When he told me something like, "I need some money and I'll give it back to you," he always did. One time the cat told me, "Sonny, I'm goin' to Jersey, and if you see me next week, I'll have at least three thousand dollars." I saw him about a week later, and he had the money. This was the way he was. He always did everything he said, so I always listened to him.

About half an hour after I'd lent Reno the half bill, he was back uptown. He was in a cab. He stopped at 146th Street and Seventh Avenue, outside the bar where I used to deal pot, and called me over. I came up to the cab, and he had two gray bitches in it. He said, "Sonny, do you want to go for a ride with us?"

"Yeah, man, but I'm gon take care-a some business."

"Can't somebody else take care of it for you?"

He winked at me, and the chicks looked kind of good, so I said, "Fuck the money, I'm gon go on this ride." So I got in the cab, and we went downtown to a hotel where Reno had already paid for a suite. These chicks were tricking, and the bitches looked good.

When we got in the hotel suite, he introduced the bitches to me and said, "This is Lydia, and Lydia wants to be a friend of yours."

I said, "I'm all for that."

He took out something, and he said, "Good. We could have a party. We can have some room service."

He took out this package of something white and threw it on the table in the living room. It kind of scared me, because I thought it was horse, and he knew I didn't fuck with any horse. I said, "What's that all about?"

He said, "We gon git high, man, and have just a party for four."

I hesitated for a while, and I was wondering what the hell was Reno doing, because he knew I didn't want to screw any bitch who was high off drugs. It was all right, but it took them too long, they never came. Horse cuts the nature, and I didn't want to bother with that. I said, "Look, man, you got in that bag what I think you got in that bag?"

He said, "No, Sonny, 'scuse me for not tellin' you, but that's coke, man. That's some-a the best coke in New York City today."

I just said, "Oh," but I thought cocaine was habit forming too, and I was scared.

Reno said, "Man, this stuff'll make your head bigger than that mother-fuckin' ceilin' up there."

I said, "Oh, Lord." I'd heard about cocaine. I'd heard that some cats went crazy and started doing a whole lot of weird shit. I remember that James Fox got high off cocaine one night and tried to stick up a police station with a toy gun. He had gotten shot twice and was doing fifteen years. Fox said he thought it was a boat he was sticking up. I was thinking to myself, Maybe this cocaine is worse than horse.

One of the chicks started opening the bag. I couldn't let this bitch get into the cocaine while I just sat there like a lame. I said, "Wait a minute, baby, pour me some."

She said, "Okay, just a minute." Then she snorted some.

So I dived on in. I took it real fast. I didn't feel anything. I wasn't even sure it had gone up my nostril. I snorted some in the other nostril and waited for something to happen. Nothing happened right away, so I said, "Maybe I need some more," but before I could get the match-book scoop up to my nostril again, the music started sounding real pretty. It was prettier than music usually sounds. I looked around. Everybody looked beautiful. Everybody looked like angels, like the nicest people in the world. The whole room had changed; it looked like a room outside or a garden house. I felt I was in the nicest place in the world with some of the nicest people in the world, and I was all set to have the nicest time in the world.

My inhibitions just sort of went out the window. I didn't have any kind of complexes. I wasn't scared of anybody or anything. We started playing. We got real friendly. The atmosphere was so relaxed. It was the most relaxed place I'd been in in all my life, and these were some of the most relaxed people I'd ever been with. I felt I knew them better and enjoyed being with them more than any of the other people I'd known.

I took Lydia into the bedroom, and we started playing for what seemed like a long time. I had a whole lot of energy, more than I'd ever had before. We played and played and played. When I'd gotten my nuts off about six times, we got hungry. I said, "Come on, let's go out and eat."

We went out to this little restaurant at Broadway and Forty-sixth Street, ate, and came back. We got high again and played some more. About three o'clock in the morning, the stuff wore off, and I started feeling tired. I felt more tired than I'd ever been. I just couldn't stay awake any longer, so I fell off to sleep. I slept until about noon. When I woke up, everybody was gone. I was the only one left in the hotel suite. I got up and went back uptown. I looked around for Reno, but he wasn't around. I didn't see him for three days.

When the cat got back on the scene, he told me he was trying to get an apartment downtown. He never mentioned the time we'd had with those whores a few nights before. It didn't seem to matter to him. I wanted to talk about it, but I felt I would have been real lame to say anything about that to him, because this must have been something he did almost every night, so I didn't mention it.

After a while, Reno asked me to go downtown with him and meet some Spanish cats. He said that these were the people into all the cocaine weight and that he was going to cut me into them. I went down there, and to my surprise, I met a cat I knew from Warwick, a Puerto Rican cat named Ventura.

I started buying cocaine in quantities. I'd usually go down there and get a spoon for forty dollars. I learned how to take it, and I didn't care after a while whether it was habit forming or not. After taking it constantly for about a month, I found out it wasn't habit forming. If the panic was on and I couldn't get any, it didn't bother me. I'd just go on and smoke some pot and forget about cocaine. But I had found my thing. I had found that my best high was with cocaine. It did more for me than pot, more than anything I'd ever had before. So I kept snorting cocaine.

It was as expensive as hell. A cap of cocaine that was the same size as a one-dollar cap of horse cost five dollars. It didn't matter, because I had money coming in from the pot. Every time I'd cop some cocaine, I'd never get less than a spoon. Then I could sell some and make my money back before I got high off the rest of the stuff. I never lost any money using cocaine.

Most of the cats my age, sixteen, seventeen, eighteen, were just coming out of the house. They were just being cut loose from their parents. The first thing they usually did was run out and start using drugs to be hip, to be accepted into the street life, to be down. I didn't have to do that, because I had come up in the street life. I knew all the old hustlers, the hustlers who had become successful now, the hustlers who used to be fences, used to be whores, the hustlers I used to sell stolen goods to when I was just ten, eleven, twelve. I knew these people from way back, and now they had big Cadillacs, they had restaurants. Some of them had little nightclubs, after-hours places. I'd see these people on the street, and we'd stop and talk. All the young cats my age envied me and looked upon me as an older cat. Most people thought I was older. They had put out the story at one time that I was a young-looking little midget, a cat who was really twenty-one or twenty-two. It was the only way some of the cats my age could explain my being so far ahead of them in street life.

Mama used to get down on me about hanging out with Reno. She'd say that she knew he'd be going to jail one day soon and that I'd be going with him. At the same time, she was always getting down on me about bringing certain chicks to the house. She used to say I always brought nasty girls to the house. It became a real hassle.

Dad knew I was doing something, but he didn't know exactly what. They didn't know I was dealing pot, because I didn't have people coming to the house. He'd say, "Yeah, you gon be up there in jail where all them other bad boys is you used to hang around with." He was always riding me.

I got tired of it after a while. I got tired of them telling me who to hang out with and who to associate with. I felt that this shit was childish, and since I was out and working, I didn't have to take it.

I got fed up one day and moved out. I told Mama I'd found a place up on Hamilton Terrace and was moving. Mama didn't believe me until I started packing my stuff. Dad didn't say anything; he started mumbling to himself. Mama started crying and said I shouldn't be leaving, I didn't have anybody outside. She said a boy of sixteen should still be living with his family.

I didn't feel that way about it. I told them that I was tired of living with them, that I just couldn't take that sort of thing any more. They were kind of old-fashioned and countryfied. The way I saw it, they couldn't understand anything. I just packed up one night and pulled out. I left Dad squawking and Mama crying and moved up on Hamilton Terrace to a nice little room. This was where all the young hustlers lived.

The only other fellow I knew in Harlem who used to sell a lot of nice pot was Tommy Holloway, and he lived on Hamilton Terrace too. He was the one who got me my room up there. Tommy dressed real nice. He showed me a lot of stuff. He showed me what fences to buy clothes from if I wanted to get the best. He even cut me into the good dry-goods thieves so that I would never get burned by fences.

This was where I felt I was supposed to be; it was where all the slick people were living. This was the set I wanted to be in.

It hurt Mama. Dad didn't care. He thought I was going to end up in jail anyway. Behind this, I could associate with anybody I wanted to. Mama kept telling me, "You can come home," every time I came around. I told her that I had my own home now and that I wasn't going to come back there any more. She said, "Come by and get a good meal." I'd stop by and give them money. After a while, they stopped asking me where I'd gotten it.

After I'd moved, Reno got busted, and he was in the Tombs. I didn't swing with anybody for a while. There was Tony Albee, who was about a year older than me, but he was just coming out. He'd been a nice boy, and he had just come up from down South in 1950. He had never gone through all the stuff that I had gone through. He hadn't been through the gang-fighting stage. He'd never smoked pot until I gave him a reefer one night. The cat was at a party, and I gave him a joint. He said he liked it, and he started trying to get tight with me, but the cat was a farmer. I didn't let him get but so tight. I used to let him run errands for me. He used to do what I told him to. If I went someplace and told him to wait, he'd wait. After a while, I started liking the guy.

He started hanging around. He said he wanted to started dealing pot, I said okay, and I gave him a couple of ounces and told him, "You can give me fifty dollars when you sell the stuff." I had to show him how to roll pot. He was a real country boy all the way.

People started saying that he was my partner. He turned out to be a real nice guy, so I didn't mind. He stayed close to me and used to try to dress the way I did. He'd buy clothes from the same people I got mine from. He'd never worn anything but cheap Charlie's shoes before, but now he started wearing custom-made. I guess he wanted to start acting just like me, and he had to start someplace. If he wanted to get into the street life, he had to start swinging with somebody who was already into it. I was into it kind of good, so I was a good person for him to start with.

When Reno came back on the street scene, he found out that Tony and

I were tight. He said he didn't like him and that I shouldn't be hanging out with a farmer. I told him that the cat was all right with me and that I was going to swing with him for a while. Reno started staying away from me, and he started telling other cats that I was swinging with a lame, an old farmer. He was putting me down. I thought, Fuck it, I don't need him. But I still liked the cat and still admired him. I'd see him, and if he needed anything, I'd whip some money on him. Or we'd get high together.

Sometimes Tony would come around and try to talk with him. Tony might say, "Hi, Reno," but Reno would ignore him and then walk.

I guess it was something that Tony deserved, in a way, because he had been a nice boy for so long. Reno and Danny and Butch and Kid and I were with the dirty side. We were always the ones that people said would probably be in jail or dead before we were twenty-one. I think a lot of those "good boy" cats believed their parents when they were telling them that kind of stuff. Guys like Reno had to get their revenge on those cats, I guess, and now the "bad boys" day had come. We were the elite in the neighborhood. We were the people who were into all the happenings, and these cats were trying to get in.

I guess we all kind of had it in for the righteous-doing folks in the neighborhood because they had messed with all of us when we were just kids coming up. They were always squealing on us and stuff like that. But I don't think anybody had as much reason to get back at them as Reno and his family. Most of them were pretty nice. Bucky was a nice guy. Mac was kind of lame and didn't have a lot of heart, but he was damn nice. He was a natural athlete. He was tall and lanky; he could play a whole lot of basketball, and he could run real fast. He had everything needed to become a good athlete, everything but confidence. Maybe if Miss Jamie had just shown him a little bit that she cared and tried to give him a little bit of self-respect, he would have made out all right. But she didn't do that, so the cat just never had any heart.

I guess it was harder on the girls than it was on anybody. Dixie started tricking when she was thirteen. She was big for her age, and "nice" ladies used to point at her and say, "Oh, ain't that a shame." But it wasn't. The shame of it was that she had to do it or starve. When she got hip and went out there on the street and started turning tricks, she started eating and she stopped starving. And I thought, Shit, it ain't no shame to stop starvin'. Hell, no.

Babe, Dixie's younger sister, was kind of ugly. She tried tricking, but she was just too ugly to make any money. Babe and Dixie were both sent to Hudson State Training School for Girls. When Dixie came out, she moved from Miss Jamie's and got a nice little place downtown. She made it on her own. Babe was too young to make it, so she just kept going back to Hudson. She said that she liked it there. It was the first place she'd been where people didn't make her feel she was out of place.

When Dixie got to be thirteen, there was nobody to tell her not to trick. She figured that since her mother was laying so many cats, why shouldn't she be tricking, especially if it was going to mean money and food. She used to feed the whole family sometimes, and that was a damn job, but the people in the neighborhood just kept looking down on her. They used to say that they didn't want their daughters hanging out with Dixie. But some of their daughters were giving away more cunt than Dixie was selling.

Reno was always in the Tombs for jostling. The Tombs used to be his winter home. He said he didn't mind being down there in the wintertime, but he liked to be out on the streets in the fresh air and living and partying in the summertime, when so much was happening out on the streets. I guess to most people, it would have seemed like a hard life to be spending all your winters down in the Tombs, but it wasn't so bad. Life out on the street for some people was harder. It was much harder to be out there working every day than to be in the Tombs. Jail wasn't hard for anybody who knew how to live down there and get by.

A few weeks after I moved to Hamilton Terrace, a panic was on. You couldn't get any pot. Cocaine was pretty nice, but nobody used cocaine much but the hustlers, and it wasn't an all-night thing with them. You could sell a hundred dollars' worth of cocaine if you made all the bars up to 148th Street. You could sell it to the pimps, the whores, all the hustlers out there at night. But there weren't many customers for cocaine on the street, not like pot. Cats who were working would hardly come up and give you five dollars for a tiny cap of cocaine or ten or twenty dollars for a little tin of cocaine. It was too expensive for the average person, and you couldn't be selling it to the hustlers every night, because they couldn't afford to be blowing all their money on cocaine.

I had a little money in the bank, but I was scared that wasn't going to last too long. So I got a job working at a joint called Hamburger Heaven. This was a real drag. It was something terrible. It was on Madison Avenue, and you had to be a real Tom. Most of the cats there were from the South and weren't too hip. They hadn't been in New York long, and they didn't know anything. Most of them were really dumb—farmers.

I stayed with that for a while. The thing that bothered me most—I didn't know it would, because I'd never thought about it before—was that only white people came in there. I started off as a busboy. Later I became a waiter—white coat, black tie, and black pants. You had to smile at the white folks, hoping they'd throw a big tip on you. You had to watch what you said, and you had to watch the way you acted, because they had an old, dumbhead waiter who was a real Tom. If you said anything to one of the customers and didn't put a "sir" on it, he'd run up there and say, "Boy, what's wrong wit you?" and all this kind of simple shit. It was pretty hard to take, but I needed a job.

I stayed on for about a year. Behind the panic coming on, I couldn't get any pot, so I wasn't dealing anything then. I still had my contacts, and as soon as stuff came in again, I would go back into business.

The first time I heard the expression "baby" used by one cat to address another was up at Warwick in 1951. Gus Jackson used it. The term had a hip ring to it, a real colored ring. The first time I heard it, I knew right away I had to start using it. It was like saying, "Man, look at me. I've got masculinity to spare." It was saying at the same time to the world, "I'm one of the hippest cats, one of the most uninhibited cats on the scene. I can say 'baby' to another cat, and he can say 'baby' to me, and we can say it with strength in our voices." If you could say it, this meant that you really had to be sure of yourself, sure of your masculinity.

It seemed that everybody in my age group was saying it. The next thing I knew, older guys were saying it. Then just about everybody in Harlem was saying it, even the cats who weren't so hip. It became just one of those things.

The real hip thing about the "baby" term was that it was something that only colored cats could say the way it was supposed to be said. I'd heard gray boys trying it, but they couldn't really do it. Only colored cats could give it the meaning that we all knew it had without ever mentioning it—the meaning of black masculinity.

Before the Muslims, before I'd heard about the Coptic or anything like that, I remember getting high on the corner with a bunch of guys and

Claude Brown

watching the chicks go by, fine little girls, and saying, "Man, colored people must be somethin' else!"

Somebody'd say, "Yeah. How about that? All those years, man, we was down on the plantation in those shacks, eating just potatoes and fatback and chitterlin's and greens, and look at what happened. We had Joe Louises and Jack Johnsons and Sugar Ray Robinsons and Henry Armstrongs, all that sort of thing."

Somebody'd say, "Yeah, man. Niggers must be some real strong people who just can't be kept down. When you think about it, that's really something great. Fatback, chitterlin's, greens, and Joe Louis. Negroes are some beautiful people. Uh-huh. Fatback, chitterlin's, greens, and Joe Louis . . . and beautiful black bitches."

Cats would come along with this "baby" thing. It was something that went over strong in the fifties with the jazz musicians and the hip set, the boxers, the dancers, the comedians, just about every set in Harlem. I think everybody said it real loud because they liked the way it sounded. It was always, "Hey, baby. How you doin', baby?" in every phase of the Negro hip life. As a matter of fact, I went to a Negro lawyer's office once, and he said, "Hey, baby. How you doin'?" I really felt at ease, really felt that we had something in common. I imagine there were many people in Harlem who didn't feel they had too much in common with the Negro professionals, the doctors and lawyers and dentists and ministers. I know I didn't. But to hear one of these people greet you with the street thing, the "Hey, baby"—and he knew how to say it—you felt as though you had something strong in common.

I suppose it's the same thing that almost all Negroes have in common, the fatback, chitterlings, and greens background. I suppose that regardless of what any Negro in America might do or how high he might rise in social status, he still has something in common with every other Negro. I doubt that they're many, if any, gray people who could ever say "baby" to a Negro and make him feel that "me and this cat have got something going, something strong going."

In the fifties, when "baby" came around, it seemed to be the prelude to a whole new era in Harlem. It was the introduction to the era of black reflection. A fever started spreading. Perhaps the strong rising of the Muslim movement is something that helped to sustain or even usher in this era.

I remember that in the early fifties, cats would stand on the corner and talk, just shooting the stuff, all the street-corner philosophers. Sometimes, it was a common topic—cats talking about gray chicks—and somebody might say something like, "Man, what can anybody see in a gray chick, when colored chicks are so fine; they got so much soul." This was the coming of the "soul" thing too.

"Soul" had started coming out of the churches and the nightclubs into the streets. Everybody started talking about "soul" as though it were something that they could see on people or a distinct characteristic of colored folks.

Cats would say things like, "Man, gray chicks seem so stiff." Many of them would say they couldn't talk to them or would wonder how a cat who was used to being so for real with a chick could see anything in a gray girl. It seemed as though the mood of the day was turning toward the color thing.

Everybody was really digging themselves and thinking and saying in their behavior, in every action, "Wow! Man, it's a beautiful thing to be colored." Everybody was saying, "Oh, the beauty of me! Look at me. I'm colored. And look at us. Aren't we beautiful?"

Around November of 1953, I went up to Wiltwyck. I hadn't seen Papanek since I'd gotten out of Warwick for the last time. I guess I didn't want to see him. I'd resigned myself to the fact that I was in street life for good. I'd be going to jail soon, and I'd be doing a lot of time. I liked Papanek, but we could only be but so tight, because I was going the crime way. That's all there was to it.

I went up to Wiltwyck for Thanksgiving to visit the people and see what the place looked like. Maybe it was a kind of homesickness that took me up there. When I left, Papanek drove me to Poughkeepsie to catch a train back to New York City.

He said, "What are you doing, Claude? Are you going to school?"

"No, I'm goin' to school next term, when it starts in February. I'm gonna go to night school." I was only joking with him.

"Yeah, that's good. You can really do it if you want to, and I'm glad to hear that you want to."

I looked at him and said to myself, Well, damn, this cat really believes me. I just didn't think too much more of it after that.

Before I left Wiltwyck, I had been talking to Nick and had told him that I was dealing pot. He was a hip guy and knew how life was on the streets and knew something about Harlem, so I just came out and told him, "Like, man, I'm dealin' pot, and I'll probably be in jail in another couple-a months or so. But right now, I'm doin' good."

He could see I was doing good. He saw the way I dressed. After that, Nick started telling me about what Papanek was saying to people about me. He said, "Papanek really thinks a lot of you. He thinks you're gonna make out just great. He keeps tellin' people that Claude Brown is gonna be a real success."

I said, "Yeah, man. Uh-huh. I'm gon be a real success. I'm liable to be the biggest drug dealer in Harlem. . . . Nobody from here is gonna make it too far. I don't think anybody is gonna make it farther than Floyd Patterson has made it." Floyd was Golden Gloves champion at that time. I said, "Maybe Wiltwyck ought to be satisfied with that."

Nick finally said, "Well, Claude, you never know how the cards are stacked up for you, and if it's in the cards, maybe Papanek is right."

I looked at Nick, and I thought, Damn, what the hell is wrong with Nick? He must be gettin' old. Here I just told the cat that I was into the street life and was dealin' pot and cocaine. I just looked at him and said, Poor Nick, to myself. Aloud I said, "Yeah, man. You never know," and I just forgot about it until I got in the car with Papanek and he started asking that business about school.

I'd always been aware throughout my delinquent life of the age thing, and I knew that I didn't have a sheet yet. I knew that I didn't have a criminal record as long as I was sent to the Wiltwycks and Warwicks. But I also knew that since I was sixteen and out on my own, the next time I was busted, I'd be fingerprinted. I'd have a sheet on me for the rest of my life. I thought, Yeah, I could still make it, but, shit, what would I want to make it for? I knew I didn't want to go to school, because I would have been too dumb and way behind everybody. I hadn't been to school in so long; and when I was really in school, I played hookey all the time and didn't learn anything. I couldn't be going to anybody's school as dumb as I was.

I got back out on the streets, and I forgot about what I'd told Papanek on the ride from Wiltwyck to Poughkeepsie. I knew what I was going to do, and there was nothing to think about. When I got back to New York, I did the same things I'd been doing. I kept on working. I kept on dealing pot. I kept on dealing a little cocaine.

One night, I was uptown on 149th Street. I had gone to see some cute little girl up that way. She was a beautiful little brown-skinned girl with long, jet-black hair. She looked like an Indian, so everybody called her Cherokee. I had come out of Cherokee's house about twelve-thirty or one o'clock, and as I started into the hall leading to the outside, somebody from behind the stairs called my name.

"Sonny!"

I said, "Yeah," and turned around. The first thing I saw was a gun in a hand. Then I saw a cat. I'd seen him around. They called him Limpy. I don't know why. He had a sort of hunched back, but he didn't have a limp.

He just said, "Sonny, I want all your shit. I don't want to have to kill you."

I knew he was a junkie, and I knew about junkies. When their habit comes down on them, you can't play with them. It's kill or be killed. I didn't have a gun at the time, because last time I'd gotten busted, I'd lent my gun to Danny.

"Look, Sonny, I don't want to kill you, man. All I want is your shit, now. It's, like, I gotta have it." He started talking real fast. He seemed to be nervous but not scared. His habit was down on him, and he was trying to say all this before anything happened. He wanted to explain.

I liked the way he respected me, and I thought maybe he was a little "religious." He must have seen a look in my eye, and he said, "Now, look, nigger, I'm not scared-a you, and I'll kill you if I have to. But I don't want to. All I want is what you got on you."

I didn't say anything, and he started toward me. I said, "Man, I ain't got nothin'."

"Look, Sonny, I don't want to hear that shit." He put the gun up to my face.

"If that's all you want, man, go on and take it."

"Where is it, man? Don't get crazy and try anything, because my habit's down on me; I got to have some drugs. The way I see it right now, it's you that's standin' between me and some drugs. And I'll kill you, nigger, if you make me."

I told him where the drugs were. I had them in an eyeglass case in my inside jacket pocket.

He reached in there, got it, and looked in it. He said, "Okay, like, you stay here, man. You in my neighborhood now, and I know the backyard; I know the people and everything around here, so don't try and act like you crazy."

He told me to just stay there for about two minutes, and he ran in the backyard. He just took the drugs and was gone. He took about a hundred and ten dollars' worth of coke and pot from me. He'd sell it for horse.

I felt bad. Nobody had ever stuck me up or shit like that. I knew that this would get around, and you couldn't deal any drugs if you were going to be letting cats stick you up and take it. I knew that I'd have to get a gun, and that when cats heard about it—cats like Bubba Williams, Big Freddie, Reno, and Tommy Holloway—they would also want to hear that the guy had been killed. This was the way the people in our set did things. You didn't go around letting anybody stick you up. Shit, if you let somebody stick you up and go on living behind it, you didn't have any business dealing drugs. Everybody who wanted some free drugs would come by and try to stick you up. I didn't want to, but I knew I had to get another piece and find that cat.

The cat pulled a fadeaway. Danny heard about it. Danny and I were still tight. He was still coming around. Cocaine couldn't do much for Danny, because Danny was strung out on smack. When you're using heroin, nothing else is going to do but so much for you. I used to always give Danny money to cop, or if I came by some horse by accident—somebody might have given me some for some cocaine—I used to give it to Danny. Danny was a cat who appreciated this sort of thing.

I saw him the day after Limpy had stung me in the hallway on 149th Street. I went up to him, and I said, "I got to get me a piece, baby."

He said, "Yeah, I heard about it, Sonny, but I want to ask you somethin', and I mean it from the bottom of my heart."

"Sure, Danny, you know, speak your piece, baby."

Then Danny said, "Look, Sonny; like, I know you, man, from way back. We came outta the house together, you know?"

"Yeah. So, what you want to ask me, Danny?"

"Do you really want to burn this cat, man? I mean, you want to waste Limpy?"

I said, "Look, man, it's like you said; we came the street way together, and you know how that shit is. You know if I don't kill that mother-fucker, I can't come out on the street any more with any stuff in my pocket talkin' about I'm gon deal drugs. Niggers will be laughin', comin' up in my collar, and sayin', 'Give me what you got.' I mean, if I did that kinda shit, if I let the cat go on livin', mother-fuckers would be tryin' to rob me without a gun. That would be the end of it all."

He said, "Yeah, I know how that shit is, Sonny. But, like, look, man, you got a whole lot goin' for you. You got a lot on the ball. I never told you this before, but I think you're smarter than all these niggers out here, Sonny. And I think if anybody on Eighth Avenue ever makes it, I think it could be you."

I said, "Danny, what you talkin' about?" That shit surprised me. This wasn't supposed to be coming from Danny. This just wasn't him, and it wasn't the stuff we used to talk about. I said, "What's wrong with you?"

"Look, Sonny, I got a piece, but I'm not gon let you have it. What I want you to do is forget about Limpy, not just forget about him, but let me take him, man, let me worry about him."

Danny had been strung out for about four years. I guess he felt that he didn't have much going for him. His folks had cut him loose; he couldn't go home. None of his relatives wanted him coming by. He was ragged all the time. He'd been in and out of jail. He'd been down to Kentucky a couple of times for the cure. He'd been to a place called Brothers Island. He'd been a whole lot of places for a cure. He'd caused everybody a whole lot of trouble. He felt that life was over for him.

"Look, Sonny; I'm already through. Like, I'm wasted. You got somethin' to live for, but me, I can't lose no more. So let me take care-a the nigger for you, and we'll be squared away. You did a whole lot for me, man. I remember the times I was sick and you gave me some drugs. I couldn't go anywhere but to you. I feel if there's one nigger out here on the street who I owe somethin' to, one nigger I should give my life for, man, it's you. And, besides, I'm not really givin' my life. I'm already fucked up. I gave my life the first time I put a little bit-a horse in my nose."

"Look, Danny, thanks a lot, man, but we're not back in the short-pants days. If somebody stings me out here, it's not like somebody bigger than me fuckin' with me in school or some shit like that. We're out here man for man and playin' for keeps, baby. Everybody's gotta be his own man, you know?"

"Okay, Sonny, like I kinda understand it, but I'm still not gon give you my piece, man, because I don't want you to do it. And if I see the nigger before you do, I'm gon beat you to him."

"Yeah, Danny, like, thanks a lot, baby," and I walked. I went up to Robby Ohara. Robby Ohara was a stickup artist, and he used to sell all the guns in the neighborhood. He lived in my building. Just about all the criminals lived in my building.

Robby had heard what happened to me, and when I came up to his crib and said, "Robby, I need a piece right away," he asked me what kind of piece I wanted. I told him I wanted something small but effective, like a .25 automatic.

He said, "All right." He went into another room, came out, and threw me a .25. He said, "You know how to use it?"

It was a Spanish-make gun, and he showed me some things about it. I took out some money. He said, "Forget it, Sonny, that nigger is suppose to be dead. That's a gift from me."

Robby was a killer, and he understood this sort of thing. I took the piece and left.

I looked for Limpy for about a week or more, and I couldn't find him. After a while, I heard that he had gotten busted trying to stick up a doctor in his office. Somebody said he'd gotten shot about four times. This took me off the hook and saved my face, but I still had the piece. I knew that the next time somebody stung me, I was going to have to kill him. I started thinking about it. It didn't seem right for me to be killing a junkie, because these cats were usually harmless. And when they weren't harmless, it wasn't really them, it was smack that was at fault.

I started talking to Tony. I said, "Look, Tony, I'm gonna give up dealin' pot."

He said, "Yeah, I'm gon give it up too," but I knew he couldn't, because he didn't have a job.

I told my customers I was going out of business, and I started sending them to Tony and other people who were dealing. A lot of cats who were dealing stuff would ask me, "Look, Sonny, you need some money? You can't get any good stuff?" I guess they just didn't want to see me stop dealing. I told them I didn't need anything and didn't want anything.

I started going to night school. I went to Washington Irving, because that was the first one I had heard about. When I'd come uptown, I'd see the cats on the corner at night. They were still making that money, teasing me, and laughing. They called me Schoolboy and said that I must be dealing pot downtown someplace, that I was pulling everybody's leg about school. Some of the cats I knew said I wouldn't go to school even when I had the truant officer after me, so why should I be going now.

But after a while, they saw that I was serious, and everybody stopped teasing me about it. I hadn't felt too bad when they were teasing me, because I knew they couldn't call me square or lame. Most of the cats who were out there on the corners dealing stuff now were the newcomers. Most of the cats I came up with were in jail or dead or strung out on drugs. I'd been out in street life long before these cats ever knew how to roll a reefer. I could do what I wanted. I could turn square now, even straighten up if I wanted to, and not worry about anybody naming me a lame. I'd been through the street-life thing. At seventeen, I was ready to retire from it. I'd already had ten or eleven years at it.

After the cats saw I was serious about what I was doing, a lot of them starting coming along with it and trying to find out about it. They'd say, "Sonny, I'm goin' back to school, too, man."

I'd say, "Sure, man, it's a lot to it. You can do a whole lot of stuff. Like, if you want to come out in the street and be a hustler, if you gon be a good hustler, man, you got to know somethin' about arithmetic and business. You got to know how to read. You could be a better hustler if you knew how to read and if you knew a little bit-a math."

A lot of cats came down there with me, but most of them couldn't stay for more than a week or two, because that math was whipping their assess. They didn't know what they were going for. I didn't know what I was going for either, but I knew I wanted to go. I suppose that was more than any of the other cats who'd gone down there knew.

They all dropped out in two to five weeks. Tony stayed the longest. He was determined. I had put him into a whole lot of things, and he just wanted to stick with me. He felt that if he stuck with me, he couldn't go but so wrong. We two started this school thing, and we stayed in there.

I was having a rough time in school. I was taking an academic course, and the only thing that I knew anything about was English, and I only knew a little bit about that. Geometry and algebra were kicking my ass. When I was going to high school during the day, I told them I wanted to take an academic course, but they said I couldn't take that because my math wasn't strong enough. They put me in a commercial course. I didn't know anything about algebra and geometry. So when I went to Washington Irving High School at night, I was starting right from the beginning. The people at Commerce were right. My math gave me twice the hell because I'd had a weak math background. But I stuck with it. I had to take intermediate algebra over, and I had to take geometry over twice. But when I did pass them, I got something like ninety or ninety-five.

I'd had a big disappointment in my love life when I came out of Warwick the third time. I wasn't in love with anybody; I hadn't been in love with anybody since I was in love with Grace, as far as I knew. And that was when I was nine years old. When I came out, I saw Sugar, and Sugar was something beautiful. She had gotten a shape on her that was the finest shape on Eighth Avenue, maybe even in Harlem or New York City. She had always had a beautiful complexion, and she always was a sweet girl. She still had her beautiful ways, and she wasn't ugly any more.

I tried to get tight with her again. I didn't beg her or anything like that. I asked her to be my girl, but Sugar said she didn't feel the way she used to feel about me. She didn't think she could be going through what she went through before. She was a big girl now, she was older, and she felt it would be silly to go back into her childhood thing with me.

I felt sort of bad when she reminded me how I had mistreated her. I didn't feel bad about having mistreated her. I felt bad about her remembering this and not wanting to go with me, as fine as she was. I just said, "Hell wit it," but I sure wanted her to be my girl. When she told me no, it was a big letdown. I felt that she wasn't supposed to say this. She was supposed to be mine. I guess this was one of the hardest things I ever had to accept. Sugar had declared her independence and become a person.

She dug this lame, some cat who worked in a grocery store. That's the way she was. She dug him, and nobody could change her mind. All the older hustlers in the neighborhood were offering her money, like a hundred dollars for one night. It just didn't bother her. I hated that nigger, even though I'd never seen him, because I didn't think any cat who was working in a grocery store deserved a girl like this. She was something wonderful. If she was yours, she was all yours. She was sensitive; she would do anything for you. But I guess I didn't deserve her either. I had had her and had let her slip right through my fingertips by mistreating her. I just said, "Fuck it; that's the way the cards fall."

I met an older girl at Washington Irving. She was about nineteen. She was married. She was hip. She had a couple of kids, and I told her I liked her. When I first met her, I thought she was younger than she was. I approached her the way I would have approached any other young girl. I stopped her in the hall one day and said, "Hey, you, young lady, hold it right there!"

She stopped and looked around as if something had happened, as if she was afraid to move. I came up to her looking pretty serious, so when I spoke, I guess she expected me to say something serious. I just walked up to her and solemnly asked, "Where in the world did you get that lovely ass on you?"

She just looked at me and dropped her eyes as if to say, "This crazy-actin' nigger! And here I am, standin' here and waitin' for it too." She smiled, turned around, and walked away.

This chick looked like an animal, a natural-born freak. She was short, a little shorter than I was. She had a beautiful shape, jet-black skin, long, jet-black hair, and slanted eyes. Her skin was real smooth. She looked like a beautiful black Chinese. The next time I saw her, I just waved and smiled. Every time I'd see her, I'd talk to her and say something that she wouldn't forget.

I came out of school one night about ten o'clock. This gray boy was trying to talk to her. He was a little older than me, but I couldn't imagine him ever getting anywhere, so I just went on up and started talking to her like he wasn't even there. She excused herself from the cat and started talking to me. I asked her if she was going my way. She said she was, so we just left him standing there looking.

We started walking toward the corner, and I asked her if I could take her out.

She said, "Yeah, but I'm married, you know."

I said, "Well, like, that's okay." I'd never played around with any married women before. It should have bothered me, I guess, but it didn't. I said, "I won't hold it against you if you don't." I took her out on that weekend, and we partied.

She was married to some cat I didn't know, so it didn't make any difference to me. She had a couple of kids, but that didn't bother me either. I just couldn't believe I was getting anything as beautiful as this girl. She had a whole lot of nature. I'd gotten high when I took her out. I had smoked some pot, and we'd drunk some liquor. I didn't think she smoked pot or used cocaine, so I just started her off drinking.

I took her down to Basin Street and to a movie, then took her to my room and knocked her off. I was ready to go after I'd knocked her off one time. But the chick was really something—she couldn't see anybody just knocking her off one time. I was young and had a lot of energy. I used to box and this sort of thing. I thought I was in good shape, but I had never busted my nuts more than three times in one night without any cocaine or stuff like that. But this chick just wouldn't let me go. She wouldn't stop. I thought, Shit, I'll probably die behind this. It was a whole lot of work, but she knew something. She knew how to keep me stimulated, and even though I was tired as hell, I could never lose that erection, and she just kept forcing me and forcing me. She was a beautiful girl, so I just kept going at it.

I wasn't too anxious to see her again, but we'd started something. I used to take her out just about every weekend. Sometimes we'd cut a class or two; we'd go by my place first, and I'd knock her off. But she was killing me. I felt that this was a whole lot of hard work.

She wasn't like the average young girl I'd been jugging. She was over-sexed or something. It was okay at first, because she was so beautiful and it was something new, but I just couldn't see doing that thing every night. I'd turned her on to some pot. She liked pot, and we used to get high just about all the time. When she got high, all she wanted to do was screw and screw and screw some more. I just couldn't take all that.

I was supposed to meet her one night, but I was tired, so I just went to school. She was waiting for me when I came out of my last class. We always used to greet each other with a "Hey, buddy." So when I came out of my last class and I heard somebody say, "Hey, buddy," I knew who it was without turning around. She said, "What happened to you tonight? I waited for you."

I told her that I had forgotten all about it, that it had just slipped my mind.

She said jokingly, "That's a bad sign."

We went to an Italian restaurant and had some sausages and spaghetti. Then we went on up to my place and started playing some sides and smoking pot. I went to bed with her, but it had become a chore. Right in the midst of everything, I just jumped up and said, "I'm sorry, baby, but the party is over."

She looked kind of stunned. She said, "Look, Sonny, what have I done? What have I said or what didn't I do or what didn't I say?"

I said, "It's nothin' that you've done, baby. It's just that I'm tired, and, you know, I just can't fight it any more. I'm tired of this thing, and I'm tired of you."

She got kind of mad, and she started screaming, "Okay, nigger, but your day'll come. I believed everything you said. I love you, and I believed you when you said you loved me. I became a tramp for you. I made my kids' mother a tramp because of you."

I just said, "Yeah, yeah, yeah, baby. You just needed somebody else and somethin' new, and I just happened to be there." That was the way I felt about it.

She just walked. She called me a couple of times and wrote me some letters, but I just never paid any attention.

I learned something in school that wasn't on the program. I learned that you just can't go and try to get some body from every chick that looks nice, because you'll get yourself involved in a whole lot of stuff that you wouldn't want to walk with. I decided that I wasn't going to get involved with any more married chicks, not right now anyway.

I started concentrating on the books. I guess I started learning a little bit. People didn't take it too seriously, my family and all the other people I knew. They just saw that, as usual, I was doing something new. Just about everything I'd done, the reason I had tried it in the first place was that it was something new. School was this way too.

The next time I saw Papanek, I was in school. He said he had known I was going to do something like that. I didn't take him too seriously. I was just there, and all there was to do there was learn. I started feeling torn between two things, the street life and the school life. After a while, I just didn't know where I was going. I didn't feel a part of Harlem any more. I had the same slang as the cats on the street, but I wasn't out there on the avenues. I wasn't in the bars any more, and I didn't do a lot of things that the other cats did. I was way behind in just about most of the happenings in the neighborhood. After a while, I thought it might be a good idea for me to move out of the neighborhood and see some other sides of life.

I'd been doing a lot of changing in less than a year. I had gotten out of the garment center, and that was the place where everybody worked. Cats used to call it a "slave." A guy who worked in the garment center wouldn't say he had a job; he'd say, "Man, like, I got a slave." That was what it amounted to. It was a real drag. I had seen old men down there, old colored cats, pushing those trucks and sweating. They looked like they were about sixty years old, but they were still pushing trucks through the snow. I knew I didn't want to be doing that kind of shit. I'd rather be in jail or someplace. Someplace where it was warm in the winter.

Since I had gotten out of Warwick, I had left the garment center, gotten a job at Hamburger Heaven, and started school. I'd done a whole lot of things. But I was still looking for something new.

After working at Hamburger Heaven for a year, I got tired of that. I just couldn't take it any more. I got tired of being the old-style nigger with the rag around his head. I didn't have any kind of skill or trade, so the only kind of job I could get was doing some labor. This shit was beginning to bother me. I knew I didn't want to do this all my life.

I was pulling further away from the Harlem scene. I didn't swing with the old cats any more. I'd go up to Harlem and party, things like that, but I wasn't for going to jail any more. One thing began to scare me more than anything else about jail. This was the fact that if I went to jail and got that sheet on me, any time I decided that I didn't want to go the crime way, that I wanted to do something that was straight, I'd have a lot of trouble doing it behind being in jail. I didn't want that sheet on me, and I knew if I kept hanging around Harlem I was going to get busted for something jive, something like smoking reefers. And it would be a shame for anybody to get busted for smoking reefers and get a sheet and have his whole life fucked up.

I decided to move out of Harlem. I started reading the papers, looking for places down around school, which looked like a nice neighborhood. I was kind of fascinated by Greenwich Village anyway. I moved to a little loft room down on Cooper Square.

It was just the thing that I needed. I'd still go up to Harlem on the weekends and party, because I didn't know any people in the Village. That was one of the reasons why I liked being down there—the cats in the street life weren't coming around, so I got a chance to open a book every now and then. I knew what street life was like, but school and the books and the Village—all this was new. I wanted to get into it and get into it good. I couldn't do it in Harlem. Being down there, I could.

When I moved down to Greenwich Village, it was no big thing. I had come out of the house early. But Mama still kept saying, "Why don't you come on home?" I couldn't make her understand that it just wasn't home for me any more.

I got a job working for a watch repair shop. Everybody in there except for two cats was Jewish. There was one Japanese guy and one Puerto Rican guy. All the others were Jewish. They were straight-up, nice people. They seemed to be some of the happiest people I had ever been around. Of course, they were all straight. They weren't into any crime or stuff like that, as far as I knew.

I liked it. It didn't pay much, only forty dollars a week, but I didn't need much money. I had all the clothes and stuff I needed, and I was free. For the first time in my life, I didn't have the feeling that I had to go to Coxsackie, to Woodburn, and then to Sing Sing. I had the feeling now that anything could happen, anything that I decided to do. It seemed a little bit crazy, but I even had the feeling that if I wanted to become a doctor or something like that, I could go on and do it. This was the first time in my life that I'd had that kind of feeling, and getting out of Harlem was the first step toward that freedom.

One night, I went uptown. I was talking to Tony in the Club Harlem, on 145th Street. We'd gotten high, and we were sitting there drinking some beer and talking. I was telling him how just one little bust could close a lot of doors for him in life, doors he would never think now that he wanted open.

Tony listened. He usually listened to me, and he took it seriously. A couple of weeks later, he came down to the Village. He got a job, and he got a loft room right next to mine. He was going to try to make it this way too. I knew he was still going uptown and dealing pot now and then, but that was all right. The main thing was that he wanted to do something. He wanted to get out of Harlem too, and he wanted a chance at life. Even though he'd never been in anyplace like Warwick or Wiltwyck, he was beginning to feel a need all on his own, apart from what I was telling him. He was beginning to feel a need to free himself from that Harlem thing.

This was a start. This was a big start.

7

When I first moved down to Greenwich Village, I didn't know anybody but Tony Albee, who lived next door to me. We used to hang out together whenever there was time. Going to school and working, I didn't have too much time to hang out. For a long time, I just fell into that groove of going to school, hanging out on the weekends, going to work during the day, getting high with Tony and philosophizing at night, peeping the Village scene from the outside, the artists, the quacks, the would-be bohemians.

Most of the time, I would go up to Harlem on the weekends, because this was the only place I knew to go when I wanted some fun. It seemed that if I stayed away two weeks, Harlem had changed a lot. I wasn't certain about how it was changing or what was happening, but I knew it had a lot to do with duji, heroin.

Heroin had just about taken over Harlem. It seemed to be a kind of plague. Every time I went uptown, somebody else was hooked, somebody else was strung out. People talked about them as if they were dead. You'd ask about an old friend, and they'd say, "Oh, well, he's strung out." It wasn't just a comment or an answer to a question. It was a eulogy for someone. He was just dead, through.

At that time, I didn't know anybody who had kicked it. Heroin had been the thing in Harlem for about five years, and I don't think anybody knew anyone who had kicked it. They knew a lot of guys who were going away, getting cures, and coming back, but never kicking it. Cats were even going into the Army or to jail, coming back, and getting strung out again. I guess this was why everybody felt that when somebody was strung out on drugs, he was through. It was almost the same as saying he was dying. And a lot of cats were dying.

I was afraid to ask about somebody I hadn't seen in a while, especially if it was someone who was once a good friend of mine. There was always a chance somebody would say, "Well, he died. The cat took an O.D.," an overdose of heroin; or he was pushed out of a window trying to rob some-body's apartment, or shot five times trying to stick up a place to get some money for drugs. Drugs were killing just about everybody off in one way or another. It had taken over the neighborhood, the entire community. I didn't know of one family in Harlem with three or more kids between the ages of fourteen and nineteen in which at least one of them wasn't on drugs. This was just how it was.

It was like a plague, and the plague usually afflicted the eldest child of every family, like the one of the firstborn with Pharaoh's people in the Bible. Sometimes it was even worse than the biblical plague. In Danny Rogers' family, it had everybody. There were four boys, and it had all of them. It was a disheartening thing for a mother and father to see all their sons strung out on drugs at the same time. It was as though drugs were a ghost, a big ghost, haunting the community.

People were more afraid than they'd ever been before. Everybody was afraid of this drug thing, even the older people who would never use it. They were afraid to go out of their houses with just one lock on the door. They had two, three, and four locks. People had guns in their houses because of the junkies. The junkies were committing almost all the crimes in Harlem. They were snatching pocketbooks. A truck couldn't come into the commu-nity to unload anything any more. Even if it was toilet paper or soap powder, the junkies would clean it out if the driver left it for a second.

The cats who weren't strung out couldn't see where they were heading. If they were just snorting some horse, they seemed to feel that it wouldn't get to them. It's as though cats would say, "Well, damn, I'm slicker than everybody else," even though some slick cats and some strong guys had fallen into the clutches of heroin. Everybody could see that nobody was get-ting away from it once they had started dabbling in it, but still some people seemed to feel, "Shit, I'm not gon get caught. I can use it, and I can use it and not be caught."

Guys who were already strung out were trying to keep their younger brothers away from stuff. They were trying feebly, and necessarily so, because guys who were strung out on drugs didn't have too much time to worry about anybody but themselves. It was practically a twenty-four-hour-a-day job trying to get some money to get some stuff to keep the habit from fuck-ing with you.

There was a time when I'd come uptown on the weekend and cats would say things like, "Man, let's have a drink," or "Let's get some pot," or "Let's get some liquor." But after a while, about 1955, duji became the thing. I'd go uptown and cats would say, "Hey, man, how you doin'? It's nice to see you. Look here, I got some shit," meaning heroin. "Let's get high." They would say it so casually, the way somebody in another community might say, "C'mon, let's have a drink."

I'd tell them, "No, man, I don't dabble in stuff like that." They'd look at me and smile, feeling somewhat superior, more hip than I was because they were into drugs. I just had to accept this, because I couldn't understand why people were still using drugs when they saw that cats were getting strung out day after day after day. It just didn't make too much sense to me, but that was how things were, and it wasn't likely that anybody was going to change it for some time to come.

Then money became more of a temptation. The young people out in the streets were desperate for it. If a cat took out a twenty-dollar bill on Eighth Avenue in broad daylight, he could be killed. Cats were starving for drugs; their habit was down on them, and they were getting sick. They were out of their minds, so money for drugs became the big thing.

I remember that around 1952 and 1953, when cats first started getting strung out good, people were saying, "Damn, man, that cat went and robbed his own family. He stole his father's suits, stole his mother's money," and all this kinda shit. It was still something unusual back then. In some cases, the lack of money had already killed most family life. Miss Jamie and her family, the Willards, were always up tight for money because she spent the food money for playing the numbers and stuff like that. This was the sort of family that had never had any family life to speak of. But now, since drugs demanded so much money and since drugs had afflicted just about every family with young people in it, this desire for money was wrecking almost all family life.

Fathers were picking up guns and saying, "Now, look, if you fuck wit that rent money, I'm gon kill you," and they meant it. Cats were taking butcher knives and going at their fathers because they had to have money to get drugs. Anybody who was standing in the way of a drug addict when his habit was down on him—from mother or father on down—was risking his life.

Harlem was a community that couldn't afford the pressure of this thing, because there weren't many strong family ties anyway. There might have been a few, but they were so few, they were almost insignificant.

There was a nice-looking little dark-skinned girl named Elsie on 146th Street. When she was a little snotty-nosed thing, she used to hang out with my sister Margie. Around 1955, Elsie was thirteen or fourteen. She was a little large for her age, and she'd just gone into junior high school. She wasn't even a real schoolgirl yet. I remember once standing on a stoop on Eighth Avenue, and she came up. I had seen her in a bar, and I had wondered, What the hell is she doin' in a bar as young as she is?

I started talking to her, asking her what she was doing. She told me she was making money, and she sounded as though she was kind of proud of it, as though she thought she was slick.

I asked her, "How much money are you makin', Elsie?"

She said, "Enough for me."

"How much money do you need?" She was thirteen, and it seemed kind of crazy to me for her to be out there tricking.

She wasn't such a beautiful girl. She was just trying to grow old fast, too fast. I had the feeling that this little girl ought to be still reading *True Love* magazines, still dreaming about romance and Prince Charming and all that kind of stuff. Here she was out here acting like a whore.

I wanted to get her to face up to what would happen. I said, "Look, Elsie, what cat's gon want you? The average nigger isn't gonna want to be seen with you in a year or so."

"No, not unless I've got money."

"Look, baby, money's not everything."

She said, no, money wasn't everything, but what money couldn't buy, nobody wanted anyway, so it might as well be everything.

The conversation just went on like this. She had all the answers. She knew that everybody needed money, and she had a good point there. She asked me, "Now, if you ain't got no money and you come uptown, do you think your family would be as happy to see you?"

This stopped me. I knew she was right.

In Harlem, practically everybody I knew had been striving for a long time to make enough money to buy a big car and expensive clothes. They'd always wanted to do these things, and the main way of doing it had been through the numbers. All the people who had a little more nerve than average or didn't care would take numbers. Numbers was the thing; it sort of ran the community.

Early in the morning, everybody used to put in their numbers before they went to work. I remember that Mama and Dad used to always go up to Miss Rose's house and leave their numbers. Sometimes, if it was getting late, they'd give me the numbers to take up. All day long, they'd be thinking about the numbers. Numbers was like a community institution. Everybody accepted it and respected it. This was the way that the people got to the money. If you were lucky, you hit a number now and then, but very few poor people were lucky enough to hit the number for anything big. A few did, but even if you didn't, you could run numbers. If you could be a numbers runner, you'd make about seventy-five dollars a week, which wasn't that much money, but there wasn't that much work to do. And when people hit, they would give you some.

But then it seemed like drugs were coming in so strong with the younger generation that it was almost overshadowing numbers. A lot of younger cats who were taking numbers would start using drugs, and then they would start fucking with people's money. They couldn't be trusted by numbers bankers any more. A whole lot of things started happening. People started getting shot and things like that over their money because cats needed it to get drugs. A lot of the junkies started sticking up the numbers writers and sticking up the controllers.

Peddling drugs had become a popular vocation in Harlem, and it was accepted by everybody, except the police, and they didn't matter. They didn't count unless you got caught, and, if you didn't get caught, nobody asked where you got your money from. That's why a lot of people went into it.

If there wasn't so much time on a drug bust, I suppose a lot of other people would've gotten into it, some of the more righteous people, who had been controlling the numbers for a long time. I remember once, there used to be a preacher down around Eighth Avenue who preached in Jersey on Sundays and during the week came to Harlem and took numbers. That was all right, but now drugs were the thing. This cat had to move on out because drug dealing was a cold business. Anybody who was dealing drugs now would have to have a gun. There was always somebody trying to stick you up, because they knew how much money you had.

If the plague didn't hit you directly, it hit you indirectly. It seemed as though nobody could really get away from it. There were a lot of guys trying to get young girls started on drugs so that they could put them on the corner. When a chick's habit came down on her, she'd usually end up down in the "marketplace," 125th Street between Third Avenue and St. Nicholas Avenue, where all the whores hung out. They sold cunt out there on the street at night.

If a young girl got strung out on drugs, she wouldn't go around trying to steal. Most girls were afraid they might get caught. Most girls would start selling body. So if a cat was strung out, if there was a young girl he knew who had eyes for him, he would cut her into some drugs to try to get her strung out too. Then he could get the chick to sell cunt for him and get enough money to keep them both high. But it was always just a matter of time before the chick would cut him loose. She'd find somebody else, usually another junkie she dug more than she dug him. She'd go on and pull tight with this cat, and she'd sell body, turn tricks, and make money to support both of their habits. This was usually the way things went.

Many times they were guys who never knew anything about stealing. They were good boys; I mean, they were never into street life. But it seemed as though drugs crawled into all the houses. It even crawled into the churches and pulled some of the nice people right out. It was a plague. You couldn't close all the doors and all the windows and keep everything out. It was getting to everybody. It was getting to cats who went to nice schools, Catholic schools. It was even getting to people whose folks used to live in the Dunbar and up on Edgecombe Avenue in fabulous houses, people who thought cats from Eighth Avenue were dirt.

You'd run into many cats along Eighth Avenue and you'd say, "Look, man, what are you tryin' to do? You tryin' to kick your habit? You want to get yourself together?" A lot of cats just didn't seem to feel that they were in a bad way, being strung out.

They'd say things like, "Man, all I want me is a slick bitch." This was a good thing to have if you were strung out, I suppose, because just about all the young cats, seventeen or eighteen, knew that if you had a slick bitch, you would always have some money. By a slick bitch, they meant chicks who would help you work a Murphy and who would sell some cunt if you got up tight; chicks who would burn other people for you, that is, go into a bar and tell a cat that the Man was on him, or some shit like that, and have him pass his drugs to her. She'd make it out with the drugs, and her man would be waiting outside. Or her man would be playing the police.

Around 1955, everybody wanted a slick bitch; nobody wanted to kick the habit much. They were strung out, and they were really going down. They were ragged and beat-up. Cats who had never come out of the house without a pair of shoes on that didn't cost at least thirty-five dollars, who had never had a wrinkle anyplace on them, who had always worn the best suits from Brooks Brothers or Witty Brothers —these cats were going around greasy and dirty. These were people who had a whole lot of pride. They were people who had had too much pride to put a dirty handkerchief in their pockets at one time. Now they just seemed to be completely unaware of how they looked. They would just be walking around dirty, greasy, looking for things to steal.

The slang was always changing for heroin. They called it duji or shit or stuff or poison. After about 1952, nobody called it horse any more. I always referred to it as the shit plague, because that had more meaning to me.

I ran into Danny in a hallway one night. He was down on his knees crying and holding his stomach. I said, "Danny, what's wrong, baby?"

And he said, "I need some shit. I need some shit."

It just stuck in my mind. I could always see heroin more vividly as shit than anything else, because it was real dirt. They would put it into their veins, and that was the same thing as putting dirt into it.

There was never a time that I could remember in Harlem when there were young girls who looked so bad as after the shit plague hit. You'd find strung-out fifteen-, sixteen-, seventeen-year-old girls who didn't look too bad at first. But then they got so bad that even cats with long cunt collars would get tired of screwing these cold junkie bitches. They couldn't come, and it wasn't much fun for a cat to screw them, even if they only wanted enough to get a three-dollar bag or a five-dollar bag. After a while, nobody wanted to screw a junkie bitch. Regardless of how fine a chick was, if cats knew she was on shit, they didn't want her.

You could tell if a bitch was a junkie by the way she looked. Their skin just seemed a little faded. Even if they weren't high, they looked dingy. If you saw a young girl up in Harlem, looking like she'd been living down on the Bowery, you'd know that she was strung out. And if she was strung out on shit, there just wasn't much she could do in bed for anybody.

You might be going downtown or coming out of the Palm Café on 125th Street one night, or you might be coming out of the Apollo, just passing up 125th Street on your way to the Baby Grand, and you'd see the chicks lined up there. Most of them used to be older girls, a couple of years back, and you'd say, "There's that same old whore." You'd know them by sight. They might stop you and say, "Say, baby, you sportin' tonight?" and you'd say, "Yeah, Mama, if I could find somebody to sport with."

But then, one night, it happens. I suppose it has happened to everybody who has escaped the plague. One night, you hear a familiar voice and turn around. Perhaps she'll see you and hide her face, something like that. It's a friend or a friend of a younger sister or one of the girls you know from the neighborhood. You almost want to cry, and you snatch her and say, "C'mon, girl, git off this corner. What the hell is wrong with you? Come on over here and let me buy you some coffee and send you home."

You want to tell them something like, "Do you know how your mother would feel?" You might get them into a restaurant to have a cup of coffee, or you might take them to a bar for a drink. You find out that it's futile to say anything to them. She just isn't supposed to be there. She hasn't got any business being a junkie bitch turning tricks. That's selling two-dollar pussy. That's not even being a whore. The whores would look down on her behind this sort of thing.

You just sit there for a while and talk to her. You say, "Look, I'm gon take you home," or "I'm gon take you down to the hospital tomorrow, and I want you to sign yourself in," this sort of thing.

They look at you and say, "Yeah, yeah, yeah. If you really want to help me, you can give me five or ten dollars, so I won't have to spend my night out here. I'm sick now."

A chick might say she turned a trick with a cat who was too big, that she got hurt and really shouldn't be out there, but that she needs some money and has to get high. The first time, you give them some money, but after you've heard that story a couple of times, you get hip. You begin to feel like a trick, like the cats out there buying that cunt.

I remember once I was talking to a little girl who used to live across the street from me on Eighth Avenue, a little girl named Sadie. I saw her out there. She didn't hide like some of the others had done. She just said, "Hi, Sonny, how you doin'?"

I said, "Hey, baby, like, what you doin' out here?"

She looked at me, smiled, and said, "Now, isn't that a silly question?"

I thought about it, and it was. Shit, I knew what she was doing out there. She was doing the same thing that all those other chicks were doing out there. She was trying to sell some cunt. This was the place for it, 125th Street, after midnight.

I took her into a bar, and we sat down and had a beer.

She said, "Now, look, I've got to make some money."

I said, "I'll give you the money. Don't go back out there."

"Okay, thanks, but tomorrow night it's gon be the same thing."

I tried to talk her out of it, but she said, "No, look, you can't help me now. The only way anyone can help me is that they give me some money to get some shit and get that monkey off my back."

I knew her family wasn't too tight, because her mother used to run an after-hours joint, and she used to be a whore when she was younger. I used to sell stolen goods to her mother. I told her, "How would your mother feel if she saw you down here?"

She said, "Shit, it just doesn't matter how she'd feel. Because after all the tricks I turned, it wouldn't make any sense for her to feel any kinda way now."

I knew she was right. I knew that a lot of mothers were learning that their daughters were becoming junkies and prostitutes to support their habits. I suppose this was a way many girls took to get even with their families, to get even for the way their mothers had lived. I thought this was the reason Sadie had done it. She was telling her mother she was going to be a worse whore than she'd ever been. I think she was succeeding at it too. Even if she wasn't she was giving it a damn good try.

I started getting a little worried about Pimp, but not about Carole and Margie. Carole had started listening to a lot of that down-home nonsense that Mama had been telling all of us for so many years. I don't know what it was, but she just got a whole lot of religion all of a sudden.

I used to feel sorry for Carole, and I used to get mad at Mama, because I didn't think she had any right to tell that girl all that old crazy shit that should have been left down there in the woods. She had Carole going around to all those old sanctified churches and all that old crazy kind of stuff. The girl lost all the self-confidence she used to have.

Carole used to be smart and never used to be afraid of anything. Now she was a different person. I used to look at her sometimes and wonder what the hell Mama had done to her all that time I was at Warwick and those places. I used to feel sorry for being away and not being able to tell her, "Look, all that shit Mama's tellin' you is nonsense and bullshit, so you don't have to listen to it." She really needed somebody to tell her that.

But now it was too late to do anything about it; she was good and sewed up in that religious bag. She was afraid not to be religious. I just could never figure out why she changed so much, what happened to her while I wasn't around.

Margie was still young, and she had always been obedient, so there was nothing to worry about there.

Pimp was thirteen, and he had wanted to follow in my footsteps for some time, but Pimp couldn't take the beatings that Dad gave him. He tried stealing—once. He tried playing hookey—once. Dad beat him nearly to death, and that was the end of that. Now he was thirteen, and he was getting in with a lot of other little boys who were also trying to come out of the house and act like they knew their way around in the street. It wasn't too bad now, because there wasn't too much expected of him. Tony Albee told me that he'd seen Pimp and another little boy drinking a bottle of wine in the hallway. I laughed at it, but I wondered to myself just how long it would be before Pimp and the other little boys he hung out with would be affected by the plague.

It was the time and the plague. Everybody knew they had to get away from something and get into something. I guess one of the reasons Tony Albee and I hung out together was that we had to get away from not having a groove. We had to get with somebody and something. We had a lot of expensive clothes, and we would go to parties. We'd party with a lot of the young girls, a lot of the whores. Every Friday and Saturday night, Tony and I would come uptown and go to a party or a dance, or we'd just get high off pot. And we would philosophize about what we were going to do one day, and about the junkies, and about the way the cops were carrying on, the way they were taking target practice on the junkies.

There was a cop up there called Schoolboy. Sometimes we'd stand on the corner and get high and talk about how the police department planned to let Schoolboy kill off all the junkies. Schoolboy was a white cop who had shot quite a few junkies. It didn't make sense to shoot junkies, because they were sort of harmless people unless you were standing between them and drugs. But Schoolboy shot junkies just for running. I don't know how true it is, but Wally said that when he had been caught on 146th Street, Schoolboy had told him to run. He said he lay down and refused to run, because he knew that Schoolboy liked to shoot junkies. He said when he lay down, Schoolboy shot him in the leg anyway.

I'd heard a lot of cats say they never were going to run from him. Sometimes cats who were stealing stuff would hear him. They'd get up close to a wall or something. He'd say, "Come over here." They'd say, "No, you gon have to shoot me here if you gon shoot me." People in the neighborhood complained about it: "They got this white cop around here killin' all these young boys." The old ladies would say this when the junkies weren't robbing their houses. If the junkies were robbing their houses, the old ladies would say, "They ought to kill all them damn no good junkies." This was the usual story with the junkies and the old ladies.

Nobody in the neighborhood liked Schoolboy, but nobody did anything. This was a sign that the neighborhood had changed. In the old days, somebody would have killed that cat. He couldn't have gone around shooting everybody like that. People said, "Yeah, Schoolboy, he's a nut, and somethin' has to be done about that cat." But right then, nothing was happening.

I heard that one lady said she saw Schoolboy shoot a young boy who was a junkie. Schoolboy had told him to stop, and the boy stopped and was just waiting for him. Schoolboy just walked up to him and shot him. The lady went down to the police station to complain about it. They told her, "Get the hell out of the precinct." There was a big stink about it in the *Amsterdam News*, the colored newspaper, but nothing ever came of it. Everybody just started squawking, "Yeah, they ain't gon do anything to a white cop for shootin' a nigger, even if it is in New York." Perhaps they had something there.

Tony felt that Schoolboy was going to be the one to get rid of all the junkies in Harlem. He was going to shoot them all. He had knocked up a colored girl up the block, and everybody knew he was going around there fucking the young girls and shooting the junkies. I guess a lot of people felt that he should have been killed, because he was no good.

When people got high off pot and philosophized about it, it almost seemed unbelievably funny. But they were right. Nobody seemed to care much about Harlem, not the people who could do something about it, like the mayor or the police.

Some of the cats I knew had gone into the police department. They seemed to be exploiting Harlem too, once they got in there. These were the same cats who had come up in Harlem. They didn't care any more either. They just wanted to go out there and get some of that money too.

Harlem was getting fucked over by everybody, the politicians, the police, the businessmen, everybody. There were a lot of things that we knew about but didn't think about when we weren't high: how nobody cared too much about cleaning up the junkies or making drugs legal so that they'd stop robbing people, since it was just Harlem and East Harlem; how nobody gave a fuck about some niggers and some Puerto Ricans, so that's why nothing was going to be done about it. It seemed that when we got high off pot and stuff and started philosophizing, we really knew things. We understood this whole thing about Harlem, but we didn't mind it too much then. You could get high, sit down, and talk about it, even laugh about it.

We'd laugh about how when the big snowstorms came, they'd have the snowplows out downtown as soon as it stopped, but they'd let it pile up for weeks in Harlem. If the sun didn't come out, it might have been there when April came around. Damn sending snowplows up there just for some niggers and people like that!

Many times we would think we had found the way to get the junkies out, but we could never have taken it down to City Hall and gotten people to listen to it. Especially since we were high. If we'd gone down there and said, "Look, Mr. Mayor, you take a stick-a this, and, baby, when you get up there off this joint, you'll see all this shit out here just the way it is. Like, you get some-a this and come to Harlem and just dig it. You got to be high off some good pot." That's all we needed. They would have said, "These niggers are crazy. Let's call up Bellevue."

We knew we couldn't do that, but we could squawk about the snow. Somebody'd say, "Yeah, this is the last place they git with the snowplows," and somebody else'd say, "Would you listen to that nigger? He must think he's livin' down on Park Avenue. You better go and take another look in the mirror. Shit, ain't nobody gon be sendin' no damn snowplows up to Eighth Avenue and 145th Street. Shit, they probably ain't got enough people up here who can vote."

There was a lot of sense to this. Even though cats get high off pot, they're not crazy. Most of the men from our community had some kind of bust on them, even if it was just for something petty. The average cat around our neighborhood in Harlem had a sheet on him, so he couldn't vote. Even most of the young cats around there who weren't strung out owed some time for something. A lot of the older people who went to work every day had sheets on them from way back for killing some other nigger in Georgia or running some moonshine.

The women, with their votes, just ran the community. They'd elect the councilmen. They'd elect our same old light, bright, damn-near-white Congressman who was always making those pretty promises that never amounted to anything, those bullshit promises. He was going to keep on doing this, and we knew it even though we were young and high. We could stand around and talk this shit, and we knew we were right, because just about the only people who could vote were the women. So this light, bright, damn near white and full of shit cat was going to be in there just as long as women had most of the vote. As Johnny D. once said, a woman's brain is between her legs, and some pretty nigger who was suave, like our good Congressman, could get up there and say, "Look, baby, I'm going to do this and that for you." The women would go right out and vote for him, because the nigger was too pretty for them not to. We kept on getting the same treatment because the women were running Harlem.

Most of the people didn't know it, and this was one of the great truths that we discovered. When you got high, you'd discover a whole lot of answers to many questions. This was one of them. We knew that the women were running Harlem. The women didn't know it themselves, but we knew it. Anyway, we knew it when we got high.

We'd get high, and we'd solve all the problems of Harlem. When it wore off, we would just have to live with them all over again.

The real reason I wanted to be in Harlem was to spend more time with Pimp. But I couldn't. There just wasn't enough time. I couldn't take him to live with me. He was still too young. I couldn't have him hang out with me. I couldn't go back home. I'd just see him sometimes and talk to him.

He got in trouble once with some kids, something childish like snatching a pocketbook. It didn't seem too important at the time. I was a little bothered about it, and I spoke to him. He said they'd just done it for kicks. I was trying real hard to keep a check on him from a distance. I knew what he was doing.

He had started shooting craps, but this was nothing, really. All the young boys shot craps and gambled. This was what they were supposed to do. But Mama was worried about it. I suppose she and Dad were getting kind of old. She used to tell me, "Oh, that boy, he stays out real late." It seemed as though they were trying to throw their burden of parenthood on me, and I kind of resented that, but I cared about Pimp. I wanted to do something for him.

The only trouble was that I had set such a high standard for him, such a bad example, it was hard as hell to erase. People knew him as my brother. The boys his age expected him to follow in my footsteps. He was my brother, and I had done so much, I had become a legend in the neighborhood. They expected him to live up to it.

I used to try to talk to him. I'd say, "Look, Pimp, what do you want to do, man?" I tried to get him interested in things. He used to like to play ball and stuff like that, but he wasn't interested in anything outside of the neighborhood. He wasn't interested in getting away. He couldn't see life as anything different. At fourteen, he was still reading comic books. He wasn't interested in anything except being hip.

I was real scared about this, but I knew that I couldn't do anything. He was doing a whole lot of shit that he wasn't telling me about. I remember one time I asked him, just to find out if he had started smoking yet, if he wanted some pot. He said, "No, man, I don't want any, and if I wanted some, I'd have it. I know where to get it." I was kind of hurt, but I knew that this was something that had to come. He would've known, and I suppose he should've known. When I was his age, even younger, I knew.

I couldn't feel mad about it, but I felt kind of hurt. I wanted to say, "Look, Pimp, what's happenin', man? Why aren't we as tight as we were before?" He still admired me, but something had happened. It was as though we had lost a contact, a closeness, that we once had, and I couldn't tell him things and get him to listen any more the way he used to do. I felt that if I couldn't control him, nobody could, and he'd be lost out there in the streets, going too fast, thinking he was hip enough to make it all by himself.

I'd take him to a movie or something like that. I'd take him downtown to the Village, and we'd hang out for a day, but I noticed something was missing. We didn't talk about all the really intimate things that we used to talk about. He wouldn't share his secrets with me any more, and this scared me, because I didn't know how far he'd gone. I wanted to say, "Pimp, what happened to the day that you and I used to walk through the streets with our arms around each other's shoulder? We used to sleep with our arms around each other, and you used to cry to follow me when I went out of the house." I wanted to say it, but it didn't make sense, because I knew that day had gone.

I gave my gun away when I moved out of Harlem. I felt free. This was one of the things that made me feel free, that I didn't need a gun. I didn't need any kind of protection, because I wasn't afraid any more. I had been afraid in Harlem all my life. Even though I did things that people said were crazy—people who thought that I must not be afraid of anything—I was afraid of almost everything.

Fear made me stop and think. I was able to see things differently. I had become convinced that two things weren't for me: I wasn't going to go to jail, and I wasn't going to kill anybody. But I knew I couldn't completely sever all ties with Harlem. My family was there, and just about all my life was there. I didn't know anybody anywhere else. I didn't know anybody in the Village. All I knew was that I had to get away.

I was only seventeen when I moved downtown, but I felt much older. I felt as though I was a grown man, and I had to go out and make my own life. This was what moving was all about, growing up and going out on my own.

Every time I came up to Harlem, it was a surprise, a frightening or disheartening surprise. If somebody hadn't died from an O.D., somebody had gotten killed trying to get some drugs or something crazy like that.

I remember once I came up to Harlem after I had been living down in the Village for about a year. I saw Turk, and he said, "Sonny, have you seen Knoxie around?"

I said, "No, man." I hadn't seen Knoxie for years, not since before I went to Warwick. He had gone into the Army. I hadn't seen him since the time he and Turk had had a fight on the corner of 145th Street for about two hours. That was about four or five years before.

Turk said, "When you see him, man, you really gon be surprised."

I said, "Why, is he bigger, or is he into somethin', is he into drugs?"

"Yeah, man, he's into a whole lot, but more than that, he's changed, man. He's changed a hell of a lot."

He smiled when he said it, so I said, "Yeah, like, I'm anxious to see the cat."

Turk said, "Look, man, he'll be in the Hole tonight. Come by and see him. That's where he deals stuff from."

That night, I went by the bar called the Hole and asked for Knoxie. The bartender said, "Yeah, he's over there."

As I started over, a peculiar-looking character looked up from the bar and said, "Hey, Sonny, how you doin', baby?" He said it in a very feminine voice. He threw his arms open wide to grab me and hug me. I didn't have that much against faggots, but I was shook. This was Knoxie. I had heard years ago that he'd gone good boy, but I could never imagine Knoxie being a faggot. But here it was.

He acted real happy to see me, but I felt a little uncomfortable. He said, "Come on, I want to buy you a drink."

I didn't want anybody to think I was his man, but I said, "Yeah, okay." We were friends, and it went past that feeling of not associating with faggots.

I stood there and talked to him. I asked him what had happened. He said, "Nothin' happened to me, baby; like, I'm happy. It got a lot of pressures off my back. I think I was cut out to walk queer street all my life, and I just found out recently, so I'm doin' it."

Knoxie put his arm around my shoulder. I sort of pulled away. I did it automatically, and I felt bad about it after I'd done it. He said, "Sonny, are you mad at me, man, for the change I made?"

"No, man, that's your life, and anything, you know, anything you want to do with your life is all right with me."

"Do you feel the same about me?"

"Yeah, we're still all right." Then I joked, "If I wanted to go party with some bitches, I'd never say 'Come along, Knoxie.'"

He laughed it off and said, "I'm glad, man, that you feel the way you do." He told me a lot of stuff about how he thought I was one of the hippest cats around there and could understand a lot of things.

I said, "Yeah, thanks."

Then we talked about the fight he'd had with Turk. He said he remembered it, that it was a good fight. I said, "I think Turk is kinda hurt behind that now."

He said that he'd seen him and they'd talked. He said that Turk took it big and was an all right cat. He understood things too. Turk had changed a lot since we were kids out there in the backyard bebopping.

Turk had started fighting in the Air Force, and he was talking about turning pro when he came out. He was pretty good; I guess he was always pretty good with his hands. He was always cut out for that. It would be a funny thing, I told Knoxie, if one day Turk became champ. I said, "Look, man, you're gonna have to change your way of life, of doin' things. We couldn't have Turk bein' heavyweight champion of the world and having once fought a faggot for two hours. That sounds damn bad."

Knoxie laughed at it. We had a drink, and he asked me if I wanted some drugs. Knoxie had a piece, so he wasn't worried about anybody trying to take the drugs from him. He said some cats had tried a couple of times. He'd been around for a while, out of the Army, and he had been dealing drugs downtown. He said some cats stopped him once, and he stabbed one of them. The word got out, and that was the only time he had ever had any trouble with junkies. It seemed as though most of the junkies thought a lot of him. If they came to him half a dollar short, sometimes a dollar short, Knoxie would let them ride with some drugs.

Here he was, a faggot dealing drugs and wearing a raccoon coat. He used to wear the coat even in hot weather. It was June or July, and the weather was damn hot. And here was Knoxie standing up at the bar in his raccoon coat, while everybody else was in shirt sleeves. Nobody thought that Knoxie was crazy for wearing the raccoon coat or for being a faggot, because there were a whole lot of crazy people around Harlem, and there were a whole lot of faggots. Nobody thought anything was wrong with faggots. Faggots were an accepted part of life.

One of the biggest thieves around there was a faggot, Broadway Rose. They tell me that Broadway used to rule Rikers Island every time he went over there. Cats used to say that if you had Broadway as your woman when you went over there, it worked in your favor. He would say, "That's my man," and nobody would mess with you.

All the kids in the neighborhood knew Broadway. He used to take them to the candy store or ice-cream shop. He even had them calling him mother.

I remember one time I was going up on the hill with Reno and Broadway was coming down. He stopped and started talking to Reno. He looked at me and said to Reno, "He's cute. What's his name?"

Reno said, "That's Sonny. He lives on the Avenue."

Broadway said, "Yeah, I've seen him around." He put his arm around me and started talking, trying to play that girl role. He said, "Sonny, I'm gon put five dollars in my back pocket, and if you take it out real slow you can have it."

I looked at Reno as if to say, "What the hell is wrong with this faggot? Is he crazy or somethin'?"

Reno kept hunching me, as if to say, "Go on, man, go on."

The whole thing was that I was supposed to put my hand in Broadway's pocket and take some time getting the five dollars out and play with his ass. This faggot was about six foot four and big as a house. Since Reno kept hunching me to go on and do it and since he was a cat who knew what was going on, I thought, Shit, this is probably the best thing to do. He must know what he's doin'.

So I went on and got the five dollars out kind of slow and thanked him . . . played the part like I dug him. I said, "Thanks, baby, maybe I'll do you a favor one day."

Broadway said, "Maybe someday I'll hold you to it."

I asked Reno afterward, "What was that all about, man? Why you gon tell me to play with some faggot's ass?"

He said, "This faggot is one of the best people you could ever know if you go to the Rock. Cats who're suppose to be real killers on the outside, when they come in there—like, if Broadway's there, he rules the Rock. A cat might think he's a killer, and Broadway might walk up to him and say he digs him, like, 'Look, you my man.' And if the cat squawks or acts like he's not gon play the game, he just punches him out, and that's that. On the other hand, if a cat comes in there and Broadway likes him and thinks he might be able to get a play out of him now and then, he'll tell everybody else, 'Look, that's my man, don't fuck with him.' They know this is law, because he runs the place."

He was big enough. Broadway must have been a good 270 pounds, a good six feet four. He used to walk sloppy and slow, but anybody who's been in jail knows you can't tell how good a cat is with his hands by the way he walks or carries himself out on the street—or even in jail, for that matter. You never know until you see him in action.

The people in the neighborhood were accustomed to faggots. Faggots were no big thing, neither were studs. There were a lot of girls who just liked girls. Some started at a young age. I remember once my little sister asked my mother, "Mama, is that a lady or a man?" It was a stud.

Mama just looked at her and said, "That's a bull-dagger, baby."

It was just like somebody telling a child, "That's a horse." This was how the people accepted it in the community. Nobody could be shocked at people being faggots. Nobody thought there was anything so crazy about it. A lot of people, if their sons became faggots or their daughters became studs, were disappointed and hurt. At first you'd hear about people putting their sons out because they became faggots, and putting their daughters out because they started liking girls. But after a while, they always came back home. The family accepted it, the community accepted it, and everybody else accepted it. But, then, there was so much going on in the community. There were a lot of old women who just liked young girls. There were a lot of old men who just liked young boys. Just about everybody knew who was who and who was what, and they just accepted it.

I never met any faggots in Harlem who were in love with anybody. With them, it was sex, and they always wanted to try this sex thing with anybody who was willing.

There were a lot of regular whores around. Sometimes you'd be in a bar.

Some chick would be sitting around. You might have sold her some drugs, like when I used to be around selling cocaine and pot. She's turned her last trick, and she's got some money. You sit at the bar with her. The place is closing, it's time to go home. It might be a girl you have known for years. You might be good friends or good business associates, or you might have been in the same class at P.S. 90. She says, "You know somethin'? In all the time we've known each other, we've never been to bed." It's not really an offer, and it's not really a passing comment. It's more or less a challenge.

Here's a bitch saying to you, all of a sudden, "I want to find out what's to you" . . . in bed. With the whores, especially if you're friends, not good friends, but if you've known each other a long time, what she's saying is, "Do you think you're man enough to come share my bed tonight?" or "I want to try you out."

You have to go along with it. Some of the chicks you might really enjoy yourself with. You become a wealthy rat. You get yourself another hole to crawl into on nights when you don't want to go home to an empty bed.

But with faggots, I just couldn't see this.

I was going through all kinds of crazy things. Harlem and life were becoming pretty confusing to me. Even though I lived downtown and worked and went to school at night, Harlem was still my point of relating to life and events and putting them together, my point of reference. It was becoming confusing because everything was changing and everybody was changing. I started trying to find out what all this changing was about.

First of all, I started looking into the junkies, the faggots, all this sort of stuff. It had been going on for a long time, and I wondered about the people. Most of the cats I knew who were junkies said they did it because they wanted to, but I knew they did it because they wanted to be down. It was a hip thing to do, to know about—to be nodding. Not only that, it seemed to me that the junkies were running from things. They were running from people and life. Nobody expected anything from you if you were a junkie. Nobody expected you to accomplish anything in school or any other area. It was a good way to run from it all. You could just say you were a junkie and you were through. You were suddenly relieved of any obligations. People just stopped expecting anything from you from then on. They just started praying for you.

I couldn't understand why people became faggots. Then I thought, Shit, somebody has to do it, and they just want to.

Some girls wanted to become prostitutes. Some were prostitutes because they were strung out and had to support their habits. Some girls just liked selling cunt. Johnny D. used to say that prostitutes were cold bitches, that there was a difference between a prostitute and a whore. A whore could never be a prostitute. According to Johnny, the reason a whore couldn't be a prostitute was that the first time somebody put some good dick to her, she'd be giving him money instead of making him pay for her body. To be a prostitute, a girl had to be kind of cold-natured and businesslike. There might have been something to this.

It seemed that Carole had started going to Mrs. Rogers' church. Mrs. Rogers was Danny Rogers' mother. She had four sons, and they were all junkies and had sheets on them. She'd had a hell of a lot of trouble with the boys. According to Dad and Papa, my grandfather, this was the way the Lord was making her pay for becoming a preacher. They said the Lord had never called a woman to preach, and any woman who got up there and started calling herself a preacher was going against the way the Lord had made things and was going to have to suffer.

Whatever the cause was, Mrs. Rogers was doing a whole lot of suffering. Danny and his brothers, Johnny, Dennis and George, had been fucking up right and left. Danny had gotten all shot up trying to stick up a liquor store to get some money for drugs. Johnny was doing something like seven years for trying to stick up a mail truck. These cats were some pretty good guys, and they had a lot on the ball, but they all got caught by the plague, all four of them.

Carole was going so strong, I wanted to find out what had gotten into her, what was going on. One day, I just decided, "I'm gon go down there and check this thing out." When I went around to the church, I saw June Rogers. It was the first time I'd seen June since she was a little girl. I hadn't hung out with Danny in a long time, and when I used to hang out with Danny, June was in a Southern boarding school. When June had almost finished school, her parents had to take her out of the boarding school because they didn't have the money any more. They had had to pay people off to drop charges against Danny and Dennis and Johnny and George, because these cats had been stealing to support their habits and had been messing with a lot of people. Mrs. Rogers was trying to keep them out of jail, and most of her money went to lawyers.

June was a beautiful girl. She was like a walking dream. If you melted her, she would have been sweeter than honey.

The first time I saw her, it turned my mind around. I knew I had to get to her. I had to make her mine. I sat there in church and listened to Mrs. Rogers talk all that godly stuff. I'd never paid too much attention to Mrs. Rogers after that time I came by her house after I'd gotten shot and she told me how lucky I was. She thought I should thank the Lord that He had put the bullet down there, because if the bullet had been just a little higher it would have hit my heart.

I always thought Mrs. Rogers was a little crazy or something. She was too involved in all that godly business for me to pay much attention to her. She might not have been gone, but I couldn't listen to it. She was the minister, but I couldn't listen to any of that "Word" she was talking about.

I had just come down there to find out how I could show Carole that this was all a lot of bullshit and make her put it down. When I got there and saw June sitting there banging on a tambourine, it just took my mind away. I couldn't think about anything. I forgot what I was there for. I went up to the collection plate and put in five dollars. She looked like a queen. She had long, jet-black hair. She had a candy coloring, like caramel or peanut brittle. She was tall and shapely. Lord, when I saw her, I wanted to get next to her so badly. . . .

I couldn't think of anything else for days after I went to that church, and I knew I was going to go back and back. I knew I couldn't take her out anywhere, because Mrs. Rogers wouldn't allow June and her younger sister, Deidre, to associate with boys. Deidre was about my age. June was about a year or two older. Deidre wasn't much to look at. I don't think too many boys would have minded her not associating with them.

I went home and, since everybody was so religious, I prayed and prayed for the Lord to give me just one chance, one chance to get June Rogers down to my place. After a week or so, I got kind of impatient and saw that the Lord wasn't going to answer my prayer. I was going to have to take some action myself if that prayer was to be answered.

I started talking to Carole. Carole was really sold on this Holy Roller thing. She was saying that "everybody needs God in their life," and that sort of business.

I said, "Yeah, baby, it's a lot to that, and I been thinkin' about bringin' God into my life."

Carole said, "Oh, Sonny Boy, I'm so glad!" and she told me that she had prayed for me time and time again. She'd prayed for the Lord to touch me and give me the message.

I said, "Yeah, baby, well, it seems like your prayers are finally bein' answered, because I think the Lord gave me the message. I feel like now the time has come for me to start goin' to church."

I told her, "I'm gon start goin' every week," and she started waiting for me to go to church with her. I started going every Sunday, religiously. I'd sit there in one of the front rows and stare at Mrs. Rogers when she started throwing up her hands and sweating and hollering about the Lord and good Jesus. I'd pat my foot and look like I was really getting the message. Occasionally, I'd even say an amen or a hallelujah. I didn't even know what it was all about, but I heard the other people saying it who were supposed to be in on that stuff, so I did it too.

Mrs. Rogers started getting the feeling that I was a real good boy. I was working, and I gave a lot of money to the church. Every time I came, I would give them five dollars or something like that. I used to tell the people that the reason I started going to evening high school was that I wanted to better myself, that I wanted to get ahead in life, and this sounded good. The real reason was that I wanted to get the hell out of Harlem. I needed a change, and I started going because of that reason. But they liked the other one better, so I told them that. Mrs. Rogers thought that was real nice. As a matter of fact, she thought that I was a nice young man who was going to be something someday and that all I needed was God. I went along with it.

After I'd been going to church about three weeks, I figured it was time for me to go into my act. I was having a fever to get next to June. I had to do it soon. I figured if I was saved, Mrs. Rogers wouldn't mind me coming by and taking June out sometime, like to a nice movie, a religious picture, something about Jesus or the Bible. I could take her to the museum or down to the Coliseum. All I needed was just one chance to get her down to my place, to my quaint little loft room in the Village. I knew she would like the idea. She was nice, and she was very religious. But I knew she had a lot of animal in her, and all I wanted was a chance to unlock that animal and let it out. There's just something fascinating about religious chicks anyway. It's the high potentiality for corruption that's so fascinating.

On the fourth Sunday, I made plans. I put on a brand-new hundred-and-fifty-dollar suit, my thirty-dollar shoes, and my ten-dollar shirt and went uptown.

I sat in the front row, and I waited for Mrs. Rogers to reach the climax of the sermon. Mrs. Rogers was a big, burly, dark-skinned woman. I suppose this was why most of her children were so nice looking—she was big, dark, and burly, and her husband was lean and real light-skinned. He looked almost white.

This Sunday, Mrs. Rogers started throwing up her big arms and raising her voice and hollering about the Lord and how good Jesus was. When she really got excited and carried away with the sermon, she said, "Talk to Jesus, everybody!" She shouted it out; she threw both fists straight up in the air and preached at the top of her voice. The veins were bulging in her forehead, and the sweat was pouring down.

June was banging on her tambourine real hard and getting excited too. Deidre was on the piano, and somebody else had a cymbal. Everybody was really going at it. I felt that this was the time—when Mrs. Rogers hit her most excited point—this was the time I'd planned to pull my saved scene.

I jumped up and started hollering, "Oh, Jesus!"

Mrs. Rogers looked at me and said, "Yes, son, call on Jesus."

I started clapping my hands and jumping up and down and saying, "Oh, Jesus! Oh, Jesus! Please, Jesus!" This was the way I'd heard the people do it before when they'd been saved. After a while, I fell on the floor and started rolling around in my brand-new suit. This looked good; I knew it had to be convincing.

I rolled down there for ten or fifteen minutes, and Mrs. Rogers came over. She took my hand and said, "Call on the name o' the Lord, son. Call on Jesus!"

"Oh, Jesus, oh, Jesus, save me!"

"Tell Jesus to come into your heart, son."

"Oh, Jesus, Jesus, please, Jesus, come into my heart."

"Call on Jesus." She just held my hand, and she said, "Call on Jesus, son, call on Jesus!" And she started squeezing it.

I wanted to call on Jesus and say, "Jesus, please tell this woman to let my hand go!" She was almost squeezing it off.

Somebody would have thought it was her up there being saved instead of me. The times when she told me, "Call on Jesus," and I was saying, "Oh, Jesus!" real loud, it was the pain. She was squeezing my hand so hard, I was screaming to get away from that. I just went on calling on Jesus, and after about twenty-five minutes of this, I felt I had convinced everybody in the church that I was good and saved. I was all set to go on and get tight with June.

I got up, and Mrs. Rogers said, "Son, the Lord is callin' you, and you almost came to Him just then. Jesus almost walked into your life. You just keep on prayin'. You just keep on prayin', and I know you gon be saved, because the Lord wants to come into your life."

I never felt so low in all my life. Here I was lying and rolling on the floor all that time, and this woman was saying I was *almost* saved. I was really disgusted, and I just never went back there any more. I felt that it wasn't worth the time and effort. If I couldn't convince this woman I was saved, I'd never get next to June; she'd never let her out of the house by herself. I just chalked it up to experience—and to a cleaning bill.

I stayed away from that religious thing and let Carole go on and walk that way if she wanted to. I felt that this was something she needed, the way everybody in Harlem needed something. Some people needed religion. The junkies needed drugs. Some people needed to get drunk on Saturday night and raise hell. A lot of people needed the numbers. Me, I needed to get out of Harlem.

8

I came uptown one night and met Danny on the corner of Seventh Avenue and 145th Street. We were just standing there talking. Danny was telling me for about the fiftieth time that he was going to kick his habit. I kept saying, "Yeah, man, yeah. I know you're going to do it eventually." I just happened to ask how Jim was doing.

He said, "Goldie?"

"Yeah, Jim Goldie."

Danny said, "Oh, man, you didn't hear about it?"

"About what?"

He said, "They're having Goldie's funeral Tuesday night. Somebody shot him in the head four times."

I said, "Who and why? What happened?"

Danny asked me if I knew somebody on 141st Street by the name of Eddie Carter. I said I didn't know him. He said this was the cat who had wasted Goldie. I asked him why, and he told me about it.

As he told me about it, I couldn't listen very well. It was kind of hard for me to believe that Jim was dead. Jim was a big guy, and he was good with his hands. He had been to Warwick. He had done a couple of years in Elmira. He'd gotten back on the street and made the big time right away. He had brothers in numbers, so when Jim came out, there was a spot waiting for him in the numbers racket. His family was running the whole show.

We all used to hang out together. Jim had had a whole lot of heart, maybe too much. He would fight anybody, and this was when we were only thirteen or fourteen. He wanted to gang fight, and he was always real game. When he came out of the Warwick Annex at Hampton Farm, he was big and burly, almost as big as a barn. I suppose just his size frightened a lot of people. He was a nice cat, and he'd always been a nice cat. Of course, if he hit a cat—and he would hit a cat if he got mad—he would usually wreck the side of his face.

I think Jim had boxing on his mind when he first came out of the Annex. I don't know what happened. I think he came out and found this spot waiting for him in the numbers and found that all he had to do was come out and stand on Eighth Avenue most of the day. He walked right into the big time. I guess he just lost interest in boxing. Perhaps it was less appealing. His brother Zack was running around with the fine whores, he had a big Cadillac, he was the big numbers man. It was a more glamorous life than boxing.

After being out for about a year, Jim got busted sitting in Zack's big Cadillac smoking reefers. When he came back on the scene two years later, he was still in the big time. I remember when he first came out of the Annex, he looked for cats from the old crowd. Rock was out on parole. He'd say, "Have you seen Rock?"

I said, "No, man, I haven't seen Rock."

He said, "Damn, I'm looking for that cat. I want to get him high."

This was the way he was. He was always trying to do something for the old crowd, the cats he use to bebop with up and down Eighth Avenue and Lenox Avenue and Seventh Avenue and Amsterdam, all around the neighborhood.

But when he came out of Elmira, he seemed to look down on everybody as small-time hoodlums. He was ready for the big time. He used to hang out with a lot of Italian cats. Everybody thought they were members of the Mafia. He'd bring them uptown. He started snobbing the old crowd. He even started smoking a big cigar. I guess he was heading for the short life. People started saying that he was a gorilla, that he was going around shaking down people, shaking down numbers controllers and cats who were dealing drugs. The word was out that he would just walk up to somebody and say, "Man, give me five hundred dollars." They tell me that Shorty Mannlin gave it to him once. Shorty Mannlin was a big-time numbers controller on 146th Street. He was Zack's competitor, and Jim just walked up to him and asked for five hundred dollars. Never laid a hand on him. He was so big, and he had a reputation. Everybody knew he was rugged.

After Jim had been out of Elmira for about a year, and even though he was only twenty-three years old, he'd gotten big time without a hustle. He went into numbers, and he would take people's plays. If they had a hit, he'd tell them that they just hadn't put it in.

Some people would get their gun and go looking for him. If he wasn't home or in his stash, people would say, "Tell that nigger don't come on the street any more until he's got my money."

One of the most dangerous things in the world is to steal from poor people. This was what Jim and some other young cats his age were doing. They would start taking numbers, and they wouldn't pay these people when they hit. They were stealing from the poor, and when you steal from the poor, you gamble with your life.

Jim had gotten a reputation for not being afraid of a gun because he had once walked into a .45. He hit a cat who had a .45 on him and about six other cats. This was a crazy thing, because everybody else was ready to give the cat the money.

We used to shoot craps down in a cellar down on 145th Street. There'd usually be a lot of money flying around. Cats would shoot three hundred dollars or sometimes five bills on a roll. When cats were happy, they'd get high, go down there, and shoot craps. A lot of people knew about it, all the hustlers anyway. Evidently, a few others from out of the neighborhood had heard about it.

One Saturday night we were down there shooting craps. Everybody was hollering and making a lot of noise. The police knew about it. If they came down there, somebody would give them fifty dollars and they were happy. About two o'clock in the morning, two cats came in, two big colored cats. I don't think anybody saw them come in or heard them. All I recall was hearing a big, strong, mean-sounding voice say, "Don't a mother-fucker move." I knew the sound of a voice that meant business. I looked up and saw a cat standing with his back to the door and a gun pointing down at us.

Over in the far corner, there was another cat. He said, "Drop all the money right there on the floor."

Most of us had some money in our hands. I dropped mine in a hurry, without any hesitation, because I knew these cats weren't playing. Everybody else knew it too. The cat who had told us to drop the money had a revolver, but the cat against the door, the cat with the mean voice, had a big .45.

A .45 is a frightening thing. Not just because it's a gun, because all guns are frightening. The thing that's so terrifying about any gun is that when you look into it, you're aware that here's this little black hole that at any time can spit death out at you and take your life. People who have a gun in their face will get up off money in a hurry, especially people who have been shot. Most stickup artists know that if they put a gun to somebody's face and make him look right into the barrel, it's going to have much more effect than a gun held way down low.

A .45 has a big hole. As a matter of fact, it's the biggest hole I've ever looked into. The big holes are twice as frightening. It's as though if some-thing were to come out of there, it would take your whole head off. This was how we all felt when we looked up into the muzzle of that .45 pointed at us. I suppose everything seems bigger when you look up at it, and we were all kneeling down shooting craps or watching the craps roll. And all of a sudden there was this big black nigger standing there with death in his hand. I wanted to say, "Here, man. Here's the money; take it in a hurry. Just turn that thing away from me."

Nobody rose or anything. The cat with the .45 was so big and mean looking, he probably could have stuck me up without a gun. There were some cats there he couldn't have stuck up without a gun. But it was surpris-ing that anybody would come in there and do this even with a gun, because most of the cats shooting craps down there had killed somebody at some time or another in their life. Just about everybody on 146th Street who was in street life had the reputation of a killer. It took a lot of nerve for anybody to come in there and even think about sticking up these cats.

The guy only spoke once, and everybody heeded him in a hurry—every-body but Jim. Jim just squatted down there, almost sitting, like somebody taking a shit in the woods. He had his money in his hand.

The cat with the .45 spoke again. He said, "Nigger, what you waitin' for? Put that money down."

Everybody froze; we all expected this cat to waste Jim right then and there. I knew, and everybody else knew, that if the guy was scared to shoot or wasn't prepared to kill anybody, he wouldn't have been there. He might have gone and stuck up some other crap game or a check-cashing place or a liquor store. He would have been safer going to stick up the police station if he was afraid to kill somebody.

Zack was there too. As a matter of fact, Zack had eight hundred dollars going on the roll, and Zack told Jim, "Jim, put the money down."

Jim didn't pay any attention to Zack. He just kept staring at the cat for a little while, the cat with the .45 in his hand. The cat said to Jim, "Man, you ain't gon put that money down?" And he stuck the gun out in front of Jim. It seemed to be not more than three feet from his face.

Jim just started rising out of his squatting position, and he said to this cat, who was still standing with his back to the door, "Man, ain't nobody gon take my money."

When he said that, the feeling went through me, Oh, Lord, there goes Jim. I thought to myself that this nigger must be crazy, because you just don't argue with a .45. You might gamble and argue with a .22 or maybe a .32, but this nigger was arguing with a .45. He had to be crazy—stark, raving mad.

Everybody tensed. The cat who had told us to drop our money was still standing in the corner and just seemed to be backing the play. The main man in the scene was the cat against the door.

The cat in the corner with the revolver said, "Look, nigger, I'll shoot you if you don't put that money down by the time I pull this trigger."

Jim didn't even look at him; he kept looking at the cat against the door, and everybody else kept looking. I got kind of worried. Aside from being the youngest, I was the only one who hadn't killed anybody.

Jim said, "You come and get me up." Everybody else started backing away.

The cat in the corner said, "All you mother-fuckers better keep still, because the next cat who moves is dead." I was scared, because I didn't know what was going on. Everybody else seemed as though they were going to back Jim's play if he made a stand for his money.

Jim started getting up. The cat said, "You get up, and you leave your money on the floor."

Jim just kept rising slowly. As he got up, the cat still had the gun in his face. He never did drop his money. He still had his money in his hand when he hit this cat. He hit him with a straight right that everybody thought had broken the cat's neck. His whole head seemed to snap right off.

I just put my head down, because this shit was crazy. I said, "Oh, Lord, we all gon be wasted right here tonight." I wished that I'd never come down in that cellar that night.

But everybody just walked away. The cat in the other corner shot his piece off one time. Nobody had been paying any attention to him before, and when he did this, Zack walked over to him and said, "Come on, man, give me the piece. Don't get hurt."

The cat said, "Look, man, I don't want you cats' money. Just let me out of here." Everybody moved back. Zack said, "Okay, we gon let you out. Go on out." The cat started backing toward the door.

Just before he got to the door, Jim got to him with a right too. It surprised me. I'd been in a lot of gang fights with him, and he'd been a cold cat. But that was years ago, and he was always nice with everybody who was around him. I had seen him stab a cat and not even make any kind of face, not even seem to be the least bit bothered about it. I once saw him stab a girl in the behind with an ice pick. It didn't bother him.

He wanted to stomp the two cats, fuck them up good, not let them walk from there. What he was saying made sense, because he was saying that this was 146th Street, and 146th Street had always had a reputation, even when I was in knee pants. When I first started running away from the truant officer when I was playing hookey from school, I could always run into 146th Street. At night, two policemen wouldn't come in there by themselves. They had trouble getting anybody but the Four Horsemen to come in there.

Bubba Williams was kind of cold too. Bubba said, "Yeah, let's break their legs." I don't know if they broke their legs or not, but Bubba Williams took these bedposts that were down there. He banged on these cats' shins until he thought that they were broken. Then we walked out and left them.

People were afraid to mess with Jim. He could do a whole lot of shit and get away with it. After a while, nobody would play any numbers with him. He would just go around shaking down people, and most of the people who used to like him started putting him down.

I didn't think anybody would shoot him, not in Harlem. I listened to Danny tell me what had happened.

He said that Jim had been taking care of a cat's gambling joint down on 112th Street. Some guys had come there looking for the cat who owned the joint. He had beaten somebody out of some money or cheated somebody. Since Jim was the substitute houseman and since the owner was his main man, he wasn't going to turn them away and tell them to come back another time. He was going to find out what it was all about, and if it was trouble, well, Jim wasn't afraid of anything.

Danny said that the cats knocked on the door and asked for Kelsey, the guy who was running the house.

Jim said he wasn't there. He never opened the door, because it might have been the police. He asked what they wanted with Kelsey, and one cat said they had some business with him. Jim said, "You tell me the business."

This cat, Eddie Carter, who was gunning for Kelsey, had heard about Jim. He knew that Jim was tight with Kelsey. He called through the door and said, "Look, is that you, Jim?"

"Yeah, it's me."

"Jim, this is Eddie. I got no squawk with you, man, but I've got to see Kelsey."

Jim said, "Look, man, like, Kelsey's my man, and if you got anything to see him about, you got to see me about it too."

Eddie asked him, "Is that really the way you want it, Jim?"

Jim said, "Yeah, man, that's the way it is."

Danny said that he shot through the door six times. Four of the bullets caught Jim in the head. Jim was a big, rugged cat. Danny said they were .45 slugs, but I couldn't believe that anybody with four .45 slugs in his head could open a door, walk out of a building, walk for a block, walk up to a policeman, and say, "I'm shot," before he dropped dead.

That's the way the story went. Danny said that everybody was expected to the funeral Tuesday night.

I said, "Yeah, man. Yeah, I'll be there."

We would come. We had to come, because we were all a part of that Harlem thing. I guess I'd want them to be at my funeral too. It was a scream. The junkies were there. I recall sitting there in the back wondering who was going to follow Jim. Chink and Dew, a whole lot of other cats, they were just nodding and nodding, scratching and carrying on. They had to be there. We had all come up together, and we were all a part of this thing, all a part of the Harlem scene in some way or another, all a part of Jim's death. I looked at Jim. He seemed to have a frown on his face, a grimace. It looked as though he were in pain, as though he were hurt behind leaving so early.

Everybody passed around the coffin. The preacher said a whole lot of shit about "he was a good strong boy." All this nonsense. All I could think about was how he had lived so quick. He was like the community Horatio Alger. He had made it big in a short period of time. He had become a real big-time gangster.

He was a funny cat. People said he could smell a crap game a mile away. I'd never been to one where Jim didn't show if there was any real money there. I thought about all Jim's funny ways and all the things he did, and there just wasn't that much to say about him. So I could understand why the preacher had to preach such a bullshit sermon, because if he was to tell the truth, all he could say was, "Jim did some time in jail. He was a member of the old Buccaneers. He grew up on the streets of Harlem, running loose, like so many other of you boys back there nodding and scratching and carrying on."

As a matter of fact, the preacher did make a crack about "some of us who will follow this coffin on" in his sermon. I felt it was uncalled for. Those colored preachers would do that sort of stuff.

He died so young, and he wasn't even on stuff. It was okay for the junkies to die that young. Everybody expected them to. They were popping off right and left from an O.D. or from getting shot or from falling out of a window. Nobody paid it any attention. The thing at the funeral that seemed to get to most people was when Jim's mother screamed out, "Oh, my baby's gone! And he didn't even use no dope.".

It seemed like a whole lot of people in the neighborhood, cats that we'd come up with, gone to school with, were being cooked in Sing Sing. It had become a thing with people in the neighborhood to talk to these cats' mothers and relatives, cats who went to the electric chair in Sing Sing. I remember when I was younger, when I was at Warwick and right after I came out, I had heard about people I knew who had gone to the chair. We all wanted to know what they had said, but now we wanted to know what they said because we wanted to find out something for ourselves. We wanted to find out if it was worth it at the last minute, if they felt that it was worth it, now that they were going to die.

When I was younger, a few years after Warwick, I wanted to know just whether these cats were really hard. I think most of the guys my age looked upon them as heroes when they were getting cooked at Sing Sing. We wanted to know their last words. Somebody told me that when they cooked Lollipop—Lollipop was a cat who was kind of crazy, and we called him Lollipop because he liked candy—just before he left, he said, "Well, looks like Lolly's had his last lick." That was it. Everybody admired him for the way he went out. He didn't scream or anything like that.

Years later, after so many guys from the neighborhood had gone to the chair up at Sing Sing, we'd gotten too old to be hero-worshipers any more. The cats we used to worship when we were younger, these were the cats we had to equal. But I think everybody was curious about whether or not it was worth it to kill somebody and save your name or your masculinity, defend whatever it was that had been offended—whether it was you or your woman or somebody in your family. It seemed as though nobody would know this any better than the cat who was going to pay with his life, and he wouldn't know it any better than when he was getting ready to pay. If a cat could say it was worth it at the time he was going to give his life for it, who could challenge it? Who could say that it wasn't worth it? This was what everybody wanted to know.

The moment that somebody heard that anybody had gotten cooked, they would say, "Well, man, what did he say?"

I never heard of anybody ever saying it was worth it. They said a lot of things, but nobody ever said it was worth it.

One day Carole called me and said that Butch had fallen off a roof. Just about all the roofs were five stories high, and I couldn't imagine anybody falling off a roof and living.

I went to the hospital to see Butch. He was all broken up. He didn't know anything. He was hung up on one of those bed contraptions that seem to be holding people together with wires, holding each joint in place. He couldn't talk, and a couple of days later he died.

I couldn't think about it. Butch had always been such a strong person to me. He was one of the people whom I admired most when I was very young, before he got on drugs. I thought he was one of the strongest cats in the neighborhood. I thought if anybody could come back off drugs, it would be Butch. I just never thought that drugs were going to be a fatal thing with Butch and Danny. Maybe with Kid, but I just knew it wouldn't be fatal with Danny and Butch. I just figured they were stronger than drugs. Maybe if Butch hadn't fallen off that roof, he might have been strong enough to come back and kick. But he'd already been down to Kentucky about seven times, and he hadn't kicked. He'd stayed in the Army for a short time, and he still hadn't kicked.

I remember going by his house to see his mother afterward. I'd heard from a lot of the fellows that she didn't want any of them coming around. There were stories that somebody had given him an O.D. on the roof and that they threw him off when they couldn't bring him around. There were stories that he was trying to break into somebody's apartment to steal some money to get some drugs and that some cats who were holding the rope had just run and let him drop in the backyard when they saw the police or when somebody came up on the roof.

When I walked into her house, there was sadness all through it. He was the only boy. His mother had three girls, and I suppose Butch was pretty close to her. I went in, and I said, "Look, Mrs. Crawford, I came to pay my respects." She didn't say anything for a long time. I didn't know what to say, because I'd never been around the parents or the family of any friend of mine who had died. I'd never had a close friend die before, and I didn't know what I was supposed to do.

I knew that as a friend I was supposed to be able to offer something. Even though we hadn't been hanging out together much for the past few years, I was still close to Butch. I felt close to him. I doubt if any of the cats he had been hanging out with could have felt anything for his family, because they were junkies. They were always dying. These cats would run away and leave each other when one of them passed out from an overdose.

I used to wish I'd been there when it happened, whatever happened. Since I hadn't been, I felt that all I could do now was try to give his family a word of comfort, say something that might help. After fumbling for words and sitting there feeling uncomfortable for what seemed like hours but really wasn't more than fifteen minutes, I got up to go.

Just as I got up, Mrs. Crawford said in her West Indian accent, "Why, Sonny Boy, didn't you start using the damn dope too? Why did my Butch have to use that damn dope and go and kill himself?" She said, "All of the boys on Eighth Avenue, just about, is killing their damn selves with that damn dope. Sonny Boy, why didn't you?"

I told her I didn't know. She didn't say it, but I had the feeling she was saying, "Why aren't you dead too? Why aren't you dead instead of my Butch? Or if he has to be, why aren't all you boys who came up on Eighth Avenue and did all the same things together? . . . You played hookey together, you stole together, and you stayed out together." She knew these things, so I guess she felt we were all supposed to die together. I suppose that when a mother's son dies, she hates all sons, all sons who are alive.

After I got out of there, I just couldn't go to the funeral. Butch was a good friend of mine, but it was too much. I was getting tired of funerals. I was getting tired of seeing cats I knew die from overdoses, cats who had promising futures, who had good heads on their shoulders, cats I ran the streets with when we were in short pants. I was tired of seeing their families looking at me and saying, "I wish he could have been like you," or something like this. I was tired of being alive, not being strung out on dope at somebody's funeral who had been strung out and finally died from it. I was tired of going there and watching what duji was doing to everybody.

People came back and told me about Butch's funeral. I looked all over town that night for Danny. I finally went around to his parents' house and found him there. His mother was happy to see me. Mrs. Rogers was always nice to me, and she always wanted me to keep hanging out with Danny. It was kind of hard, seeing as how he was a junkie, and junkies couldn't be trusted too much.

Mrs. Rogers asked me if I had been to the funeral. I told her no. She said, "Why? He was a good friend of yours." She looked at me for a long time, and she said, "Why didn't you go to that boy's funeral?" She was angry with me.

I said, "I saw him before, in the hospital, and I saw his family yesterday." Then I saw myself, and I thought, Damn, I don't have to explain to you. She didn't know anything about him or me. She didn't know anything about how I felt about him, and she had no business asking that. I got angry with myself for feeling as though I had to explain my not being at his funeral to her.

I could halfway understand her fears and her anger, because I guess she figured if I had forsaken Butch, perhaps I wouldn't appear at Danny's funeral if he should ever take an O.D. or be shot by a cop or fall off a roof. After a while, I just walked away from her and went into Danny's room.

Danny wasn't high. He was packing. I sat on the bed, and I said, "Danny, where you goin'?"

He said, "I'm going to Kentucky."

I said, "Yeah, again, man?"

"Sonny, I think I've seen something." He grabbed me by my shoulders as though he wanted me to know that he wasn't just talking this time. He grabbed me by my shoulders and started squeezing. He said, "Sonny Boy, Sonny Boy, look at me."

I looked at him; I thought he was going crazy for a while.

He said, "Sonny Boy, you know what my mama told me?"

I said "No, Danny."

Danny told me that she had said that Butch's death was the way God was giving the message to him and Kid. He said he was going to kick his habit. He was going to really kick it this time. He was going to Kentucky, and when he came back, he was going to be through with drugs.

I said, "Yeah, Danny. I think you just might do it this time."

He sounded serious. I guess he had been serious all the other times too, although we had never really talked about it before.

I went with him to a cab. We talked about the time he and I and Butch and Kid had done things together—when I cooked shrimp in hair grease, that sort of thing.

As Danny got into the cab, I prayed for him. I found myself praying that he had gotten the message, if not from God, from someplace, at least into himself. I had the feeling that he'd found something.

When he got into the cab, he held out his hand and said, "Sonny Boy, say good-bye to Danny the Junkie, because when I come back, I'm gon be a new man. I'm gon be bigger than drugs. I'm gon be bigger than Harlem. I'm gon be bigger than anything that's against me."

When Danny got in the cab, I felt really alone. I decided to go uptown and look for Tony. I just had to find somebody, because Harlem had become sickening to me. Butch was gone; Danny was gone, in a way; and Kid, I felt that he would be following Butch soon.

I was wondering what had happened to the Harlem I used to know, to my Harlem, the Harlem of my youth, to our Harlem, Butch's Harlem, Kid's Harlem, Danny's Harlem. Young Harlem, happy Harlem, Harlem before the plague. I had to find something to show me that my Harlem was still there, that it wasn't just falling apart. I had to find something that was still intact.

I couldn't find Tony or anybody else. I wanted to talk to Pimp. I wanted to find out just how he had taken this thing, if he was aware of what was going on. I went to my parents' house and sat and talked with Pimp. I asked him if he knew that Butch had died. He said that he'd been to the funeral. He told me about somebody else on 146th Street, a guy I didn't know, who had died from an O.D. about two weeks before.

I asked him if he was still drinking wine. He said that he was. Then I asked him if he'd started smoking yet, because he was about fifteen. He said that he smoked a cigarette now and then and that Mama said it was okay.

"Look, nigger, don't play with me."

"No, Sonny, you know I ain't smokin' no pot yet."

"Why? Aren't you curious? Come on, let's get high for a first time."

"No, I've found out what it was like. I know it. I'd rather spend my money on other things."

Then I told him that I was going to come up the next day and spend the evening with him.

He said, "Yeah, I could show you a lot of things."

Pimp tried to talk to me, so it seemed, but I don't think I gave him the right answers. He told me things that I thought he didn't really feel. He was trying to emulate me. He was tired of Dad nagging him. He said, "Man, that cat gets on my nerves."

It seemed that his favorite conversation with me was tearing Dad down. I didn't want to encourage him in it, but this was what he wanted, and if I didn't do it, I felt as though I wasn't giving him what he wanted. I couldn't give him what he wanted, because he had to stay in that house and learn how to get along with Dad. He wasn't old enough to get a job and move out. If he started staying out in the street and getting himself into trouble, he wouldn't have had anyplace to go or anything to do.

He would talk that talk, and I'd try to change the subject. Or I'd say, "Yeah, man, he seemed that way to me too at one time."

Then, he'd say things like, "No, Sonny, you can't say that now, because you outta here; and, like, you know, I know you didn't feel that way when you were here. You been out of it for so long you forgot what it's like."

I knew that there was some truth to it, and I could almost agree with him. I did, to myself, but I couldn't let him know. I couldn't say, "Yeah, man, you're right. You're gonna have to get out. You're gonna have to put the house down and get away from them."

Pimp was getting big and wanted to declare his independence, but he was just too young. I couldn't encourage him, and my failure to encourage him was pulling us apart. I was afraid of this, but there was nothing I could do. I felt as though I was losing out on all fronts in Harlem. I was losing my bearings there, and I was losing whatever hold I'd had on my old stamping ground, my home town, my family, and my friends. I was just losing my place.

I decided to run. There was nothing else I could do. I was going to go back down to the Village and just stay there. I was going to try to find something new, because every time I went up there, it was almost sickening.

When I went back home after that night, I decided I wasn't going to go uptown for a while.

I gave up pot. It used to make me think too much, and the things I thought about bothered me. So I wouldn't get high. I just stayed down there in the Village. I went to school and read a lot. I drank a lot of wine. I tried to stay away from Harlem and forget it, but I couldn't do that. I guess it was too much in my blood to stay away for long.

Something happened to me just about that time. I was staying downtown, and I'd call up to see how people were. There was a guy I knew from Washington Irving Evening High School. I called him up one night, and we were talking over the phone. I heard a record playing on a disc-jockey program coming from the Palm Café. I asked him, "Man, what's that playing?"

It sounded like someone just playing the piano. He told me it was a record playing, just a disc-jockey program. I said, "Okay, I'm going to keep talking, and when the program goes off, I want you to get the name of that record, because I want to get it." When it went off, he told me that it was Bud Powell playing "A Memorial to Charlie Parker."

I liked a few jazz cats then, and I was living right down the street from a place called the Five Spot. I used to go in there and listen to musicians like Thelonious Monk, Randy Weston, Cecil Taylor, Don Schumacher, and those cats, that Village circuit of musicians. I hadn't become too involved in it then. But when I heard this record, it sounded like the most beautiful piano solo I'd ever heard in my life. I decided that I wanted to get a piano. I wanted to play.

It might have sounded like a crazy thing. Here I was, nineteen years old and I was going to start playing the piano. But this was the way I felt about it. I told a lot of people, "Man, I got to get me a piano."

Tony said, "Yeah, man, that's just the thing, because you bound to be good at it." This was Tony. He would say something like that.

A lot of other people said, "Man, you kinda old for piano lessons, aren't you?"

I said, "I don't care, man. I got to have me a piano."

I didn't tell people why I wanted it. I wouldn't say, "Yeah, I heard this cat Bud Powell playing over the telephone, and I have to get me a piano because I want to play like that." But this was how I first got the bug to blow a piano.

I had started getting out. I had stopped going up to Harlem every weekend. Sometimes I'd stay away three or four weeks at a time. I'd stay downtown. I was still in the talking stage in this piano thing. I knew I wanted a piano, but I didn't know too much about just how I was going to get it or when or anything like that.

I never heard anybody else who I thought was as good as Bud Powell, but every time I heard somebody good, I got this big urge to play the piano all over again. It would last for a couple of days, but I wouldn't do anything about it. I didn't get the piano right away.

I stayed downtown, and there were a lot of crazy things happening right there in the house. I remember once I had come in, and it was cold. It was a private house, and I had left the front door open but didn't know it. I had a little kerosene stove to heat up my room. After I finished lighting the stove, I sat down on my bed and started to eat a sandwich, a kielbasy sandwich. This was something I had found out about when I moved. I used to eat a lot of those sandwiches.

I heard a voice in the hall. Somebody said, "Hey, come out here. Open that door and come out of there or I'll shoot."

I didn't pay any attention to it. I thought it was one of the cats who lived in the house, just clowning. I said, "Yeah, well, go ahead and shoot."

I heard something like *Blam!* The door flew open. Something hit the door, and I knew somebody had shot. I just froze; I was about to take a bite, then everything just stopped.

Then somebody said, "Are you comin' out?"

I said, "Wait a minute! Wait a minute! What you shootin' for?"

He said, "Come out of there with your hands up."

I put my hands up and walked out. There was this dumb rookie cop standing out there with a gun in his hand and shining a flashlight. I was standing there trembling like a leaf in the wind. "Don't shoot, man. What you gon shoot me for?"

"What are you doing here?"

"I live here."

By that time, the cat who owned the house, an artist named Pops, who lived downstairs, had turned on all the lights and was running upstairs. Since he was a white cat, the cop figured right away he owns the house.

He started searching me with the gun still in his hand. Pops jumped back. He probably figured that if the cop turned on him with the gun, he was going to shoot.

The cop said, "Hey, does this guy live here?"

Pops said, "Yeah, he lives here. What's wrong? What's he done?"

The cop said, "He went and opened the door." This sounded stupid to all of us. I was still standing there shaking, because this guy was crazy. I felt he shouldn't be running around loose with a gun and coming in people's houses shooting just because they had opened a door. This was what had happened.

Afterward, he just went on downstairs. But this was only the beginning.

The next incident took place a few days later, maybe about a week later. It was early in the morning. Somebody had come in late at night and left the door open. I had gotten up about five o'clock in the morning and was going downstairs to the bathroom on the second floor to shave.

When I opened the bathroom door to go in, a flashlight beam hit the wall on one side of me. Then it moved over into my face. The voice behind it said, "Hold it right there."

I said, "Yeah, what's wrong?"

"Do you live here?"

"Yeah, I live here."

"Is there a light around here anywhere? Turn on the light."

"Yeah, there's one right here." I turned on the light.

Then I saw this cop. He was in his thirties. He was bent over. You could see that he was sloppy drunk; the guy was stinking. He smelled like wine, but I'd never seen anybody get that drunk off wine. He was bobbing and weaving; he had a gun in one hand and a flashlight in the other hand.

I had a safety razor down in my hand, and I was thinking, Oh, Lord. Here's this nut. He's just liable to fall. And he's just liable to shoot me, the liquor's just liable to shoot me.

He started squinting, as though he couldn't see too well. He said, "Hey, what's that in your hand?"

I was afraid to snatch it up too fast, because the guy might have gotten excited and started shooting. I said, "This is just a razor, you see." My hand wouldn't move. I wanted to raise it up and show it to him, but I was too scared to move.

"Do you live here?" Then he said, "No, you don't live here because there's a white couple who lives in this house."

"Yeah, I rent a room from them."

He said, "I'm gonna wake 'em up." And he started shouting, "Hello, hello there!"

I got kind of scared. I was hoping that somebody would come out in a hurry. If he didn't see anybody, I was afraid he might start shooting. After about six loud calls, this guy roused everybody in the house. They all came down. Pops came down and said he was going to write his councilman.

The cops down there were terrible, but we were living right near the Bowery, so we couldn't expect but so much. They wouldn't put any good cops down there—if there is such a thing as a good cop.

Sometimes I wanted to run back to Harlem, but I couldn't find anything up there any more. I didn't want to get high; I didn't want to go around to the old places. I didn't want to be with those people any more, because I didn't feel I was a part of it.

Cats wouldn't say certain things around me any more. The truth was that I didn't want to hear a lot of these things, and I guess a lot of them sensed it. Cats would whisper when they were talking about drugs or about some other kind of business. Everybody started feeling as though I wasn't a part of the Harlem scene any more. I started feeling like it too.

When I did go back up to Harlem after staying away for about three or four weeks, I met some young cats who were musicians. They'd been in the neighborhood a long time, and I'd seen them around, but we'd never said anything much to one another. I'd sold them some pot a few times, but we'd never really swung together.

Now these cats were blowing their horns, their axes, whatever they had. I remember that Flip was playing saxophone, and he was damn good. David was playing some nice drums. There were a lot of cats around there who were doing things.

I started talking to Flip one night. He asked me to come down to Connie's on Seventh Avenue, and hear Sonny Rollins blow. I'd heard about Sonny Rollins, but I wasn't any great jazz enthusiast.

I went there one night and sat and listened to these guys blow. Anybody could sit in. After a while, it became a regular thing for me to go to Connie's and listen to these cats. I liked some of the stuff they were doing. This gave me a stronger urge to blow piano, or blow a box, as they used to say. It still was just something I wanted to do but didn't know how to go about. I had to find another out, someplace else to go, something to do away from Harlem.

I was passing by a place on Broadway in mid-Manhattan one day. It was a gym where a lot of well-known personalities went. I didn't know the difference. It just seemed to be a place where people went to lift barbells, and I thought this would be the thing for me.

I had just started seeing other parts of New York. When I took the job with the watch repair firm, I used to deliver watches to parts of New York City I didn't even know existed, like Flatbush. I'd never been to Flatbush in my life before. I'd never known that there was such a pretty section in New York City. I used to go over there when it was spring and everything was in bloom. I liked being in a place where everything was so clean. It used to make me feel like me. I was lost, the colored folks were lost, because there were no Negroes in this nice clean section of town, nothing but Jewish people.

I wanted to see a lot more of New York. Sometimes on Sundays I'd go way up in the Heights just to see new sections of town.

This day when I was in mid-Manhattan and saw the sign about the gym, I went up to look at it, to see what it was all about. The fellow who owned the gym walked up to me. I had noticed that there were no colored cats in there. I felt a little out of place, but everybody who was working out at the time seemed to be all by himself. This encouraged me. It wasn't as though it was one big happy family, all white cats, and I'd be the only colored cat there. The cat told me that it was fifteen dollars a month and that you could come up and train as often as you liked. I said, "Okay, I would like to try it."

I started going every other night. I would knock off from work, go to the gym, and then go to school. I started feeling pretty good. Sometimes I'd be tired when I got off from work. Then I'd go up to the gym and work out for a little while, and I wasn't tired any more. I'd go home and get a good night's sleep. I'd be sleepy, but I never felt really tired.

After I was at the gym for a couple of months, I met a guy. He was a sort of funny-looking guy. I'd never paid any attention to him, but I think he'd been up there a couple of times before. He was about twenty-seven, twenty-eight. We were sitting in the locker room getting dressed. He spoke to me. I had a thing about speaking to those gray cats first. I wouldn't, because I didn't want my feelings hurt. I was made to feel pretty silly sometimes. You'd say hello and they'd look at you as if you were crazy, so I never spoke to them first. I just didn't know how to approach them. I used to think that maybe my voice was too low-pitched for them. Most of these cats were nice clean gray boys, and I knew I was kind of crude, right off the streets of Harlem. I didn't know how to talk to these cats. They were polished. I was pure Harlem.

Somebody had put a trombone under the bench that I was sitting on. This funny-looking gray cat—he wasn't really funny looking; he just wore glasses and looked real serious—said, "Is that your trombone?"

I said, "No."

"Somebody blows trombone in here?"

"Yeah, I guess so." Then I said, "I'd like to play piano myself."

The cat said, "Well, why don't you play piano? What's stopping you?"

"Oh, man, I'm kind of old."

He started telling me about somebody he knew who had started playing piano at the age of thirty-eight and had gotten quite good at it by the time he was forty-five.

"Yeah, well, he must have been a pretty determined fellow."

"Yeah, he was. You could do it if you wanted to."

"Yeah," and I had the feeling that this guy wasn't playing.

"If you want me to, I can give you the name of a guy who'll rent you a piano and give you a good deal if you want to buy it."

"Yeah, thanks a lot."

"If you have any trouble finding a teacher, I can recommend some good teachers to you." The guy was very serious, and I knew he wasn't playing.

I said, "Yeah, I'd appreciate it."

He wrote this down and gave it to me. Then he introduced himself to me, so I told him my name. His name was James Finley. He was a musician. He was also a composer who had written a couple of hit tunes. He'd written a couple of scores for Hollywood films, this sort of thing. He was a young man who had been out on his own for a long time, and he was doing a lot of things for himself. He believed in getting things done.

He showed me how to get a piano and a music teacher, a lot of things. He was a quack psychologist, apart from being a good musician. He was a Freudian. He introduced me to psychoanalysis, a lot of things, a whole new world. I was fascinated by the guy because he had accomplished so much while he was young. He had started at Juilliard when he was about fifteen.

The teacher he recommended was top-notch. When I was ready to change, he recommended other top-notch teachers. After a while, I'd just find my own. This was all right too. After I really got started in music, I didn't need anybody to recommend them. I knew where I was going.

I became more engrossed in the piano than in anything else I'd ever been involved with in all my life. I was grateful to Jay, because he had started me. Before, it was just a talking thing. I might have talked and talked about it for years and never have gotten a piano and started taking music lessons.

When I started taking the music lessons, I was studying with white music teachers. After I'd been at it six months or a year, I'd go uptown and play with the cats. These guys didn't have any formal teaching. They'd been around joints where the cats were jamming all the time, and they'd pick up a little bit here and a little bit there. They were getting good by just being around people who were always playing.

We would talk a lot. Many of the guys said that the reason Bird blew so well was that he stayed high, that it was drugs that made him blow so well; so if somebody wanted to really blow, he had to use drugs. A lot of them believed it. They would point out that just about all the good jazz musicians used drugs. Everybody had this big thing about colored cats and all the soul they had. They would say, "None-a them gray boys can blow any real jazz."

I had trouble with rhythm. I just couldn't seem to get into it with these cats; they were way ahead of me. They had all these eighth notes and sixteenth notes going, up-tempos. Every time I tried to speed up things or do something fancy, I'd get lost. These cats would be saying, "Sonny, you got to stay away from them gray boys and them gray teachers, because, like, they stealin' your soul, man. You got to get you a colored teacher if you really gon learn how to blow some good jazz."

I started looking around for a colored teacher, and I found one. I went to the Professor. The Professor wasn't a professor, but he was a good music teacher, damn good. That's why everybody called him the Professor. The first time I went to him, he made me feel that maybe there was some truth to all the stuff those cats were saying, because the first thing he said when I told him I was having trouble with rhythm was, "Boy, you havin' trouble with rhythm? You must not be as colored as you look, huh?"

I thought, Well, damn, this cat's a real musician and knows something about it, so I guess there is something to that color thing in music. After I got this teacher, I figured I was all set to get into this soul thing.

I had started hanging out with a new group. I found a new groove in the Harlem thing. I was with the young jazz musicians now. I was still living down in the Village, but now I had a companion in my room with me. It was a piano, something that I had needed for a long time. I played the piano from four to eight hours a day, and I liked it. I really liked it. I felt that I was into something. Every time I learned a new tune, I would struggle and struggle with it, but I could see the progress. For the first time in ages, I felt as though I was really doing things, learning new things. I felt that now I was going places and doing something. I was ready. I had everything back in its right perspective. I had Harlem in its place. I had the job in its place. I had school and everything. I felt whole. I was ready to take on the Harlem scene again.

9

One night in the fall of 1956, I was walking down Lenox Avenue, and I saw somebody coming toward me. The face looked familiar, but the way he was walking . . . there was something about him that just didn't resemble anybody I knew. As he got closer, he started smiling, and I recognized him. It was Billy Dobbs.

Billy walked up to me and said, "Peace, brother."

I thought, Oh, shit, here's another one of those cats on this Muslim kick. I said, "Hey, man, how you doin'?"

He said, "Oh, I'm doin' fine, Sonny. I'm doin' better than I've ever been doin' in my life."

"That's good, Billy. I'm glad to hear it." I was all prepared for a sermon or a long spiel about the Muslim thing, Allah, and Elijah Muhammad, all that bullshit. I didn't want to hear it. I had heard enough of that. It just didn't get to me. Those cats were crazy, the way I saw it.

Billy started talking, and I was surprised. I had never thought that Billy could get into that thing. The last time I'd seen him, Billy was strung out. He had at least a forty-dollar-a-day habit. He was far away from any kind of religion then, unless it was drugism. Billy said he'd found a whole lot of peace.

"Yeah, man, everybody's finding some peace."

"Have you found any, Sonny?"

I said, "Yeah, man. I just had a nice piece last night, a fine bitch, man," and I went on. I was doing this because I didn't want to hear any of that nonsense about peace. I was just being nasty to avoid all that.

"Sonny, I remember when you were talking to me about getting away from drugs, when you started going to school. Now I want to do something for you. I want to show you how to find your way, if you haven't found it."

"Thanks anyway, Billy, but I think I've found my way."

"Have you got a minute, man? Could I have a minute of your time?"

"Yeah, sure, go on. What's on your mind?" I didn't want to hear that stuff, but I didn't want to be rude to the cat.

When I had decided to go to school and get out of street life in Harlem, I talked to Billy. He was dealing heroin at the time. I told him, "Look, man, you know what's going to happen? Sooner or later, you're going to start dabblin' and you'll be strung out." I tried to tell him to give it up, but he said, "No, man, what am I going to do if I give up dealing drugs?" I thought he was convinced that he was going to be doing that for the rest of his life, so I just stopped talking to the cat. Now here he was, deep in this religious thing and trying to sell me on it too. It was damn surprising.

"Tell me something, Billy. What happened to you, man? How did you get into this Muslim thing?"

"I'm not a Muslim, man. Those people are a little mixed up."

When he said that, I sort of raised an eyebrow and thought, Well, damn, I thought one of those groups was bad enough around here, and now we got something else. Everybody's going crazy in his own right. I said, "Well, what you into, man?"

"Have you ever heard of the Coptic faith?"

"No, man. The Coptic? There's no such thing."

"Yeah, man. There's a Coptic."

"You mean Catholic, man." I thought the cat was just pronouncing "Catholic" wrong.

"No, Sonny, I mean Coptic. This is the true black man's faith. It comes straight from the black continent. . . . Haven't you ever heard of Haile Selassie?"

"Damn right, everybody's heard of Haile Selassie. So what's that got to do with the Coptic faith?"

"He's head of the Coptic Church. Haven't you ever seen those signs up along Lenox Avenue and Seventh Avenue whenever Haile Selassie comes to town? They've got up the banners saying, 'Welcome, Conquering Lion of Judah,' and all this sort of thing."

"Yeah, I've seen them."

"That's the Coptic, man, who put up all that stuff. This is what I'm into."

"How did you get involved in this?"

"Somebody pulled my coat, man, in a dark moment when I was heading down the road to destruction."

I said to myself, Oh, Lord, here comes some more of that shit about "how I was saved," and what not. Whenever junkies kicked for a little while, they'd go into this crazy kind of shit.

Billy said, "You know Lonnie Jones, who use to live on 146th Street?"

"Yeah, man, I know Lonnie. I haven't seen him in a couple of years at least."

"Lonnie saved me. He was the cat who pulled my coat to this brand-new, hip way of life."

"Oh, yeah?" I was a little surprised, but not too much so, because Lonnie had been a guy who I thought was not cut out too well for the Harlem scene.

"Yeah, man, that's no stuff. Lonnie is a priest in the Coptic faith."

"A priest! I always thought Lonnie was cut out for something different, but I didn't think he was made to become a priest in anybody's religion."

"Yeah, man, he's a priest."

"Well, I'll be damned! You never know what people are going to do next!" It wasn't too surprising in Lonnie's case, because Lonnie was a good boy. He didn't steal and stuff like that. He was in the Buccaneers with us, with most of the cats in the neighborhood. I think he was just in it because his brothers were. Just about everybody he knew was in it, so he had to get in the clique too.

I remember once when we were bebopping on 148th Street with some cats called the Chancellors. We only had three guns with us when we went uptown that night, and the person who had one of the guns was Lonnie. I was with him, Rock, Danny, and a couple of other cats. There were two brothers on 148th Street who everybody knew were killers. They were called the Lordly brothers. The Lordlys had stabbed and shot a lot of cats. People knew that you couldn't play with them. You didn't go up there and wave a gun in front of their faces or stick them with knives or try to scare them. These cats were dangerous. If you went to war with them, you had to kill them.

We had gotten cornered in a hallway up on 148th Street, me, Danny, Lonnie, Butch, and a couple of other cats. About ten or twelve Chancellors were coming after us. Some of us were trying to get out the back door, but it was locked. Lonnie had a gun, and these cats were coming in through the front door. Lonnie hollered, "You niggers don't move or I'll kill every last mother-fucker."

I tried to say, "Look here, man, do something in a hurry." I knew if these cats got to us, we were through. Lonnie kept hollering about what he was going to do and shaking, and they kept coming on. He kept telling them not to take one more step, and these cats were taking five steps at a time.

Rock stopped them; he snatched the gun and shot Junior Lordly. Everybody else stood back, and he kept shooting. We got out of the back door, and all the other Chancellors ran back out the front door. We went up on the roof and got out of there, but I don't think we would have gotten out if we'd waited for Lonnie Jones to shoot. This was the sort of cat he was. He had no business gang fighting anyway.

I said to Billy, "Come on in this bar and I'll buy you a drink."

He hesitated. He said, "No, man, I don't think any more."

"Damn, man, that sounds like that's something really powerful that you're into."

"Yeah, man. I don't need alcohol; I don't need drugs; I don't need anything any more. When I came out of Kentucky about a year ago, I didn't know what I was going to do, Sonny. I didn't know if I was going to go back on drugs, start drinking wine, or what. But I found out that I didn't need anything but this." He took something out of his shirt. It looked like a little metal triangle on a chain. He said, "Do you know what this is?"

"Yeah, man, it's a triangle."

"No, man." He turned it over. It was a pyramid with the Sphinx engraved on it. "This is the symbol of the Holy Land and a symbol of our religion."

"That's all right, man. Tell me some more."

"Actually, this is the symbol of man also."

"Since you don't want to go in a bar, why don't we just have a cup of coffee? You can tell me about this."

We went into a restaurant. He started telling me that this was something that had originated in Ethiopia and that this was the true black man's religion. He asked me if I knew a cat by the name of Father Ford. I said, "No, I don't know him."

"You've probably seen him. He's a short dark-skin cat, and he's really weird looking. I know you've seen him, because he's been around here for years, hollering the truth like a madman, hollering in the wilderness."

"No, man. I never met the cat."

"Well, anyway, we have classes on Wednesday and Friday nights around Father Ford's house. He lives on 142nd Street. Man, why don't you come by on Friday or Wednesday night, like next Wednesday night, and check it out?"

"Yeah, man, I'd like to do that. Give me the address."

I was so surprised at Billy that I just had to find out about this thing, because something that could take a cat who was a stone junkie and turn him around like that, I wanted to know what it was all about. I decided to go around there that next Wednesday night.

When Wednesday night rolled around, I went to the address that Billy Dobbs had given me, 142nd Street between Lenox and Seventh Avenue. It was a basement apartment. Lonnie Jones answered the door. He looked surprised. He said, "Hey, Sonny, how you doin'?" He had a long goatee. Billy Dobbs had one almost just like it.

I said, "Hi, Lonnie. How are things?"

"Oh, fine, fine. I'm glad to see you here, man. I thought everybody was lost down here." Then he said, "How'd you find out about it? What brought you down?"

"I ran into Billy Dobbs, and he told me to come down. He gave me the address."

"Oh, yeah, one brother finds another." Then I heard somebody call him St. John.

"St. John? What is all this saint business about?"

Billy Dobbs had told me that Lonnie was a priest in the Coptic faith now, but I had forgotten about it. This brought it back to mind. I thought maybe they called them all saints, all the priests.

He went into the other room, and he called me after he got in there. He said, "Sonny, come here. I want you to meet somebody."

I came in the room, and there was this little short black man, whom I had never seen before. He was short, skinny, and spooky looking. He had one eye that he couldn't see out of, and it was turned around; you couldn't be sure whether the back of the eyeball was facing you or not. It looked a little nasty. He looked ugly and frightening at the same time.

When Lonnie introduced me, he said, "This is Father Ford."

I said, "Hello, Father. How are you?"

He just looked at me, nodded, and said, "Welcome to our house, son, and peace." I felt kind of funny. I didn't know what I was supposed to say. I looked at Lonnie.

He went on talking about what they were going to do. They were having lessons in Amharic and in numbers, this sort of thing. He was showing some other students, as he called them. There were some younger people, teenagers; there were a lot of kids around, too, and quite a few adults. This was supposed to be some kind of Bible class, or whatever they were teaching, and language class. Everybody was being taught Amharic, the native language of Ethiopia. I didn't know what was going on. But nobody cared that much. They weren't going to stop just because I didn't know what was going on.

When the class was over, Father Ford said, "Son, I want you to wait and let me give you a proper introduction to the Coptic." When most of the people had left, Father Ford asked me if I knew anything of the black people.

I said, "You mean Negroes?"

"No, I don't mean Negroes. I mean the black people, some of whom are called Negroes."

"I don't know. I know about as much as anybody else, I suppose, but a lot less than many."

"Well, do you know anything about the black man's faith?"

"Do you mean the Baptist faith or something?"

"No, that's not the black man's faith." He started frowning and grimacing as he talked about the Baptist faith. He said, "All these Western beliefs have been given to you by the white idiots who are running the world today. Do you know that the first civilized people were black? . . . You've heard of the Egyptian civilization, haven't you?"

"Yeah, I heard of the Egyptian civilization."

"That was the beginning. That was the very first civilization, even before the Chinese." He said that the ancient Egyptians who built the first civilization were black people. They were blacker than the Egyptians of today. They fell because they clashed with their brothers, who were Ethiopians. He said in the beginning there was one great civilized continent, Africa. There were two great powers, Egypt and Ethiopia, and these two powers clashed. A house divided cannot stand, and they fell.

"It was the practice in those days for the victor in any battle to take slaves and sell them to other people, like the yellow people in Asia. That's what was done with the Ethiopians when they lost the battle between Ethiopia and Egypt." He said there were a lot of long-forgotten mysteries that every black man once knew the answers to. He said, "Did you know this?"

"No. Mysteries like what?"

"Do you know what the Pyramids symbolize?"

"No."

"I'll bet you your first ancestors knew, and I'll bet you your great-great-great-great-grandfathers knew before they were brought to this land."

"They might have, but I don't know anything about it now. So what does it stand for?"

He still didn't answer my question. He asked me if I knew what the Star of David symbolized, and I said I didn't. He took out a dollar bill. He said, "You've seen this pyramid before, haven't you?" and he pointed to the back of the one-dollar bill.

"Yeah."

"Did you ever know whose eye that was? That's the all-seeing eye of God."

There were only seven or eight of us left there then. He seemed to hypnotize everybody; his voice filled the room. Everybody got very quiet, and it seemed as though if the dog made a sound, he could look at the dog and the dog would shut up. His voice had a commanding effect on everybody, I think. I know it had a hypnotic effect on me. I could remember everything he said, and he wasn't talking especially slow.

Then he started talking about the pyramid and the all-seeing eye and how man could rise to this power of all-seeing wisdom, as he put it, the omnipotent wisdom of God. I was stopped. I was really fascinated at this point. After explaining this, he went on talking. I was still listening, but I was looking around at the room. I felt as though I'd gotten high, like somebody getting high off some kind of drug. I looked around at all the pictures of symbols. There was a big poster on the wall of the Star of David, another of the Sphinx, and another of one of the Pyramids. There were pictures all over the room of black crucifixes and of Haile Selassie nailed to the cross.

After telling me about the all-seeing eye, Father Ford went on to speak about the symbol of the pyramid. He said that the pyramid straight up symbolizes woman, the inverted pyramid symbolizes man, and the two of them together are a six-pointed star, or the Star of David. The Star of David symbolizes life, because man and woman, in their holy union, symbolize life.

Then he told me that Haile Selassie, or somebody from the house of Haile Selassie, was the promised Messiah that the New Testament speaks of. He said, "They don't know too much about it actually. They're expecting some white God to come down here with blond hair and blue eyes. But you can't expect too much of the white people, because they were barbarians not too long ago."

He asked me if I'd heard about the love affair—he didn't call it the love affair, but that was what it amounted to—between Solomon and Sheba. I said I had, so he asked me if I knew that Sheba had come from Ethiopia. I said, "Yeah, I heard about that too."

He said in Ethiopia today, there was a piece of the ark of the covenant that had been given to Moses and that had been kept by Solomon. It had been stolen by the son that Solomon and Sheba had, and it was now kept in Ethiopia. Ethiopia was the true Holy Land today. One day, when the promised Messiah came, he would come from Ethiopia. He said that life was a cycle—it would get back to the black man's rule. I became more and more enthralled.

He said that everything about us was full of spirits, and these spirits were just waiting for some way to express themselves in life. I felt that there was nobody in the room but me. This cat was talking this stuff, and it really sounded good. It sounded new and different. I hadn't heard anything that sounded so fascinating in all my life.

He told me about the cycles of life. He said, "When it goes back again, and life is traveling on in this cycle or evolution, the evolution will not be complete until the black man is back on top again." This was what the Christians in their faith thought was the Second Coming of the Messiah. He said, "It is the coming of the Messiah, but it's the coming of Haile Selassie or someone from the line of Haile Selassie. Then the evolution shall be complete. All one has to do is watch Ethiopia, and he shall see the coming of the millennium and of complete peace on earth that the Christian Bible speaks of in confusion."

After this, he told me about the symbol of the snake. "The snake that was symbolized in the Garden of Eden was merely a sperm." He asked me if I'd ever looked at a sperm under a microscope. I said I hadn't. He said, "Well, it has a tail. There're a lot of sperm cells wiggling around, and they all look like snakes. This is the snake in Genesis that caused Adam and Eve in the Christian mythology to lose face with God and be thrown out of the Garden." He said that there were a lot of things that no black people would ever believe if they hadn't been subjected to Christian domination and indoctrination for the last few hundred years.

Father Ford said that the sperm starts down the brain, it goes into what he called the genital sac, and then it starts tempting. It makes you tempt women, because you get riled up when the sperm cell starts moving down. That's how Christian mythology took it as the snake tempting woman. The snake was man getting excited, the beast in man.

He went from there to the mystery of the Sphinx. Father Ford said that the body of the Sphinx was that of a lion, to symbolize the beast in man. He said that the head on the Sphinx was that of a man, or godlike, to symbolize the potentiality in every man. He said that a man could rise from his beastly nature, which he was born with and which he was basically, and fulfill, through exercising his mental power, his potential for omnipotent wisdom, or godlikeness.

I was still fascinated, but nothing else was said. Guys got up and started moving around. I looked at the clock in the room; it was a little after two o'clock in the morning. I had been there since eight o'clock. It didn't seem that I had been there so long. Maybe it was just that what he was saying was so interesting and so enthralling that I just lost all track of time. I wanted to tell him, "Go on. Go on, man. Talk some more." I hadn't heard anything that I had listened to so attentively in I don't know how long.

When I went home that night, I told Tony about it, and Tony said he just had to see this. I brought him with me the next night I went to Father Ford's. Then he started going regularly. He was just as fascinated by it as I was, but Tony said he didn't think he could get but so involved in this thing, because these people didn't drink, they didn't smoke, they didn't do anything. He said St. John—that was Lonnie's priest name—and Billy Dobbs had told him that they could get high if they just thought, by exerting mental power. Tony said he didn't think he had that much mental power, and he was going to have to keep on smoking pot to get high. Since these people didn't go for that, he knew he wasn't going to be in this thing. I thought that after a while he would be able to get high without smoking and could get into it. I had stopped smoking, so it didn't bother me.

When I started going regularly, St. John gave me lessons in Amharic. It seemed really easy. I was still going to high school at night, and I thought that French was easy, as far as languages went, but Amharic was much easier than French. There were only thirteen characters in the alphabet. They sounded strange at first, primitive utterances like "ugg" and "uhh" and "omm." I couldn't make the sounds at first. I thought it was a crude language, but after I started practicing and getting the hang of it, they were just sounds. In order to write a word in Amharic, you'd take one letter and make a slight deviation. You'd just make one of the lines on "A" a little longer and you had the word "am." After a while I was convinced that Amharic was the most melodic language I'd heard.

I wanted to go to Africa more than anything else in the world. I wanted to visit the Holy Land, and I wanted to see where this thing had come from. I wanted to see the piece of the ark that they had in Ethiopia. I started feeling frustrated, because I knew I'd never get to Africa. It seemed to be the farthest place in the world. I wondered if anybody in Ethiopia knew anything about us in Harlem and what we were doing. I wondered if they really accepted us as a part of the thing.

After a while, I began to feel as though the whole thing was just a crazy masquerade. I thought that if I ever went up to Haile Selassie and bowed down and paid my respects to him in Amharic, he would probably look at me as if I were crazy and resent my using the language, being a Negro and all. The few Africans I'd met just didn't seem to dig Negroes.

I started thinking, This is all a big farce. I started tapering off in my attendance. First I would go once a week, then every other week. Then I just stopped going altogether, after about four months.

I ran into Billy Dobbs at Broadway and Forty-seventh Street, in front of a frankfurter joint. We went in, and he said, "How you been, man?"

I said, "Okay. How you been?" I figured now was the time he was going to ask me why I had stopped coming to Father Ford's, why I'd lost interest in the Coptic. He didn't ask me. I sat there and looked at him. I noticed that he looked a little different. He had a two- or three-day beard on his face, and he looked a little greasy. He hadn't looked this way since he had kicked his drug habit. As I sat there, I was thinking that he'd undergone some kind of change.

He asked me if I knew some girl by the name of Ann, who lived on 147th Street, a tall light-skinned girl, nice looking, kind of shapely. I said, "No, man. I don't know her. Why?"

"She's my brother Doug's woman."

I said, "Oh, yeah? How is Doug, and what's he been doing?" I hadn't seen Doug in about three or four years. The last time I saw him, he was jostling, working the Murphy. I never was tight with Doug. He was about five or six years older than me.

Billy said, "Man, he ain't doin' nothin'. The nigger is strung out. He's not trying to kick his habit. He's not trying to do anything." At first, I didn't pay much attention to the hostility in Billy's voice. It seemed to be the ordinary animosity that a cat would have for a brother who was strung out, because when somebody in the family got strung out on stuff, everybody had to suffer. The junkie would steal from everybody in the family and scheme on everybody to get money to support his habit.

Then he said, "Ann is a damn nice girl."

I didn't know what this thing was all about, but I knew he wanted to talk about this girl. I said, "Yeah, man, she sounds like somethin' nice to look at."

"She's more than that. She's got a couple of kids, but she's a nice girl. I mean . . ." Then he grabbed my arm and started getting excited about it. He said, "Sonny, I mean, she ain't no bitch. She's got a couple of kids, but she ain't no bitch. She's a nice girl. She's a good-doin' woman; she wants to be a good mother."

"Yeah, uh-huh, I understand, man."

"I knew her first."

"Oh, yeah? You knew her first outta who?"

"I knew her before Doug met her. I knew the chick in high school. He came on and pulled her. He don't know how to treat her, man. He treats her like she's just an average old funky bitch out there. The cat gets high in front of her. He comes up to her place, and he brings the junkies up there, you know? They all get high in front of her, in front of the kids. He leaves his works around there; he does all kinds of shit. He brings stolen goods up to the chick's house and leaves it there."

I said, "Yeah, well, you know how it is when a cat's strung out. They don't consider anybody too much. You know how that is. You were strung out too." I got the feeling that Billy resented this, because he wanted me to give him some kind of support in what he was saying.

I just sat, and Billy went on ranting. "Sonny, the nigger steals everything she's got, man. He takes the money she's got to feed the kids with, and all kinds of things like that. He steals everything in the house, pawned her television, stuff like that." I just sat there and didn't say anything.

He looked at me as if to say, "Man, aren't you going to agree with me or at least say something?" Then he said, "Now the nigger wants her to go out on the corner and sell body for him. He's gon make a whore out of her just to support his habit. And she ain't that kind of chick, man; she ain't no bitch."

I realized he wanted me to encourage him to take his brother's woman, but I didn't feel as though I had the right to do this. I couldn't say anything.

He started pulling on my arm and telling me, "That nigger ain't no good, man. He ain't never treated no bitch good in his life."

"Yeah, uh-huh. Look, Billy, have you talked to Father Ford about it?"

He looked at me and smiled. He said, "Come on, Sonny, man, you know how those people are in that Coptic thing."

I got the impression that he had somehow been disillusioned with the

Coptic faith. I said, "Look, man, I got to go," and I guess I sounded a little angry when I said it.

He looked at me and said, "Okay, Sonny. I'm sorry, man."

"There's nothing to be sorry about. Look, Billy, I'll see you around. And whatever you do, good luck to you." I started walking out, and he called me.

He came up behind me after he paid for the franks and the orange drinks. He said, "Look, do you come uptown any more, man?"

"Yeah, I'm up there quite a lot, and I don't see you around."

"Do you ever come around the Low Hat Bar on Seventh Avenue?"

"The bar?" I was surprised, because I knew that he wasn't drinking when I cut into him about six months before, at the beginning of the year.

"Yeah, man. I'm around there quite a lot now."

I knew he had put down the Coptic faith. It seemed that it couldn't hold anybody but for so long.

I didn't see Billy any more until about a month later. I saw him uptown. He was with Ann, and he introduced me to her. She was a nice-looking girl; she looked like she was everything he had said she was. She might have been a good-doing woman and all that. Billy looked happy.

About four months later, I saw him standing on a corner nodding. I didn't know what had happened, but I felt that he should have stayed with the Coptic faith. If nobody else should have, Billy should have. And maybe he should have let his brother keep that good-doing woman.

That same year that I gave up that business with the Coptic faith Dunny, Tito, Alley Bush, and Mac got out of jail. They had all changed. Harlem had changed on them a hell of a lot. They didn't know what was going on. I felt a little sorry for them.

When I had gotten busted with Alley Bush on that last thing, I was glad that I was too young to go to some place like Coxsackie. He'd been gone three whole years. Three years was a long time; it was a real long time. I saw that it had done something to these cats' lives. Alley Bush was only about sixteen when he went away, and now he was nineteen. He seemed real backward, as though he hadn't grown any. Dunny seemed to think that the world had waited for him, just stood still while he was in Coxsackie. And Mac, he didn't know exactly what he was going to do. He was lost.

I asked him, "Mac, what you gon do? You gon get a job or something?"

He said, "I don't know, man. I guess I'll deal drugs." This was what everyone in the neighborhood was doing. Nobody seemed to know how to do anything else. He said, "All I know is that I'm gon move."

They all looked up to me because I was on my own. I told them I hadn't been living with my parents for about two years, and they all said, "Damn, Sonny, that's great, man. I want to find me a place too. I want to get me a place somewhere."

So I said, "Yeah, man, you can do it."

I figured it would be a good thing if everybody got out of Harlem. But most of these guys didn't know anything but Harlem, and they couldn't go anywhere.

Mac had always been miserable living with his family, but he had never had the nerve to walk before. He could finally admit to himself that his mother was no good and that she had mistreated them all. This was something that was damn hard for him to do. Mac used to always try to defend her. When all the other kids in the family had rebelled, he was still defending her.

Mac said, "I don't know what I'm gonna do, but I want to get me my own place. I want to have me a refrigerator that's always full of food, you know?"

I said, "Yeah, man, I know." There was never any food in the refrigerator in his house, and the kids had to fight and scheme on one another to eat up anything they got before anyone else came there, because it was so seldom that his mother ever bought any food. In a way, this was a lot for him to want, just an icebox full of food.

Tito said he wanted to deal drugs, make some money, and get a job. He said he'd have to find a place. His mother had never cared for him. He was always striving to make his mother like him and want him around. He always wanted to make her proud of him. He'd pull a big score and give her all the money he got from it. But if he got busted, she wouldn't even come to jail to see him. He still tried to hold on to the belief that she cared for him.

Tito said he didn't know where he was going to stay, and I said, "Look, aren't you going to stay with your moms and your brother?"

He said, "Man, I don't even know if they alive, and I don't care. I hope they aren't."

"What you talking about? What kind of shit is that to be saying about your relatives?"

He said, "Yeah, man, I know it may sound hard to you, but you know somethin', Sonny? I was up in Woodburn for three years and three months, and I didn't get one letter, man, not even around Christmastime, from my mother or my brother. It would be easier for me to take, man, if they were dead or something. I could understand that. But I'd hate to think of them being alive and couldn't even send me a Christmas card. I don't even want to know where they at, nothin'. I don't want to know if they alive or not, 'cause I'm afraid they just might be."

I could understand his feelings. He said he was going to get into some drugs or something. He asked me if I knew somebody, and I told him that I'd cut myself loose from all that. I didn't have any connections.

He said that was okay, because as soon as he had some money he knew where to go. He had cut into some people in jail who could turn him on to some nice weight. I gave him some money, and he gave it back to me. He said that he'd make it on his own, that all he wanted to do was get high. I took him to get high.

After that, it seemed that Tito, Dunny, Mac, and Alley Bush all went their separate ways. We were too old to hang out any more, and the Harlem we'd known had gone. In three years, it had all gone. Everybody had changed so much, and we didn't need one another any more. There was nothing else for us to do but say good-bye to the old way of life that we had known and to try to find something new.

Dunny seemed to have matured less than all the other guys. I guess jail didn't make much impression on Dunny because Dunny was hip, and he knew how to get along. He said it was hard. But if it was hard for him, it was probably twice as hard for everybody else.

Dunny told me once, "Sonny, don't ever go to jail in New York State, because the jails, man, are all run by Northern crackers. You might as well be down in Alabama someplace if you're gonna go to jail." He had been in Coxsackie and Woodburn, and he said that in both of them it was the same thing.

He told me a whole lot of things. The guards—the hacks, as they called them—were hillbillies. These hillbillies disliked anybody who came there and acted too suave or had handkerchiefs that were expensive, anything like that. According to Dunny, a Negro who was too suave had a hell of a hard time to go. The hacks were always kicking his ass for no good reason.

He told me about one cat he had met up in Coxsackie. He said he was a young cat, about eighteen or nineteen, who had hoboed his way to New York from Texas. Dunny said that this cat's name was Moe and that he had a whole lot of scars on him. Every time they'd catch him hoboing on trains or hitchhiking in some Southern town, they'd beat his ass. The sheriff or some of those cracker cops would beat him just for kicks. A lot of times, they put him in the hospital. He said it took Moe three months to get up here from Texas, because they were always kicking his ass and putting him in the hospital. In Alabama, they broke his leg and put him in jail for two days before anything was done for him. When Moe was at Coxsackie, he told Dunny that the jails in New York were no better, and maybe a little worse, than some of those he'd been in in the South.

Dunny said, "Yeah, Sonny, don't ever go to jail in this state, because they even have segregated jails."

I didn't know this about New York State, but I believed he was telling the truth.

He said, "Yeah, they put the white boys one place and they put the niggers in another section. The niggers get all the shitty jobs, and the white boys . . . man, they live good. It's just like it is out here."

"Damn, man. It can't be that bad. In jail, everybody's doing time."

"Yeah, man, but everybody isn't doing the same kind of time. There's white time in jail, and there's nigger time in jail. And the worst kind of time you can do is nigger time. They've got more niggers up there than anything else, but niggers ain't got no business in jail. They gon get fucked over worse than anybody."

"Yeah, Dunny, I'm really gon do my damnedest to stay outta jail." I told him I was going to evening high school, trying to get a diploma, and he said he was thinking about that too, "because there's not much money out here."

First of all, he had to get a job. He said as soon as he got a contact, he was going to deal drugs and make a little money. Then he could go to school. I told him it wasn't such a good idea to put it off. He said, "Look, Sonny, I need some money, man. Can you give me eight hundred dollars right now?"

"No, man, I can't."

"I've got to have the money." He said he wanted to get married to Trixie.

I said, "Okay, man, you go on and you get married and you deal drugs. But I think that if you gon deal drugs, and plan on gettin' married behind that, you're liable to get busted." I told him that it was hot out there and that cats were getting busted right and left for dealing drugs. I told him it didn't make sense. I said, "If you gon deal drugs, man, deal some cocaine or some pot, because you don't have to be dealing with the junkies. The junkies are gonna start crowdin' around your house and all that sort of business. If you deal drugs, they point the way for the police to go and bust you."

He said that he had a way that he was going to avoid all that. He wasn't going to have them coming to him. He would be at a certain place at certain hours; they'd come and cop there. He was going to have a new place every day or every week or something like that.

After that, I didn't see Dunny too often. I wanted to tell him that I didn't think it was a good idea for him to marry Trixie. But if a cat wants to do that, it's kind of hard to tell him not to. Then again, I thought Trixie might have been in love with Dunny. They might have been the perfect match.

I didn't see too much of any of the guys after that. I was going on my way. These cats were out there searching for themselves, not knowing how they were going to make it, trying a whole lot of ways. The most I could do was wish them good luck.

I'd see one of the old cats occasionally. The first one I heard had gotten busted and was back in jail was Tito. I think Turk told me that Tito had gotten busted for drugs, and he was doing something like one to five in a federal prison at Danbury, Connecticut. I knew that Tito didn't mind. He didn't have anything out on the street. He wasn't in love with anybody. He had a couple of chicks, but they weren't the kind of women that made a cat serious about not going to jail or that made a guy want to get a job and straighten out his life. He didn't care about his family, and they didn't care about him, so, actually, there was nothing to keep him out on the street.

I figured that Alley Bush would be the first to get busted, because Alley Bush was a little crazy. He used to do a lot of stupid things. He might have gotten busted for something silly like stealing apples or breaking a window in the police station. But Tito was the first one.

Mac was second. Mac got busted for dealing drugs too. These guys had made a little bit of money, but none of them stayed out there long. Everybody got busted within six months after they started dealing drugs. That's how it was. These cats didn't know what was really going on when they came out. All they knew was that they had to make some money, and since the money was in drugs, they were going to try to make money that way.

I felt sorry for them, but I knew that I couldn't tell them anything. One reason was that we weren't as tight as we used to be. We weren't tight at all. I'd see Turk. He said he was going to become a professional fighter. I remember seeing Dunny and telling him that Turk was going to turn pro after he got out of the Air Force. Dunny laughed at it. He said, "Yeah, man, can you imagine that?" like it was a big joke. Turk had always had a lot of heart. I think the reason Dunny laughed was that Turk wasn't that good with his hands. He always figured that Turk couldn't even get started good with him, so how could he be a professional?

But Turk had knocked out a lot of cats in the Air Force, and he was making a name for himself. He had a lot of people wanting to manage him when he came out. When he came out of the Air Force, Turk was a completely changed cat. He didn't have any of the old larceny in his heart. He didn't want to do any of the old things. He wasn't so childish any more. He was more social. He knew how to hang out with people, how to socialize with a lot of different people. He used to bring gray boys around. His fight trainer was an Irish cat. He used to bring him up to Harlem; he'd bring him to a bar, and he'd fit the cat right in with everybody.

Turk had grown a hell of a lot. He had gotten real big, and he was ready to do things. I didn't know whether he would be good as a professional fighter; as a matter of fact, I had some doubts about it until he came out and started fighting. Everybody in the neighborhood kept going to see him fight, but nobody paid it much serious attention at first. I suppose most of the older cats who knew him kept laughing, but this is the way it goes sometimes.

I kept coming uptown, and I kept going to school and working. I ran into a cat I hadn't seen for about three years. This was a cat I had gotten tight with up at Warwick. We called him T. He was using drugs, but he wasn't strung out, and he said that he wasn't going to get strung out, because all he did was snort. He said he would stop using drugs altogether rather than start skin-popping. He knew he would never get strung out because he would never be putting stuff in his veins. He had this method for not getting hooked.

T. was a pimp now. Not any real big-time pimp; he just had some funky little girls turning tricks for him down on 125th Street in the bars in that neighborhood. It was enough to pay for a dumpy hotel room, keep him in cocaine and support the chicks' habits.

He had some cocaine one night and wanted to turn me on. He said he had some fine girls. "Like come on, and we'll party." I told him no. He said, "What's wrong, Sonny, you scared-a some good cocaine?"

I laughed at it. I said, "No, man, I'm not scared." The truth of it was that

I was more afraid of those chicks he had than the cocaine, because they were funky girls. They used to call those kind of girls skunks because they were so dirty.

He introduced me to one of his girls. He said she was his main woman. We were sitting in a bar on 125th Street, and the chick came up to him and slid onto a stool next to him. He said, "Sonny, I want you to meet the woman I love, the woman who's going to be my wife as soon as I can get her to go down to Kentucky and come back. She's got a slight habit."

I said, "Hello, woman T. loves."

Her name was Gloria. She looked like she might have been nice looking at one time, but she was played out. The average chick who's been using drugs for some time looks like a played-out old prostitute, even though she may be young and may have been tricking for just a few months or so. It's the drugs that make them look so wasted, more so than the night life or going around hooking.

She had to go to work, so she left. He kept on talking to me after she was gone. At first I didn't pay too much attention to what he was saying about marrying her, because I figured nobody in his right mind would do that, go out and marry some chick who was a hooker. This didn't make sense.

T. and I were still good friends even though I hadn't seen him in a long time. So I said, "Look, T., you can't be serious, man."

"Why not?"

"Well, because the chick is . . . I mean, you know why not, man. If you gon marry her, you must not intend to live in Harlem. Look at all the shit you'd have to go through. All the cats who've jugged her, and that sort of thing. You just can't."

We sat there for a long time arguing about it. Then he just said, "Look, Sonny, the chick may be a whore, but she's my whore, and I love her, and I'm gon marry her." I saw that he was mad. He raised his voice when he said this.

"Yeah, man. Well, that's okay. You go on, man. And when you walk down the street and everybody points, what you gonna do? Fight all the niggers in Harlem about her?"

"Look, man, I don't care about anybody pointin'. I don't know, but my mother could have been a whore and I would have loved her. You can't tell me I'm not gon love a woman because she's a whore. That's just her work, man. It doesn't mean a damn thing to me. Maybe it means she's gone to bed with a whole lot of cats, but they didn't take it with them. It's still there, and I want it. She's my whore, and I love her."

This stopped me. I said, "Yeah, man." Suddenly it made a whole lot of sense. "Yeah, you're right. You can't stop lovin' a woman because she's a whore." I believed it; it seemed like the most sensible thing in the world. If he had said that two hours before, I wouldn't have had any argument. It made a hell of a lot of sense for somebody to love their mother even if she was a whore. This was what it was all about. I didn't try to stop him any more. We finished our drink and left.

I thought about Dunny and Trixie, and I thought that these people were really mature; I felt childish, the way I'd been thinking about people not loving whores and all that kind of nonsense. It seemed stupid to me. I realized that even though I had been out there in the streets and had met all kinds of people, I hadn't learned to accept people, not really accept them. I had still thought of a whore as being something unlovable. It was as though T. had been pinning diapers on me when we sat there at the bar and he told me about the mother and the whore thing. I was kind of grateful to him for that.

It seemed that every time I came uptown, I learned something. The best way to look at Harlem was to be on the outside and have some kind of in. I'd come up occasionally, look at it, see the changes and the stuff that everybody was going through, and be able to feel it. The only way you could feel it was to have had the chance—I don't know whether it was good or a misfortune—to experience it and to know what the people were feeling.

The more I learned, the more beautiful it was. The more I came up, the more I had the feeling that I wanted to come back and stay and give it something. I didn't know what. I didn't feel as though I had that much to offer, but I just knew I wanted to give it something. The more I came up and the more I saw of the people . . . I just felt closer. People would do things and say things that made me like them more and more.

One day I was walking on 143rd Street. I was remembering a lot of things about the block. I was with Tony, walking up the street. I met somebody I hadn't seen in seven or eight years. It was Hildy. Hildy was a lady who used to keep us when Mama worked. She used to keep me and Carole and Margie and Pimp. She lived on 145th Street then, and she drank a lot. She used to drink wine. A lot of people would call her a wino, I guess, but I just couldn't think of Hildy as a wino, because she was always a nice person, real nice. That's the only way I could think of her.

On this day, Hildy was standing around the stoop with some more people who looked like winos.

I stopped and said, "Hello, Hildy."

She looked around and said, "Sonny Boy! My Sonny Boy!" She grabbed me with both arms—she was kind of a fat woman—and she started kissing me. I would have been embarrassed had it been anyone but Hildy, I guess.

"Sonny Boy, you really grew."

"Yeah, well, I guess everybody does."

She pointed to the building that she was standing in front of. She said, "I live right here, you know. Right down in the basement. I want you to come and see me sometime, and I want you to bring Pimp to see me. How is that little rascal? I'll bet he's gotten bigger."

"Yeah. He's gotten bigger and badder." We joked about it.

I introduced her to Tony as an aunt of mine. I think it really made her feel good, and I was glad that I had done that.

She told some of the other people on the stoop that I was her nephew. They looked and said, "Yeah, uh-huh." It made her feel proud; she was proud of me. As I walked away, I told her that I was going to bring Pimp by to see her and that I was going to tell Carole and Margie where she was living, this sort of thing.

"Sonny Boy, would you wait a minute?"

I asked Tony to wait at the corner and turned around and went back. I thought she was going to ask me for some money or something. I wouldn't have minded giving it to her, but when I went back, she grabbed me by the arm and started walking a little way away from the crowd with me. She said, "I want you to come back real soon, and I want you to bring Carole and Margie and Pimp, but don't tell anybody I live in the basement."

I don't know why, but I felt a little hurt when she said this. I wanted to tell her, "Look, Hildy, you don't have to be ashamed of living in the basement or anyplace else. They've got people living on Central Park South and Sutton Place and Tudor City who're not half as good as you are." I wanted to hug her and comfort her and tell her, "You don't have anything to be ashamed of."

I just smiled and kissed her on the cheek and said, "Okay, Hildy," and I left.

That was only one of the things that I loved about Harlem, the meeting old people and old things. There was always something new to do. Somebody would always come along now and then and make me feel that it was getting better. Harlem was getting better. The people throughout Harlem were getting a lot more compassion for one another.

People were protesting, but not that the police should take all the junkies and put them in jail. As a matter of fact, they were petitioning to get a place to cure the junkies, to get more facilities at the hospitals for helping drug addicts to kick their habits. Before, all the people wanted to do was put them in jail or shoot them. It just wasn't this way any more. People were getting a little bit of tenderness.

As time went on and I kept going to Harlem, I was still out of it, but I was getting more feelings for it each day I lived out of it.

Around the end of 1957, I saw Danny. I think he had been back for a month before I saw him. He had straightened out. He'd been in Kentucky for fourteen months, and he was still clean. Danny had been down there a few times before. He'd been to a lot of places, and he had kicked it before. But this time, there was something different about him. He was more determined. When I saw Danny, he was really clean. He had new clothes; he was really dressed. He was decked out like a Madison Avenue executive.

The cat was happy. He grabbed me and started hugging me, all that nonsense. We went into a bar and had a drink. Danny said, "Sonny Boy, you know what? I'm offa drugs; I'm offa drugs for good!"

I said, "That's damn nice, man."

"No, man, it's not like before. I'm tellin' you I'm offa drugs and soundin' like I'm just sayin' that like I've said it so many times before. But it's not that way. I've been through it. I've had it."

"What do you mean you've had it, Danny? Did you get the calling from the Lord or something?"

He said, "Look, man, you know me better than that. I'm just through. I know that I've had it. I was strung out for seven years, and it seemed like I was strung out all my life. When I was down there and I couldn't get any drugs, I did a whole lot of thinking this time. It seemed like when I was strung out, I was living on the outside of life. There was so much shit happening that I didn't know about. I didn't know what was going on. I'd hurt my whole family, man, I'd hurt them something terrible. Sonny Boy, I'm twenty-three years old now, and I got to do something. I haven't been doing anything, so I'm going to get a job. I'm going to straighten up. As a matter of fact, I think I'm going to get married soon."

"Oh, yeah? That's damn nice, Danny."

"You don't believe me now, but just wait a couple of months. Have I ever stayed off drugs for three months or even one month?"

"No, not that I can recall."

"Okay." He took fifty dollars out of his wallet and laid it on the bar. He said, "Sonny, I want you to take that."

"What for?"

"I want you to take it, and I want you to hold it for three months. Take down the date and time and put it on a piece of paper with the fifty dollars. Three months from now, I want you to give me that fifty dollars if I'm still clean, only if I'm not messin' with that poison again."

"Okay, Danny, I'll do that." I took the money, but I was kind of concerned about what Danny was doing with a fifty-dollar bill. I figured he must have been dealing drugs; he must have been dealing a whole lot of drugs. I said, "Look here, Danny, what are you doing?"

"I'm back in business, man. I'm clean, and I know I won't get strung out. I feel so secure about this thing that I don't have to stay away from drugs. I can stay right here in Harlem, and I can even deal drugs, sell it to the cats I use to get high with, Sonny. That's just how secure I feel in this cure that I've got now. I know it's over with. All those other times when I was kickin', I'd go down to Kentucky or I'd go to Brothers Island, and the psychiatrist would say that I had complexes and all this. That was a lot of B.S., Sonny. I just used drugs because drugs was good. I liked it, and I wanted to. It made me feel better than anything else. It made me feel as though I was complete, man. I just wanted to use drugs; I didn't want to do anything else. I didn't want to stop doing it.

"But when I was down there, I did so much thinking, I just had to stop. I had to stop causing my family all that trouble. My moms is getting old. Have you seen my moms lately? Have you seen how much gray hair she got? Shit, I got to do something for that woman before she dies. She's suffered a whole lot for me, man. Half of that gray hair up there is on account of me."

When Danny said that, I had the feeling that he was serious, that this was it. But at the same time, I was still kind of leery about him dealing drugs and staying off it. Cats didn't do that. Just about everybody who dealt drugs for any length of time had to start dabbling, and eventually they got strung out.

"Danny, man, do you have to deal drugs? There are a lot of better ways to . . . it's safer to get away from it altogether."

"Yeah, but if you do that, you're not really cured. The only time you're cured, man, is when you can sit around people who're getting high off drugs and you know the good feeling, but still it doesn't move you to get high. I had seven years of that, man, so I know I'm not missing anything if I sit around and see people get high."

"Yeah, uh-huh. Okay, Danny, if you do it, man, that's a mother-fuckin' miracle. But I just hope you can do it."

He said, "Okay, Sonny, you just hang on to that fifty dollars."

I did and three months later, I had to give Danny that fifty dollars back. This was a big surprise because he was out there with everybody. It's easy, I suppose, to kick a habit and stay off it if you get away from the old environment, but Danny was doing what I had thought impossible. And I suppose just about everybody who knew anything about junkies thought it was impossible too. He had kicked his habit, he was dealing drugs, and he was successful at it. This was a most admirable feat to anybody who knew anything about drug addiction and had watched drugs rule an addict for so long and so destructively as it had Danny for all those years when he was strung out.

It was a damned admirable feat when the victim became the master of the poison that had had him by the throat. But Danny did it.

Cats used to say, "Man, I'm gon to do like Danny. I'm gon kick my habit. I'm gon make drugs work for me." He began to be a living symbol of victory over drugs even though he was still dealing drugs.

I suppose he wasn't an asset to the community in the eyes of the law or in the eyes of the good-doing folks who do all the talking, the guardians of our society and community. But he was an asset to the junkies, and I think many of them knew it. If it weren't for Danny, many cats would have had no kind of hope. He had compassion for the junkies. He didn't do cutthroat business. If a cat wanted a five-dollar bag and he only had four and a half, Danny would tell his lieutenants, "Don't wring it out of anybody, and don't tell a cat to go get a gun and get him some money if he can't make it any other way."

Everybody liked him not only for defeating the drug habit but for the kind of cat he was. I always knew that Danny had it. I always knew this, but I never thought I'd see him bring it forth. But he did it.

Danny never thought it was such a miracle or any fantastic feat. He just said, "Look, man, it was something I had to do."

One time he said, "Remember the time I went into the liquor store and pulled a stickup with the toy gun, Sonny? Well, I was doin' shit like that every day, climbing into people's apartments while they were sleeping and robbing them because my habit was down on me. I was going down from the roof into somebody's fifty-story-apartment window on some kind of thin rope."

He said, "Every day, I was goin' out there, risking my life, gambling, for just five dollars or enough to get straight, enough to get me enough to buy some duji and stay high for a day. It went around in a cycle. If the phone rang while I was out—my three brothers, they were fuckin' up too; my moms couldn't sleep; there were four of us out there for her to worry about—every time the phone rang, she figured somebody was gon say, 'Your son is dead.'

"We'd all gotten shot trying to pull stickups or running from the cops after we had stolen something. The best thing we could have done to make it easier on Moms was to die. When you stop and think about this shit, you know what you have to do. I knew I had to go on and throw just one big brick—kill myself, take an overdose, or something—or put the shit down. I couldn't do the shit any more; I couldn't do it to my moms, to my family. Everybody was suffering too much on account of me. I remember one day. You know my older sister, don't you? Vivian."

"Yeah."

"Her little girl, man, my niece, she's about five years old now, but she was only about three years old then. I'd been out all day trying to scrounge up enough to get high. I finally got enough to get me a ten-dollar bag. I came home and cooked my stuff. The family use to hide all the belts and all the cords. You know how Moms is, man, she didn't know that much about drugs. She figured if I couldn't get any belts or shit like that . . . she even use to hide the spoons so I couldn't cook my drugs in it. They figure it's gon be that hard. They were doin' all kinds of crazy stuff to stop it, but they just didn't know what was goin' on.

"This day when I had finally got my stuff together and came home to take off, I went into my room. I had had me a belt. The people had taken most of my belts, my ties, any kind of cords that I could use to tie up my arms and get the vein to bulge. I had cooked up everything, and I looked for a belt, but my belt was gone. I figured, I'm gon go in my father's room and get a belt. I put the drugs in the spoon, put a matchbox under the spoon to keep it level, and left it on the bedside table in my room. I went in the front room to get the belt. It seemed like I was only gone for about a minute.

"Vivian was in her room ironing some clothes. My niece, Debby, was comin' out of my room as I was coming down the hall. When I saw her coming out of the room, I said, 'Oh, shit, I should've locked the door!' I ran back to my room.

"The spoon wasn't there, man. You don't know. I panicked behind that . . . when I saw the spoon gone off the bedside table. The floor was kind of wet, man, looked like it had some water on it. I said, 'Oh, Lord, no, it can't be that! I know that's not my stuff.' I fell down on my knees, and I prayed when I saw that liquid on the floor. I prayed one-a them hopeless prayers, like 'Lord, please don't let it be my stuff.' The spoon was gone from the table.

"I knew, I just knew. I put my tongue down on the floor in the liquid and tasted it. I coulda almost died. My habit just started coming down on me altogether then and started eatin' through me. My whole stomach tightened up in me, and I knew I was gon die. I got down on my hands and knees, and I crawled on my knees into Vivian's room, and I grabbed Debby. I was gon throw her out the window with the last bit of strength I had.

"Vivian was ironing, and she hit me in the head with that hot iron. I didn't wake up until they woke me up in the hospital about three hours later. I was so glad when I woke up that I was in the hospital and hadn't done what I was going to do."

He said, "Sonny, when I was down in Kentucky, I use to lay awake at night and have awake nightmares just thinking about it. I knew, man, now I had to get up off it. I think if I wasn't so young before, I would have done it a long time ago. I was just too young."

I believed Danny. I believed a lot of cats out there were too young. We talked about drugs and about the cats coming up using drugs and not really knowing what was happening. Danny seemed to really know something about it, and I said, "Damn, man, if you could write about this or talk to the younger cats comin' up, it might stop somebody, turn 'em around."

Danny said, "No, Sonny, that's not gon help, because everybody has got to try that thing for themselves. Either they're hip enough to know before they start that they can't win, or they have to find out for themselves. If anybody could tell 'em . . . look at all the examples they've got. It doesn't make sense for anybody to be starting to use drugs, when they've seen all the cats who were dying." Danny started naming the cats, like Skully, Butch, Wattlo, like Sonny Bobbins, all the cats in the neighborhood who had died off drugs.

He said, "Man, these should be enough examples for everybody; the cats who use to be big time, and now they're down and out and noddin', this should be example enough for anybody, if examples were gonna help. Here's the living story. Look at some of the cats around here, like Father Time."

Father Time was an old junkie. He'd been around for years. He didn't want to kick; he didn't want to do anything but use drugs. He was harmless. Most of the cats who dealt drugs would give Time some, because he was a good-doing cat, and everybody wanted to keep him on the street. The cats who dealt drugs used to feel it was luck to give Father Time drugs.

I think it had started years ago, when Johnny D. was dealing drugs. He had given Father Time some drugs one time. The law was waiting at Johnny's house to bust him. Father Time had started begging him to give him some drugs. Johnny only had one last bag on him, but he let Father Time talk him out of it. He was just in a good mood. He gave it to Father Time and went upstairs.

The Man was waiting for him, but he didn't have anything. So it became a tradition with all the drug dealers to give Father Time some drugs. Almost every night, somebody would give him a bag of drugs. He just sat around on the stoop. The other junkies used to try to get tight with him, hoping that when the drug dealers gave him some drugs, he would turn them on. But Father Time never got tight with anybody.

He never talked. He never talked about anything. I guess this was why all the drug dealers liked him. He used to see a whole lot on Eighth Avenue. In fact, it was just about impossible to stay on Eighth Avenue all night long, like Father Time did, and not see a hell of a lot. He had to know what was going on, but since he never talked, nobody ever knew how much he saw.

Danny said, "If examples or stories were gonna help any, Father Time would be the living example and the living story. You see the pants that cat wears, man? I bet he hasn't changed them in three months. The cat doesn't bathe, and he stinks. Unless somebody takes him out in the backyard and turns a hose on him, he'd never get no water on him. That's how the cat is, he's so strung out.

"Do you think all these young boys going around trying to be hip, who want to use drugs, who want to nod, who want to be down, want to get away from this scene, to get older in a hurry, you think they don't know, Sonny? They can see. They got two eyes, just like you and me, man. They dig Father Time; they dig the whole scene, all these other cats noddin'. They know who died last month and who died last year. They know just who got killed over some drugs. But that's not gonna help them, man. They have to find out for themselves. What they don't know is all the individual hell that a junkie goes through. And this is something that they got to know, man, before they really understand what they're doing.

"Yeah, they're just a bunch of little chumps, man, just the way I was, scared to live. Scared, that's all it is. You can't talk people out of fear, man. You just can't do it. You got to let them grow up and one day stop runnin'.

"That's all it was with me, Sonny. I stopped runnin'. You know how it is; you run and run from a cat, down the street or around the corner. Then one day you come out of your house and you say, 'Damn this. I'm not gon run from that mother-fucker any more. He's just gon have to kick my ass, or I'm gon have to kick his ass.' That's the same way it is with drugs out here. When you come out of your house every day and you're a young boy on Seventh Avenue, Eighth Avenue, Lenox Avenue, or any of the other avenues around here, you got to walk up to that big gorilla, that big gorilla named duji.

"Every man's got to pick his own time, Sonny. Every man's got to pick his own time to stop running."

10

If anyone had asked me around the latter part of 1957 just what I thought had made the greatest impression on my generation in Harlem, I would have said, "Drugs." I don't think too many people would have contested this. About ten years earlier, in 1947, or just eight years earlier, in 1949, this wouldn't have been true.

In 1949, I would have answered that same question with the answer, "The knife." Perhaps all this could have been summed up in saying, "The bad mother-fucker." Throughout my childhood in Harlem, nothing was more strongly impressed upon me than the fact that you had to fight and that you should fight. Everybody would accept it if a person was scared to fight, but not if he was so scared that he didn't fight.

As I saw it in my childhood, most of the cats I swung with were more afraid of not fighting than they were of fighting. This was how it was supposed to be, because this was what we had come up under. The adults in the neighborhood practiced this. They lived by the concept that a man was supposed to fight. When two little boys got into a fight in the neighborhood, the men around would encourage them and egg them on. They'd never think about stopping the fight.

There were some little boys, like myself, who when we got into a fight— even though we weren't ten years old yet—all the young men, the street-corner cats, they would come out of the bars or the numbers joints or anyplace they were and watch. Somebody would say, "Little Sonny Boy is on the street fightin' again," and everybody had to see this.

Down on 146th Street, they'd put money on street fights. If there were two little boys on one block who were good with their hands, or one around the corner and one on Eighth Avenue, men on the corner would try and egg them into a fight.

I remember Big Bill, one of the street-corner hustlers before he went to jail for killing a bartender. When I was about seven or eight years old, I remember being on the street and Bill telling me one day, "Sonny Boy, I know you can kick this little boy's ass on 146th Street, and I'll give you a dollar to do it."

I knew I couldn't say no, couldn't be afraid. He was telling all these other men around there on the street that I could beat this boy's ass. There was another man, a numbers hustler, who said, "No. They ain't got no boy here on Eighth Avenue who could beat little Rip's ass on 146th Street."

Bill said, "Sonny Boy, can you do it?" And he'd already promised me the dollar.

I said, "Yeah." I was scared, because I'd seen Rip and heard of him.

He was a mean-looking little boy. He was real dark-skinned, had big lips and bulgy eyes, and looked like he was always mad. One time I had seen him go at somebody with a knife. A woman had taken the knife out of his hands, but she cut her hand getting it. I knew he would have messed up the cat if he could have held on to that knife.

He knew me too, and he had never messed with me. I remember one time he told me that he was going to kick my ass. I said, "Well, here it is. Start kickin'." He never did. I don't think he was too anxious to mess with me. I didn't want to mess with him either, but since Big Bill had given me this dollar and kept pushing me, I couldn't have said no. They would have said I was scared of him, and if that had gotten back to him, I know he would have messed with me.

I fought him for three days. I beat him one day, and he beat me the next day. On the third day, we fought three fights. I had a black eye, and he had a bloody lip. He had a bloody nose, and I had a bloody nose. By the end of the day, we had become good friends. Somebody took us to the candy store and bought us ice-cream cones.

Rip and I got real tight. If anybody messed with him and I heard about it, I wanted to fight them. And it was the same with him if anybody messed with me.

This was something that took place in all the poor colored neighborhoods throughout New York City. Every place I went, it was the same way, at least with the colored guys. You had to fight, and everybody respected people for fighting. I guess if you were used to it and were good at it, there was nothing else you could do. I guess that was why Turk became a fighter. He had fought so long and had been so preoccupied with fighting that he couldn't do anything else. He had to get this fighting out of his system.

With cats like Turk and many others who came up on the Harlem streets, the first day they came out of the house by themselves, at about five or six years old, the prizefight ring beckoned to them. It beckoned to them in the form of the cat around the corner who had the reputation or the cat who wanted to mess with your little brother or your little sister. If you went to school and somebody said, "I'm gon kick your ass if you don't bring me some money tomorrow to buy my lunch," it was the prizefight ring beckoning to you.

I remember they used to say on the streets, "Don't mess with a man's money, his woman, or his manhood." This was the thing when I was about twelve or thirteen. This was what the gang fights were all about. If somebody messed with your brother, you could just punch him in his mouth, and this was all right. But if anybody was to mess with your sister, you had to really fuck him up—break his leg or stab him in the eye with an ice pick, something vicious.

I suppose the main things were the women in the family and the money. This was something we learned very early. If you went to the store and lost some money or if you let somebody gorilla you out of some money that your mother or your father had given you, you got your ass beaten when you came back home. You couldn't go upstairs and say, "Well, Daddy, that big boy down there took the money that you gave me to buy some cigars." Shit, you didn't have any business letting anybody take your money. You got your ass whipped for that, and you were supposed to.

You were supposed to go to war about your money. Maybe this was why the cats on the corner were killing each other over a two-dollar crap game or a petty debt. People were always shooting, cutting, or killing somebody over three dollars.

I remember going to the store for my father on a Sunday morning. He'd given me a quarter to get him some chewing tobacco. I had to walk up to 149th Street, because no place else was open. I went up to this drugstore on 149th Street, and there were some cats standing around there. I was about eight, and they were about ten or eleven.

One of them said, "Hey, boy, come here," one of those things. I was scared to run, because I knew I wouldn't be able to outrun them all. I figured that if I acted kind of bad, they might not be so quick to mess with me. So I walked right up to them. One cat said, "You got any money?"

I said, "No, I ain't got no money."

I guess I shouldn't have said that. He kept looking at me real mean, trying to scare me. He said, "Jump up and down." I knew what this was all about, because I used to do it myself. If you jumped up and down and the cat who was shaking you down heard some change jingling, he was supposed to try to beat your ass and take the money.

I said, "No, man. I ain't jumpin' up and down."

He grabbed me by my collar. Somebody said, "He's got something in his hand." That was Dad's quarter. One cat grabbed my hand. I'd forgotten all about the guy who had my collar. I hit the boy who had my hand. Then the cat who had me by the collar started punching me in the jaw. I wasn't even thinking about him. I was still fighting the other cat to keep that quarter.

A woman came out a door and said, "You all stop beatin' that boy!"

I had a bloody nose; they'd kicked my ass good, but I didn't mind, because they hadn't taken my quarter. It wasn't the value of money. It couldn't have been. It was just that these things symbolized a man's manhood or principles. That's what Johnny Wilkes used to like to call it, a man's principles. You don't mess with a man's money; you don't mess with a man's woman; you don't mess with a man's family or his manhood—these were a man's principles, according to Johnny Wilkes.

Most girls in Harlem could fight pretty well themselves, and if other girls bothered them, they could take care of themselves. You couldn't let other cats bother your sisters. In the bebopping days in Harlem, if the girls had brothers who were scared to fight, everybody would mess with them and treat them like they wanted to. Cats would come up and say things like, "You better meet me up on the roof," or "You better meet me in the park."

It went deep. It went very deep—until drugs came. Fighting was the thing that people concentrated on. In our childhood, we all had to make our reputations in the neighborhood. Then we'd spend the rest of our lives living up to them. A man was respected on the basis of his reputation. The people in the neighborhood whom everybody looked up to were the cats who'd killed somebody. The little boys in the neighborhood whom the adults respected were the little boys who didn't let anybody mess with them.

Dad once saw me run away from a fight. He was looking out the window one day, and the Morris brothers were messing with me. I didn't think I could beat both of them, so I ran in the house. Dad was at the door when I got there. He said, "Where are you runnin' to, boy?"

I said, "Dad, these boys are out there, and they messin' with me."

He said, "Well, if you come in here, I'm gon mess with you too. You ain't got no business runnin' from nobody."

I said, "Yeah, Dad, I know that. But there's two of 'em, and they're both bigger than me. They can hit harder than I can hit."

Dad said, "You think they can hit harder than I can hit?"

I said, "No, Dad. I know they can't hit harder than you." I was wondering what was behind this remark, because I knew he wasn't going to go out there on the street and fight some boys for me. He wasn't going to fight anybody for me.

He said, "Well, damn right I can hit harder than they can. And if you come in here you got to get hit by me."

He stood on the side of the door and held on to the knob with one hand. I knew I couldn't go in there. If I went downstairs, the Morris brothers were going to kick my ass. I just stood there looking at Dad, and he stood there for a while looking at me and mumbling about me running from somebody like some little girl, all that kind of shit.

Dad had a complex about his size, I think. He was real short. Maybe that's why he played that bad mother-fucker part so strong. That's probably why he always had his knife. This was what used to scare me about him more than anything—the scar on the neck and his knife. I used to associate the two of them together.

Every night when Dad went to bed, he'd put his watch, his money, his wallet, and his knife under his pillow. When he got up, he would wind his watch, but he would take more time with his knife. He had a switchblade, and he would try it a couple of times. Sometimes he would oil it. He never went out without his knife. He never went to church, but I don't think Dad would have even gone to church without his knife. I guess it was because of that scar on his neck; he never was going to get caught without it again.

The Morris brothers were hollering, "Sonny, you ain't comin' down? Man, you better not come down here any more, 'cause I'm gon kick your ass."

They would take turns hollering up and telling me all this. Dad was standing there in the doorway, and I had a headache. I had a real bad headache, but I knew that wasn't going to help. Dad started telling me about running from somebody who was bigger than me. He said, "You'll probably be short all your life, and little too. But that don't mean you got to run from anybody. If you gon start runnin' this early, you better be good at it, 'cause you probably gon be runnin' all your life."

I just sat down there on the cold hallway tile, my head hurting.

Dad said, "Get up off that floor, boy."

Mama came to the door and said, "Boy, what's wrong with you?"

Dad said, "There ain't nothin' wrong with him. He just scared, that's all. That's what's wrong with him. The thing that's wrong is you try and pamper him too much. You stay away from that boy."

Mama said, "That boy looks like he sick. Don't be botherin' him now. What you gettin' ready to beat him for?"

Dad said, "Ain't nobody gettin' ready to beat him. I'm just gon beat him if he come in this house."

Mama came in the hallway and put her arms around me and said, "Come on in the house and lay down."

I went in and I laid down. I just got sicker until I went downstairs. They really did kick my ass. But it was all right. I didn't feel sick any more.

I remember one time I hit a boy in the face with a bottle of Pepsi-Cola. I did it because I knew the older cats on 146th Street were watching me. The boy had messed with Carole. He had taken her candy from her and thrown it on the ground.

I came up to him and said, "Man, what you mess with my sister for?"

All the older guys were saying, "That's that little boy who lives on Eighth Avenue. They call him Sonny Boy. We gon see somethin' good out here now."

There was a Pepsi-Cola truck there; they were unloading some crates. They were stacking up the crates to roll them inside. The boy who had hit Carole was kind of big and acted kind of mean. He had a stick in his hand, and he said, "Yeah, I did it, so what you gon do about it?"

I looked at him for a while, and he looked big. He was holding that stick like he meant to use it, so I snatched a Pepsi-Cola bottle and hit him right in the face. He grabbed his face and started crying. He fell down, and I started to hit him again, but the man who was unloading the Pepsi-Cola bottles grabbed me. He took the bottle away from me and shook me. He asked me if I was crazy or something.

All the guys on the corner started saying, "You better leave that boy alone," and "Let go of that kid." I guess he got kind of scared. He was white, and here were all these mean-looking colored cats talking about "Let go that kid" and looking at him. They weren't asking him to let me go; they were telling him. He let me go.

Afterward, if I came by, they'd start saying, "Hey, Sonny Boy, how you doin'?" They'd ask me, "You kick anybody's ass today?" I knew that they admired me for this, and I knew that I had to keep on doing it. This was the reputation I was making, and I had to keep living up to it every day that I came out of the house. Every day, there was a greater demand on me. I couldn't beat the same little boys every day. They got bigger and bigger. I had to get more vicious as the cats got bigger. When the bigger guys started messing with you, you couldn't hit them or give them a black eye or a bloody nose. You had to get a bottle or a stick or a knife. All the other cats out there on the streets expected this of me, and they gave me encouragement.

When I was about ten years old, the Forty Thieves—part of the Buccaneers—adopted me. Danny and Butch and Kid were already in it. Johnny Wilkes was older than Butch, and Butch was older than Danny and Kid. Johnny was an old Buccaneer. He had to be. When he came out on the streets in the early forties, it must have been twice as hard as it was a few years later. Harlem became less vicious from year to year, and it was hard when I first started coming out of the house, in 1944 and 1945, and raising all kinds of hell. It was something terrible out there on the streets.

Being one of the older Buccaneers, Johnny took Butch, Danny, and Kid as his fellows. He adopted them. I guess he liked the fact that they all admired him. They adopted me because I was a thief. I don't know why or how I first started stealing. I remember it was Danny and Butch who were the first ones who took me up on the hill to the white stores and downtown. I had already started stealing in Harlem. It was before I started going to school, so it must have been about 1943. Danny used to steal money, and he used to take me to the show with him and buy me popcorn and potato chips. After a while, I stole money too. Stealing became something good. It was exciting. I don't know what made it so exciting, but I liked it. I liked stealing more than I liked fighting.

I didn't like fighting at first. But after a while, it got me a lot of praise and respect in the street. It was the fighting and the stealing that made me somebody. If I hadn't fought or stolen, I would have been just another kid in the street. I put bandages on cats, and people would ask, "Who did that?" The older cats didn't believe that a little boy had broke somebody's arm by hitting him with a pipe or had hit somebody in the face with a bottle or had hit somebody in the head with a door hinge and put that big patch on his head. They didn't believe things like this at first, but my name got around and they believed it.

I became the mascot of the Buccaneers. They adopted me, and they started teaching me things. At that time, they were just the street-corner hoodlums, the delinquents, the little teen-age gangsters of the future. They were outside of things, but they knew the people who were into things, all the older hustlers and the prostitutes, the boot-leggers, the pimps, the numbers runners. They knew the professional thieves, the people who dealt the guns, the stickup artists, the people who sold reefers. I was learning how to make homemades and how to steal things and what reefers were. I was learning all the things that you needed to know in the streets. The main thing I was learning was our code.

We looked upon ourselves as the aristocracy of the community. We felt that we were the hippest people and that the other people didn't know anything. When I was in the street with these people, we all had to live for one another. We had to live in a way that we would be respected by one another. We couldn't let our friends think anything terrible of us, and we didn't want to think anything bad about our friends.

I think everybody, even the good boys who stayed in the house, started growing into this manly thing, a man's money, a man's family, a man's manhood. I felt so much older than most of the guys my age because I had been in it for a long time before they came out of the house. They were kids, and I felt like an old man. This was what made life easier on me in Harlem in the mid-fifties than it was for other cats my age, sixteen, seventeen, and eighteen. I had been through it. I didn't have to prove anything any more, because I'd been proving myself for years and years and years.

In a way, I used to feel sorry for the cats coming out of the house at sixteen and seventeen. I knew they were afraid. I'd always been afraid too, and I wasn't afraid of what they were afraid of. I wasn't afraid of not using drugs. I sort of knew that I wouldn't have to kill anybody.

I suppose I was luckier because, when I was young, I knew all the time that I couldn't get in but so much trouble. If I had killed somebody when I was twelve or thirteen, I knew I couldn't go to the chair; I knew they couldn't send me to Sing Sing or anyplace like that.

Then the manhood thing started getting next to cats through drugs. I saw it so many times. Young cats wanted to take drugs because they used to listen to the way the junkies talked, with a drag in their voice. I used to see some of the younger cats on the corner trying to imitate the junkie drag, that harsh "Yeah, man" sort of thing.

It was changing. By 1957 the fight thing had just about gone. A man didn't have to prove himself with his hands as much as he had before. By then, when I met cats who had just come out of jail, out of Woodburn, Sing Sing, Coxsackie, and I asked about somebody, they'd say, "Oh, yeah, man, I think I know the cat," and they would start describing him by features, his height, his voice, that sort of thing. But as late as 1953, if I asked somebody, "Do you know a cat by the name K.B.?" The guy would say, "Yeah. He's left-handed, and he always fights with his left hand cocked back?"

This was something that was dying out. Now people would ask if you knew somebody by scars or the way he talked, something like that. The fighting thing didn't seem to be important any more. The only thing that seemed to matter now, to my generation in Harlem, was drugs. Everybody looked at it as if it were inevitable. If you asked about somebody, a cat would say, "Oh, man, he's still all right. He's doin' pretty good. He's not strung out yet."

I never got too involved with drugs, but it gave me a pretty painful moment. I was walking down Eighth Avenue, and I saw somebody across the street. It was a familiar shape and a familiar walk. My heart lit up.

The person looked like something was wrong with her, even though she was walking all right and still had her nice shape. It was Sugar. She was walking in the middle of the street.

I ran across the street and snatched her by the arm. I was happy. I knew she'd be happy to see me, because I hadn't seen her in a long time. I said, "Sugar, hey, baby, what you doin'? You tryin' to commit suicide or some-thin'? Why don't you just go and take some sleeping pills? I think it would be less painful, and it would be easier on the street cleaners."

I expected her to grab me and hug me and be just as glad to see me, but she just looked around and said, "Oh, hi." Her face looked bad. She looked old, like somebody who'd been crying a long time because they had lost somebody, like a member of the family had died.

I said, "What's wrong, baby? What's the matter?"

She looked at me and said, "You don't know?"

"Uh-uh, uh-uh."

I looked at her, and she said, "Yeah, baby, that's the way it is. I've got a jones," and she dropped her head.

"Well, anyway, come on out of the street."

"I don't care. Claude, I just had a bad time. You know a nigger named Cary who lives on 148th Street?"

"I don't know him. Why?"

"He just beat me out of my last five dollars, and my jones is on me; it's on me something terrible. I feel so sick."

I was so hurt and stunned I just didn't know what to do. I said, "Come on, Sugar, let me take you someplace where I know you can get some help. Look, there's a man in East Harlem. His name is Reverend Eddie, and he's been doing a lot of good work with young drug addicts, and I think he could help you. He could get you into Metropolitan Hospital or Manhattan General, one of the places where they've started treating drug addicts. Come on, you got to get a cure, baby. This life is not for you."

I pulled on her, and she said, "Claude, Claude, I'm sick. There's only one thing you can do for me if you really want to help me. There's only one thing anybody can do for me right now, and that's loan me five dollars to get me some stuff, because I feel like I'm dyin'. Oh, Lord, I feel so bad."

I looked at her, and she was a part of my childhood. I just couldn't stand to see her suffer. I only had one five-dollar bill and some change. I said, "Look, baby, why don't you get off this thing? Because it's gonna be the same story tomorrow. You'll just be delaying it until another day."

"Look, Claude, I'll go anyplace with you, but I can't go now. In a little while, I'm gon be laying down in the street there holdin' my stomach and hopin' a car runs over me before the pains get any worse."

"Shit. Come on with me. I'm not gon give you another five dollars to go and give it to somebody and get bit again. Come on with me. Come on to 144th Street. I know somebody there who's got some drugs, and I understand it's pretty good. I'll get you some drugs and take care of that. Then we're gon see about doin' something for you."

"Okay. You get me high and I'll go anyplace with you after that. But first I want to go downtown. You could come with me, down around Times Square. I really appreciate this, and I'm gonna give you ten dollars."

"Shit. You gon give me ten dollars? Why don't you just go on and . . ."

"No, I ain't got the money now. I got to go down there and turn a trick. I'll give you ten dollars, or I'll give you twenty dollars if you need some money. I'll turn a few tricks for you tonight."

I wanted to hit her when she said that, because it meant she thought of me as somebody who might want her to turn a trick, somebody who would accept her turning a trick for him. But I knew that it wasn't so much me. This was what she'd been into, and she'd probably turned a whole lot of tricks. She probably thought of everybody that way now, as somebody who she could turn a trick for. I suppose that's all anybody had wanted from her for a long time.

I was hurt. I said, "Come on." I took her to Ruby's, on 144th Street. Ruby was a chick I knew who was dealing drugs. I said, "Look, you can get high right here."

I told Ruby who Sugar was. I introduced Sugar to her. I told her I wanted to get Sugar high. Ruby said, "No! I'm surprised. Damn, Sonny, you sure waited a long time to start dabblin', didn't you?"

"No, baby, it's not for me; it's for Sugar."

She said, "Oh, yeah? She looks like she's in a bad way."

Ruby told us to sit down in the living room. She had a bent-up spoon that she cooked stuff in for the poison people. She cooked some for Sugar. While Sugar was waiting for her to cook it, I asked her, "Sugar, what's been happening? The last time I heard about you, you were dancing with a popular troupe, and you were doin' good."

"Yeah, I was dancin', but I haven't done any dancin' in a long time."

"I guess not. What happened? You were doin' so good. You had finished high school. I thought you were really gonna do things; you were a damn good girl." I asked her what had happened to the young cat that she had eyes for when I wanted her to be my woman, about five years before.

"Oh, that was just one of those childish flames. It burned itself out."

"Yeah? I heard you'd gotten married. Wasn't it to him?"

"No, it wasn't to him. He wasn't mature enough for anybody to marry."

"Well, what happened with the marriage?"

"It's a long story, Claude, but I guess I owe it to you."

"No, baby, you don't owe me a thing. Save it if that's the way you feel about it."

"No, I want to tell it to you anyway. I guess you're the one I've been waiting to tell it to. . . . Do you remember a boy on 149th Street by the name of Melvin Jackson?"

"No, I don't know him."

"Anyway, he use to be in a lot of trouble, too, around the same time that you were raisin' all that hell. I think he was a year or two older than you.

When you were at Warwick, he was at Coxsackie. He came out about a year after you did.

"He was a lonely sort of guy. He seemed to really need somebody. Claude, you know what I think? I think all my life, I'd been looking for somebody who needed somebody real bad, and who could need me. Who could need all of me and everything that I had to give him."

I said, "Yeah, baby, I think I know."

"We got married in '55. For about a year, we were happy. Marriage was good. I thought this was something that would last and last for a long time."

"Yeah."

"Claude, I hope you don't have anyplace to go tonight. The first thing I want to do after I get high is go down and turn a trick and get some money."

"Look, girl, stop saying that. Stop saying that before I beat your ass."

She looked at me and smiled and said, "Yeah, won't you do it? I think I'd like that, just for old time's sake." And she went on with telling me about the marriage.

"For the first year, we were happy. He was working and I was working. After about a year, he started going out nights and stayin' real late. He'd get up out of bed at one o'clock in the morning, go out, and come back about four or five. At first, I thought it was another woman or something like that. I thought it was for a long time, until I found out.

"At first he just started goin' out and stayin' for a few hours. After a while, he started goin' out at night or early in the morning and not comin' back for two and three days. I got worried. After a while, I couldn't work. I had a miscarriage about a month before he started staying out all night long. I was kind of sick. I was weak, and I would get worried and couldn't go to work in the morning.

"Once, when he came home, I asked him where he'd been. He just said, 'I had to go out, baby.' I knew he knew a whole lot of shady people, because he'd been in street life for a long time, most of his life. And he knew a whole lot of characters who I didn't want him to bring around the house and who he was respectful enough not to bring around.

"I didn't ask him too much about these people. I didn't try to butt into his business, because we just had this understanding. We never talked about it. That's just the way we understood each other.

"I knew him, and I knew he loved me. I think he loved me more than anybody ever loved me in all my life before. That's what made it so bad when he started staying out at night. All that love I had finally found, the love that I'd been seekin' so strongly all my life, was being threatened. It made me sick. I'd wake up in the morning, feel that he wasn't there, and I became so scared I felt like a little kid hidin' in the closet from monsters.

"My eyes just started pushin' the water out. Heat waves would swell up and come out of my eyes in tears. That's how I felt. It wasn't a thing of body with him. It wasn't a thing of this flesh stuff. He didn't even know that I had a body when I first met him. He didn't like me; he couldn't stand having me around. One day, he said something kind, and I realized that it wasn't just me that he disliked. It was everybody. And he was lonely. He needed somebody, and I knew that the somebody could've been me.

"I'd never felt so un-alone, you know, until I met this guy. I never felt as though I had anybody or anything but him. I would've lived with him or done anything he asked. I would've went out on the street corners and tricked for him if that was what he wanted me to do, because he became a part of me, and I wanted him just that badly.

"But he really loved me; he didn't expect anything out of me. That wasn't the worst part of it. I thought he was getting money from me to give to another woman, because sometimes he'd be going into my handbag in the middle of the night, and he'd take money out of it. Then he'd be gone. Maybe he'd come back later that night, or maybe he wouldn't come back until the next day or two days later. It scared me.

"Well, anyway, one night, he was layin' next to me, sleepin'. I should've suspected it, because I came up in Harlem, and I knew what was goin' on. I don't know, I guess I was so frightened about this other woman thing that I couldn't see the symptoms. He seemed to be almost losin' his nature. He would . . . you know how if a guy wakes up in the morning, and he's a young guy, he usually has a piss hard-on. But he'd be as soft as a rag all the time. I was wonderin' if it was just that he was gettin' tired of me. Maybe I was making him lose his nature, because he didn't want to be bothered with me any more. I just got so afraid of this . . . and I should've known. I should have known what it was.

"Anyway, he didn't eat. I became more afraid of this thing. I became afraid to ask him, 'What's wrong?' I wanted to say, 'What's wrong, Mel?' But I was scared. I was so afraid he might say, 'Look, I'm tired of you, and I got to get out of this thing.' I thought it was gonna come one day anyway. He was gonna tell me, 'Look, I got another woman, and I got to leave you.' But it was gettin' to be too much for me to keep quiet about, because when he woke up at night and started leavin', I would be awake most of these times. I'd be tellin' myself for a week, 'Look, I'm gonna ask him the next time.'

"But still I was scared; I was scared of losin' him. I'd already lost him in that love thing. He always was quiet, but now he was more quiet than he'd ever been. It seemed as though he didn't want to kiss me. If I played with him in the bed, he'd get mad, that sort of thing.

"One night, he got up, and I asked him. I said, 'Mel, turn on the light, please.' He had been nervous. I hadn't been sleepin' for over a week, because I use to lay awake just wonderin', Is he gonna go out tonight, or maybe he's gonna come back to me? Our sex life had been dwindling away to almost nothin'. I thought, Maybe tonight, maybe tonight he'll play with me. I kept hopin'.

"When he got up to dress, that night I asked him to turn on the light, he was real nervous. He just said, 'Bitch, go on to sleep, and don't bother me!'

"I was kind of hurt, because he'd never said anything like this to me. We were real sweet to each other. This was crazy. I could've never imagined him saying it to me. When he said that, I had to jump up and turn on the light. I had my scream all ready. I told you what I was gonna tell him about the other woman, and all that sort of thing

"When I opened my mouth, I could taste the tears, and I heard myself talkin' to him in a real soft voice. I was sayin', 'Mel, please tell me where you goin'.'

"He said, 'Look, baby, go on to sleep, and don't worry about me. Try and forget me. Imagine that I never even lived, 'cause I think my life is ruined. I don't want to ruin yours. I'm goin' out tonight, and I'm not comin' back.'

"I said, 'Where're you goin'? Tell me something.'

"He got mad. He'd been gettin' irritable for a long time. He just snapped at me; he said, 'Shit, if you got to know, I'm goin' to my first love.'

"When he told me this, it stunned me. I felt as though I'd been hit in the face by a prizefighter. Everything was quiet. I was stunned, and I think he knew it. It was as though lightning had struck the house, and now all was silent.

"Then I said, 'Mel, I thought I was your first love.'

"He just said, 'No, baby, you're not my first love.' He said, 'Stuff is my first love.'

"I said, 'What do you mean "stuff"?'

"He said, 'You've heard of shit, haven't you, duji, heroin?'

"I wanted to cry. I wanted to cry. But it didn't make sense, because I was already cryin'. I didn't know what to do. I just said, 'Oh, no, no, it couldn't be.' He left."

When Sugar said that bit about "he left," she tried to smile. I felt uncomfortable. Then she said, "It seemed that I stood there in that dark room for hours with the word 'stuff' echoing in my mind. I knew but one thing in life for a whole week. All I knew was that I had to learn about stuff. I had to find out what it was that could make the man I loved love it more than he loved me. Well, Claude, baby, you can see I found out. Yeah . . . I really found out."

Ruby brought in the works; she had a makeshift syringe with a spike on the end of it. She was holding it upside down. I'd given her the five dollars when I first came in. She handed the spike to Sugar, and Sugar paid it no mind. She just rolled down her stocking and pinched her thigh. I saw the needle marks on her thigh.

She looked at me and smiled. She said, "Do you want to hold the flesh for me?"

I said, "Thanks for the offer," and smiled, but I just didn't want to help her get high. I watched as she hit herself with the spike, and I thought about the fact that just a few short years ago, to put my hand on those thighs would have given me more pleasure than anything else I was doing back in those days. I could never have imagined myself saying no to an offer to feel her thighs. Those were the same thighs that had all the needle marks on them.

I watched the syringe as the blood came up into the drugs that seemed like dirty water. It just filled up with blood, and as the blood and the drugs started its way down into the needle, I thought, This is our childhood. Our childhood had been covered with blood, as the drugs had been. Covered with blood and gone down into somewhere. I wondered where.

I wanted to say, "Sugar, I'm sorry. I'm sorry for the time I didn't kiss you at the bus. I'm sorry for not telling people that you were my girl friend. I'm sorry for never telling you that I loved you and for never asking you to be my girl friend." I wanted to say, "I'm sorry for everything. I'm sorry for ever having hesitated to kiss you because of your buckteeth."

Sugar took the spike out, and she patted herself. She started scratching her arm and went into a nod. "That's some nice stuff," she said.

I got up, went over to where Sugar was sitting, bent over, and kissed her. She smiled and went into another nod.

That was the last time I saw her, nodding and climbing up on the duji cloud.

11

When I went uptown now, I always had a definite purpose. I was going up to see Pimp to try and get him interested in something. I would take him out to the Flatbush section of Brooklyn and to Brighton, and we'd just walk. We'd walk around in Washington Heights. Sometimes on Sundays I liked to take him bike riding with me and show him other parts of New York City, hoping he could really get to see something outside of Harlem.

I was kind of worried about him now, because he was at that age, fifteen, where it was time to start doing something to be older and get into street life and do the things that the other cats out there were doing.

He knew that I was playing piano. I'd bring him down to my place sometimes and play for him. I'd take him to joints like the Five Spot. I showed him Connie's. He kind of liked it, but it didn't really impress him. He'd say things like, "Yeah, I'm gonna learn to blow a trumpet; I like a trumpet," but I knew that this wasn't really his thing.

I knew he had problems now. He had that problem of staying home and taking all that stuff from Dad. Mama had told me that he had had a fight with Dad. He was fighting back now. He was declaring his independence. I couldn't say anything. I didn't know what to do when he started complaining about how Dad and Mama and Papa, my grandfather, were still in the woods and he was growing up. He was getting away from all that old down-home stuff, and he didn't go for hearing it all the time around the house. I knew he was right, because I'd had the same feeling. You feel as though they're trying to make something out of you that you couldn't be and didn't want to be if you could, as though they're trying to raise you as a farm boy in New York, in Harlem.

I knew he was right, but I couldn't agree with him. I couldn't say, "Yeah, man. You got to get outta there." I wasn't sure that he was ready to leave, and I didn't have anyplace for him to go.

He would come down to my place after he'd had a fight with Dad and stay for a night. I knew Mama was all upset, because she'd get on the phone and start calling until he got there. She'd be real upset every time he stayed out after twelve o'clock. She was afraid that he was going to run away. She'd had her troubles with me, and I guess she figured history was repeating itself. Mama had really been through something with me, and I knew this. She had not had any trouble out of Carole and Margie. She'd always said she hoped she wouldn't have any grandsons, because if she had it all to do over again, she'd never have any boys.

I knew she had one reason for saying that, but I didn't want her to have another. I was trying to cool Pimp. I didn't feel that this cat was really ready to make it out on his own. He'd been a good boy all his life, and good boys weren't supposed to be pulling up and leaving home at fifteen.

I had to stop him from coming down to my place, because he was liking it too much. He'd come down, I'd give him money to go to school, money to blow. It was better than being home, because he didn't have anybody to answer to. I never asked him where he'd been or where he was going. He could stay out as late as he wanted to. Cats were always jamming at my place, all the young jazz musicians, the cats playing at the joints around where I lived. They'd be coming up all times of the night, getting high smoking pot and having jam sessions.

There'd be all kinds of bitches up there. We'd be partying way into the wee hours. This was a hip life, the way he saw it, and he wanted to get in. But I knew he wasn't ready for anything like this. It might have had a bad effect on him. The last thing I had to worry about was having my morals corrupted. But Pimp was younger, and he wasn't ready for this thing, the way I saw it. I was afraid for him, so I had to pull a mean trick on him to stop him from coming.

One night he came down, and he said he was tired of Mama and Dad and wanted me to look for a place for him. This was about twelve-thirty.

I said, "Okay, man," and pretended that I was serious about finding him a place. It was a cold night. I said, "Look, I only have one blanket." I put him in the little room across from me, and he almost froze. The next morning, he was in a hurry to get out of there and get back uptown to his warm bed.

I still didn't think he was ready, and more than that, I just didn't want him to hurt Mama as much as I had. I decided to go up there and talk to him, find out just what was going on. I could ask Mama about it, but she'd say, "That boy just thinks he's grown; he's gon fight his daddy, and he gon go outta here and stay as late as he wants." Mama couldn't understand Pimp any more than he could understand her.

I tried to talk to her. I said, "Look, Mama, Pimp grew up here in New York City. He's kind of different. He didn't grow up on all that salt pork, collard greens, and old-time religion. You can't make a chitterlin' eater out of him now."

Mama said, "Now, look here, nigger, you ate a whole lot of chitterlin's yourself, and chitterlin's wasn't too good for you back there in the early forties when your daddy wasn't doing too good on his job."

"Look, Mama, why don't you listen sometime, just for a little while. I'm telling you your son's got problems, Mama. It's not problems down on the farm. He's got problems here in New York City. And the only way he's going to solve these problems is that you try and help him."

"Oh, boy, sometimes I don't know what's wrong with you. You gon get involved in all that psychology you're always talkin' about and go stone crazy."

"Yeah, Mama, forget it." I just couldn't talk to her.

This day that I'd come up to talk was right after a big snowstorm. It was pretty cold; there was a lot of snow in the street. Traffic was moving at a snail's pace, almost at a standstill. Mama was complaining about how cold it was.

"Mama, why don't you complain to the landlord about this?"

"I called the office of the renting agency twice, and they said he wasn't in. When I called the third time, I spoke to him, but he said that it wasn't any of his problem, and I'd have to fix it up myself. I ain't got no money to be gettin' these windows relined."

"Mama, that's a whole lot of stuff. I know better than that. Why don't you go up to the housing commission and complain about it?"

"I ain't got no time to be goin' no place complainin' about nothin'. I got all this housework to do, and all this cookin'; I got to be runnin' after Pimp."

"Look, Mama, let's you and me go up there right now. I'm gonna write out a complaint, and I want you to sign it."

"I got all this washin' to do."

"Mama, you go on and you wash. I'm gon wait for you; I'm gon help you wash."

Mama started washing the clothes. As soon as she finished that, she had to put the pot on the stove. Then she had to fix some lunch. As soon as she finished one thing, she would find another thing that she had to do right away. She just kept stalling for time.

Finally, after waiting for about three hours, when she couldn't find anything else to do, I said, "Look, Mama, come on, let's you and me go out there."

We went over to 145th Street. We were going to take the crosstown bus to Broadway, to the temporary housing-commission office.

We were waiting there. Because of the snowstorm, the buses weren't running well, so we waited there for a long time. Mama said, "Look, we'd better wait and go some other time."

I knew she wanted to get out of this, and I knew if I let her go and put it off to another time, it would never be done. I said, "Mama, we can take a cab."

"You got any money?"

"No."

"I ain't got none either. So we better wait until another time."

"Look, Mama, you wait right here on the corner. I'm going across the street to the pawnshop, and when I get back, we'll take a cab."

She waited there on the corner, and I went over to the pawnshop and pawned my ring. When I came back, we took a cab to Broadway and 145th Street, to the temporary housing-commission office. When I got there, I told one of the girls at the window that I wanted to write out a complaint against a tenement landlord.

She gave me a form to fill out and said I had to make out two copies. I sat down and started writing. It seemed like a whole lot to Mama, because Mama didn't do too much writing. She used a small sheet of paper even when she wrote a letter.

She kept bothering me while I was writing. She said, "Boy, what's all that you puttin' down there? You can't be saying nothin' that ain't the truth. Are you sure you know what you're talking about? Because I'm only complaining about the window, now, and it don't seem like it'd take that much writing to complain about just the one window."

"Mama, you're complaining about all the windows. Aren't all the windows in the same shape?"

"I don't know."

"Well, look here, Mama, isn't it cold in the whole house?"

"Yeah."

"When was the last time the windows were lined?"

"I don't know. Not since we lived in there."

"And you been livin' there seventeen years. Look, Mama, you got to do something."

"Okay, just don't put down anything that ain't true." She kept pulling on my arm.

"Look, Mama, I'm gonna write out this thing. When I finish, I'll let you read it, and if there's anything not true in it, I'll cross it out. Okay?"

"Okay, but it just don't seem like it take all that just to write out one complaint."

I had to write with one hand and keep Mama from pulling on me with the other hand. When I finished it, I turned in the two complaint forms, and we left. Mama kept acting so scared, it really got on my nerves. I said, "Look, Mama, you ain't got nothin' to be scared of."

She said she wasn't scared, but she just wanted to stay on the good side of the landlord, because sometimes she got behind in the rent.

"Yeah, Mama, but you can't be freezin' and catching colds just because sometimes you get behind in the rent. Everybody gets behind in the rent, even people who live on Central Park West and Park Avenue. They get behind in the rent. They're not freezin' to death just because they're behind in the rent."

"Boy, I don't know what's wrong with you, but you're always ready to get yourself into something or start some trouble."

"Yeah, Mama, if I'm being mistreated, I figure it's time to start some trouble."

"Boy, I just hope to God that you don't get yourself into something one day that you can't get out of."

"Mama, everybody grows into manhood, and you don't stop to think about that sort of thing once you become a man. You just do it, even if it's trouble that you can't get out of. You don't stop to think. Look, forget about it, Mama. Just let me worry about the whole thing."

"Okay, you do the worryin', but the landlord ain't gon come down there in Greenwich Village and put you out. He gon put us out."

"Mama, he ain't gon put nobody out, don't you believe me?" I pinched her on the cheek, and she got a smile out.

After a couple of days, I came back uptown. I asked Mama, "What about the windows?"

"Nothin' about the windows."

"What you mean 'nothin' about the windows'?" I was getting a little annoyed, because she just didn't seem to want to be bothered. I said, "You mean they didn't fix the windows yet? You didn't hear from the landlord?"

"No, I didn't hear from the landlord."

"Well, we're going back up to the housing commission."

"What for?"

"Because we're gon get something done about these windows."

"But something's already been done."

"What's been done, if you didn't hear anything from the landlord?"

"Some man came in here yesterday and asked me what windows."

"What man?"

"I don't know what man."

"Well, what did he say? Didn't he say where he was from?"

"No, he didn't say anything. He just knocked on the door and asked me if I had some windows that needed relining. I said, 'Yeah,' and he asked me what windows, so I showed him the three windows in the front."

"Mama, you didn' show him all the others?"

"No, because that's not so bad, we didn't need them relined."

"Mama, oh, Lord, why didn't you show him the others?"

"Ain't no sense in trying to take advantage of a good thing."

"Yeah, Mama. I guess it was a good thing to you."

I thought about it. I thought about the way Mama would go down to the meat market sometimes, and the man would sell her some meat that was spoiled, some old neck bones or some pig tails. Things that weren't too good even when they weren't spoiled. And sometimes she would say, "Oh, those things aren't too bad." She was scared to take them back, scared to complain until somebody said, "That tastes bad." Then she'd go down there crying and mad at him, wanting to curse the man out. She had all that Southern upbringing in her, that business of being scared of Mr. Charlie. Everybody white she saw was Mr. Charlie.

Pimp was still in this thing, and I was afraid for him. I knew it was a hard thing for him to fight. I suppose when I was younger, I fought it by stealing, by not being at home, by getting into trouble. But I felt that Pimp was at a loss as to what to do about it. It might have been a greater problem for him.

It seemed as though the folks, Mama and Dad, had never heard anything about Lincoln or the Emancipation Proclamation. They were going to bring the South up to Harlem with them. I knew they had had it with them all the time. Mama would be telling Carole and Margie about the root workers down there, about somebody who had made a woman leave her husband, all kinds of nonsense like that.

I wanted to say, "Mama, why don't you stop tellin' those girls all that crazy shit?" But I couldn't say anything, because they wouldn't believe me, and Mama figured she was right. It seemed as though Mama and Dad were never going to get out of the woods until we made them get out.

Many times when I was there, Mama would be talking all that nonsense about the woods and about some dead person who had come back. Her favorite story was the time her mother came back to her and told her everything was going to be all right and that she was going to get married in about three or four months. I wanted to say, "Look, Mama, we're in New York. Stop all that foolishness."

She and Dad had been in New York since 1935. They were in New York, but it seemed like their minds were still down there in the South Carolina cotton fields. Pimp, Carole, and Margie had to suffer for it. I had to suffer for it too, but because I wasn't at home as much as the others, I had suffered less than anybody else.

I could understand Pimp's anxieties about having to listen to Grandpapa, who was now living with Mama and Dad, talk that old nonsense about how good it was on the chain gang. He'd tell us about the time he ran away from the chain gang. He stayed on some farm in Georgia for about two or three weeks, but he got lonesome for his family. He knew if he went home, they would be waiting for him, so he went back to the chain gang. The white man who was in charge of the chain gang gave him his old job back and said something like, "Hello there, Brock. Glad to see you back." He said they'd treated him nice. I couldn't imagine them treating him nice, because I didn't know anybody in the South who was treated nice, let alone on a chain gang. Still, Papa said the chain gang was good. I wanted to smack him. If he weren't my grandfather, I would have.

I felt sorry for Pimp, and I wished I were making a whole lot of money and could say, "Come on, man. Live with me and get away from that Harlem scene, and perhaps you can do something." But before he made the move from Harlem, he'd have to know where he was going, every step of the way, all by himself.

He was lost in that house. Nobody there even really knew he was alive. Mama and Dad were only concerned about the numbers coming out. Papa, since he was so old, would just sit around and look for the number in Ching Chow's ear in the newspaper comic section. When the number came out, he'd say, "I knew that number was comin'. I could've told you before."

I used to watch Pimp sometimes when I'd go up there. Papa would be talking this stuff about the number, and it seemed to be just paining Pimp. It hadn't bothered me that much. But I suppose it couldn't have. I used to be kind of glad that they were involved in this stuff. I guess I had an arrogant attitude toward the family. I saw them all as farmers. It made me feel good that they were involved in this stuff, because then they couldn't be aware of what I was doing and what was going down. The more they got involved in that old voodoo, the farther they got away from me and what I was doing out in the street.

Papa used to make me mad with, "Who was that old boy you was with today, that old tar-black boy?" Mama used to say things like that about people too, but I never felt that she was really color struck. Sometimes I used to get mad when she'd say things about people and their complexion, but she always treated all the people we brought up to the house real nice, regardless of whether they were dark- or light-skinned.

I knew that Pimp was at an age when he'd be bringing his friends around, and Papa would be talking that same stuff about, "Who's that black so-and-so?" If you brought somebody to the house who was real light-skinned, Papa would say, "They're nice," or "They're nice lookin'." All he meant was that the people were light-skinned.

I remember one time when Papa was telling his favorite story about how he could have passed for white when he first came to New York and moved down on the Lower East Side. He became a janitor of a building there. He said everybody thought he was white until they saw Uncle McKay, Mama's brother and Papa's son. He was about my complexion or a little lighter than I was, but anybody could tell he was colored. Papa said if it wasn't for McKay, he could have passed for white. This story used to get on my nerves, and I thought it was probably bothering Pimp now too. Sometimes I wanted to tell him, "Shit, man, why don't you just go on someplace where you can pass for white, if that's the way you feel about it? And stop sitting here with all us real colored niggers and talkin' about it." But if I'd ever said that, Mama would have been mad at me for the rest of my life.

I wondered if it was good for him to be around all that old crazy talk, because I imagined that all my uncles who were dark-skinned—Uncle McKay, Uncle Ted, Uncle Brother—felt that Papa didn't care too much for them because they were dark-skinned, and I supposed that Pimp might have gotten that feeling too. I had the feeling that this wasn't anyplace for kids to be around, with some crazy old man talking all that stuff about light skin and how he could have passed for white and calling people black.

Many times, Mama and I talked about Pimp. She'd say, "I don't know what's gon happen to that boy." She'd always be telling him he was going to get into trouble.

I wanted to say, "Why don't you leave him alone and stop talking that?" She'd say, "That boy's gon be up in Warwick just as sure as I'm livin'."

I said, "Mama, look, don't be puttin' the bad mouth on him." I could tell her about the bad mouth, because this was something she knew, and she'd get mad. This was the only way to stop her from talking that stuff sometimes.

She'd say, "Boy, what's wrong with you? You think I'd put some bad mouth on my children?" She'd get real excited about it.

I'd say, "Look, Mama, that's just what you're doin'. The police ain't sayin' he's goin' to Warwick; the judge ain't said he's goin' to Warwick; nobody's sayin' he's goin' to Warwick but you."

She'd say, "I'm trying to stop him from goin' out of here gettin' into some trouble."

I said, "Mama, ain't nobody talkin' about him goin' out of here gettin' into some trouble. Ain't nobody talkin' about him doin' nothin' but you. You're the only one who says he's gonna get in trouble. You're the only one who says the police gon get him soon and that he's gonna go to Warwick. Nobody's sayin' it but you; and all that amounts to is the bad mouth, because you're saying it before anything's happening."

Tears would come to her eyes, and she'd stop talking about it. That was good, because all I wanted to do was stop her from talking that nonsense about Pimp getting in trouble and going to Warwick and all that kind of foolishness. I knew that talking about the bad mouth would bother her. I didn't like to be mean to Mama, but this was something she understood. I knew she had all these boogeyman ideas in her head.

With Dad, I suppose it was just as bad at home. He would never read anything but the *Daily News*, and he always read about somebody cutting up somebody or killing somebody. He liked to read about the people in the neighborhood, and he'd point the finger at them. He'd say, "There goes another one." Just let it be one of my friends and, oh, man, he'd ride Pimp about it.

He'd say, "You remember that old no-good boy Sonny use to hang out with? He went to the chair last night," or "He got killed in a stickup someplace." He'd tell him, "You remember that old boy Sonny Boy use to bring up here years ago?" Pimp would never answer. "Well, they found him around there in the backyard on 146th Street dead, with a needle in his arm, last night. All of 'em just killin' theirselves. They ain't no damn good, and they ain't never had no sense. They didn't have enough sense to go out there and get a job, like somebody who knows something, and act halfway decent. They just gon hang out around here and rob the decent people, and break into people's houses. Somebody had to kill them, if they didn't kill theirselves. So I suppose they just might as well go ahead and use too much of that stuff and kill theirselves, no-good damn bums, old triflin', roguish dope addicts. They all ought to kill theirselves."

He'd be preaching this at Pimp as though he were one of them. It bothered Pimp. It would bother anybody. Dad never messed with me with this sort of thing. I was on my own, I was clean, and I was certain that I had as much money in my pocket as he had, if not more. I was his equal, and he couldn't run down all that nonsense to me.

Living in that house wasn't too hard on Carole and Margie, but for a boy it must have been terribly hard. Everybody was far away, way back in the woods. If Mama heard that one of her friends had come home and found her husband in the bed with some other woman, she'd say, "She should've poured some lye on her." If somebody had poured some lye on her, she'd say, "Yeah, that was good for that old heifer, that old no-good whorish hussy."

This was the way they felt about it. This was all the stuff that came from the backwoods. I suppose the Harlem tradition, the way of life in Harlem, had come from the backwoods. All that mixing up lye and throwing it in somebody's face, all that was just as backwoods as working roots. These people just seemed to believe in that, like cutting somebody's throat. They didn't seem to be ready for urban life.

They were going to try to guide us and make us do right and be good, and they didn't even know what being good was. When I was a little boy, Mama and Dad would beat me and tell me, "You better be good," but I didn't know what being good was. To me, it meant that they just wanted me to sit down and fold my hands or something crazy like that. Stay in front of the house, don't go anyplace, don't get into trouble. I didn't know what it meant, and I don't think they knew what it meant, because they couldn't ever tell me what they really wanted. The way I saw it, everything I was doing was good. If I stole something and didn't get caught, I was good. If I got into a fight with somebody, I tried to be good enough to beat him. If

I broke into a place, I tried to be quiet and steal as much as I could. I was always trying to be good. They just kept on beating me and talking about being good. And I just kept on doing what I was doing and kept on trying to do it good.

They needed some help. The way I felt about it, I should have been their parents, because I had been out there on the streets, and I wasn't as far back in the woods as they were. I could have told them a whole lot of stuff that would have helped them, Mama and Dad and Papa, everybody, if they had only listened to me.

I remember how Dad thought being a busboy was a real good job. When I was working at Hamburger Heaven, I stayed there for a year, and I don't know how I did it. I was working for nine hours a day, six days a week, and going to school at night. He still felt that this was a good job, because he'd never made any money. He'd never made more than sixty dollars a week in his life until recently. I suppose when he was my age, he was only making something like thirty dollars a week and thought it was a whole lot of money. He figured if I was making forty-five dollars a week, that was a whole lot of money. The cat was crazy. I would spend forty-five dollars on a pair of shoes. To him it was a good job because when he was nine years old, he'd plowed the fields from sunup to sundown.

I came in one night and told Mama. I said, "Mama, I'm gon quit this job at Hamburger Heaven, because it's getting too damn hard on me."

Dad was sitting over in the corner in his favorite chair reading the newspaper. He wouldn't look up, because we could never talk. We just never talked too much after we had our last fight.

I said I was going to school, and that plus the job was kind of rough on me.

After Dad couldn't take any more, he lifted his head out of the paper and said, "Boy, you don't need all that education. You better keep that job, because that's a good job."

"Yeah, Dad, it's good as long as you can take it, but if it kills you, there's nothing good about that."

He said, "Hard work ain't never killed nobody, unless they was so lazy that thinkin' about it killed 'em."

I said, "I know one thing. It's not gon kill me now, because I already quit it."

He said, "Yeah, well, it sure seems funny to me, you quittin' your job, talkin' about you can't do that and go to school. You ought to stop goin' to school. You didn't want to go to school when I was sendin' you there. Your Mama would take you in one door and you'd sneak out the other door. Even the truant officer couldn't keep you in school. Boy, I think you're dreamin'. You better stop all that dreamin' and go out there and get yourself a good job and keep it while you got it."

I knew that I couldn't talk to him and tell him what was really on my mind without going to battle with him, so I just said, "Yeah, Dad," to end it right there.

I remember when Pimp was thirteen or fourteen. He was in the eighth grade. He came home one day and said, "Mama, I think I'm gonna become an Air Force pilot and fly a jet plane." It seemed a normal thing that any little boy might say to his mother and get some kind of encouragement, but that didn't happen in Pimp's case.

Mama told him, "Boy, don't you go wantin' things that ain't for you. You just go out there and get you a good job." A good job to Mama was a job making fifty or sixty dollars a week, and that was as much as any-body should have wanted, in Mama's opinion. Sixty dollars was damn good money. That was enough to retire off, the way they used to talk about it.

I guess I could understand their feeling this way. Their lives were lived according to the superstitions and fears that they had been taught when they were children coming up in the Carolina cotton fields. It was all right for them down there, in that time, in that place, but it wasn't worth a damn up in New York. I could understand why Mama couldn't understand Pimp and his troubles, because Mama had only gone through the fifth grade. Dad had only gone through the fourth grade. How could they understand Pimp when they couldn't even read his textbooks?

Mama and Dad and the people who had come to New York from the South about the time they did seemed to think it was wrong to want any-thing more out of life than some liquor and a good piece of cunt on Satur-day night. This was the stuff they did in the South. This was the sort of life they had lived on the plantations. They were trying to bring the down-home life up to Harlem. They had done it. But it just wasn't working. They couldn't understand it, and they weren't about to understand it. Liquor, religion, sex, and violence—this was all that life had been about to them. And a prayer that the right number would come out, that somebody would hit the sweepstakes or get lucky.

It seemed as though if I had stayed in Harlem all my life, I might have never known that there was anything else to life other than sex, religion, liquor, and violence. Sometimes I would try to tell Mama things in the slang terms. They had their own down-home slang expressions. I couldn't understand theirs too much, and they couldn't understand ours. The slang had changed. In this day when somebody would say something about a bad cat, they meant that he was good. Somebody would say, "That was some bad pot," meaning it was good. You really got high. Or somebody would go to the movie and see Sidney Poitier in a film, and they'd say, "Man, that's a bad-doin' nigger." They didn't mean that he was running out in the street cutting somebody's throat, carrying a gun, and cursing. But this was all that a bad nigger meant to Mama and Dad and the people their age. It was the bad-nigger concept from the South, but it didn't mean that any more.

I couldn't get it over to Mama that things were changing. The bad nigger to my generation was a cat like Paul Robeson. To Mama, that was a nigger who was crazy, who would go out and marry some white woman. Mama and Dad would associate a nigger like this with the ones they saw hanging from a pine tree down in the Carolina woods with blood on his pants. They'd say this wasn't a bad nigger to them, this was a crazy nigger, one that was going to get himself hanged.

I could sense the fear in Mama's voice when I told her once that I wanted to be a psychologist.

She said, "Boy, you better stop that dreamin' and get all those crazy notions outta your head." She was scared. She had the idea that colored people weren't supposed to want anything like that. You were supposed to just want to work in fields or be happy to be a janitor.

I remember something she told Pimp. I think she thought she was giving Pimp something that he needed, and she felt big about it. "Now if you just get a job as a janitor, I'll be happy and satisfied," she said.

I jumped up when she said this, and I said, "Doesn't it matter whether he's satisfied or how he feels about it?"

Mama and Dad looked at me as if in two minutes' time I'd be ready for Bellevue, or maybe they'd better call right away. They'd always look at me and say, "You better stop talkin' all that foolishness, boy. What's wrong with you? You better get all that stuff out of your head."

I remember the times I tried to explain these things to Mama, just what was happening in Harlem, just what was happening between my generation and hers. I would tell her, "Look, Mama, don't you remember when I use to play hookey from school, steal things, and stay out all night? Do you know why I was doin' that?"

She would look at me and ask, "Yeah, why?" sarcastically, as if I couldn't possibly tell her anything. I didn't understand anything that she couldn't understand.

I'd tell her about rebellion, and she'd say, "Look, don't be tellin' me about no rebellions and all that kind of business. You might know some big words, but you don't know what you're talkin' about. I know a whole lot of people go around using them old big words, and they don't know a damn thing what it's all about."

I'd say, "Look, Mama, when people start ruling people and they rule 'em wrong, in a way that's harmful to them, they have to stop them. They've got to rebel; they've got to get out from under their rule. Sometimes it requires a fight, but it's always going to require a little bit of commotion, a little bit of anger, and sometimes violence.

"You've got to stop them before they destroy you. That's all that's going on around here. Everybody is rebelling. You see all the young boys going around here using drugs. They're rebelling, that's all it is. They're rebelling against their parents. If there were any drugs around here when I was a little boy, I would've been using 'em too. I had to rebel. I had to get away from all that old down-home nonsense you been talking."

She'd say, "Boy, you don't know anything about that, and you ain't got no business calling it nonsense."

"Yeah, uh-huh. That's okay, Mama. Look, I'm trying to explain to you how this is. You gon listen?"

"I am listening, but I ain't hearing nothin' but a whole lot of foolishness."

I'd say something like, "Mama, you know and I know, these parents are talking about being good and doing right, but they're not being good. You know everybody is screwin' somebody's wife or screwin' somebody's husband around here."

"You must know more about what's goin' on around here than I do, 'cause I don't know no such thing."

"Look, Mama, don't you realize that whenever anybody starts talkin' some nonsense about 'be good, be good' and you can see that they're not bein' good, you're not gon pay too much attention to it? Right?"

She knew I was right, but she just didn't want to hear it. She'd say something like, "Boy, what you talkin' about?"

And I'd have to shout and say, "I'm talking about how you gon tell kids to be good when the kids are too hip not to see that the parents aren't being so good their damn selves!"

She'd say, "Now, you wait a minute here, nigger. Don't you be gettin' so smart with me!" This was the way the discussion always went.

After I stopped and looked real disgusted, Mama would be ready to listen then. She would try to smooth my ruffled feathers. She'd say, "You mean to tell me that the only reason these kids is going around here messin' up, killin' themselves, and causin' their families a whole lotta trouble is that everybody's preachin' one thing and doin' another?"

I'd say, "It's something like that, but not all. Listen, what you mean is they're causin' their parents a lot of trouble. This is the way that most parents look at it. I don't think any parents look at the situation as if they could be causin' the kids some trouble and causin' them some embarrassment because they're going out doing the things that they're not suppose to do. But this is just what's happenin'."

Mama would say, "Ain't no kids got no business judgin' their parents."

"Mama, a lot of 'em aren't judgin' 'em. They're just going out and doing what they want to do too. They're not judgin' them; they're just gettin' revenge."

"Well, they ain't got no business tryin' to get revenge, because parents are grown, and they ain't got to answer to nobody's children." Then Mama would get all wound up, and she wouldn't listen to anything.

The attempts at discussion always ended with me feeling more depressed about Pimp. I wondered if Pimp was going to be able to get a job in about a year, because he kept talking about quitting school and making some money. I didn't think he was ready to go downtown. But he had to, because there wasn't any money to be made uptown, not honestly. If he quit school, there was nothing for him to do but go down to the garment center and push one of those trucks, like everybody else who quit school.

I wondered if he'd been listening to the cats on the street when they talked against going downtown. If he had, it would be twice as hard, because the stuff that those cats used to talk about that downtown thing was strong stuff for a young boy's mind, a young colored boy.

I remember Reno used to say, "Man, I'll never come out of jail owin' any time. They'll just have to keep me until I can walk away clean, not owin' nothin' to nobody, 'cause I don't want to go downtown. Goldberg is never gonna get over me with the whip."

This was the first time I'd ever heard "Goldberg" used this way. I said, "Who's Goldberg?"

"You know. Mr. Jew. That's the cat who runs the garment center."

"Oh, yeah." But I didn't get the connection right away.

"Goldberg ain't gon ever get up off any money. Goldberg's just as bad as Mr. Charlie. He's got all the money in the world, Sonny, believe it or not. Look across the street. He owns the liquor store, he owns the bar, he owns the restaurant across there, the grocery there. He owns all the liquor stores in Harlem, 'cause that's where all the niggers' money goes, and he's gon get all that."

"Yeah, man. You may have a point there."

"I know I got a point, man." He really got excited. He said, "The only time I'm goin' downtown, man, I'm goin' to steal me some money from Goldberg, not to beg him for it. That's just what you're doin', man. That cat's got all the money in the world, and what he'll give you is carfare back downtown for another day's slavery."

"The only way you gon get some-a that real money from him is to get you a gun, go down there and put it to that mother-fucker's head, and take it. That's the only way you gon get any of that dough from Goldberg."

I used to listen to Reno sometimes, and I'd get scared behind the way he use to get all excited. I'd say, "Cool it, man. This stuff is not to be told too loud, because the kids might hear it."

If Reno was in a bad mood—if he didn't have any money and he wasn't high—he'd say, "Man, Sonny, they ain't got no kids in Harlem. I ain't never seen any. I've seen some real small people actin' like kids. They were too small to be grown, and they might've looked like kids, but they don't have any kids in Harlem, because nobody has time for a childhood. Man, do you ever remember bein' a kid? Not me. Shit, kids are happy, kids laugh, kids are secure. They ain't scared-a nothin'. You ever been a kid, Sonny? Damn, you lucky. I ain't never been a kid, man. I don't ever remember bein' happy and not scared. I don't know what happened, man, but I think I missed out on that childhood thing, because I don't ever recall bein' a kid."

The only way I could stop Reno when he got wound up like this was to say, "Come on, man. Let's go get a drink," or "Let's go get high." That would take him down off his soapbox.

Reno was only one. There were a whole lot of other cats out there who felt the same way that Reno felt about going downtown, about working for Goldberg.

I remember when I was down in the garment center and used to see George Baxter down there. He used to tell me, and the cat would be almost crying, "Man, a cat got to take a whole lotta shit for fifty dollars a week." Just about every time I saw him, he'd say, "Man, I don't think the stuff that a man has to take down here is worth fifty dollars a week; it's worth a lot more, at least ten times more."

He used to say that he was going to leave, that he was going to get up off of this thing. But I didn't think he was going to leave the garment center, because Baxter was sort of a nice guy. But he did. He was one of the guys I knew who tried it and gave it up to come back uptown and deal drugs. There was more money in it. Cats used to say it made them feel better than being down there, being messed over by Goldberg all the time.

I remember Baxter used to say all the time, when I'd meet him uptown after he'd given up the garment-center gig, "Man, if you keep goin' downtown every day, you'll be a boy all your life. I use to be afraid, Sonny, I use to be deathly afraid of bein' a boy all my life. I use to have nightmares, man, about me bein' old, about sixty years old and almost bent, knockin' around there, sweeping the floors for Goldberg in that dress house of his. He's comin' in there pattin' me on my back and callin' me 'boy,' sayin', 'Come over here with your broom and sweep up this thing for me, boy.' It use to get to me. I use to jump up out of bed screamin', 'Mr. Goldberg, please, Mr. Goldberg, don't call me boy. Please, Mr. Goldberg, don't pat me on my back.'

"Sonny, I think if I had stayed down there in that garment center much longer, man, and continued to be Goldberg's boy, I might've lost my mind. I had to get outta there."

Before he got busted, he used to say, "Man, I might not be out here on the streets for long. I'm gamblin' and I know I'm gamblin'. Every time I come out of my house, I got to look around for the Man. Before I go in my house, I got to look around to see if any junkies are waitin' to sting me. I got to be careful about everybody who comes up to me and asks me for a sale. I'm livin' on pins and needles, man, but I can stand up a whole lot straighter. Nobody calls me a boy, and I know even when the Man walks up on me and busts me out here, he's gon do it in a fashion that I can appreciate.

"If they take me downtown and put me in the lineup, they're not gonna say 'boy.' They're gonna say, 'Stand there.' If a cat ever runs up on me in a hallway and says, 'Freeze, nigger,' he's not gonna say, 'Freeze, nigger boy.' Man, the nigger thing is all right, but the boy thing, that's too goddamn hard to live with, Sonny. It was almost killin' me, man; it was almost killin' me.

"You go down there into this thing—I guess I had a boss as nice as anybody—and Goldberg would say, 'George, do you know where I might find some nice honest colored girl who could come in and help my wife clean up the house?' He didn't mean help, man, he meant somebody who would come in and actually clean up the house for his wife. It was a drag, man. He said the other girl had to leave because her daughter was having a baby. He said, 'You saw the girl who was here. She was a very nice girl, and she'd been with us for a long time, for three or four years.'

"Man, you should've seen this girl. This girl was about sixty years old. Her hair was gray, but she was colored, so she was still a girl. She was twice the age of Goldberg's wife. It hurt me, man, when I saw her. This colored girl was sixty years old, and she was cleanin' this house for his wife. I felt like, damn, if that was my wife, I'd beat her ass and make her help that woman clean up that house, man. But I knew, after I saw that woman and he'd asked me if I knew some girl who could help his wife, I wanted to say, 'Hell, no!' But I needed the job, so all I could say was, 'No, man, I don't know any girls. I don't know nothin'. I don't know anything about that.' I felt like I was gon lose my mind if I had stayed in that stuff.

"I don't remember my father too well. He use to work on the docks, and he died in the chair, man. I guess you knew; everybody in the neighborhood heard about it. He died behind some gray cat tryin' to fuck over him, tryin' to make him look like a Tom. It's somethin' I've always had a big thing about, man. And my brothers, they can't stand to be around gray people. That's why they all stand around 143rd Street and take numbers. I guess we couldn't make it outside of some Harlem somewhere. We weren't cut out to play that boy role. I suppose there's a lot of people who aren't."

As I used to listen to George, I'd think I had fallen in there and played that role without giving it much thought. But then I became aware of what I knew about the garment center and about Goldberg and his relationship to the Negro, the "boy" who worked for him. I had the feeling that he never saw us. He never saw our generation. He saw us only through the impressions that the older folks had made.

He never even tried to see us, and he tried to treat us the way he had treated them. Most of the older folks were used to it. They didn't know

Goldberg from Massa Charlie; to them, Goldberg was Massa Charlie. I suppose the tradition had been perpetuated when the folks moved to the North and took the image of Massa Charlie and put it into Goldberg. Perhaps Goldberg was unaware of it.

When I worked at the watch repair shop, if I said anything that would indicate that I thought a little of myself, or if I didn't seem damn grateful when somebody said, "I'm gonna give you a five-dollar bonus for Christmas," they all seemed to think that I was being arrogant in some way or another. They all seemed to feel, What is wrong with this nigger? They all seemed to have the impression that niggers weren't supposed to act like that. They'd think, This nigger's crazy. What kind of Negro is he? Doesn't he know his place?

In the evening, I'd run out of the shop with my books in my hand and say I was going to school, and they would crack jokes about it, as if to say, "This Negro must be dreaming. Doesn't he know that Negroes are supposed to just be porters?"

It wasn't just our parents and Goldberg who weren't ready for my generation. Our parents' coming to Harlem produced a generation of new niggers. Not only Goldberg and our parents didn't understand this new nigger, but this new nigger was something that nobody understood and that nobody was ready for.

There was trouble everywhere, every time. Everyplace I looked, I wasn't understood. I felt like a misfit on just about every job I went to. Everyplace I went, it was like a first time. It was always a new thing. I always had to establish a new relationship with everyone. I always had to find out where I was and what things were like. I always wanted to run. It was so difficult. There was nothing that was old. I really didn't have any familiar ground. I guess, in a way, my generation was like the first Africans coming over on the boat. There was still the language problem. The Harlem dialect was something that I was a little afraid to use. When I first went down to the gym on Broadway in mid-Manhattan, I was very self-conscious about it.

I knew that these were gray boys, and I felt I had to be careful around them or else I might frighten them. Sometimes I was made to feel silly. I was careful to pronounce my r's and say "you are" and "you're not." I'd say, "Hello. How are you?" very properly. Occasionally somebody would say, "Hi, How you doin'?" and I'd feel ridiculous. There was always this uncertainty, this thing of feeling your way through. I became aware that I was a new thing. The average cat who ventured out of Harlem would be afraid and run back. It was safer dealing drugs or doing something like that. And there was much less embarrassment.

I couldn't take my job in the watch repair shop after a while. Everybody was reading the papers about the Emmett Till case, and they'd say, "Gee, that's terrible." But I knew that if I went out to the Flatbush section of Brooklyn or Brighton Beach, where all these cats lived, they'd probably lynch the landlord if he rented me an apartment. This was the relationship between the Jew and the descendants of Ham. We were all right. We were supposed to work for them; we were good enough for this, good enough to clean their houses. They were supposed to sympathize with us. I think sometimes the sympathy used to bother me more than anything else, this attempt at being liberal-minded.

I just got tired of it one day. I felt I was going to crack up, just blow up. I said, "Look, I'm tired. You take this job; you just take it and shove it," and I walked out of the shop. I didn't know where I was going. I didn't have any money; I didn't have anything, but I couldn't feel too bad about it or the least bit frightened. I was aware that I hadn't had anything all my life. I'd had jobs, money, and expensive clothes, but I still hadn't had anything.

I didn't even have a slight understanding of what it was all about, what I was trying to accomplish, what I was supposed to accomplish. I had no idea of where I was going. I went to Central Park and started walking around. I didn't understand anything about me. It was crazy to expect Goldberg to understand. I couldn't feel any kind of animosity toward anybody, toward anybody in the world. I'd hoped that one day I could go back and say, "I'm sorry if I offended you people," and that they would forgive me. I realized that I had said some pretty nasty things to them. They were all little people, and I was demanding that they suddenly become big, tremendous, and understand this gigantic problem that the entire nation was trying to resolve and had been struggling with for years.

I was demanding, "Now, look, Goldberg, look here, now. You understand this problem because you've been here all this time. You've been close to me. My mother been buying the pig tails and the neck bones from you as long as I can remember. She's been paying you the rent, she's been pawning stuff to you whenever we got up tight. So if anybody should give us some kind of understanding, you should."

But Goldberg didn't owe us anything. If I had said this to him, he probably would have said, "Look, what do you want from me? What do you want? I owe you nothing." And he would have been right, because he didn't owe me anything. I had been demanding a whole lot of understanding, but, shit, I didn't understand him, so why should he understand me?

One night I stayed uptown, and about six o'clock in the morning I left to go home to get a bath and shave and go look for a job that day. I planned to go to school that evening. I had a little briefcase with me, with my French textbook in it, and a couple of notebooks.

I was coming up 145th Street toward Eighth Avenue, and I heard somebody call me. It was Jake Snipes. He was coming out of a Japanese restaurant with a takeout order. I said, "Hey, Jake, how you doin'? What you doin' out so early in the mornin'?"

He started telling me about his chick who wanted some chop suey. "At five-thirty in the mornin'. Ain't that just like a bitch, man?"

"Yeah, man, that's just like a bitch. You sure she's all right?"

"Man, she better be all right. This chick's got to make me some money."

I smiled. Jake was a pimp.

"Damn, Sonny, you look kind of under the weather, man. What's it all about?"

"Man, I got to get out here and find me a gig."

"Damn, man, why don't you stop workin'? All your troubles'd be over."

"I'm not like you, Jake. I don't have any chicks out here hustlin' for me. I got to get me a job and work. That's the only way I know, man."

"Damn, Sonny, you sure changed a whole lot."

"Yeah, well, that sort of thing will happen, and sometimes you can't do anything about it."

"Look, Sonny, why don't you come on up to my house, man? I got a freak up there. You get in the bed with this chick one time, and I guarantee you that you'll lose your mind. You'll probably want to fight me over this woman."

I knew he was just trying to cheer me up, so I smiled and said, "Man, I know it before I even go up there. I'm so sure of it, Jake, that I don't even have to try it."

"Look here, Sonny," and he pulled something out of his pocket. "I want you to taste that."

It was a tinfoil, and I knew what was in it. I said, "Coke, huh?"

"It's not just coke. Look at it."

I opened it, and it was brown cocaine.

"Sonny, when was the last time you had some brown cocaine? It couldn't have been recently, because there ain't been none in the city in the last four months."

"No, it hasn't been recently, Jake. It's really been a long time, man."

"Look, man, forget about that job and come on up to my crib. I'll turn you on to a freak; she is a stone animal, Sonny. She'll mess your mind up. You'll never want to leave there, and behind some of this good cocaine, you just might decide to stop workin' altogether."

"Okay, Jake. Fuck it, man. I'll just take you up on that."

"Good, good," and we started walking.

He said, "What you got in the briefcase, man?"

"Oh, just a textbook and some notebooks. I go to school in the evening."

"Oh, yeah? You really sold on that thing, huh?"

I said, "Well, it's somethin' new, man. It's somethin' else to do."

"Yeah, man, you always were one for books."

We were walking toward Eighth Avenue, and as we got near the corner, a little boy was coming up the street walking his dog. I didn't pay any attention to the little boy and the dog until they stopped right in front of me. Jake walked on and waited a few paces away.

I looked down at the boy. He was looking at me and smiling. Suddenly he just said, "Hey, what do you do?"

"Who are you? A member of the police department or somebody?" I said it jokingly.

He said, "No. I just want to know what you do."

"Why do you want to know what I do?"

He said, " 'Cause I want to do it too. I want to be like you."

I looked at him, and I was kind of surprised, because I didn't recall ever seeing him before. I asked him, "Why do you want to be like me? Have you ever seen me before?"

He said, "Yeah, I saw you a lot of times."

I was kind of moved by the whole thing, but at the same time I was a little hurt because I couldn't say anything to him that might have been inspiring to him or given him something to set his sights on. I said, "Would you do me a favor?"

He said, "Yeah." He smiled and looked real anxious, as if he was glad I'd asked him.

I said, "Would you just go on down the street, keep walking your dog, and don't want to be like me? I'm just lookin' for a dog to walk. All my life, I've been lookin' for a dog to walk."

He looked kind of sad. He walked around me and pulled his dog.

I felt different. I'd forgotten about the job and all that sort of thing. I'd forgotten about Jake too. I looked down the street after the little boy had gone. He'd only walked away about a minute before. I looked down the street, and he was gone. I didn't even remember what his face looked like. All I remembered was the little dog. It was a white dog, the kind they used to have in my first-grade reader, the kind nice little white kids would have, a little white dog with a black patch on his eye. And they would call him Spot.

I stood there thinking for a while, wondering if there were any other little boys who watched me and wanted to be like me. I was hoping that there weren't any others, not yet anyway. As I stood there, just thinking, I heard Jake's voice calling me.

He said, "Come on, Sonny. You comin'?" I walked up to him. Jake was getting ready to turn the corner, and he asked me, "What was that all about?"

I said, "That was about what I've got to do, man. I got to go."

"Where you gon go, man. I thought you'd forgot about the job for now. I thought you were gon come on up and knock off this bitch and get high off this cocaine."

"No, Jake, thanks anyway, but I don't have time for freaks right now, and I don't have time for any cocaine right now. I've got to go and do something, and I've got to do it before another little boy with a dog comes up and asks me what I do."

He looked at me in that peculiar sort of way I had come to expect, the way the cats on the block looked at me when I first started telling them that I was going to evening high school and that I was going to stop dealing drugs. They all looked at me and said, "Yeah, man," with a look in their eye that said, "Is this cat crackin' up?"

Jake looked at me and smiled and said, "Okay, Sonny. Take it easy, man. I'll see you around."

"Later, Jake, and thanks, man, thanks anyway."

I didn't see any more of Jake after that. I heard about three months later that he'd gotten busted for using drugs. It was the same old story.

It was good to see Turk. I'd see him and he'd tell me about his upcoming fights. He was doing good. He'd started knocking out some pretty good light heavyweights. It did me good to see him around and know that it could be done. He was living proof that we could make it—the cats who had come our way in Harlem and had thrown the bricks that we had thrown in our youth. We weren't all cursed or destined to end up in jail.

I suppose that I was the living proof of it to him too. Whenever I saw him, we talked for a long time. I could tell him my dreams. He was the only one who could accept me as I was, and he wouldn't say, "Well, damn, Sonny, you've changed," or look at me in that peculiar way.

I could accept his dreams. When he told me that he was going to become heavyweight boxing champion of the world, I believe it. I guess I wanted to believe it, because I wanted him to believe me when I told him what I was going to do.

It became a thing. Whenever I started feeling sad or that everybody was losing out in Harlem or that all Harlem was going to pot and nobody was making it any more, I'd go to the Uptown Gym, on 125th Street, and I'd watch Turk work out. I'd talk to him afterward. We'd have a cup of coffee or a glass of wine, and we'd talk about our plans. I always felt good afterward.

The gym was right next to the Apollo Theatre, and one day when I was with Turk, I happened to bump into someone going into the Apollo. As I turned around to apologize, I looked right into Rickets' face. It was the first time I'd seen him since I'd left Wiltwyck. I grabbed him, and he grabbed me. We were real excited. I introduced him to Turk, and they said hello. I told him we were going over to a restaurant to have a cup of coffee and asked him to come along.

He said, no, he was going into the Apollo, but give him my address and he'd come around. He asked me if I was working, and I told him that I wasn't. I told him that I was just up there visiting and watching some people.

He asked me what was I doing, and I told him, "Nothing, just knocking about." I had gotten out of the habit of telling people I hadn't seen in years that I was going to school. I just didn't think any of them took it seriously enough. Most of the cats would laugh at it, and then the word would get around. I couldn't tell anybody that any more.

I told him that I just wasn't doing anything, and I asked him where he had been. He looked at Turk, and I guess he figured he was all right, so he said, "Man, I just got out of Sing Sing. I did three years on a one-to-five bid. Damn, man, everybody is up there, and all the cats are lookin' for you, man, askin' about you."

When he said this, Turk sort of laughed, and he said, "Yeah, Sonny, I guess you're missed, man."

"Yeah, well, tell them not to give up hope, Rickets, when you go back, because I may get there yet."

"Yeah, man, cats put out stories about you were doin' time in another state. Somebody said you'd gotten killed. They had a whole lot of stories about you going around up there."

He told me that K.B. was up there, that there were a lot of my friends up there. While he was talking, I said, "Stop it, man, you tryin' to make me homesick or somethin'?"

"It's pretty nice up at Sing Sing."

"Damn, how nice can it be?"

"I mean, you know, just about every cat is up there."

He went on into the Apollo, and Turk and I walked on down the street. Turk said, "You know, Sonny, sometimes when I think about all the other cats, like Dunny and Tito and Mac and Alley Bush and Bucky, it's like, man, I feel as though I'm one of the luckiest people in the world. I know that somewhere in my life I must have done something good for somebody, because if I hadn't . . . I'm walkin' around here free, and all those cats, they didn't raise any more hell than I did. . . . I don't think anybody cared any more for me than they cared for them, but I'm here, man, so it had to be only by luck."

I said, "Yeah, man, I can understand that. You know I can, because I'm alive by luck."

Turk looked at me and smiled. He knew. We had a whole lot in common that I didn't have with other cats. The one time in my life when I was most afraid of dying, Turk was with me. Perhaps it was the most dramatic moment in my life, and maybe it had had a great impact on him too. We had this experience together, and it was a bond.

I remember when I first came back from the hospital, most of the other cats thought that Turk and I wouldn't like each other any more because I had squealed on him that he was with me when I got shot. And I was pissed off at him because when I got shot, he'd just asked me if I was going to tell the law that he was with me. But for some reason or another, I just wasn't mad at Turk, and he wasn't mad at me.

The first time I saw him after I got back, he was down in the cellar of 2754. Everybody used to go down there and get high. This was our hangout. I walked in there, and all the fellows greeted me with, "Hey, Sonny." Everybody but Turk started rushing to me. He stayed back in the crowd. He looked at me as if he didn't know if he should speak to me or if I was going to speak to him or what. I didn't know exactly how I felt about it either, but after a while, when everybody else came around and started greeting me as if I were a celebrity, I felt as though I had to go over and say something to Turk and let him know how I felt about it, that it could have been me or it could have been him.

If he had gotten shot, I might have taken the same attitude that he took about me. I suppose it was just the thing to do. He might have told on me; maybe he wouldn't have. But I didn't have any hard feelings about it. I just walked over to him, and I stuck out my hand. He said, "Hi, Sonny." And we smiled.

After that, Turk and I were tighter than anybody.

12

I saw Danny a few nights after that. We talked and had a drink. As I was getting ready to go, Danny said, "Have another one on me, Sonny."

"No, thanks, Danny. I got to make it. I'm still a workin' man."

"Yeah, I know that. I think it's kind of nice too." He smiled. "Wait a minute, Sonny. Have one more drink."

When Danny did that, I had the feeling that I was supposed to stay, that there might have been somebody waiting for me outside or something and he was trying to keep me from it. I said, "Yeah, man. I got about another fifteen minutes to blow." I sat down, back at the bar with him. I had another drink, and Danny kept looking in the mirror, watching everything behind him.

When the bartender poured another two, Danny thanked the cat and looked down at his glass. Then he said, "Sonny, how's Pimp doin'?"

When Danny asked that, I got scared. I had a feeling why he asked me to sit down, and I had a feeling that he'd been wanting to say something about this all night. I said, "He's doin' fine, man, as far as I know. I haven't seen him in a good little while, but I know he's still got a nice job."

Danny said, "Yeah, I've seen him sometimes, and he seems to be dressin' nice, so he must be into things."

I said, "Yeah, I'm a little disappointed in the cat, though, because he wouldn't finish school. I tried to get him to go back to school in the evening, but he says he's not ready to do that yet. He keeps talkin' that talk about he might go back later on and that kind of shit. You know how that is."

"Yeah, Sonny. I know how that is," and he looked back down at his glass.

"Why, Danny? Have you seen him lately?"

"Oh, yeah. I see him around most of the time, Sonny. He seems to be lookin' good to me, man; he's takin' care of himself, you know, stayin' clean."

"Yeah, uh-huh, that's what I thought, man. I hope he is."

"Yeah, how old is he now, anyway, Sonny?"

"Pimp's about seventeen."

Danny said, "That's a bad age, you know, Sonny. That's a real bad age, man, for a young cat to be at in Harlem, you know. You come out of your house and you're seventeen years old, you come out on Eighth Avenue, you feel like you're a stud on trial, man, on trial by the world."

"Yeah, Danny, I guess any age that's young is bad in Harlem. What makes seventeen such a bad age for Pimp, Danny?" I kept looking straight at Danny, trying to look at Danny's eyes. They never came up. He kept avoiding my stare. I said, "Danny, you know, I expect, man, if you got anything on your mind, I expect you to tell me. If you didn't, I'd be kind of pissed off. You know how we've always been, man. If I was ever in a joint and somebody ever fucked with my family, like my sisters or Pimp, you know, if you didn't take up for them, when I came out I would've been lookin' for you. I know it would've been the same thing in my case, because that's what we expected from one another. In the same way, I always expected you to pull my coat if somebody in my family was in danger, you know."

"Yeah, Sonny, but I know how you've always felt about Pimp, man. It's just that I never knew how to mention it to you."

I got kind of mad. I said, "Danny, why don't you stop fuckin' with me and say what's on your mind, nigger." I got kind of loud, and people turned around and looked at us.

Danny kept looking in the mirror. He just said slowly, softly a couple of times, "Cool it, Sonny. Sonny, baby, cool it."

I looked in the mirror at his eyes, and I said, "I'm sorry, Danny." I've always had a lot of respect for Danny, and I guess it was mutual, because we had thrown a lot of bricks together. I had even more respect for him after he had kicked his habit.

After I quieted down, and the conversation got back to normal, Danny said, "Sonny, I was up to Ruby's house a few nights ago, and I saw Pimp there. He was there with some little girl on 144th Street."

I said, "So what, man? I've been up to Ruby's house, and that doesn't mean a mother-fuckin' thing. Anybody can go up there." I started getting loud again. I saw that I was getting excited.

"Yeah, Sonny. Forget it, man. But now you see what I meant when I said I didn't know how to say anything. And now you see how you would take somebody's pulling your coat."

"No, man. That's not it. That's not it at all. Was he doin' anything?"

Danny looked at me for a while, and he said, "Sonny, tell me, this is

Danny. We stole our first mickies together from Gordon's fruit stand. Tell me, Sonny, what do people go up to Ruby's house for? I could go up there to see about some business. You'd be going up there if you were gon turn somebody on. But it's got to have something to do with some drugs, right? I'm goin' up there to give her her weight for the week, you know. When somebody else goes up there, just from the street . . . she doesn't open the door for everybody, Sonny. You know that."

"Yeah, Danny. I guess I know."

"Man, you must know what's goin' on."

"No, man. How the hell are you gonna say I must know what's goin' on?"

"Well, you said you see him all the time. Don't you see anything different?"

I said, "No, man. He's still working, so he can't be strung out, right?"

"Yeah, Sonny, that's right, if you want to take it that way. If that's all you're worried about, man, you might as well forget it, because you know you can't do anything for anybody when they're strung out. Nobody can do anything for anybody who's strung out. The only person who can do anything is the man out there who's dealin'. So if you ever talk to him, Sonny, talk to him now."

I just sat here and looked in the mirror for a long time. I wondered about me, and I wondered where I'd failed. I remembered all the days when we were young, the time Pimp and I had spent together. I remembered when Mama brought Pimp to Wiltwyck to visit me and Pimp punched K.B. in the mouth. Everybody laughed and said, "He must be fast if he can hit K.B. in the mouth and not have him get out of the way." Pimp was only about seven or eight then. He was something.

But I had known for some time that I had lost him. I guess I should have known it when I saw him. He was hanging out with Murray. Murray just didn't seem to have enough heart to be hanging out with Pimp. He used to marvel at the fact that I was Pimp's brother. This was nobody for Pimp to be hanging out with. He should have been hanging out with strong young cats who knew where they were going, knew how to get around the places that they didn't want to go, and knew how to get around doing the things that they didn't want to do. Pimp should have been hanging out with cats like me, I suppose. I should have been there to guide him, but I couldn't be in Harlem all the time leading him around by the hand.

I thought I had gotten him ready. I thought I had taught him enough. Maybe he just came out of the house too late; maybe Mama held on to him too long. Maybe a lot of things. But there was one thing that I was certain of, and that was that he was in trouble now. And I didn't know how to help him. I didn't know where to begin.

I sat there looking in the mirror across the bar and thinking. When Danny said, "Take it easy, Sonny," I heard him and I didn't hear him. I couldn't answer because I was too hurt, and my mind was too preoccupied with thoughts of Pimp and his youth, the days when we were happy together, and why I never thought the plague would ever get to him.

I was going to find that nigger, and I was going to beat him and beat him until he stopped breathing. I was going to beat that mother-fucker until he realized what he was doing, if I had to beat him to death. Something kept gnawing at me. How the hell could I beat him? I remembered seeing him as a little baby; I remembered slapping him too hard once, when I was about thirteen. His nose bled. . . . But I was going to beat him. I was going to beat that nigger with my fist, because he didn't deserve any more slaps.

I wasn't even going to tell him why. I was just going to tell that mother-fucker to throw up his hands. I was going to find him and say, "Pimp, throw up your hands. Throw up your hands or go in your pocket." I wondered how I was going to beat him, when I'd taught him everything he knew.

As I looked for him, everybody I asked . . . I guess they saw it. I tried to cool myself, because as I went from place to place asking people if they'd seen Pimp, they'd look at me, and they'd say, "No," as though they knew that I wasn't looking for him to bring him any cheerful greetings. I became almost convinced that nobody was going to tell me where he was, so I went around to his girl's house.

I asked Shirley if she had seen Pimp. She said she thought that she'd seen him on 143rd Street, but she wasn't sure, because she called to him and he didn't answer. She said she didn't know what was wrong; she was waiting to see him too.

I said, "Yeah, well, maybe he had something on his mind."

I left her, and I went to 143rd Street. Somebody told me that he was in the poolroom on Seventh Avenue and 144th Street. When I got there, I saw Jack Davis. Jack Davis was a cat I had known from way back. He was in my class in junior high school. I asked him if he knew Pimp. He said he did and asked me if I wanted to get something.

I said, "Oh. Why? Is he dealin' stuff now?"

"No, man, but he was just around here a little while ago looking for Johnny McNeil, and Johnny McNeil is dealin' stuff."

I said, "Oh." It kind of hurt me that Johnny would deal Pimp some stuff, because Johnny knew that Pimp was my brother. When Johnny came out of the Army and was up tight and didn't know what he was going to do with himself, I started teaching him the street life. I taught him how to Murphy, and I taught him a few other games. I taught him how to scoop cocaine.

I was mad. Now I was looking for Pimp and Johnny too. I was going to beat both of their asses, and especially Johnny's, because, if it hadn't been for me, that nigger would have been just about starving. He didn't know anything. He didn't know a damn thing, and he probably never would have known anything if I hadn't taken pity on him and taught him something. That no good son of a bitch.

I knew that if Johnny was dealing stuff, he'd probably have a piece on him, because he usually carried one of them even when he wasn't dealing. He was just a mean cat that way. Johnny wasn't that good with his hands. He was a cat that didn't believe in fighting. Anytime anybody hit him, he'd go for his piece and shoot.

But I was determined. I was going to walk up on Johnny and Pimp together, and I was going to hit Johnny first. I was going to walk up to them smiling, like Bubba Williams taught us in the streets. Bubba always said that if you ever wanted to waste a cat, smile at him for a month. But I was just going to smile at Johnny for one minute, just long enough to get close enough to him to hit him in his kidneys.

I was mad. How the hell could he? He knew Pimp was my brother. Everybody around there knew I didn't want him to be using any stuff. Pimp knew I didn't want him using it, more than anybody else. He was the main one; he was the one I was really disappointed in, because I thought he had so much more sense.

I wondered what Mama would say when she found out. She probably thought that all her troubles were over, that she'd made it with her boys, that they were all right after all. She'd had her bad days. I felt that she'd had all she could take and that Pimp wasn't going to give her any more, not if I could help it. I was going to kill that nigger first.

I went into the Low Hat Bar, on 146th Street and Seventh Avenue. When I looked in there, I didn't see Johnny McNeil, but Pimp was there. Pimp was standing near the jukebox with a cigarette in his hand and dark glasses on. I thought he was going to scratch himself. Then I saw that he was in a nod.

I walked toward him. I was just going to walk up to him, snatch him by the arm, pull him over in a corner, and talk to him. But as I walked up to him, I saw him going into a nod, a deep nod. I stopped about four feet away from him, and I just couldn't move. I don't know why. The anger was there, but it was mixed with something else. The something else just paralyzed me. It wouldn't let me move.

Here was Pimp in a nod, in a nod, the little brother that I loved, the little brother I had fought so many fights for, the little brother who used to come and get me to go and swing on whoever fucked with him, regardless of how big they were.

I stood there and watched his head go down. I thought I'd hit him as he was coming up and take him off his feet. But he got all the way up in his nod, and I couldn't move. I just stood there looking at him, and then a phrase ran through my mind: Absalom, Absalom.

13

Saturday night. I suppose there's a Saturday night in every Negro community throughout the nation just like Saturday night in Harlem. The bars will jump. The precinct station will have a busy night. The hospital's emergency ward will jump.

Cats who have been working all their lives, who've never been in any trouble before, good-doing righteous cats, self-respecting, law-abiding citizens—they'll all come out. Perhaps it'll be their night in the bar, their night in the police station, maybe their night in the emergency ward.

They tell me that young doctors really try hard for a chance to do their internship in Harlem Hospital—it offers such a wide variety of experiences. They say it's the best place in the city where a surgeon can train. They say you get all kinds of experience just working there on Saturday nights.

It's usually the older folks who practice this Saturday night thing, or some of the younger cats who haven't come out of the woods yet, young cats who drink a lot of liquor, who didn't quite finish junior high school, who still have most of the Southern ways . . . the young cats who carry knives, the young cats who want to be bad niggers. It's usually the guys around eighteen to twenty-five, guys who haven't separated themselves yet from the older generation or who just haven't become critical of the older generation. They follow the pattern that has been set by the older generation, the Saturday night pattern of getting drunk, getting a new piece of cunt, and getting real bad—carrying a knife in your pocket and ready to use it, ready to curse, ready to become a Harlem Saturday night statistic, in the hospital, the police station or the morgue.

The intern who comes to Harlem and starts his internship around April will be ready to go into surgery by June. He's probably already tried to close up windpipes for people who've had their throat slit. Or tried to put intestines back in a stomach. Or somebody has hit somebody in the head with a hatchet. Or somebody has come into his house at the wrong time and caught somebody else going out the window. That's quite a job too, putting a person back together after a four- or five-story fall.

I suppose any policeman who's been in Harlem for a month of Saturday nights has had all the experience he'll ever need, as far as handling violence goes. Some of them will have more experience than they'll ever be able to use.

To me, it always seemed as though Saturday night was the down-home night. In the tales I'd heard about down home—how so-and-so got bad and killed Cousin Joe or knocked out Cousin Willie's eye—everything violent happened on Saturday night. It was the only time for anything to really happen, because people were too tired working all week from sunup to sundown to raise but so much hell on the week nights. Then, comes Saturday, and they take it kind of easy during the day, resting up for another Saturday night.

Down home, when they went to town, all the niggers would just break bad, so it seemed. Everybody just seemed to let out all their hostility on everybody else. Maybe they were hoping that they could get their throat cut. Perhaps if a person was lucky enough to get his throat cut, he'd be free from the fields. On the other hand, if someone was lucky enough to cut somebody else's throat, he'd done the guy a favor, because he'd freed him.

In the tales about down home that I'd heard, everybody was trying to either cash out on Saturday night or cash somebody else out. There was always the good corn liquor that Cy Walker used to make, and there was always that new gun that somebody had bought. The first time they shot the gun at so-and-so, he jumped out of the window and didn't stop running until he got home—and got his gun. You'd sit there and say, "Well, I'll be damned. I never knew they had all those bad niggers in the South. I always thought the baddest cat down there was Charlie." But it seemed as though on Saturday night, the niggers got bad. Of course, they didn't get bad enough to mess with Charlie, but they got bad. They were bad enough to cut each other's throats, shoot each other, hit each other in the head with axes, and all that sort of action. Women were bad enough to throw lye on one another.

Saturday night down home was really something, but, then, Saturday night in Harlem was really something too. There is something happening for everybody on Saturday night: for the cat who works all day long on the railroad, in the garment center, driving a bus, or as a subway conductor. On Saturday night, there is something happening for everybody in Harlem, regardless of what his groove might be. Even the real soul sisters, who go to church and live for Sunday, who live to jump up and clap and call on the Lord, Saturday night means something to them too. Saturday night is the night they start getting ready for Sunday. They have to braid all the kids' hair and get them ready. They have to iron their white usher uniforms and get pretty for Sunday and say a prayer. For the devoted churchgoers, Saturday night means that Sunday will soon be here.

Saturday night is a time to try new things. Maybe that's why so many people in the older generation had to lose their lives on Saturday night. It must be something about a Saturday night with Negroes. . . . Maybe they wanted to die on Saturday night. They'd always associated Sunday with going to heaven, because that was when they went to church and sang all those songs, clapped and shouted and stomped their feet and praised the Lord. Maybe they figured that if they died on Sunday morning, the Lord's day, they'd be well on their way.

Everybody has this thing about Saturday night. I imagine that before pot or horse or any other drugs hit Harlem good and strong, the people just had to try something else, like knifing or shooting somebody, because Saturday night was the night for daring deeds. Since there was no pot out on a large scale then, I suppose one of the most daring deeds anyone could perform was to shoot or stab somebody.

Many of the chicks in the neighborhood took some of their first really big steps on Saturday night. Some cats—or as a girl I knew might say, "no-good niggers"—talked many girls into turning their first tricks on a Saturday night just because the cats needed some money. That's how that thing goes on Saturday night. I recall talking a girl into a trick on a Saturday night. She said it was her first, but I like to tell myself it wasn't. If it was, that was okay. She was a part of Harlem, and Saturday night was a time for first things, even for girls turning their first tricks, pulling their first real John.

Saturday night has also been a traditional night for money to be floating around in places like Harlem. It's a night of temptation, the kind of temptation one might see on Catfish Row at the end of the cotton season on the weekend. Most of the people got paid on Friday night, and Saturday they had some money. If they didn't get paid on Friday, there was a good chance that they'd be around playing the single action on Saturday in the afternoon. By the time the last figure came out, everybody might have some change, even if it was only eight dollars—one dollar on the 0 that afternoon. It was still some money.

Then there were all the crap games floating around. The stickup artists would be out hunting. The Murphy boys would be out strong. In the bars, the tricks would be out strong. All the whores would be out there, and any decent, self-respecting whore could pull at least two hundred dollars on Saturday night in some of the bad-doing bars on 125th Street.

As a matter of fact, Reno used to say, "The cat who can't make no money on Saturday night is in trouble." There was a lot of truth to it, because there was so much money floating around in Harlem on Saturday night, if anyone couldn't get any money then, he just didn't have any business there.

It seemed as though Harlem's history is made on Saturday nights. You hear about all the times people have gotten shot—like when two white cops were killed on 146th Street a couple of years ago—on a Saturday night. Just about every time a cop is killed in Harlem, it's on a Saturday night.

People know you shouldn't bother with Negroes on Saturday night, because for some reason or another, Negroes just don't mind dying on Saturday night. They seem ready to die, so they're not going to take but so much stuff. There were some people who were always trying to get themselves killed. Every Saturday night, they'd try it all over again.

One was Big Bill. When I was just a kid on Eighth Avenue in knee pants, this guy was trying to get himself killed. He was always in some fight with a knife. He was always cutting or trying to cut somebody's throat. He was always getting cut or getting stabbed, getting hit in the head, getting shot. Every Saturday night that he was out there, something happened. If you heard on Sunday morning that somebody had gotten shot or stabbed, you didn't usually ask who did it. You'd ask if Big Bill did it. If he did it, no one paid too much attention to it, because he was always doing something like that. They'd say, "Yeah, man. That cat is crazy."

If somebody else had done it, you'd wonder why, and this was something to talk about and discuss. Somebody else might not have been as crazy. In the case of Big Bill, everybody expected that sooner or later somebody would kill him and put him out of his misery and that this was what he was trying for. One time Spanish Joe stabbed him. He just missed his lung, and everybody thought he was going to cool it behind that. But as soon as the cat got back on the street, he was right out there doing it again.

Even now, he's always getting in fights out on the streets on Saturday nights. He's always hurting somebody, or somebody's hurting him. He just seems to be hanging on. I think he's just unlucky. Here's a cat who's been trying to get himself killed every Saturday night as far back as I can remember, and he still hasn't made it. I suppose you've got to sympathize with a guy like that, because he's really been trying.

Harlem is full of surprises on Saturday night. I remember one in particular.

I was down on 116th Street. I was going to visit someone, and I decided to call before I got there. I went into the bar on the corner to call. I saw a familiar face in the bar. We had stopped hanging out together when I was about nine and never started again. We just weren't that tight any more. We'd had our fights. We were all right; we'd speak if we saw each other. I was just surprised to see him in that neck of the woods. I didn't think he ever went anyplace outside our neighborhood. I guess a lot of people had the same idea. It just goes to show how little we all knew about him.

I walked up to him and said, "Hey, Dad, how you doin'?" I guess he was just as surprised to see me down there, and I thought he was going to ask, "Hey, son, what you doin' down here?" I was all set to tell him, "I got a friend down here who owes me some money, and I need it tonight, because I got to take this chick out, so I came down to see him."

But he didn't say it. He just asked me if I wanted a drink. He didn't act too surprised to see me. He was out, and this was Saturday night. He'd been in Harlem a lot of Saturday nights, and he'd gotten that big, nasty-looking scar on his neck on a Saturday night.

Despite the fact that he didn't ask me what I was doing there, I said, "I got to get uptown. I got to call somebody to wait for me. I hope this chick don't stay in that phone booth too long."

He said, "No, I don't think she'll be in there on the phone too long."

I didn't pay much attention to it. I said, "She looks like one of those who can really talk."

He just said, "Yeah," and kind of smiled.

I looked at the woman again. She looked as though she might have been about thirty-three, something like that. I would look over there every couple of minutes. She would look over to the bar at me and smile. I just forgot about the phone and started talking to Dad about my job and what I'd done that night, how I was catching hell, how everything I touched just turned to shit, sort of halfway crying.

It dawned on me that he had been standing there all by himself when I came in, and I'd never known him to do this. I never thought that he would go to a bar by himself, especially some strange bar, just to stand around and drink. He usually brought his liquor home when he wanted a drink.

I said, "Say, Dad, you waitin' for somebody down here?" I knew a friend of his who worked with him. Although I hadn't seen him in a long time, I figured they were still friends. I knew his friend, Eddie, lived down there, so I said, "Dad, you waitin' for somebody? Is Eddie around?"

He didn't answer the first question, but to the second one he said, "No, I haven't seen Eddie now in about a month."

I said, "Yeah? Well, doesn't he still work on the job with you?"

He said that Eddie had an injury; some crates fell on him. "It's not too bad, but he can't be doing that heavy work around the dock, so he stayed off. He's collecting compensation for it. He's taking it easy, the way I hear it."

I said, "Oh." After that, I thought about the first question, but I figured it wouldn't be too wise to repeat it. I thought, Well, maybe he's waiting for his woman. And I laughed, because I always thought of Dad as the kind of cat nobody but Mama could take. With her, it was just habit.

After a while, the woman from the phone booth came up. She said, "Hi."

I looked at her and said, "Oh, do I know you?"

Dad introduced her. He said, "Ruth, meet my oldest son."

She smiled and said, "Hello. So you're Sonny Boy."

I said, "Yeah."

She said, "I knew it was you the moment I saw you sittin' there next to your daddy on that stool. You two look so much alike. If he was about ten years younger, he could pass for your older brother."

I said, "Yeah, that's something that people are suppose to tell fathers and sons, huh, that they look like brothers?"

She threw both of her hands on her hips and looked at me in a sort of defiant way, but jokingly, and said, "Supposin' it is, young man? That's beside the point. I'm telling you that you and your daddy look alike, even if this is what people are suppose to tell you. Now, you can believe it if you want to. All I'm interested in is saying it, and I said it. You can take it from there."

I looked at her and said, "Okay, I believe it." I had the funniest feeling that this woman knew what was going on. I knew this was his woman.

I couldn't feel anything about it. I guess I'd just never given too much thought to the idea of Dad playing around. I couldn't imagine anybody else ever wanting him. In the case of Mama, I think, if it had been her, I would have felt good about it. She deserved to get out and get somebody who would treat her like she was something, like she was a person. Because of this feeling about Mama, I suppose I should have felt bad that Dad was being unfaithful, but I didn't. I didn't see any way in the world to dislike this woman. She seemed to be a nice person.

Dad asked her if she wanted a drink.

She said to me, "What you drinkin', junior?" I told her I was drinking a bourbon and soda with lemon. She said, "Umph. That sounds like something with a whole lot of sting in it. Maybe I'll try one."

She moved closer to Dad and put her hand around his waist. She looked at me as if to say, "Well, young man, that's the way it is. So how you gonna take it?"

Dad never even looked at me. He just picked up his drink, as if to say, "Shit, he's old enough. If he's not, fuck him." He emptied his glass, put it down, and called to the bartender.

When the bartender came to bring Ruth one, Dad got another whiskey, straight. We sat there for a while and started talking. The woman didn't seem to be the least bit ill at ease. She seemed completely relaxed, and she looked pretty, in her own way. She was kind of plump, but she looked like she might have been a very nice-looking girl when she was about twenty.

I guess she was pretty for Dad. He was forty at the time, so I suppose anything under thirty-five would have been real nice for him. They seemed to have something. He had a patience with her that I'd never seen him show with Mama. I didn't think he was capable of showing this to any woman. She seemed to be able to play with him, and he took more playing from her than I'd seen him take from anybody else.

It made me wonder just how long had he known her and just what was going on with them. All I could see was that, whatever they had with each other, they were really enjoying it. I decided that was enough. I didn't feel as though I had the right to judge them or even have an opinion about them. Whatever they were doing, it seemed to me that they weren't doing it to anybody but themselves. Mama would never be hurt, because there was a good chance that she'd never know. New York was a big city, and they seemed so tight that they must have been tight for a long time, a real long time.

I asked her, "Pardon me, Ruth. Haven't I seen you uptown? Do you live up around 145th Street?"

Dad still never looked at me. He said, "Sonny Boy, I think you better grab that phone there now. The booth is empty. If you don't get it while it's empty, you're liable to be here all night."

I got up and went to the phone booth. When I came out, Dad and his lady friend were gone. That was understandable. I guess I really messed up with that question about 145th Street.

I didn't feel bad toward Dad. It was just that I had never seen it as being possible for him to pull a chick on the outside, a nice-looking chick like this Ruth. She seemed to be a person with a nice personality, and she didn't look bad for a woman her age. Maybe she did something for Dad too. He acted like a different person altogether with her. Maybe she was the one who made him relax. He must have been a different person. I'd never seen him act like that with anybody. At home he was always shouting and raising hell, threatening somebody, a real terror.

I was kind of sorry that I had started prying into the woman's business. I knew I'd never seen her uptown. I suppose Dad knew it too. I was supposed to act as old as he had treated me. One of the things had been to treat the lady like she was just a friend of Dad's and to be cool behind it. But then I had just gone on and messed over her. I knew this was something I'd never get a chance to do again. I knew I'd never get a chance to say, "Look, Dad, I'm sorry I said that, and I shouldn't have," because I knew that this wasn't supposed to be mentioned ever, not even to him.

The next time I saw him, I would just have to speak first, about something that was far removed from the night at the bar and from Ruth. But I hoped that I would get a chance to let her know somehow that I was sorry that I hadn't played my part properly.

I didn't feel as though he was hurting Mama. I felt she didn't know about it, and what she didn't know wouldn't hurt her. Maybe it was just that she wasn't missing anything, because I didn't feel they were in any great love anyway. It just didn't bother me as I might have thought it would. It just seemed to be one of those Harlem Saturday night surprises.

I remember the Saturday night when Dad kicked Pimp out of the house and told him not to come back. Pimp had fallen to sleep on the toilet with a needle in his arm. I guess he'd taken a light O.D.

Mama was telling me about it. According to her, Dad came in and panicked. He opened the bathroom door and saw Pimp halfway on and halfway off the toilet with a needle in his arm. Mama said he just starting calling so loud for her to come there, she thought he was dying. Mama tried to make a joke out of it. She said she thought maybe he'd fallen down in the toilet and was having trouble getting out. I tried to laugh, but all I could get out was a snicker.

Mama said she tried to slap Pimp out of it. She thought for a while he was dead when she saw him. She just refused to accept that her child was dead from using dope. She ran into the bathroom and started slapping him and calling his name real loud, as though, even if he was dead, he would hear her and come back.

She started hollering for the doctor, and she started hollering about an ambulance. Dad said, "No, don't be callin' no ambulance or no doctors around here. We ain't gon have no police coming in here."

Mama started hollering, "The boy might be dead! The boy might be dead!"

Dad said, "Huh?" He'd stop and say, "He ain't dead. He ain't dead. It's just that old dope." They both panicked.

When Mama finally got Pimp to wake up, after so much slapping and calling his name, Dad was convinced that it was time for Pimp to go. I guess he should have been convinced. It must have been a pretty frightening thing, even for him, though he wouldn't admit it, to come into the bathroom and see his son slumped over a toilet with a needle in his arm, after having heard so much about the junkies dying from using dope, after having been to so many funerals, after having asked so many times about this kid and that kid who came up with his older son and being told that he'd died from dope—it must have been a pretty frightening thing.

Pimp had deceived just about everybody in the family for a long time. After a while, we all knew, but I knew before anybody else that Pimp was dabbling. I was the first one to say, "Come on, man. You got to do something."

I guess Pimp sort of knew that I suspected him of using stuff. The first time after I saw him high that night in the Low Hat, I took him to a bar. He didn't know that I had seen him nodding. I said, "Come on, let's have a drink. I want to talk to you. Let's sit down and have a drink."

I asked him what he'd like to drink. I remembered that he used to like rum. I think he just took a rum and Coke because he knew I remembered it and thought I might get suspicious if he didn't.

When he took his first sip of the rum and Coke, he grimaced. He said,

"Man, it's, like, I'm so tired. I'm so tired, Sonny, this stuff almost knocks me out."

I looked at him and said, "Yeah, man. It can do that to you."

Then he looked down and started fumbling with his glass, as if he knew I was suspicious of him. The next thing he said was, "Man, you know, I ain't had no good rum in a long time."

When he said this, I paid it no attention. I knew he was going to try to bullshit me. I looked straight at him as he went on talking. I said, "Pimp." I sort of quietly shouted it at him.

"Yeah, Sonny?"

"How long have you been dabblin' in stuff?"

He looked at me for a long time. He got kind of quiet, and he dropped his head. He said, "Oh, about four months, man."

"How far are you? How much stuff are you usin' a day?"

"Oh, man, I buy a bag about every other day, but I don't get high every day."

"Are you snortin' or skin poppin'?"

"Man, I'm just startin', and I can keep a bag two or three days."

"Uh-huh. That's good, because now is the time for you to stop. You got to stop now, before you really get yourself into some trouble."

"Yeah, yeah." He was glad to hear this. It seemed as though he had heard something that he had been waiting to hear, he had been given some kind of signal. He seemed to feel that all he had to do now was agree with everything I said and everything would be okay. He was going to prevent any violence from taking place by just being agreeable.

"Look, Pimp, you got a job, and you're still working. You're doing good now. Now is the time when you can quit, because if you keep on dabblin', man, you're gon actually go to the dogs. After a while, you won't be able to quit, and you won't have anything to quit for, because once you blow your job, your clothes, and everything you've got, it just won't matter that much. You got a nice girl, man. And maybe you'll want to get married or something. But what you're doin', man, you're gon blow everything."

"Yeah, Sonny, I know what you mean, man. I've been tellin' myself. I've been planning on stopping this stuff for the last two weeks. As a matter of fact, last week . . ."

I just knew he was lying. He was saying all this so relaxed, and he seemed so pleased with the way he was telling it. But I could tell he was lying. I knew. He didn't know how to lie, not to me anyway.

He said that he had bought some Dorphine tablets and that he had taken his first two today. He was going to keep taking the Dorphine tablets and start cutting down on other drugs from day to day, and in a couple of weeks or so, he'd be ready to sign himself into someplace.

I asked him if he'd ever heard of Norman Eddie, in the East Harlem Protestant Parish. He said no, he hadn't. I said, "Well, he's doin' a lot of good work with drug addicts, and if you're really interested, I think I could get him to work with you, man. You could kick it now, before it really gets a strong hold on you."

Pimp went right on bullshitting me. He said, "Yeah, Sonny, that's what I want to do. You go ahead and see this cat and let me know what's happening."

I was crushed. He didn't understand it at all. He just seemed to look at me as if I were someone who was trying to deprive him of something. And he wasn't even going to pretend to defend it, even though he wanted it terribly. He was just going to sit there and say, "Yeah, yeah, yeah, uh-huh. I'll go along with you. You're right; that's so right. I'm going to be doing it, so there's nothing else to talk about when you stop trying to sell me on it."

Even though I could see this, I still felt I had to try. He was my brother, and I could make him kick it. He couldn't help but kick it if I was in his corner, if I really wanted him to. I was going to put everything I had into it.

When Mama called me that Saturday night and told me what Dad had said to Pimp, how he couldn't come back in the house any more, and how afraid she was for him, I said, "Look, Mama, he'll be coming back."

She said, "No, he ain't gon come back, because he was really hurt. I think he's just gon go someplace and try and take enough of that stuff to kill himself or something."

I said, "No, Mama, junkies don't kill themselves. They've got something to live for. They got to live for another high, for the next one. He'll probably come down here." I knew he wasn't coming, but that's what I told her. "Mama, he'll probably come down here, and when he does come down, I'll put him up for the night and call you and let you know."

Mama said, "He just might go someplace and get himself into some trouble in the meantime, before he gets down there. Why don't you go out and look for him for a little while. He's probably around there on 144th Street. And let me know if you can't find him. Call me and keep in touch with me, because he ain't had a bath all week, and he got on those old dirty pants. That shirt he has on, he put it on day before yesterday, and it was white. It looks like it's black from the dirt and grime. He ain't had nothin' to eat in a long time. I don't know if he even had anything to eat yesterday, and he's probably hungry."

I wanted to tell her, "Look, Mama, junkies don't care about eating. They don't care about clothes. They don't care about baths and stuff like that. It just don't matter to them. All they care about is some heroin, and this is the only thing that's gon do them any good, Mama. You got to face the fact that he's at that state where soap and water's not gon do him any good. Clothes ain't gon do him any good. Food ain't gon do him any good. He's just dead, and maybe the thing that'll do him the most good is the O.D., the O.D. that he's waitin' for." But I couldn't tell her that. I just couldn't seem to bring it out.

I knew it was no use, but she got me to promise that I'd look for him. She was a woman, and that was her child. I couldn't tell her that many other women had sons and daughters out there dying too. It wouldn't have meant anything to her, because this was the first child that she had out there who was a drug addict. This was the only one out there she was concerned about, the only one that mattered.

I went uptown to start looking for Pimp. I looked everywhere. I went to all the places where junkies might go, looked in all the dope dens, in all the backyards where the junkies might sleep. Nobody had seen him or heard about him. Some people hadn't seen him in days. I kept on looking and hoping. When Mama called me, it had been about eight-thirty or nine o'clock. When I hadn't found Pimp or anybody who had seen Pimp by three-thirty, I became a little worried.

I started fearing for him. When this happened, I started getting mad at myself, because I felt myself going right back into the same pattern again. I knew that if I had seen him then and he was in pain or said his habit was down on him, I would have had to give him some money to get him some stuff. I probably would have fallen right back into Pimp's trick bag and helped send him to Kentucky and waited for him to come back and start all over.

Still, the longer I looked for him, the more worried I became. And the more worried I became, the more angry I became with myself for worrying, for going back on my word, for weakening, for weakening from Pimp and his weakness. This was what he had always played on with me. He'd beg me for my clothes, to pawn them, because he knew I worried about him.

He'd intimidate me with my concern for him. He'd tell me he was going to have to go and try a stickup or something like that. Many times, after he'd left, I'd say, "Nigger, go on. Go on and pull a stickup. Go on and do what you want to. Just hurry up and get it over with; like, pull a stickup and get shot, or go on and throw a brick. Rob somebody's house and get thrown out of a window, or just go on and take that O.D. But whatever you do, please do it in a hurry. Please do it in a hurry and get off my back."

That was what I should have told him, but I guess every junkie looks pitiful to his brother. Pimp always seemed to be the most pitiful creature in the world when his habit was down on him. He looked so helpless. I knew I could never turn my back on him if I saw him when his habit was down on him. I was almost certain that this morning would be another case like that.

There was nothing else to do but go on uptown and tell Mama that I couldn't find him but that we still had Pimp, we still had our problem.

When I got there, I hesitated to knock on the door. I felt ashamed to go in there and tell Mama, "Look, I couldn't find him. I couldn't find hide nor hair of him. Nobody's seen him or heard from him."

She expected me to bring her some hope. That's why I went out to begin with, because I figured I could bring him back or at least find him and ease her mind. But I had to come back with nothing, not even knowing where Pimp was.

When I finally got around to knocking on the door, Dad opened the door. I think he had just come in. Not from looking for Pimp—he had come in from his Saturday night. He looked at me as if he was a little disappointed or something. Maybe he expected the police to come and bring Pimp home or bring his body home or bring the information that he was dead. It was just me, and he seemed to resent the knowledge that my presence brought him: that we still had our problem.

Dad went into the bathroom, and I went into the front room. Mama was sitting at the front window. I just came in, walking slowly, and said I couldn't find him.

Mama said, "Yeah, he might just be someplace dead, in some strange backyard. Maybe some of those junkies could have taken him and thrown him in some boiler down in the cellar. Like they did around on 144th Street last year, when that boy took a lot of dope and went in that coma. They

301

put him in that boiler, just about cooked him. Yeah, he just might be layin' around in one of them boilers cookin' right now."

I didn't say anything, because I knew what Mama was doing. I felt sorry for her. She was trying to prepare herself for the worst by saying all that stuff. I knew she didn't believe it, and she didn't want to believe it. She just wanted to hear herself say it, just in case somebody brought some sad news. If she told herself that this was what had happened to him, and something happened to him that wasn't as bad, it had to be good.

Then Dad came in and said, "Woman, why don't you stop all that foolishness? You don't have to be worried about them damn junkies. Them damn junkies take care of theirselves twice as good as you can. You see that they be out there so long, look like they be dying, and they be hanging around there for years. Why don't you stop talkin' all that foolishness?"

Mama didn't seem to hear Dad. She looked out the window, saw the daylight creeping in, stroked the cat—about the tenth cat named Tina—and seemed to realize that Saturday night was gone. Mama stroked the cat lightly and looked out the window, greeting the daylight with a question. She said to the dawn, "Lord, where can my child be this mornin'?"

14

I first heard about the Black Muslims in 1955. They had started talking at night down on 125th Street and Seventh Avenue. This seemed to be the speakers' corner in Harlem. Everybody talked down there, all the politicians. Anybody who had to address the Harlem public got up on a soapbox on 125th Street and Seventh Avenue.

The Coptic speakers had been down there at the beginning of the fifties and the years just before. They were still down there, but they were being overshadowed by the Black Muslims. I never paid too much attention to them. All I knew was that these cats were building up this black superiority thing. I'd heard it before. But I hadn't heard it so vividly. At the same time, these guys were tearing down anything that was white. As a matter of fact, they seemed to resent the clouds for being white.

They were really carried away, and they were coming on strong with this thing of "Buy Black." They were talking about boycotting all the white stores and taking over Harlem economically. I suppose it was frightening to all the white shopkeepers down there. They'd come to their doors and stand and look, as if to say, "Why don't the police do something about it? These niggers seem to be talking the same sort of thing that Hitler was doing."

There was nothing that could be done, because they weren't causing any violence, and they weren't inciting any violence, not at that time anyway.

No one thought there would be much to this thing. I figured this was just the next phase in the Harlem Black Nationalist movement. I thought, They had the Garveyites in the twenties, then there were the Coptics in the forties and early fifties, and now this. It's just another thing that's going to die out soon.

A few cats I knew were joining. They seemed to be impressed with the badge. It was all sort of childish, the way I saw it. I remember, about 1955, I went by Seventh Avenue, and these cats were picketing a theater. I think it was at the RKO Alhambra. These cats were picketing because the theater was showing the film *Hannibal the Great*. They were picketing because Hannibal,

according to the Muslims, was a black man and they had a white actor star-
ring in the movie. It just didn't make sense to me; I thought all these cats
were crazy, and I couldn't do any more than laugh at them.

Every other week or so, I'd pass by 125th Street and Seventh Avenue. I'd
see them, and I'd see the people who'd stand around listening. It was like a
mass street-corner prayer meeting. They'd be talking about this Allah business and about somebody named Elijah Muhammad. The people would be
looking and saying, "Yes, yes," like some of those affirmatives they shouted
out, grunted out, and nodded out at a Baptist church prayer meeting.

As I went down there, week after week, it seemed as though the crowd
was getting larger. Younger guys were beginning to listen to this sort of
thing. Then I started meeting people around there I hadn't seen in years.

I recall seeing Floyd Saks there. Floyd was up at Wiltwyck with me. He
was a good painter; as a matter of fact, he was very talented. I figured that he
could go places. When I met Floyd on 125th Street one afternoon, I didn't
know he was a Muslim. He told me that he had a studio and had painted a
few models, that sort of thing. He wanted to take me up to his studio and
show me some of his work. I hadn't seen him in a long time, and I wanted
to talk to him anyway, so I went on up to his studio. He had a piano up there,
and I sat down and played. Then he showed me some of his work.

He had painted pictures of lynchings in the South, and he had painted
a lot of biblical characters—a black Moses, a black Jesus Christ, and a black
Abraham. Everybody was black. I asked him if he ever painted anybody who
wasn't black. Floyd said that he hadn't and that he wasn't going to paint any.
He wasn't interested in anybody but colored people.

He started telling me about the superiority of colored people, and I
asked him if he was a member of the Coptic. He said no. He'd heard of
them, but they didn't know what was going on. He asked me if I'd heard of
the Muslims.

"You mean the Moslems?"

"No, man. Everybody thinks it's the Moslems, but it's the Muslims."

"You mean those cats out there on Seventh Avenue and 125th Street,
don't you?"

"Yeah. They're into things, man. A new day has dawned on us. Allah has
sent Muhammad to free us."

"To free us from what, man?"

"To free us from these white devils down here, who've stolen our heritage and poisoned our minds."

I looked at him. I said, "Are you all right, Floyd?"

"Yeah, man. It doesn't sound like the things that you've been hearing. Did you know that you were a black god?"

"Oh, man. It sounds as though they have stolen the Coptic line."

"No, man. They know. You may not believe me, Claude, but the white man was made by a colored scientist, in a test tube, man. He isn't even real. He's like a Frankenstein monster."

"Floyd, perhaps I'm just a little skeptical. I suppose I'm just a born skeptic, but I find that hard to believe, man. For a long time now, I've been believing that man is man, be he white or black. And that every man originates from sperm."

He said, "It was only the original man that originated from sperm. The other man originated in a test tube."

I said, "Man, do you know what he put in that test tube? If this is what happened, it must have been a test-tube baby, like they have modern test-tube babies. Only this one must have come out with a lighter pigmentation, for some reason or another."

"No, man. He was made out of some chemicals and stuff."

I said, "Floyd . . ."

"Yeah, you're a nonbeliever like a whole lot of these people, man. They don't even know that they're not free. You remember that I had said that Allah had sent Muhammad to free us, and you said, 'Free us from what?' Here you think you're free. If you really think you're free, man, all you got to do is go to jail one time. You find out how it is. You ain't got that much going for you once you get out of jail."

"Oh! You been to jail, man? Is that where you been all this time since you got out of Wiltwyck?"

"No, man, but I was over on the Rock for a few months. As a matter of fact, that's where I got the word."

I said, "Oh?"

He said, "Yeah. I was walking around lost too . . . until I went over there and heard the message. They got a lot of brothers over there. The movement's going strong there. A lot of cats are finding out where it's at in the joint. Most of the people out here, man, if they were only to get the opportunity to go over to the Rock for a while, it might open their eyes."

"There're a lot of people out here, Floyd, who think their eyes are open already."

"Yeah, but they're not open to the right things. Do you think that the

Claude Brown

black man on this street is really making any progress? I mean, toward any freedom, with all these bars out here and with all the liquor stores. It seems as though that's where all the money's going. You know what happens? The white man works us to death here in Harlem, in New York, man, all over the world—all over the country anyway. He works us to death all week long and gives us a little bit of money, and we don't even keep that. You know what we do with it, Claude? We go downtown come Friday and Saturday night; we go down to the bars and the liquor stores, and we give it right back to him—for nothing. We act like we don't even want it. The black man is just a sleeping man. Unless he listens to the word of Muhammad, he's going to be lost all the time."

"Damn, Floyd, this thing seems to have happened to a whole lot of people. Nobody's colored any more, and nobody's Negro. It seems as though everybody is a black man."

"Well, what's wrong? Are you afraid of being a black man? We're all black men."

"Yeah, man, you're hollering about the black man. You sound almost as bad as Adam Clayton Powell. Light-skin as you are, you're going around hollering about black man. Somebody's going to say, 'Look, fellow, get a hold of yourself and look in a mirror.'"

"Look, I'm dark-skin. They got me on all the records, on the statistics, as a black man. If I go down to City Hall and ask for a marriage license and put down there 'colored,' they'll make me put down 'black,' man. They don't want to hear none of that colored thing or Negro. They got the race there, and they want 'white' or 'black.' So whether you like it or not, Claude, we are black men in this country, and that's all we're gon be. If you're a wise black man, you'll listen to Muhammad's message from Allah, here and now, and unite. The time has come for all black men to rise up, band together, and do something for themselves."

"Yeah, well, Floyd, what would you suggest? Right now?"

"Man, the first thing we got to do is stop buying anything but the necessities from the white man. Anything that you can get from a black man, go on and buy it. Man, you know what's wrong with the people out here? They don't realize who they are. They don't realize what they are. We're not Negro, and we're not colored. These are words that somebody else gave us, that the white devils gave us . . . to help rob us of our own identity. We're black men, and we've even been taught to be ashamed of it, when, actually, we should all be proud of it.

"You don't know . . . I bet you don't know anything about yourself. You think your name is Brown, huh? That's not your name. That's just the name that some old white man gave to your forefathers when they brought them to this country, stole their heritage, and blinded them to their identity."

He told me that my name was probably Abdul or something-or-other, a Muslim name.

"We all got those other names, man. We got to stop being Negroes. The only way we gon stop acting as Negroes is that we stop seeing ourselves as Negroes. The first step toward not seeing ourselves as Negroes is to reject those names they've given us and the term 'Negro' . . . those Anglo-Saxon names that they give to us and call us Negroes by them. Then they treat us like Negroes. Man, I'm deathly afraid of being a Negro in this country, because the Negroes get messed over, messed over right and left."

Then Floyd started talking about how the white man had robbed the black man in Africa of his heritage and put him into slavery by feeding him all this white religion. He said, "The black man's got no business with Christianity. They've even got us looking up at some white Jesus. Jesus was black. It says so in the Bible. It says that Solomon was black; it says that Moses was black. But here they've told us a lie. They took the Bible and rewrote it for themselves, telling us that they were white so we'd be looking up to them for being white. If you look up to Jesus and Jesus was white, you got to look up to these white men because they're white. Right?"

"I think there's a little more to it than that, Floyd."

"Yeah, there's a lot more to it. This whole religion is foreign to a black man. A black man's got no business kneeling down and praying to some old crazy figurines and talking that old 'Our Father,' 'Jesus,' and that kind of business. This Christianity thing is the worst thing that ever happened to Negroes. If it wasn't for Christianity, Negroes would have stopped praying a long time ago. They would've started raising a whole lot of hell. They would've known. There would've been thousands of Nat Turners and Denmark Veseys. But most of the Negroes were too damn busy looking up in the sky and praying to some blond-haired, blue-eyed Jesus and some white God who nobody was suppose to ever see or know anything about. You look at it around here. The Negro's got a whole lot of religion, the so-called Negro, the black man. He's got more religion than anything else.

"But he's still poor; he's still being abused. So why the hell don't the white man take some of that religion he's been preaching to us all the time and give us some of the money? Why don't he take some of that religion and use it himself, to make himself less mean and stop killing all those people, lynching all those people down there in Georgia, Mississippi, and Alabama? If there was anything to this white man's religion, he wouldn't be so damn wicked. How can he be so righteous, how can the religion that he's living by be so righteous, if it's going to let him come in here and take a whole country from the Indians, kill off most of them, and put the remainder of them on reservations?

"Look around you. What's it taught Negroes to do? All this Christianity? Nothing, nothing that could benefit them. All it's taught Negroes to do is bow their heads to Mr. Charlie, buy bleach creams, straighten their hair, buy a Cadillac car that they can't afford, and follow some white Jesus to a mythical place called heaven. Ain't this a damn shame?"

He said, "Look, I want you to come on over here with me to the bookstore, Michaux's bookstore. They're speaking out there. Some brother is speaking out there tonight."

"Look, Floyd, I've heard these cats before, man. All they're saying is things that I've heard before, and I haven't been sold on it yet."

"Yeah, that's because you're still lost as to your identity and just where you're going and what's to be obtained in life. If you're ever going to really get anything in life, man, you've got to get out . . . separate yourself from that white man. Give him back his bullshit ideals, and give back the values that he's given you to bullshit you by and to keep you stupid. First of all, Claude, you got to let go that white god, because that white god's going to fuck over you just like it's been fucking over every black man in this country ever since we got here.

"The hip people, those who saw it, they're going on, and they're exploiting black people too. The colored preachers who go around preaching about that white god, they're the ones who dig it, man. They saw it right from the beginning, right after slavery. When a cat started preaching, shit, this meant that he didn't have to work any more. He got the calling. It was an easy life. They're not kneeling down and praying to that god; they're holding out their hands. They're preaching and talking about saving, patting sisters on the ass and saying sweet things to them, and going into their pocketbooks. They got the sisters working and bringing them all that fucking money. That's the same thing that Mr. Chuck's been doing all these years, Claude.

"You ever been out in them Jewish neighborhoods? In Long Island, in Brooklyn, in the Bronx, man, they don't have a whole lot of bars and liquor stores. Hell no! They have their synagogues; they have their bakeries, their grocery stores, their delicatessens, and shit, but they don't have a lot of bars and liquor stores. Man, those people aren't that easily bullshitted. They know where it's at. You know why? They know how to get that money; they know the value of money. They're not going to be just going out here talking about 'glory be to God.' They know they got to get that money.

"The black man is a lost man, and Muhammad is trying to show him the way. I'm telling you, Claude, if we're going to make it, man, you've got to listen to the word of Muhammad. He's the only one who seems to know. Do you know what he's done? He has taken junkies, man, here off the street, taken them downtown and put them in suits, man. I mean, he's dressed them up, given them jobs, and made cats who were strung out with long habits respectable people again. He's given them a cause, man, to fight for. He's taken the stigma off them.

"That's what's got a lot of people around here strung out, man, and fucked up in their minds. They don't know who they are. They think they're Negroes; they think they're lost. They ain't got nobody to look up to but that white god. That's hard to accept, man. Can you imagine being a Negro in a place where the only Supreme Being is a white god, and he's in the white people's corner, and the white people are fucking over you? You might as well kill yourself.

"The junkies have to use drugs, man, to stand this life. I couldn't do it myself, man, without using drugs. I don't see how you do it. Everybody with a little bit of sensitivity would have to use something or else kill himself. I couldn't accept being a Negro. I know I'm no damned Negro. That's why I was going to jail and doing all that fucking up for a long time, because I thought I was a Negro in a white world ruled by a white god. Once I found out that I was a black man and that God was a black man, I can walk with anything now. I know I'm too powerful to be made a slave ever again. My mind is free. When you get freedom of the mind, nobody can fuck with you. Nobody can enslave anybody who's got freedom of mind. All they can do is kill you.

"Those white people can't do anything to me now, man. The most they can do to me is kill me, but they can't make me a slave any more. They can't make me believe that it's right to go and spend my money in the bars. They can't make me believe that Jesus is white. They can't make me believe that I should go to church and all that kind of shit and live to go to heaven. Uh-uh, man. My mind is free, and this is what freedom of mind means. Whatever you do, man, you do it black, because you know you're a black man, and you know that God is black. When you got that knowledge of the power of blackness in this world, nobody and no force can fuck with you, because you've got the black god in your corner."

Floyd said, "Salaam aleichem, brother. Remember, Allah is black."

About six months later, I ran into Bulldog. I hadn't seen him in about three or four years. He was as big as a house. He looked like he must have been boxing or wrestling professionally. He'd gotten huge since I'd last seen him.

I said, "Bulldog. How you been?" I didn't ask him where he'd been or anything like that, because I usually had a pretty good idea, by this time, where cats had been when I hadn't seen them for a while. I was glad to see him. I grabbed his hand and shook it. I asked him if he wanted to go have a drink with me.

He said that he couldn't do that. He started off, "I just got out of jail, man."

I said, "Yeah? That's nice." Since I was with someone who wasn't accustomed to meeting people who'd just come out of jail, I tried to change the subject. I said, "Come on, let's go in the bar."

Again he said, "No, man. I just got out of jail."

I said, "Yeah, well where were you?"

He started telling me that he hit a cop one night, and they thought he was crazy and put him in Bellevue. Some attendants there started messing with him. He took on three or four of them, so they sent him to Materwann for about two years. He'd come out, and now he was a Muslim.

I said, "Wow! It seems as though this Muslim thing is getting to everybody."

He started telling me about it. He said, "You know, man, I don't eat no pork, and I don't drink no more. That's why I can't go in the bar with you and have that drink."

"Yeah, okay, B.D. I can understand that. Do you want to go someplace and have a cup of coffee?"

He said, "All right."

We had a cup of coffee, and he started telling me about how he had just come out of jail, all over again. Then it dawned on me that maybe they let Bulldog out a little too soon. He kept repeating, "I just got out of jail." If you asked him something else, he'd say, "I'm a Muslim." He had a beard, which he seemed real proud of. He kept pulling on it and stroking it as though it were something precious.

After a while, he told me about his new name. He said, "You know, Pashif's my real name now."

"Okay, Pashif." I shook his hand and said, "Salaam aleichem."

"Oh! Are you a Muslim too, man?"

"No, Brother Pashif, but I've heard a little about it. I've met a few people, and I know quite a few."

"Do you know Alley Bush?"

I said, "Yeah, why?"

"Alley Bush is a Muslim too."

"Oh, yeah? I haven't seen him in a long time, and I wondered what happened to him."

"Yeah, he's out here, and he's a Muslim. As a matter of fact, he's supposed to make a speech on 125th Street and Seventh Avenue tonight."

"Yeah? I'll have to come back and hear this. I'd like to see him."

I left Bulldog. I came back that night, because I wanted to see Alley Bush. There he was, speaking on his box. Knowing Alley Bush, I didn't think he could ever be really involved in this thing. I thought he was just jiving about it.

After he was finished, I went up to him and said, "Come on, man, let's go down and have a beer or something."

He said, "No, man. I can't do that, because . . . I could do it, but we'd have to go about three blocks away, because some of my brothers might see me."

We went and had a beer, and he started telling me about the white devils and all this kind of business. He started telling me about the great plans he had for getting up a colored army and starting a revolution. He said, "The country is ready, and what we need now is a revolution."

I thought, Damn, everybody seems to be going kind of crazy with this thing. Where is all this stuff coming from? So I asked Alley Bush if he had been in jail lately.

"Yeah, I just got out about three months ago."

I asked him if that was where he became a brother. He said yes and that his name was Bashi now and that his father had been a Muslim. I knew his father hadn't been a Muslim when I'd seen him. Alley Bush was a real great liar. He just couldn't help lying. If you asked him the simplest thing, he just had this compulsion to lie.

We sat there sipping, and he started asking me when I was going to forsake this world of the white devils and go and join the black brothers "in our struggle for freedom of the mind and freedom in our own way of life and freedom in a land of our own where we can take our rightful place among the gods."

I was taking all this with a grain of salt. Occasionally I'd laugh, and he would get a little angry. He started raising his voice and almost screaming this stuff about the white devils and the great black man. This was funny, because Alley was a very light-skinned guy, and he'd always been aware of it.

It seemed as though, under this new Muslim movement, everybody was becoming real black and becoming proud of it. Maybe this was a good thing. Maybe it was bringing all the shades together and making us realize that we're all colored, regardless of complexion.

It seemed to me that everybody who was coming out of jail was a Black Muslim. While he was raving, I was thinking about this. I said, "Damn, Alley, what the hell is going on in the jails here? It seems that everybody who comes out is a Muslim."

He said, "Yeah, man. When you're out here, you're so involved in the way the white man has been teaching you to live and doing shit that he's been brainwashing you to believe, you just can't see where you're going. You can't do the things that you ought to do, you know? But there, when you're in jail, man, you've got a lot of time to think about it. Then you can really see how this white man is fucking with you. The white cats in jail, man, they don't have to take all the shit that we have to take. They get the better jobs, and they get everything. It's just the black man, the black man, wherever he is, they're gon try and fuck with him. Actually, if the black man wasn't a god, he wouldn't have lasted this long, all the shit he's had to take in this country. Yeah, this is what it takes.

"You know what we got to do here, Sonny? We got to take Harlem out of Goldberg's pocket. You know Harlem is in Goldberg's pocket?"

"Yeah, Alley, that's been said before."

He said, "That's not my name. That's the name that the white devils gave me, man. When you call me that, you remind me of the fact that I've been robbed of my heritage. It's a painful thing, so I wish you wouldn't call me that. I wish you'd call me by my Muslim name, my real name, my true and honest name, given to my black father in the black land by a black god, many, many centuries ago."

"Okay, Bashi. Pardon me."

"What we need here, Sonny, is a revolution. If all goes well with me, we're going to have it here in this country before long. I'm trying to get a lot of militant black men who are ready to stop taking this shit. I've been in jail with them, and I know that these guys are ready for a revolution. They're ready to die, because they know we ain't got a chance in this world anyway, seeing as how the white men are running it.

"But if we revolt now, even if most of us have to die, our sons and grandsons might have a chance in it. The only thing that's going to get Harlem out of Goldberg's pocket is that we take 125th Street and leave it all to the proprietors, but move the main thoroughfare to 145th Street. If all the Negroes would pool their money together and start purchasing all the real estate on 145th Street, in about two years time we could have it. We could have 145th Street being the main thoroughfare, and it would all be owned by black people.

"That's power, and that's why Goldberg's got all the power now—because of money. They've got millions and millions of black dollars being spent right down here on 125th Street. That's what you heard me holler about up there tonight. That's what makes me so mad when I see it. And the niggers just keep going in there giving him more of their money, and he's not giving them a damn thing, man. All he's going to give them is some low-quality goods. Shit, it seems as though the nigger would have enough sense by now, man, to see that if he's ever to get anything in this country, he's going to have to start thinking for himself and start being a little selfish.

"The time is now, man, to get together. You see me out here, Sonny, and you see all the other black brothers out here. We've forsaken this white world altogether. I couldn't go downtown and work, man. I couldn't stand to be around white people for one hour a day.

"Do you really think you're out of slavery? Then all you got to do is go down as far as Maryland, brother. Go in some of those restaurants down there and ask them for a cup of coffee. They'll look at you like you're a runaway slave or something. And they might treat you like one.

"Man, we sit down here tonight, and we talk. I'm angry. With you, brother, I think you're one of these complacent niggers out here who managed to get by and not have it bother them directly. So you figure you're not out here. Yeah, I'll bet you're walking around here thinking you're free. When the shit comes down on you, you're going to be one of the angriest niggers out here on this street, man.

"As a matter of fact, I'm gon watch you. I'm gon watch you, because you've been going through all this shit, and you been going through it almost anesthetized. I'm going to keep watching you, because I know, when the shit gets to you, it's gon hit you real hard, real hard, because it's all going to come down on you at once . . . everything that's been piling up. You may not realize it, man, but you're angry.

"Sonny, every black man in this land is angry now, especially in Harlem. There's no way for them not to be. You look around you, brother. You can't get any money. You come up, a little boy, in this place. You go downtown to work. They want to treat you like you're still a little boy. All the time when you're growing up in this great New York City, man, your childhood is just filled with exploitation by those white devils out there. Everyplace you go, brother. You got to go to the white butcher shop; you got to go to the white grocery store. They've got colored barbershops. That's all they let us have, Sonny. The only reason they let us have a colored barbershop is because those white devils don't know nothin' about cutting no colored hair. They don't really know nothin', man.

"The people ain't got no soul. I'm telling you, brother. They're not even real. Yeah, I'm telling you, man. Those people are behind us. Colored people have got all the feelings, man. You see all these niggers running out here talking about they want some white girl. Damn, I don't want me nothin' but a nigger woman. I don't see how anybody couldn't want one, seeing as how they're the only ones who've got any soul, man. You been around all these people with soul for so long. They're into it with Allah. That's right.

"You come up all this time, Sonny, all your life in Harlem. And there is the white landlord, man, who your folks got to be worried about paying the rent to. There is the white grocer, who your moms got to be going down pleading with that mother-fucker to give her some credit so she could feed her kids. They got to be going and taking their stuff to the pawnshop to some damn white pawnbroker, who they got to beg for a few dollars, because he knows they're up tight and need the money, and he's gon try and take their shit for nothing at all.

"They got to be going to a white fish market, that's gon be gypping them. They got to go to the white butcher, who's gon be selling them some old dried-up mother-fucking neck bones and pig tails and pig feet. They wouldn't even think about selling that shit in any white neighborhood. They don't even sell it for dogmeat in white neighborhoods. You go to the movies, the movies are owned by the white people. Everything here is white.

"If you're not mad, I feel sorry for you, Sonny, because you're crazy, and you're lost, man. So there, black man, you've got to be mad, brother."

"Alley, man, you can get mad about this shit, but if you can't do anything about it, it's gon fuck with your mind, you know? Unless you stop being mad because you realize you have to stop, for your own good."

"How the hell are you gon stop bein' mad when you've got a foot up in your ass?"

I said, "Look, man, if you're going to live, you got to try and take the foot out of your ass. There's some things, man, that anger doesn't mean a damn thing to. You can get mad if you want to, but why bother if nobody's going to pay any attention to you? Alley, the way I feel about it is that we—you, me, the cats we came up with, probably all the cats that were in jail with you—we were angry all our lives. That's what that shit was all about. We were having our revolution. The revolution that you're talking about, Alley, I've had it. I've had that revolution since I was six years old. And I fought it every day—in the streets of Harlem, in the streets of Brooklyn, in the streets of the Bronx and Lower Manhattan, all over—when I was there stealing, raising hell out there, playing hookey. I rebelled against school because the teachers were white. And I went downtown and robbed the stores because the store owners were white. I ran through the subways because the cats in the change booths were white.

"I was rebelling every time I went to someplace like the Children's Center, like the Youth House, like Wiltwyck, like Warwick. I was rebelling, man. And all I met in there were other young, rebellious cats who couldn't take it either.

"But nobody was winning. That revolution was hopeless. The cats who had something on the ball and they could dig it in time, they stopped. They stopped. They didn't stop being angry. They just stopped cutting their own throats, you know? That kind of revolution was impossible. It was doomed to fail, right from the word go.

"Now, look at it realistically, Alley. How the hell are you gonna come in here and say, 'Look, white man, we're living in your world, but I want you to let us have a revolution'? This is what it would amount to, because the black man's just in no position to revolt against anything here. You know what that's all about, Alley. You've been around; you've heard of this before. People have always been talking that shit, but nobody's gotten up and started any revolution. In the old days, in the slave uprisings, these people were ready to die."

Alley said, "Wait a minute! Wait a minute, Sonny, I'm ready to die too, man. Shit, I don't feel as though I've got any more now than the folks in slavery had. I don't feel that their pain is any more than mine. Shit, why shouldn't I be ready to die?"

"Look, Alley, if you just want to die, why bother to go out there and do it in the name of freedom?"

He said, "Man, because I want everybody to know that they're not free. I want you to know; I want my sisters to know; I want my brothers to know; I want the whole generation to know that we're not free."

"Alley, man, didn't you find out anything when you were in jail? Didn't you find out anything about the rebellion or the revolution and why we were losing all that time? Why all those cats in there lost?"

He said, "Yeah, I found out why. I found out why, because half of those mother-fuckers in there was goin' to church on Sunday, praying to a white god."

"Listen, Alley, the rebellion has gone along the wrong lines."

"Yeah, it's goin' along the wrong line, Sonny, because it's still going along that white line. Those mother-fuckers don't even know what they're fighting in there. Half of those cats in jail, they were out here stealing from colored people. Now, ain't that a fuckin' shame? They were out in the street stealin' from black people. You know, you've got niggers up there who've hit black men in the head and taken their wallets. You know why? It's because all other Negroes see the way that the white man is treating the black man. He's just got to try and treat them the same way too. Everybody's down on Negroes because of what the white man has made this society think of Negroes. . . .

"I'm damn surprised at you, Sonny. Man, all the way up, since the time I met you, you were a real hell raiser. As a matter of fact, the last time I got back to Harlem, I was looking for you, and I was hoping that you had gotten the message from Muhammad . . . because I knew you'd be good in this thing. But now, man, I don't know. If anybody had ever told me that Claude Brown was talking that peaceful shit and he's not angry, I would have said they were lying. I think one day, it's gon come out, brother . . . the same shit. It's gon come out in you too, and I think it's gon come out so strong I'm gon be afraid to be around you. I think that stuff is gonna come out . . . that violent stuff in you, like that riot that you started up at Warwick."

I said, "Man, I told everybody I never started all that stuff."

He said, "Yeah, but you didn't have to tell me. When they told me it was a riot between the Puerto Ricans and the colored cats, I just knew you had to be behind it, you know. That's the way you are, Sonny, and I think when you get the message from Muhammad, Harlem's gon move, brother. We gon have fire on the streets, man."

"I've already got the message, Alley. And it's not from Muhammad. As a matter of fact, I'm hoping I can give it to you, but I think I'll have to wait until you become a little disenchanted with Muhammad."

He said, "Look, brother, I've got to go. I'm going to see you. I want you to stay out of these bars and stop giving that white devil our money."

"Yeah, Bashi, I just might think about that. All I've got to do is find me a good colored-owned bar."

Alley said, "Salaam aleichem."

"Salaam aleichem, Bashi."

It seemed as though over the next few years, say from 1955 through 1959, just about everybody who came out of jail came out a Muslim. By 1959, I had come to the conclusion that few Negroes could go to any of the city prisons in New York and not come out a Muslim.

There was one common thing that I noticed about all the cats in the Muslim movement. They seemed to be the cats who were very uncertain about where they were, who they were, or what they were going to do, the cats who had never been able to find their groove. The guys who went to jail, they just knew they were criminals, and that's all there was to it. They were never going to do anything to be good. They weren't going to do anything halfway good. Nobody could tell them anything. They were guys who were messing up because they just didn't know of any other way to let off steam. So the Muslim faith seems to have been just the thing for them.

But the real cold criminals, none of those guys came out Muslims. After a while, this was a way you could tell cold hoods. If a guy was a real stickup artist, he was a real stickup artist. He didn't mess with drugs; he didn't mess with the Muslim faith; he didn't mess with anything but crime.

In a way, it was a good thing that the Muslim faith was gaining ground in Harlem, because it gave something to the junkies and to the prostitutes. When a junkie came out of jail or when he came back from getting a cure, it was the rule to just come back on the streets and do the same things that he had been doing all along. Now it was different.

All the time before, the junkie never had anyplace to go when he came out of jail or out of the hospital. Now the junkies had a place to go, those who could accept the teachings of the Muslims. It wasn't hard to accept, not for most of the junkies. Junkies weren't cold criminals at heart, not Harlem junkies. Maybe this was why they became junkies—because they couldn't see going into the crime life. I've seen very few real criminals that ever dabbled in drugs. If a guy was criminally inclined and started messing with drugs, he usually became a junkie and no longer a criminal. There was a difference. The junkie was a junkie first and above all other things. His criminal activities were merely means to an end.

The Muslim movement was cleaning them up, giving them a lot of food for thought, feeding them with a philosophy—if you could call it that—that provided some type of moral fortitude. Now they had a place to go. They went to 125th Street and Seventh Avenue, started preaching the word and saying "Salaam aleichem" to everybody, and growing beards.

It was a new thing, and it was a strong thing too. It was something, I suppose, that most cats in Harlem could accept, because it was an angry thing. I guess any angry organization would have more appeal to male Harlemites than any other kind of organization.

Then, there was this thing in the new name. It was always fascinating to everybody. It was fascinating to the new recruits. It gave them a sense of being somebody, a sense of importance. All the time before they became Muslims, I suppose there was a feeling of insignificance that led them into self-destruction in one form or another. It was just not being anybody. Now they were somebody, a part of something. I suppose that's all they needed.

All the Muslims now felt as though 125th Street was theirs. It used to belong to the hustlers and the slicksters. They're still there, but Seventh Avenue belongs to the Muslims. I think everybody knows this now. This group just came down and claimed it. They started setting up their stands and giving speeches. People started listening, and it just became known that if you wanted to hear a good antiwhite sermon on Saturday night, all you had to do was go to 125th Street and Seventh Avenue.

It made everybody feel as though they had something. I suppose there were many people who had been mistreated by the white boss during the day. They could come out on Seventh Avenue and hear something that would be consoling . . . hear some of the "Buy Black" slogans and "hate the white devils" speeches.

The Muslims would try to embarrass people who weren't buying black or boycotting the white people. They weren't gaining too much ground as far as getting the people to stop buying from white store owners, but they got them to start believing this thing about buying from colored, giving the money to colored, and that colored people should stick together.

I recall one evening I had come uptown to see my folks. I had heard on the news and seen in the evening paper something about a riot down at the United Nations earlier that day.

This was about the time that Patrice Lumumba had been killed. Lumumba had come to Harlem the summer before. The Muslims had gotten him to speak on 125th Street. Everybody in Harlem was pretty fond of Lumumba, especially the Black Muslims.

The incident at the United Nations started off as a peaceful demonstration and turned into a riot. It was led by a young light-skinned fellow who—The New York Times said—had features more Arabic than Negroid, and since he was garbed in some royal Arabic attire, the paper speculated that he was most likely a prince or the son of some Arabian prince.

When I got to my parents' house that evening, Dad started telling me that he'd seen "that crazy boy who use to come around here."

I said, "Dad, which crazy boy is this?" because I knew he was always calling somebody crazy. He thought, at one time, that just about all my friends were crazy.

He said, "You know, that crazy light-skin boy who was up at Wiltwyck with you and use to come here and have a party with Suzy Q. He use to kiss the dog all the time, that sort of thing."

"Oh! You mean Alley. I haven't seen him in a little while. He's down on 125th Street most of the time."

He said, "Oh, yeah. Well, I saw him on TV just a little while ago. He was down there at the UN, with some old funny-lookin' clothes on, making some trouble about that man dying down there in Africa, that man Lumumba."

I said, "Oh! So that was Alley who started all that trouble down there at the UN? I wish I'd seen it."

Dad said, "The news will be back on at six-thirty, and they'll probably show it again. So why don't you hang around. You can see it. He was there. I know it was him, because I saw him, as big as day."

When the news came on, there was Alley looking very solemn. I knew he was very fond of Patrice Lumumba, as were all the Muslims who had met him when he was in New York. But I didn't think Alley would go down to the United Nations and start a riot or anything like that. But evidently he did.

He came back to Harlem a hero. The next day, *The New York Times* ran an article about Alley probably being the son of some Arabian prince. The Harlemites who knew him had a good laugh.

It was a good thing for Alley, I suppose, because he was heard. He made the goddamn white man know that he was angry.

The thing that I noticed about the Muslim faith that seemed to stand out over that of the Coptic was that people didn't leave as soon. I would see guys being members of the Muslim faith for years. It just kept expanding; it was more and more. If I stayed away from Harlem for a few months, when I came back, there were many more people who hadn't been Muslims when I left who were now Muslims, women and men. It was a thing that just seemed to keep expanding, and it also seemed to hold people.

Then the Muslims started getting places in Harlem. They opened up dry cleaners with lower prices than other places. They opened up their restaurants. They had good food—fried chicken, pies, anything but pork. It was always delicious, because it was home cooking, but without the pork. The prices were very reasonable. As a matter of fact, they were more reasonable than just about any of the places in Harlem except the fish-and-chips joints. I supposed that eventually the Muslims would open up a fish-and-chips joint.

The policemen in Harlem seemed to resent the Muslims, but they also seemed to be afraid of them. Especially the white police. They weren't violent. I'd never seen or heard of any Muslim violence before 1960. The policemen would come down, and they would watch. Everybody was afraid of the Muslims at first, all the politicians and the law-enforcement agents. They weren't advocating overthrow of the government. They weren't advocating riots. They weren't advocating anything but economic boycott of white stores and giving money to colored enterprises. White policemen would stand around, and they would look at these people as if to say, "These niggers are dangerous, but what's gonna happen?"

Sometimes white people would come out, and they would stand around and listen. Many people who weren't interested in what the Muslims were saying for the sake of enlightenment—the preachers or ministers or professional people in the community—would stand there and look around.

Most people would just laugh at them, but as they started getting bigger crowds and having bigger rallies, people began to wonder, "Should they be stopped?"

The police always looked as if they wanted to snatch them down from their soapboxes, but they never had any reason. Many times, these guys would stand up there and purposely single out white policemen and say, "Look at them. Look what they're doing to us. They've got us all bunched up here in some little hole in the wall. That's what this is. This is a hole in the wall on the island of Manhattan, where they stuck the majority of the black people. And they got their white devils to guard us. You see 'em? This is just like being in jail, and you people think you're free."

One of them would point at a white policeman and say, "Look at the white devil, standing around us with a gun, and all we're doing is talking to one another. Ain't this somethin'? We can't even talk to one another in this little hole in the wall that they call Harlem, and stuck us into, without them putting some guard at the door, guarding us with a gun. That's what he's doing there, standing up there near that lamppost. That's just the way the guards do in jail." (The guy probably knew, because there was a good chance that he'd been in jail at one time or another.) Then all the people in the crowd would turn around and look at the cop.

This was enough to scare the hell out of anybody. But there was nothing the cops could do to stop them, because they had permission to speak. Even the colored cops were made to feel uneasy. The speakers would point to them and say, "Yeah, you put a badge on some black men, and they'll do anything that the white men wants 'em to do to other black men. You can put a badge on some black men, give them a gun, and tell them, 'You go out there and guard your black brother. And if he does anything wrong, you shoot him.'"

Most of the time, the colored policemen would laugh, or they would try to fake a laugh. Many times you could tell that they were pretending. The crowd would usually laugh at them when the Muslims said these things. Many people would turn around and look at the cops and laugh in their faces.

Had the police tried to arrest them, I think everybody would have resented it. The Muslims had become a part of the community. They became the Seventh Avenue speakers. After a while, no one would come down there to speak but them. At the time when the Muslims first started coming down there, Seventh Avenue was something like Union Square, down on Fourteenth Street. All types of Harlem radicals would get up and speak. Sometimes they'd have debates. Sometimes one speaker would get up and vigorously contradict what the speaker before him had just said. Then, about 1956, people were afraid to get up on Seventh Avenue and try to contradict anything that the Muslims had said, because just about all the people down there around that time were Muslims, and they didn't want to hear anything other than what the Muslims were saying. It was very hard for anybody to contradict anything that the Muslims were saying, because, right away, they would be labeled an Uncle Tom. What the Muslims were saying was a colored thing. They were saying, "Let's get more and more for the black man." Anybody who got up there and opposed this was a traitor to the race. He was saying, "Give to the white man, even more."

Then the Muslims started coming around with their newspapers. I think that even the people who weren't interested in or were indifferent to the Muslim movement sort of sympathized with them. If the Muslims were trying to sell papers, people would buy papers, just to give some money to the cause.

The Black Muslim movement was closer to most Harlemites than any of the other organizations, much closer than the NAACP or the Urban League. These were the people who were right out there in the street with you. They had on suits, but their grammar wasn't something that would make the average Negro on the street feel ill at ease. The words that they used were the same words that the people on the street used. You could associate these people with yourself; you knew some of them. Since the leaders of this group had come from the community, the crowd could identify with these people more readily than they could with anybody else.

The Muslims were the home team. They were the people, talking for everyone. This was the first time that many of these people had ever seen the home boys get up and say anything in front of a crowd. This was the first time that many of these people had ever seen home boys who had been junkies, pimps, or thieves speak to crowds of people and sound so serious about it. It became a community thing.

I suppose the Muslims did the same thing in other places, other Harlems throughout the nation. They must have gotten members and speakers right out of the community. This was a way in which they couldn't lose, because when a guy got up on 125th Street and started talking about how Goldberg who's got the haberdashery right there on the corner paid him something like forty dollars a week for two years, when he was a grown man, and how he started working for Brother So-and-So, down at his rib joint on 116th Street, and is now making seventy-five dollars a week, everybody's got to get up and say, "Yeah, yeah. That no-good Goldberg ought to go."

The people would holler, "Yeah! Yeah! Them goddamn Jews killed my Jesus too!" It's easy to build up this sort of feeling among the home folks when one of the people in the neighborhood, the boy who used to work in the butcher store and became a Muslim, says, "Mr. Greenberg didn't sell you any good meat. Some of that meat was years old. Some of that meat had been in there for days, and it was almost blue, because it had spoiled so long. But he'd shellac it or something to make it look like it was unspoiled, to make it look like it was almost fresh."

The people could believe these speakers. They knew them. They knew that they had worked at these places and that they should know what they were talking about. The Muslims became a very influential force in Harlem. They would never have been able to take over, because they couldn't acquire any political power. For one thing, many of their recruits had been in jail. Once a person goes to jail for a felony, he loses his voting rights. But if the Muslims were to run a candidate for Congress in Harlem, there might be a good chance that they could get enough support. I know if they had done this in 1960, they could have gotten quite a bit of support from sympathizers. Today they might stand an even better chance.

I haven't seen too many of my Muslim friends lately, but I imagine they're still involved. I hear about the things that they're doing now. The Muslim movement is a good thing. It's good because these cats know they're angry, and they're letting everybody else know they're angry. If they don't do any more than let the nation know that there are black men in this country who are dangerously angry, then they've already served a purpose.

15

There was a piano in the auditorium at Washington Irving, and sometimes I used to go there in the evening and play it before I went up to my classes. I'd just tinkle on it softly so that I wouldn't disturb anybody. One evening, when I was coming out of school I was stopped. Somebody just said, "Hey, there." It was a girl, and she sounded as if she knew me.

I looked around and pointed to myself, as if to say, "You mean me?"

"Yeah, you, the virtuoso." She was a white girl, and I'd never seen her before. I didn't know who she was. She wasn't an especially attractive girl. She had a kind-looking face, but you couldn't say any more than that. I went over to her, and she said, "I was listening to you play this evening. You're quite good."

I said, "Well, thanks, anyway, but I'm not that serious about it."

She said, "Well, maybe you ought to be. I tried playing piano for years, and I never made that much progress. How long have you been at it?"

"Oh, about three years." She looked at me as if to say, "You're joking!" I still had the feeling that this girl was just trying to flatter me. I said, "Why? How long did you think I'd been playing?"

"From the sound of it, I thought you had been playing at least five years or more."

I just looked at her, sort of skeptically, and said, "How long did you play?"

"I played for about eight years."

"Eight years? That doesn't sound too long. You look as though you're only about sixteen as it is."

"That's nice to know." I liked the way she said it, very calmly, as if she was going to act mature. And she was doing okay at it.

I said, "Do you still play?"

"Occasionally. I think I'd like to be a teacher, teach music."

"So, what are you doing here, at Washington Irving?"

"Oh, I have to get another course to graduate, and I have to go in the evening because they don't have it up there."

"Oh? They don't have it up where?"

She said, "I attend school at Music and Art during the day."

"I know some one who used to go there. By the way, I'm Claude Brown. Who are you?"

She told me her name was Judy Strumph. I said, "I'm glad to meet you, Judy. Are you going out?"

She said, "Yeah, I'm going to the subway." I asked her where she wanted to go in the subway. She said, "I'm going home."

"Yeah, I figured that much, but where's home?"

"It's uptown."

"Why don't you just come over here in the cafeteria with me and have a cup of coffee?"

"Okay, I have some time."

She seemed very relaxed. She wasn't overly friendly, and she wasn't frightened. It was interesting to meet a young girl like this. She looked about seventeen.

We went into the Automat and had two cups of coffee and a couple of slices of pie. We sat and talked. She was very interesting; there was something beautiful about her manner. She was too plump to be attractive. Her hair was kind of kinky; it wasn't long, blond, or soft. She was just a very plain-looking girl. She could have been a country girl, or maybe a hillbilly, from her looks.

We talked about music, and I told her what I'd been doing. She told me that she had been playing piano and violin since she was a very little girl. Everybody in her family played some musical instrument.

I asked her if she liked jazz. She told me she liked it but didn't know too much about it. She said her brother had a lot of jazz albums; the only artists she knew of were the ones he had the records by. She said she had never been to a jazz concert because no one had ever offered to take her.

"If you'd like to go, I'd be happy to take you sometime."

"Yes, I'd like to, but I couldn't go on a school night because I have to get home. I live uptown from here, so I would prefer that it's on a weekend or sometime like that."

"Okay, that's all right. We'll make it on the weekend." She seemed kind of puzzled when I said, "Meet me down here this Friday night, about eight o'clock."

"Okay, but I don't have a class on Friday night."

I said, "I know, but since this is a place that we both know, it'll be easy for you to find me down here. So if you come down here and meet me, you won't have any trouble."

She looked at me for a while, and she said, "Why couldn't you come to my house and pick me up?"

"Judy, I don't think that would be a very wise thing to do. I like you, and maybe you like me. We could probably be good friends. But I don't think this is something you should spring on your folks right now."

"Oh, my folks are rather broad-minded. We're Jewish, you know."

"I didn't know, but I sort of suspected it."

"My parents are not prejudiced, and they would treat you nicely They would show you the same hospitality they would show any other fellow."

"Judy, this is usually the way it is in theory. Many parents don't know how they really feel about Negroes until something like this happens, right in the home. They feel that Negroes are nice people, and they sympathize with them, but they feel they shouldn't be around their daughters or their sons. 'They're nice people as long as they stay away from us.' There are exceptions. I've met some and they were beautiful people. It's possible that your family might be an exception, but just in case they aren't, let's not let them ruin anything that we might be interested in."

"You sound as though you've had experience."

"No, but I've heard about these cases."

She said, "Okay, I'll meet you down here on Friday night."

Friday night came around, and I had my doubts about whether or not she'd show up. I didn't really feel certain that she would want to come down there.

I went to class and left early. I came out about eight o'clock. She was standing there with a pretty dress on. She was a very serious-looking girl. There was something attractive about her, but I think it was attractive only after you had spoken to her. She was the kind of girl you would never notice before you spoke to her.

Someone was talking to her. It was a white fellow. I didn't know just what I should do, whether I should just walk by, wait, or what. She was standing just inside the door to the building. I walked around in the lobby for a little while and tried to get her attention, but she didn't see me.

So I went over into the hall leading outside the building. I just looked at her. She said, "Oh, hi, Claude. Are you ready?"

The fellow looked at her, and he looked at me. She said, "I'll see you around," and she just walked away from him.

I felt more admiration for this girl right then and there. She had a knack for doing things. She seemed like a chick who could have done anything. She had so much poise and self-confidence. I just knew I was going to enjoy being out with her.

"Look, I'm going to take you to a place down on Fifth Street. Are you hungry?"

"A little."

"Okay, let's go to the Italian Kitchen and have something for dinner. Do you like wine?" She said she liked Manischewitz, and I said, "Yeah, you would." She smiled. I felt good being with her; I really felt good.

While we were sitting in the restaurant talking, I said, "Judy, that's a nice dress you've got on."

"Oh, do you really like this dress?"

"Why do you think I said it was nice?"

"I don't know. I thought you were trying to be nice."

I said, "No. I like it; I really like it."

"Look, Claude, if you don't like something I'm wearing, or if you object to something I do, or if something I do displeases you, please let me know. I'll change it. If you don't like my shoes, or if you don't like my handbag, or anything, tell me. Even if you don't like my hairstyle, you tell me that too . . . because I want to look the way you like me. I want to do what you would like me to do."

I was sort of moved. Girls had said a lot of things to me that, I suppose, were more meaningful or more emotional, but nothing had ever moved me like this before.

Just about all my life before, most of the girls I had gone with, most of the girls I had taken out, they were bitches. I'd never gotten involved with a white girl before, and I always had all kinds of skepticism about that nigger thing. You could argue with a colored girl anytime, and if she said "nigger," nobody would mind too much. But I never knew what I would do if I was arguing with a white girl and she called me a nigger. I didn't know how I'd take it, whether I'd want to hit her or something.

But after Judy said what she had, I was certain that it wouldn't mean a damn thing. It wouldn't mean any more than if a colored girl said it. If you get close enough with people, you can say anything. After the little bit about the dress and what I wanted her to do or wear, I just wanted to grab her, hug her, and just say, "You're wonderful." She was across the table, so all I could do was squeeze her hand. She looked at me and smiled. I guess she got the message.

We went down to the Five Spot. She was a different sort of girl. She was nice, she was uninhibited, and she had so much self-confidence that it just got next to me. She told me she'd never been in a nightclub before and not to hesitate to tell her if she did something wrong.

"Oh, relax, Judy. Some people, anything they might do wouldn't be wrong. And I feel that you're one of those people."

She smiled and said, "Thanks, anyway, but don't forget to let me know."

We went in and sat down. She said she'd never drunk anything but wines before, kosher wines, that sort of thing. I said, "Okay, we can just order your wine."

She said, "No. I'd like to try something, but I don't know that much about drinks. Why don't you order something for me, something that would be tasty and safe."

"Okay, I'll do that." I ordered her a *crème de cacao*, and she thought it was tasty. We sat there and listened to Thelonious Monk and his group play for a couple of hours.

We walked all around Greenwich Village. We walked around the Fountain Circle at Washington Square. It was a real different thing just being with someone like her. I had the funniest feeling that I could never approach her sexually. But she was so unrestrained and so unafraid that I just had to be less inhibited with her. She would grab my arm or my hand. Her eyes just glowed all the time. She could look at me and ask me anything she wanted.

I knew I could never tell Mama anything about this. She and Carole and Margie would have gotten down on me about being "white-woman crazy." I could hear Mama now. "You stay away from those white women. They ain't never lynched no white man over a colored woman. You just better stay away from those white girls, because you'll get yourself in a whole lot of trouble."

I showed Judy the restaurant where Eugene O'Neill used to hang out. We went to places where they had cats painting or reciting poetry to jazz.

When I showed her the Circle, I told her how the folk singers would get in the middle, with their banjos and their guitars, and sing on Sundays; how it was mixed—everybody would come down, white and colored. She said she'd have to come and see it.

We walked and walked for most of the night. I hated the thought of having to say good night to her. I wanted to do things. I guess I was just scared. Maybe I was just afraid of the fact that she was white. But this was something new. I was thinking, I don't know what to do with a white girl. But I had a feeling that she didn't think of herself as a white girl. She didn't think of herself as any different from me.

She was so natural-acting, I just had to react to her. When we sat down at the Circle in Washington Square and I told her that I would bring her down there the following Sunday, she said, "It sounds like something marvelous, like something they'd have in foreign countries." She started getting that faraway look in her eye. I just grabbed her and kissed her.

She sighed and said, "Well! That was nice. You know, I always knew that it would be."

"How do you mean you knew?"

"I just had that feeling before it happened that when you kissed me, it was going to be something exceptional."

"Yeah? You're an authority on kissing already?"

"No, but I knew it would give me a feeling like I never had before. I knew it would be a real good feeling." She just looked at me. I still had my arm around her.

She said, "How about an encore?" I kissed her again. We just sat there and held each other for a while. Then she said she thought she'd better be going home. She was supposed to be out with a friend of hers, and she didn't want her mother to start calling the friend.

I said, "Yeah, well, that's understandable." She told me she would call me Saturday, which was the following day. I said, "Okay, I'll be looking forward to it."

I took her to the subway. I wanted to take her home, but I realized I couldn't do that. I rode uptown with her to Eighty-sixth Street and said good night there.

I felt good. I really felt as though I had met something wonderful. I had just never met a girl like that. It was everything. Everything was different about her. Compared with her, most of the colored chicks I'd known seemed crude and harsh. They were chicks who you couldn't be but so sweet to, because they weren't sweet themselves. Her voice and manner were warm.

She seemed to be more feminine than most of the women I knew, and more of everything a woman was supposed to be.

She did call that Saturday, and she talked about the time we'd had and how she'd enjoyed it very much. And she thanked me. She thanked me for asking her out. This was kind of funny. It made me laugh, but these little things made me think of her as more and more beautiful all the time. She seemed to be the sweetest girl in the world. I just kept talking about it, in my head, and every time I thought about it, I would laugh, not just smile, even if I was out in the street someplace. I guess people looked at me and thought I was a little crazy.

I brought Judy down to the Village on Sunday and took her over to the Circle to see the folk singers carrying on. She really thought this was something great. Everybody there seemed so free. She wanted to take off her shoes and go into the Circle too.

I said okay. I had to let her do what she wanted to do, and hope that she wouldn't go too far. She took off her shoes.

I said, "Come on. You want to sing?"

She said, "No, I've got a terrible voice. I don't sing, but I'd like to listen."

"Come on, you can get closer to the crowd."

"No, I just want to stand here."

"Well, aren't your feet hot?"

"No, it feels comfortable. This is something I've wanted to do all afternoon, but there aren't many places like this. Everybody else has their shoes off, so I don't look conspicuous here."

We both smiled. That thought ran through my head again: Wow! I must have done something good, somewhere in my life, and this must be the goodness I'm reaping for it. We talked about the people in the Village.

She asked me, "Why did you, that time when I told you I was Jewish and my parents were Jewish, why did you say that you suspected it?"

"Look around you, here."

"Yeah, so what?"

"The Village is like a showplace for interracial couples. You're a square down here if you're going with somebody of the same race. It's all a fad, I think, with these people. I don't think most of them dig any of the people they're going with. They're just down here trying to be different, and if you're really going to be different, you've got to get you a companion of a different race."

Claude Brown

She said, "I'm not so sure that's true. Maybe it's just that down here all these people have found something good . . . and people who happen to be of a different race. It's something they wanted, and this is the only place they can come to and not be looked on as something queer. So they all just come down here."

I said, "Yeah, that's a possibility, too, but I've been living down here now for about three years, and most of the younger people out here, they're just experimenting. They're taking a taste of the different fruits. Every few months, they have different boyfriends, different girl friends."

"That may be true with many of the people down here. Still, that doesn't answer my question."

I said, "I don't know exactly what it is, Judy, but there seems to be a strong attraction between Jewish people and Negroes. Most of the white girls who you see around here going with colored fellows will be Jewish. And most of the white guys you see going with colored girls will be Jewish guys."

"Oh, I didn't know that. I don't know of anybody who has done anything like that. I thought it was a very unusual thing."

"It is, but when it does happen, it's with Jewish people."

"Oh, I thought it was something that rarely happened with Jewish families, because Jewish people have strong family ties. I have a cousin who married this Puerto Rican fellow. Her family just doesn't have anything to do with her any more. I still like her, and I see her. She can come by my house, and my parents say it's okay, but my aunt and my uncle say that she isn't their child any more."

"Yeah, well, that's the way some parents might take it."

"If my parents were to do that, and I was in love with somebody, I think we'd be disowning each other, because if they couldn't accept someone I was in love with, it would only indicate to me that they didn't really love me."

I looked at her, and I tried to smile. I said, "Yeah, that's a big stand to take. It takes big parents to accept it. You'll have a rough way to go."

We just sat there. Before I'd realized it, we were talking about something new, something different. Suddenly, it had gotten serious.

"You know, Judy, many times I think that if a Negro fellow really loved a girl . . . and she was white, he would . . . if he really loved her . . . I think he wouldn't want to marry her."

Judy said, "Why not? I think anybody who loves anybody, regardless of color . . . if they really love them, they couldn't help but marry them."

"No. You see, what I'm talking about is most Negroes know that life is hard for a Negro anyway; it's terribly hard unless you've got some money, and most Negroes don't have any money. And if a Jewish person marries a colored person, this is murder. Life is going to be twice as hard for both of them. Then, just think about the kids you'd have. Damn. Can you imagine a kid being born a Jew and a Negro? You've struck out before you even start. It seems like a cruel thing to do to a child, bring a child into the world of Jewish and Negro parents."

She looked at me silently for a while. Then she said, "Do you really believe this?"

"Sometimes I feel that way."

"Well, let me tell you that when you feel that way, you're wrong. You're just taking a defeatist attitude. If you loved somebody, and you really loved them, you'd just have to find a way to make it work so you both could be together and be happy."

"Yeah, well, maybe." I looked at her for a while. I thought, Wow, this young girl is really on fire, really on fire! I said, "Yeah, Judy, maybe you're right. Then again, I don't know whether I'd be game enough to do something like that myself."

"Wait a minute, Claude. You mean to tell me that if I were to fall in love with you, there would be no hope for my ever becoming your wife?"

I look at her, and smiled. "Well, you've got us getting married already, huh?"

"No . . ."

"Don't rush me, lady, please don't rush me to the altar. I've been afraid of this sort of thing all my life."

She smiled and said, "Oh, no, no, no. I wasn't suggesting anything. I was just trying to find out."

I just grabbed her around the neck, playfully, and I said, "You just let your parents try and take you away from me, and I'll chase you to the ends of the earth. Just to spite 'em, I'll marry you, and we'll have a houseful of half-breeds. We'll have a houseful of nigger and Jewish kids running all around. Every Christmas, we'll let them send your parents a Christmas card with their pictures on it."

Judy laughed.

After a while, she said, "Claude, didn't you tell me you live around here somewhere?"

"Yeah, I live right over there on Cooper Square."

"What does it look like?"

"What does what look like?"

"Cooper Square, and the place you live."

"It's down the street from the club we went to Friday night. As a matter of fact, I showed you the School of Engineering at Cooper Union, and also the School of Science and Art."

"Oh, you live near there. Why don't we go, and you can play something for me?"

"I'll do it later."

"Oh, no, you're just going to procrastinate about it. You don't want to show me how well you can play. Are you ashamed or something?"

"No. You could probably play better than me."

"Okay, then, come on and let me show you how well I can play."

For some reason, I was hesitating. I didn't know what I'd be able to do with her, or what I'd want to do with her. I said, "Okay, Judy, you come with me. We'll see how good you are on the piano. I'll bet you're very talented. I've always had the suspicion that you were too modest."

I took her up to my place. We met Tony coming out. I introduced Tony to Judy. He was polite, with his beard and all, but I don't think he was too impressed. It was just a white girl. Tony said he'd see me later.

It was really a drab-looking room I had down there on Cooper Square, but I had a lot of nice paintings. The landlord was a painter, and he had made reproductions of masterpieces. They were hanging up all over the room.

Judy looked at them; she looked at just about everything as she came in. She said, "This is a very quaint place."

It was a loft room with the slanted ceiling near the window. The window was between the two drops in the ceiling. It was late afternoon when we came in there. The sun was just going down. There was a little breeze.

She thought it was beautiful. She just raved and raved about it. As she looked out the window, I came up behind her and said, "The Third Avenue El used to be there when I first moved down here. It was miserable."

She said, "Why, I'll bet it was beautiful even then." She looked around at the room and said, "I'll bet many a great artist has stood here and looked out this window. Probably during the Depression."

She was really excited about it. I just stood there and watched her. She seemed to be going through some kind of fantasy. The place looked dreary to me, but Judy said, "Wow! It's beautiful. Everything about it is beautiful.

As a matter of fact, it seems ideal for the painter, for the musician, or even a writer. It's a place where you can get away from everything."

"Oh, yeah. I've had some pretty nice lonely moments down here."

"I'll bet you've never been lonely."

"No. I have all my paintings to keep me company."

Judy said, "Play something for me on the piano."

"What would you like to hear?"

"I don't know. Anything nice."

"Have you ever heard "These Foolish Things Remind Me of You'?"

"Oh, yeah, I've heard that. Can you play it?"

I sat down and played it. She raved about it. I didn't think it was that good, but I sort of expected it from her, because she was that way.

After that, I asked her to play. She said she wanted me to play another one for her. I played another one. She was sitting over in the corner, in the rocking chair. I had had a rocking chair and a chair at the desk. These were the only two chairs in the room, other than the bench for the piano.

She said, "There's something about this room that seems to be you."

I stopped playing, and I said, "Something like what?"

"The books that you have, and the piano, with the metronome sitting on the top, the paintings that you have. It's just the coloring and everything."

"It's not really. All the paintings and just about all the furniture, except for the piano, were here when I came."

"Yeah, but it seems to have blended in with you."

"It's probably that I blended in with the furniture."

All the time, she just kept rocking. She said, "I want to hear you finish playing that, whatever it was you were playing. What was it?"

"It's a tune called 'I'm in the Mood for Love.'"

"I've heard the tune. . . . I've never heard it played that way."

"Yeah, well, this is what jazz does to tunes."

She laughed.

As I was playing, I heard the rocking chair stop. The piano was right next to the bed. Tony used to say I treated it like the woman I loved; I kept it near the bed so that it would be the first thing I touched when I woke up and the last thing I touched when I went to sleep. I used to put in long hours on the piano.

When I was sitting there playing, I didn't hear Judy get up; I just heard the rocking chair stop squeaking. Then I heard her plop down on the bed. She said, "Do you ever lie here and look up at the ceiling?"

"No, I don't look at the ceiling too much. Sometimes I lay there and read. Sometimes I just lay there and think."

"What do you think about?"

I was still playing and she was lying on the bed looking. I'd just noticed something about her. She had a very big chest; her breasts were large, and she looked ready, very ready. I don't know why, but I had a crazy feeling about her. I didn't want to look at her, because she looked so good, so tempting there. I had seen chicks with much finer bodies, but they never seemed to have the mind and womanly sweetness to go with it. It wasn't just the body or her big breasts; it was all the things we'd done that day, all the things we'd said, the kind of telephone conversation we'd had the day before. I looked at her and smiled.

She reached one hand up, and she put it on my leg. I said, "Okay, Judy, it's your turn. What're you trying to do, distract me? Did you think I was going to forget?" I started joking. I said, "You're going to get up and play something for me."

She got up and played. She said, "This is the first movement from Beethoven's *Sonata Pathétique*."

I said, "Wow! I should have known with all the modesty you have. It's usually the people with the most modesty who can play best."

I kept talking, and she kept looking at me. She had a look in her eye that sort of let me know that she wasn't in the mood for playing piano and talking. I knew what she wanted, but I just couldn't. It seemed as though I would have been treating her like an average bitch, just one of the whores you'd pick up out there on the street. I just couldn't do that; I just couldn't do it. I said, "Look, Judy, why don't we go out and get something to eat? I'm hungry. There's a nice delicatessen over on Second Avenue. We could go and have a hot pastrami sandwich and a beer or something."

She said, "Okay, if you want to."

"Yeah, I want to."

We went and had the pastrami sandwiches and the beer. When we came out, I said, "Come on, there's a park I want to show you. It's up on Eighteenth Street and Second Avenue. It's one of the nicest parks around here."

She came along, but she looked a little disappointed. I knew she wanted to go back to my place.

We walked and walked until it was time for her to go home. Then we went to the subway at Fourteenth Street and University Place.

I said, "Look, Judy, why don't we just let the relationship take its course?

I would never think of rushing you into anything. If something just happened on the spur of the moment, I wouldn't be certain whether I caught you off guard or whether you wanted to, or what. I want to get everything you've got, everything. But when I get it, I want to feel absolutely certain that you want me to have it." I kissed her, and she smiled. I had the feeling that we understood each other.

"Claude, I think that the luckiest thing that's happened to me is that I met you. I thought that at first, but now I'm more convinced of it than ever. I feel more certain every day that it has been the luckiest experience in my life."

She used to say things like this, and it always made me feel good. I wanted to devour her right there on the spot. I told her, "I feel pretty lucky too," and we just stood there, in the middle of the subway entrance, kissing. We went down the stairs holding hands.

I rode up as far as Fifty-ninth Street with her, then came back downtown. When I came home, I saw a light on in Tony's room, so I knocked on the door. I asked him, "Man, how are things?"

He said, "Okay. How are things with you?"

I smiled and said, "All right."

He said, "Yeah, I sort of thought they would be. Sonny, it looks like you're becoming a regular Villager now, man."

"How's that?"

"Well, you're into this thing, man. You got your art, and you got your beard . . . even though it's only three days old and you might shave it off tomorrow. And you even got your white girl now."

I thought he'd said it in a joking mood. I said, "Yeah, man, I guess I am." I wasn't ready to joke about it now; I just wasn't ready to joke about it. I didn't know I would feel that way. Tony and I were tight. I always felt that I could say anything to him, and I suppose he always felt that way too. Well, he was saying it, and I didn't know how to take it.

He said, "Sonny, man, how is she?"

"How you mean how is she?"

"Well, did you pop her? You must have jugged her by now, haven't you?"

I said, "Uh-uh, man. I don't know."

"Damn, man, what you doin' with it?"

I didn't answer. I didn't want to talk about it. I hadn't thought about it before, and I didn't know until Tony started talking about it, but I just knew that I couldn't make her a topic of conversation for the fellows.

He said, "Well, what you doin' with it? Holding hands, man? You mean to tell me that you got a gray bitch there and you gonna hold hands?"

"Mind your fuckin' business. What you got to do with it?"

"Cool it, baby. I think that chick is fucking up your mind, Sonny."

"You just mind your mother-fucking business. Whatever she's doing to my mind, you just don't have a damn thing to do with it, man. Don't ask anything about it. Just keep her name out your mouth."

Tony was going over to pour himself a glass of wine. He stopped and looked at me. He said, "That's the way it is, Sonny?" That's all he said, but he meant more than that. He was really asking, "Damn, man, I can't even talk about her? She's got priority over me?"

I didn't answer. I just looked at him. He poured some wine, and he poured me a glass too. I was still just standing there in the doorway. I took the glass of wine, and I said, "Look, Tony, I'm sorry, man. I'm sorry I shot off like that."

"That's okay, Sonny. I think it's nice, man. She looks like a nice girl. I wish I could meet a bitch I could shoot off about."

I didn't say anything more about it. We just drank some wine and talked about the people uptown who'd gotten busted lately, who'd gotten strung out, that sort of thing.

The next time Judy came down, I knew that I would have to try to make her happy, and I wanted to. I wanted to really make her happy. She was a sweet little girl, and she was ready. I played with her. She was kind of scared at first. She told me, "Claude, I want to, but I'm scared." I told her that there was nothing to be afraid of, because I wouldn't let her get hurt or anything, that I would be gentle.

It was a terrible night. She was a virgin, and she was going through all that clawing business, crying and carrying on. But she got used to it. She got used to it and got to like it.

We had a great relationship for about six months. Summertime came around, and she just stopped coming down. I almost panicked, because she was the best thing that had ever happened to me. I got a friend of mine, Chet, to call her house. I figured, Chet being Jewish too, he would know how to talk to her parents and give them the impression that he was a nice young man.

Chet didn't seem to want to tell me what had been said on the phone. He'd talked to her mother for about fifteen minutes. I was trying to hear, but Judy's mother wasn't a loud woman. I kept pulling on him and saying, "Listen . . ." He kept putting up a hand, as if to say, "Just a minute. I'll let you know as soon as I get off here."

When Chet hung up the phone, he looked at me and stammered for a while. Then he said, "Uh-uh, Claude, Judy isn't in town any more."

"What do you mean she isn't in town any more, man?"

"Her parents sent her to Connecticut to stay with some relatives. They think it'll just be for the summer."

"Well, didn't they have the address? Couldn't they give it to you or anything? Couldn't they give you something, man?"

"No, her mother wouldn't give me the address."

"Well, what happened? Did she think you were me?"

"Yeah, she thought I was you."

I said, "And so what was wrong with that?"

"She thought that I was Claude Brown, and she thought that I was colored."

"Yeah, and so what?"

"She said . . . I wouldn't want to repeat it, Claude."

"Man, look, tell me. I'm not going to take this kind of shit laying down. Do you know how I feel about that girl, Chet?"

"Yeah. Look, man, you got to face facts, baby. She's not here. She's gone. They sent her away. They told me she's in Connecticut, but she just might be in Florida somewhere."

"Look, I'm going to call them."

"Claude, please don't call them, please, if not for your sake, then for mine. I think her mother is just liable to say something that might hurt your feelings. Don't call."

I looked at Chet, and I could feel tears swelling up in my eyes. Chet sort of looked away, and I said, "Thanks, Chet, thanks, baby, anyway." He didn't say anything.

For a long time, I was sorry I'd ever stopped that time when Judy called to me in the hall with that "Hey, there." I remembered it for a long time. For a long time, I expected the phone to ring or thought I'd get a letter. Nothing came.

16

I decided to run. The most natural thing to do was to take refuge in Harlem. I was hurt, and I was running home. I was going to stay away from white people and the white world.

I joined a new group of young jazz musicians. We weren't good enough to play club dates for pay yet, but we were good enough so that the people who liked jazz wouldn't mind listening to us. We all hung out together, and we liked playing. The cats who were still in this young-jazz-musician groove around Harlem were really serious about music. They had to be serious to stick with it.

The attitude had changed about drugs. These guys didn't believe that drugs had anything to do with playing good jazz. Many of the cats did when we first started out. But it seemed as though the guys who felt that drugs had something to do with it didn't make it as musicians. The cats who were still hanging in there were just good jazz musicians, damn good.

This was the group of cats I started hanging out with. We would go places together. We'd go to little gigs, and we'd do a lot of things; they cut me into a lot of different musicians and a lot of cute chicks, dancers and singers, people in show business. It was a hip group of people, who knew how to be happy. I liked them more than I liked anybody else.

They didn't want to be a part of street life. Some of them had just awakened to this fact. They were the same cats who had lived according to the code of the street. Now they were the only young people in the community who were doing anything worthwhile. They were married, they had good jobs, and they were always dressed presentably. They had to stand out, because most of the young people in the community were junkies. Anybody who wasn't a junkie stood out.

They became a new class, the young elite of the Harlem community. A few of them had government jobs. They worked for the city or the Federal government, those who'd finished high school and didn't have a sheet on them. Many cats had a sheet on them; they had been in street life for a little too long, past that sixteenth year. Even then, they straightened out. But to get a good job, making a good salary, I suppose they had to go into phases of employment where the sheet didn't mean too much, like into the entertainment world or music. Occasionally, some of the guys would get a good job from a private employer who believed in them. These were the lucky ones. There were some guys who had talent but didn't necessarily want to be musicians. But since they didn't want to be in street life either, the only thing that was open for them was a field like music.

I became a part of this. I had been making it for a long time, but I hadn't noticed that there were so many other cats who had put down street life too. They were hip; they'd already made a name for themselves and gained street respect when they were coming up in Harlem. Now they were settled cats; not settled in the sense that they didn't want to go anywhere and didn't want to do anything, but settled in the sense that they weren't going to go out and get in trouble and go to jail.

I admired these cats, and I thought that they had done more, far more than I had, in staying right there in Harlem and meeting all the pitfalls of street-life temptations and eluding the plague. I think everybody in the community sort of looked up to these young cats and respected them. I guess many of the older generation would look at them and wish that their sons or their nephews or whoever they had were like these nice young men. It was an admirable thing, because there were so many who had gotten wasted by the plague.

I felt that this was a new Harlem. I saw it as a sort of by-product of the plague generation. All those cats who stayed there and eluded the plague were strong. They were dynamic and beautiful cats. They all stood out, ten feet tall, because they had the strength of character not to be swallowed up in vice and crime. They were such a small segment that the drug generation had overshadowed them, but when I saw them, I knew that everybody in the community was aware of them and admired them. I was glad to be a part of this.

It made me feel strong just being in Harlem and being a part of this, even though I knew in my heart that I hadn't achieved what these guys had. I had run away, I had hidden. That's how I'd gotten away from it. Still, I felt good. I just wanted to be around them, as though some of their strength might rub off on me.

Whenever I went up to Harlem and saw somebody like Turk, I knew that all the junkies admired him, and all the kids and the older generation too. Here was a neighborhood boy who had really made good. Turk had become quite a reputable boxer now. Just about everybody in the neighborhood watched him on TV when he had a fight. Many, including me, had even gone down to watch a couple of his fights at the Garden. I guess it was a symbol of the achievement that was possible in the community. Damn, somebody from Eighth Avenue could make it.

One day we were coming out of the building where Turk had an apartment. He couldn't get out of the house good before the junkies would pounce on him. Every junkie who saw him would come around with his hand out. Turk would reach in his pocket and keep giving out.

I stood on the side and watched this one day. After the junkies had scattered, gone on their way, I spoke to him about it. I said, "Turk, baby, you got a big heart, but I sure hope you don't end up like Joe Louis."

He smiled and said, "Sonny, it seems crazy to you, doesn't it?"

I said, "Yeah, man. It damn sure does. Down my way, man, you could go broke like that. On Third Avenue near the Bowery, they've got a whole lot of panhandlers down there. I have to light all my cigarettes in the house, man. If I come out on Third Avenue with a pack of cigarettes, I can't walk two blocks. Before I've gone a block and a half, the panhandlers have got the whole pack of cigarettes. They just seem to smell cigarettes and they come out begging. By the time you get two blocks, all you've got is a match, man. They've got the cigarettes and gone. Cigarettes aren't that expensive, man, but I was just wondering how long that pocket you kept going into was going to hold up."

Turk laughed. He said, "It's not what it may appear to be, Sonny. I brought this money out just for this purpose. It's seed money. Actually, I'll get all the money back that I gave away, ten times that."

"Yeah, man. As long as that good right holds out."

"No, man. Have you ever heard of seed money, Sonny?"

"No, man. I've never heard of any seed money."

"Man, brace yourself. I'm going to tell you a secret that you could get rich off of."

I looked at him as if to say, "Are you all right, man?"

He said, "I know you're going to think I'm crazy, but I thought so too the first time I heard about this seed money. Believe it or not, Sonny, this is the way that most of the cats all over the world who are rich got rich, man.

They got rich giving money away. The supreme powers that be, man, God, or whatever you want to call it—I call it fate myself—these supreme powers let you make a tenfold claim on them for any money that you give away, man, or for anything that you give away . . . behind a noble motivation."

"Look here, Turk. I think you better start blocking better, baby, because you're in the heavyweight division, and those boys are hitting kind of hard. I think it's beginning to tell on you."

He smiled. He said, "Yeah, man, I told you that you'd say this. As a matter of fact, I said something like that the first time I heard it, but this is the truth, man. When I come out and I give this money to these cats, or to anybody who asks for it that's up tight, I'm giving to mankind. It's like I'm planting the seed money in the soil of life, and the soil of life is kindness and good deeds. I think the supreme powers that be have just given it to me, like they've given it to all the wealthy men in my time and throughout the ages. They had some sort of kindness, man. I think fate knows who to bestow good fortune on."

I looked at him for a while, and I said, "You know something, Turk? It's hard to believe, man. I talk to you now, and I listen to you. It's hard to believe that you were in that shit with us back there. I just can't make the connection with you then and you now."

"Yeah, Sonny, the truth is that none of us had any business in that. Not a cat I grew up with had any business in there. Tito's got no business in Sing Sing. And did you hear that Dunny was in Attica?"

I said, "In Attica? What's he doing in Attica? Dunny is only about twenty-four years old."

"Yeah, but Dunny was always a hard cat. Some people, when they grow up . . . I think me and you, we got a little more human as we grew up. We softened to life. We started becoming people, believe it or not. We were crazy. Shit, running around with guns and knives and shit out there in the street. Sometimes I stop and look back and say, 'Oh, shit. Was that really me?' It's hard to believe it now, Sonny. I look at you now, man, and people tell me you're thinking about going to college."

I said, "Yeah, I've been thinking about that."

"When I first heard it, I said, 'Damn, is that the Sonny who I use to go out there and bebop with, and who was always trying to be so cold?' Now, Sonny, I know that you were a fraud. Yeah, that's right, a twenty-two-carat fake. And so were all of us. This was something we figured we had to be, because we'd come up in all that shit. As we went on, most of us just got softer, became more mature. I guess that's what maturity is, seeing that all that shit was crazy.

"In Dunny's case, Sonny, he . . . I don't know, man, but I think he had missed out on too much in life, and he just kept getting harder instead of getting softer. He got madder, madder with everybody in the world, so it seemed. I heard he was up at Sing Sing and up at Woodburn; he was up at Comstock, a whole lot of places, but they couldn't keep him anywhere— even Auburn. They have killers up there, man, some stone killers. They had Johnny Wilkes up at Auburn, and James Fox is still up there."

I said, "Oh, yeah? What happened to Johnny Wilkes? I thought he was still up there."

"You didn't hear about Johnny Wilkes?"

"No, what happened?"

"He killed a hack, and they had to send him to Materwann. His mind is gone, man. They say he hasn't recognized anybody since then. He was a real mean cat."

"Yeah, a lot of people said that, but I was never able to see Johnny as a mean cat, Turk. I figure I knew him better than most people."

"Yeah, I guess you did, Sonny. I know you knew him better than me, but I could never see that cat as nothing but a cold killer."

"Yeah, I guess he seemed that way to most people."

"The way I heard it, man, this hack was messing with him, and he'd told the hack that he was going to kill him the next time. This hack pushed him once after that, and he just turned around and threw him off a balcony . . . those tiers; you know, those things they have in jail, Sonny."

I said, "I wouldn't know," and we both smiled.

"Well, shit, you've seen the movies, haven't you?"

"Yeah, Turk, I guess I've seen it."

He said, "Well, man, he just threw the cat off it. Then they took him away. They put a straitjacket on him. It took six guards to cool him down. I hear it was over a year ago, and he's still bouncing around in a rubber room. He hasn't recognized anybody since then."

"Damn! That's an ice-cold end. I never would have expected that for Johnny."

"I'm sorry I told you now."

"No, man, I guess he had to go some hard way or another. He was always unhappy. Maybe that was his way of getting away from it all, Turk."

He said, "We changed, man. Most of us changed. I saw Mac about three weeks ago. The cat's working. He's got a job with a paint firm. He's happy; he's married and got a daughter. Actually, Sonny, he should never have gone to Coxsackie. He just never had any business in this thing. All of us, believe it or not, we were nice guys. Maybe that was our trouble, that we were afraid because we were such nice guys. I guess that's what this maturity thing is about, growing up and being able to face being what you are."

"Yeah, Turk. Maybe that's it."

Turk said, "Sonny, I'm glad that you come up more often now, because you're the only cat I know who I can talk to like this. Most of the cats around here . . . I just talk the shit that you're suppose to talk. I seldom say the things that are really on my mind, man. When you come up, I can talk to you, anything that's on my mind. You may say I'm crazy, but I know you don't really think it, and I know you're going to say something that I might tell you is crazy."

I punched him lightly on the shoulder.

Turk said, "Man, don't do that, Sonny. If we were in the ring, I'd be afraid of you."

"Why?"

"I'd be thinking you were trying to make love to me."

"Yeah, all that boxing and all that psychology is getting to you. You better watch out." We laughed.

"Sonny, I thought you had put us down, man, had gone white on us."

"Yeah, man, I think I could've done it, if it wasn't for the fact that I was so obviously colored. I'd have trouble passing, being my complexion."

"Yeah, I saw Tony, man. He told me that you had some cute little white girl down there, and I thought you had given up the colored folks completely."

"No, I guess I was trying something different, Turk, but I know better now. I have dreams about getting away from that Harlem thing. I mean, getting it out of my mind . . . and wanting to get close to people. I guess the first thing I'd like to do is get a decent girl."

"Damn, Sonny. That's nothing, man. You don't have to rush."

"Yeah, man. You can go on and talk that shit because you're married and got a good-doin' wife and a wonderful little girl."

"Damn, look at you, Sonny; you're only about twenty-one. You've got years."

I said, "Yeah. It would seem like that, wouldn't it? Look, Turk, I don't know about this spiritual thing, but I'm going to try planting some of this seed money. I'm going to try planting some of this seed money just to see what kind of a tree I'll grow."

It was as though I had found my place and Harlem had found its place. We were suited for each other now. I decided to move. I didn't exactly decide. Somebody decided to move me. The landlord I was paying the rent to took the guy who owned the building to court. He lost the case, so everybody had to go.

A few months before, I had quit my job in the watch repair shop, and now I was working with a group of fireproofing people on Long Island. They were contract painters, and they fireproofed and soundproofed ceilings. It paid two dollars an hour for nonunion men, and that was pretty good for me. It paid the rent and permitted me to continue playing the piano in my spare time.

It was all right for a while, until I realized what was happening. After I became accustomed to the job, I found out I just couldn't stay there. I was doing more work than anyone else and getting less money. It seemed that they always kept one Negro around to do the heavy work, the jobs nobody else wanted to do. So I decided to get fired and collect unemployment compensation for a while. I was collecting something like forty-two dollars a week, and that was all right. That would pay my rent and the bills, and I had a lot of time to do other things. I could practice the piano for eight hours or more if I wanted to.

I started selling cosmetics about that time. It wasn't so much for the money—there wasn't that much money in it—but for the experience. I ran into a fellow on the street, a guy I had gone to evening high school with. He was a Harlemite, and always hustling. They called him Shorty. Shorty used to be always on the go, always trying to make that next dollar, and he always had a lot of plans. He was always telling me about his plans for getting ahead. He wanted to go to college. He wanted to become a businessman in Harlem and do something for Harlem. Shorty was the kind of guy who I felt could do what he wanted to do.

He was always selling some kind of cosmetics, and he was a good salesman. He used to tell me about the people he met selling cosmetics. After a while, I became so interested in this, I thought it was something I'd like to do, just to meet the kind of people that Shorty told me about. He said that he could take me up to the place he was selling for, Rose Morgan Cosmetics.

He asked me if I knew Rose Morgan. I said I didn't know her, but I'd heard of her. I knew she was the woman who was married to Joe Louis once.

He said, "Yeah, that's the woman. She's a good businesswoman, man, and she's a fair person. Why don't you come on up and meet her? I'm sure you'll really be impressed by her, Sonny, because you're the kind of guy who could dig something like this. She wants to do something for Harlem and for the people too."

I said, "Yeah, I'd like to meet her."

He said, "Okay, well, come up to this address tomorrow morning at nine o'clock." He gave me the address of a shop up on 145th Street between Amsterdam and Broadway.

I went up there and saw her. I liked the people who were working there. They started telling me things about how to sell cosmetics. As a matter of fact, I was told to come there every morning for an hour lecture on just how to sell cosmetics and beauty products.

I started selling the cosmetics. At first it seemed kind of slow and dull. I couldn't make any money, and it wasn't very gratifying to be made to feel that you weren't a good salesman. I told Shorty about it, and he said, "You got to keep trying, man."

I went around with him for a half a day once. He was showing me how he approached customers. I got a few hints from him, and I started working long hours. Sometimes I would do this all day and part of the night. I liked it. I'd just be certain that I got four hours in on the piano during the day.

I had gotten my diploma from high school, and now I wasn't certain what I was going to do. I wanted to go to college, but it seemed like a dream. I didn't have any money. I didn't think I was good enough to get a scholarship from anywhere. There were a lot of things happening that made me sort of look at my desire to go to college as just one of those dreams that couldn't possibly come true.

There I was. I had gotten my diploma, I was twenty-one years old. It was kind of old for going to college, but I took the college entrance exam up at Columbia University. I told the folks about it. I should have known they wouldn't understand, but they were the only people I had, so who else could I tell?

I said to my father, "Look, Dad, I've passed the entrance exam for Columbia University."

He said, "Columbia University? Ain't that that school up on Broadway around 110th Street?"

"It's around 115th Street and Broadway."

He said, "Yeah, yeah, I know where that is. I passed it sometimes when I was going to work."

"Yeah, that's the same school."

"Well, that's nice. Did you hear what the first figure was?"

I felt like somebody who is looking for a bar and ends up in a church. I felt as though I'd brought the wrong news. I said, "No, I didn't hear the first number, Dad. I didn't hear anything."

"Well, it's probably better that I don't know it. I'll bet I didn't make it."

I thought to myself, I guess he didn't hear me either, or it just didn't make any difference. This is crazy. I couldn't expect him to understand. I shouldn't have expected anybody to understand.

I didn't say anything more about the school thing. It was nice to go, and that was all there was to it. I didn't have any money, and I knew it took money to go to school. I decided to just sell cosmetics and play the piano.

In selling cosmetics, I became involved in Harlem, really involved. I was in Harlem all day. Most of the night, I'd hang out up there with the cats I knew. I'd moved up to Ninetieth Street. I got closer to the people. I was able to see them better.

I was always walking around with my sample case. Sometimes I'd knock on somebody's door like the Fuller Brush man, and I would say, "Good morning, madam. I'm here to interest you in Rose Morgan beauty products," or something like this.

If it was an elderly lady, she'd probably say, "Boy, why don't you stop all that foolishness and go get yourself a job?"

I'd go on. It was a thing that I was really beginning to enjoy. I went around to all the beauty salons, and after a while, I got to know just about all the beauticians in the neighborhood, all up and down Seventh Avenue and Eighth Avenue.

I would give some things to chicks on credit. Some of them would pay, and some of them would have no intentions of paying. After a while, you could tell, before you gave them any credit, just who would pay and who wouldn't.

I'd go into bars at night and sell cosmetics to barmaids. I'd even sell them to the whores up on St. Nicholas and Amsterdam Avenues and down around 125th Street. Some of the prostitutes I knew from way back. They'd say, "Sonny, I'm gon buy something from you just to help you out, just for old times' sake," or something like that.

I remember once I walked into a bar up around 145th Street near St. Nicholas. I met somebody I hadn't seen in a long time. It was Jackie.

She had her back to me when I walked in. I walked up and said, formally, "Pardon me, young lady," and tapped her on the back.

She turned around, and she said, "Sonny!" She jumped up and threw both arms around me. She got off the stool and told the cat she'd been talking to that she'd be right back. "This is a cousin of mine, and I haven't seen him in a long time," she said. "Come on, Sonny, come with me."

I said, "Where you goin', baby? I'm on business here."

"Oh, you got one of those little bags. You selling something too? . . . Sonny, look, you just come on with me right now. I've got a trick in here. I've got a good trick, and I'll make this nigger buy me everything you've got in that bag. But come on outside. I want to kiss you first. It wouldn't look good right here, just being a cousin."

We went outside and talked for a while. I asked her what she was doing and where she'd been. She told me that she'd just gotten out of jail and that she'd asked about me. She went up to my parents' house. She said, "I should've known better than to ask your mother. I was hoping that maybe she wouldn't answer the door, that maybe your brother or one of your sisters would open the door. I didn't know that they'd moved."

I said, "Yeah, both of my sisters are married now, and they don't live with my parents any more. And my brother, well, that's a different story."

She said, "Yeah, Sonny, I'm sorry, baby. I saw him."

"Yeah, well, you know, that's how it goes." I was standing up against the wall, and I had my case on the ground between my legs.

She kissed me and leaned all over me and said, "Look, here's my address. I want you to come on up tonight. I'll be home as soon as the bars close. Look, Sonny, I'm gonna go in here, and I'm gonna tell this trick that I need a whole lot of stuff. Now, you tell me what you've got in that bag, and I'm going to tell him that I need just about everything."

I told her a few items that I had. I took her address and told her I'd come by her house about four-fifteen that morning. I had no intentions of going by, but it was nice to see her; it was real nice to see her.

She went back into the bar. She told this guy, "My cousin's selling cosmetics, and I want you to buy something for me." She picked out about twenty dollars' worth of stuff, and this cat kept on buying it. This trick seemed to be in his forties. Jackie knew that she had a good thing.

I left after I made the big sale.

I'd see a lot of whores, and I got to know them. My best customers were the whores and the beauticians. I guess they were the women who used the most makeup, or they were more conscious of makeup.

Sometimes I'd run into different whores, and I'd say, "Come on, why don't you buy somethin'?"

They might say, "No, baby, I can't buy nothin' yet. I haven't made any money. Why don't you come back about one o'clock, after I've turned a few tricks?"

I'd say, "Sure, baby, I'll be back," that sort of thing. Sometimes I came back, sometimes I didn't, but it was always an all right thing.

I went by to see Jackie, but not the night I said I would. I went by her house a couple of days later. She opened the door, looked at me, and said, "You lyin' nigger!"

I said, "What's wrong, baby? I just couldn't make it."

"I'll bet you couldn't. You could of told me that when I was in the bar. I rushed home. I was out of there about three o'clock. I went and I got something for me and you. I had a lot of liquor and stuff. And, Sonny, I was all set to party. I just knew we were gonna have a good time. And you didn't show."

I said, "What did you get?"

"I got some nice pot. I got some cocaine. I had all the liquor we needed. We could've partied all day and half of the next night."

"Yeah, Jackie, that was real sweet of you, baby. I wish I had come, and I know it was my loss, but I couldn't make it."

"What do you mean you couldn't make it? What happened? What were you doin'?"

"I went and got drunk."

"Wait a minute. Yeah, I guess I was crazy. Sonny, you're not married, are you?"

"No, I'm not married yet."

"Oh, I was wonderin'. I know I'd forgotten to ask, and I just ran right into your arms, I was so happy to see you."

"I was happy to see you too."

She said, "Yeah, well, I didn't stand you up."

"But, baby, I couldn't help standing you up."

"You still didn't tell me why."

I said, "Oh, baby, I just couldn't make it. You get up tight sometimes. You get into something and you can't get away."

"Well, I've got something nice. Do you want to get high?"

"No. Look, Jackie, I don't smoke any more, and I don't snort any coke."

She stood there and looked at me for a while. She said, "Sonny, are you for real?"

"Yeah, baby, I just don't need it any more."

"What do you mean you don't need it any more? Damn, Sonny, everything is changing too much for me. You! It's just too much. You were the one nigger I dreamed about when I was in jail. I put your picture up over my bunk."

I said, "Yeah, yeah, and I'll bet you masturbated behind it every night."

"Oh, baby, you know I did!"

"Aw, come on, Jackie, I think I told you that one the first time I came out of the joint."

"But, Sonny, damn, you know how I feel about you. You were always the main nigger for me. You were the only one who made me feel as though I was really somethin' special."

"Yeah, well, I always felt that you were something special, Jackie. I still do."

She said, "Still, why did you . . ."

"Let's forget it. I'm here now."

"Yeah, you're here now. You're talkin' about you don't snort any cocaine any more. You don't smoke any pot. Did you get any religion? Sonny, you're not one of those Muslims now, are you?"

I said, "No, baby, it's got nothing to do with religion, none of that sort of thing."

"Well, Sonny, what happened?"

"Nothin', I'm just older, Jackie."

She said, "Yeah, yeah, look at you. You're gray all around the edges."

"No, I don't mean that. It's just that I've matured, and, Jackie, those things . . . like smoking and using coke and trying to get a quick piece of cunt . . . it was all a part of my childhood."

She said, "Aw, come on, Sonny. Damn, Sonny, I use to always dig you for bein' a straight-out nigger, and now here you gon come and tell me some shit like that. How old you gon get? Shit. Colored men, they never stop fuckin', I don't care how old they get. They might stop usin' pot, and they might stop snortin' cocaine, but here you gon tell me you so old at twenty-one. You can stop snortin', you can stop smoking pot, but you can't tell me, Sonny, that you're so old you're gon stop screwin'.'"

I said, "No, I guess I'm not that old, baby; it's . . ."

She said, "That's what I was afraid of, likin' somebody."

I said, "Look, life goes on, Jackie. I'm certain you didn't wait all this time just for me. You didn't even know I was comin' in that bar, baby."

"Yeah, but that's beside the point, Sonny. I tried to find you as soon as I got home. The first place I went was to your house. You didn't answer any of my letters or anything, and I still went to your house, first stop."

I said, "Jackie, about not answering your letters, as a matter of fact, I didn't get any."

She said, "I kind of halfway figured that, when I found out that you weren't living with your folks. I knew they would never give you any letters that I'd written to you."

"That's about what happened."

She said, "Well, Mr. Righteous, can I fix you a drink?"

"Sure."

She fixed me a Scotch, and we talked about old times. I asked her about her plans. She said she didn't know. She figured she'd just keep on doing what she had been doing.

I said, "You can't intend to trick all your life, can you? One day you'll get old, baby."

"Everybody's gonna get old one day, Sonny. I think the main thing is doing what you want to do, as long as you can, before you get too old to do it. This is what I want to do. Sonny, I sure wish it could be us again."

"Yeah, I guess I kind of wish that too, Jackie, but you just can't turn back the clock."

"Yeah, I guess I should have known, Sonny, when I saw you with that little satchel. It just doesn't look like you, walkin' around and carryin' some bag, sellin' cosmetics."

"Yeah, well, I guess everybody changes."

"Sonny, did you ever miss me much, or did you ever think of me much?"

"Yeah, I thought of you quite a bit. As a matter of fact, I think it was the dreams of you that kept me warm on those cold winter nights when I first moved away from home."

"Yeah, I'll bet."

I said, "Damn, I wish you'd been around then."

"Yeah, I wish I'd been around too, Sonny."

I asked her where she'd been, and she said someplace called Westfield. She told me about some girls she knew from around the neighborhood and asked me if I knew them. They were up there. She said it was a real ball. She met some nice people.

I said, "Yeah, I usually met nice people too. That's how it goes. Sometimes you meet some of the nicest people in those places."

We were quiet for a while. I guess I was trying to find a way to end the conversation and say good-bye. After I got there, I felt it would have been better not to have seen her any more after that night in that bar. Then if I had seen her again, I could have kept telling her that I was coming by, but never getting there. Eventually, she would have gotten the message. It would have been easier on both of us. But I had come by, and we were both just sitting there. I knew she was wondering how she should treat me, and I was wondering what I should say, trying to think of something nice that I could say to her.

She started asking me about people. She said she'd heard that Turk was making a name for himself as a heavyweight fighter. I said, "Yeah, he's doing real good." She said she'd heard he'd married that little stuck-up girl on Eighth Avenue. I said, "Sally? I never thought she was stuck up."

Jackie said, "No, you wouldn't have."

"Yeah, he married Sally. They've got a real cute little girl."

Jackie said, "Yeah, I've seen her. She's a pretty child, but I think that's all because of Turk. It's got nothing to do with that old stuck-up . . ."

I said, "No, Sally has changed too. She was young then, and, I suppose, you would . . ."

"Aw, I bet she didn't change that much."

"Look at it this way, Jackie, she must've changed somewhat, because she married Turk, didn't she? And Turk was always one of the dirty little boys out there on the street. Right?"

"Yeah, well, I don't know. Maybe she did change. What happened to Tito?"

"Tito's doin' time, baby, doin' a lot of time, in Sing Sing."

"I use to always feel sorry for him. I remember one time, Sonny, I gave Tito some body because I felt sorry for him."

I looked at her sort of suspiciously and said, "Yeah, I'll bet you did."

"I would never tell that to anybody else but you. I knew you wouldn't believe it, but I knew you could understand it if anybody could."

"I'm glad you waited this long to tell me, because if you'd told me back then, I would've beaten your ass."

"Would you, Sonny, would you really have?"

"You know I would have."

"Yeah, I guess you really did care for me."

"Yeah, I guess I did."

I told her that I had to go to see some customers. She didn't want me to go, but she knew we didn't have anything more to talk about. She hesitated, and then she said, "Sonny, whatever happened to Alley Bush and his crazy self?"

I said, "Oh, Alley is a Muslim now. He's down there on 125th Street and Seventh Avenue hollering and raising hell."

"Everybody has grown up and gone his own way, huh?"

"Well, I guess that's what life's all about, Jackie. Look at you. You seem to have grown and gone on your own way."

"Sonny, I don't know what I'm doin'. I know that I've got to do it, and that's all I know. Whatever it is, regardless of how little sense it makes, I've go to do it. . . . Okay, if you have to be so straight, can't we still be friends, even though we've got different ways to go?"

"Jackie, the way I feel about you, you'll always be one of my dearest friends." She smiled. I said, "I've got to go, but I'll see you around."

She went to the door, and as I came by, she kissed at me. I touched her on her lips and said, "Take it easy, baby."

I had a funny feeling about everything, about the past, about my childhood, and I kind of wondered if Jackie had been real, if the childhood had been real, if we had all gone through all that stuff. I wondered if it weren't really just a dream. I couldn't understand Bucky's not being around. It just never made sense. I guess you just had to take it as it was.

I started meeting a lot of new people when I was selling cosmetics. There were some discouraging moments, but I felt that I had good products to sell to people. Chicks would swear they didn't even have enough money to buy food. They'd say they had only a few pennies, and they really wished they could afford it. Some chicks would start talking that talk about how much they wished they could afford it, and then they'd start opening their robes a little more.

What was so discouraging was that some women wouldn't come out and just say that they didn't like the stuff or didn't want any. They'd swear to all kinds of gods that they didn't have any money. Then the numbers man would come up and knock on the door to get his list of digits for the day, and the same chick who was just telling you that she only had money to buy a little bit of food for the day and didn't know how she was going to make it to the end of the week would start reaching in her brassiere or her stocking and pulling out dollar bills from everywhere. That was just the way it went. I didn't feel too bad. I'd been in Harlem just about all my life, and I knew how people felt about the numbers. I knew that if they did nothing else, they were going to play numbers.

Sometimes you'd meet some girls you really liked. There were other moments when you'd hear about some of the things that happen to women. It made it seem as though women in Harlem were really getting messed over right and left.

I went to a woman's house one morning, and she said she didn't have any money. I said, "Well, this is the day that you told me to come by."

"Yeah, but dammit, I ain't got no money."

I just stood there in the doorway and looked at her for a while. She kept screaming, "Everybody! Everybody's got their hand out in this goddamn town!"

"Look, lady, I'm sorry. I'll come back some other time."

As I turned, she stopped raving. She said, "Wait a minute, wait a minute, mister. I'm sorry. I had no business blowin' off and cussin' at you like that. You ain't did nothing to me. I ain't got nothin' against you."

I said, "That's okay. I'm glad to have been here, if you had to let it out. Sometimes it helps."

She said, "How much do I owe you for that soap?"

"A dollar seventy-five."

"Want to come on in a minute? I'll get my change purse."

I came in and sat down. She said, "Damn. You work so hard, and you try so hard to earn a living and make enough money so you can send your kids to school and keep some clothes on their backs, and these no-good damn doggish men ain't gon try and help you. Not only is they not gon try and help you, they gon try and stop you from doin' anything."

"Yeah, well, that's the way it goes sometimes."

"That old no-good damn doggish husband of mine had to go and get himself in jail, just for bein' so goddamn doggish."

"Yeah, I suppose all men have a little bit of dog in them."

I remembered the times I'd followed Mama from one room to another when she'd be cleaning house. She'd turn around and say, "Boy, why don't you stop walkin' up under me? Go sit down, or go someplace and play or somethin'."

I'd be following her around, asking questions. Mama would be walking from one end of the house to the other, cleaning, talking to herself, cooking, and looking in the pot. She'd be saying, "That old no-good high-yella hussy. I'm gon throw some hot water on her or somethin'."

I'd say, "Mama, what's a hussy?"

She'd say, "Boy, why don't you go on out from here and leave me alone?"

I'd be quiet and wouldn't say anything, and Mama would go back, and she'd start talking. I'd walk behind her. When we got to the other end of the house, I'd say, "Mama, what's a heifer?"

She'd say, "Child why don't you . . . a heifer is a cow. Now, would you please go someplace and leave me alone?"

I'd just be more puzzled. I'd say, "Mama, you gon throw some hot water on a cow?"

"No, I'm talking about that old light-skin heifer that's always comin' around here to see your daddy." She'd stop and sit down, maybe take me on her lap, and say, "One day, you'll probably understand . . . when the dog in you starts comin' out."

I'd say, "What dog in me, Mama?"

"Every man's got a little bitta dog in him. Your daddy got a whole lotta dog in him too."

"Yeah, well, I sure hope I ain't got no dog in me, Mama." Mama would just laugh. She'd rock me a few times, put me off her lap, and start walking from one end of the house to the other, cleaning up here and cleaning up there.

I didn't understand that dog thing, not right then anyway. Then one day I heard a girl say, "A nigger is nothing but a dog." And I remembered Mama telling me, "Boy, don't be so doggish," when I would bring home one girl one day and another girl the next. I got the meaning of the dog in the man. "Yeah, all men have a little dog in them," I repeated to myself.

"Yeah, but they ain't suppose to be that doggish," the woman said now.

I didn't initiate the conversation, and I didn't feel as though I were in a position to ask her anything, so I just sat there.

She continued after a little pause. She said, "Here I'm sending my fifteen-year-old daughter to school, and this nigger gon be goin' to jail for fuckin' his daughter."

"Yeah, well . . ." I felt uncomfortable when this came out. I felt as though I had to say something pretty fast. I just said, "Yeah, well, you can't trust those stepfathers sometimes." I figured it must have been a stepfather.

"No, that ain't none of her stepfather. That's just her natural daddy, just a doggish old nigger, that's all."

I just didn't know what to say behind that.

"I just think about it. He might have been doing it for a long time, until my son caught him."

"Yeah, well, sometimes when people get drunk they don't know what they're doing."

"He wasn't no damn drunk." Then she started crying. She said, "He's just a dog!" She put her head down and went on crying.

I felt foolish being there and wanting money, when this woman had troubles much bigger than the dollar and seventy-five cents that she owed me. I just left.

I had to get out, get to the beauty parlor, see some of the smiling beauticians. I always dug those chicks. They seemed to be the strong women in Harlem. They had a lot of confidence. They were pretty slick, and they thought they knew everything. I liked to be around them when I felt kind of blue. I used to think about these women. I used to wonder how cats who came up in Harlem with mothers like these could be anything but strong men, because they came from such strong women.

17

Three days after Dad had put Pimp out, Mama got a letter from Bellevue Hospital. They had him down there.

A panic had hit Harlem. Whenever the inflow of drugs in the country is slowed down to where there's none on the streets, the junkies panic. The junkies go around and break into doctors' offices looking for drugs. They stick up drugstores and pharmacists. They stick up dentists. They stick up everybody with a white coat, everybody even remotely associated with medicine. Some junkies even start punching holes in their arms, not with hypodermic needles, but with just regular needles. They go through all kinds of things.

The panic was on two days after Dad had put Pimp out. About three days afterward, Mama got this note from Bellevue Hospital saying that they had her son. It was a relief for everybody.

Mama went down to see Pimp, take him some cigarettes, and find out what it was all about. He had gone into Harlem Hospital's emergency section the night before and attacked a doctor. He started crying, "Give me some shit or kill me." His habit was down on him, and, like most junkies, he panicked. They gave him some morphine that night, then sent him over to Bellevue, where there's a ward for treating addicts.

Mama said she went down and talked to him. She told me I could go down and see him Sunday. I didn't pay too much attention to what Mama said. Every time Pimp got himself halfway straight, he was always telling her that he was going to kick his habit. Mama started talking that talk about, "I really believe this time that Pimp is ready to do right."

I looked at her. I was a little annoyed that she could be still so stupid. She just went on. We were sitting in the living room. She said, "Yeah, I really think he's learned his lesson now. They had him in a straitjacket for about six hours after he went into Harlem Hospital. Now he's all right, and I really think he's going to make it. He's quieted down. He don't have that nervous look about him no more. I think if anybody was ever ready to get off that stuff, he's ready."

I didn't say anything. After a while, Mama paused. I guess she was waiting for some kind of reply or some kind of agreement. I said, "Yeah, Mama, sure he's ready to get off it," and that was all.

She said, "Yeah, I knew he wasn't gon be no junkie like all the rest of these old crazy junkies out there. I told that boy when he first started messin' with that stuff, I said, 'Pimp, are you usin' that stuff?' When he started eatin' all that sugar and not eatin' no food and lookin' sleepy all the time, but, Lord, I sure am glad that boy woke up to himself and found his senses and gon stop messin' around with that old dope out there."

I just got mad, and I couldn't take it any more. Before I realized what was happening, I was shouting at her. "Mama, why don't you stop bein' so damn stupid! You know the nigger ain't gon put it down. He already said that three times. Now how many times somebody got to tear his ass to show you that he's not gon to?"

"Boy, you know you ain't got no faith in your brother. That boy ain't stupid. He can make it. He made up his mind, and I believe he's gon do it now."

I said, "Do what, Mama?"

She said, "Everybody deserves another chance."

"Chance, shit, Mama, you know that's bullshit. The nigger done went out here three times and blew. Every time he gets back on the street, he talks that same old shit about doin' it."

I hadn't realized what I was saying. There I was, ranting and raving. I didn't even know where I was. I was burned up. Here she was, a damn idiot. She'd seen the junkies, and she knew what was going on, but here she was saying, since it was her son, everything was going to be altogether different. I was pissed off at her refusal to see that her son was a junkie. Shit, junkies are junkies, and all junkies talk that shit about kicking their habits.

While I was raving, I heard Dad say, "That's the goddamn truth. That's one nigger who ain't got no sense. He's just a damn fool, and that's all he's gon be is a damn fool. He don't want to do nothin' but get out there and take a whole lot of dope with the rest of them junkies and go around and nod, and be scratchin' all the time, lookin' like he's sleepy. He can't do nothin'; he can't hold no job or nothin'. He ain't comin' back in this house, I don't care how many tears anybody sheds around here, and I don't care who believes what he says. Christ could believe it if he wants to, but I ain't gon believe it. I know damn well he ain't comin' back in this house no more."

When Dad started ranting, it sort of woke me up to myself and what I was saying. I looked at Mama, and she looked so pitiful. It was as if I'd been beating her and Dad had jumped in and started beating her too. I felt kind of shitty. As a matter of fact, when I heard him, all my anger just left. I wasn't mad at Pimp or Mama any more. I'd just had to get this thing out. I felt that what I had said was more than enough and that Dad was just sort of running it into the ground.

It seemed as though the only way I could stop him was to say, "I don't know, Mama. Maybe you're right. He might be ready now. Everybody wakes up some day. You remember how bad off Danny use to be, Danny Rogers, and he straightened up, and he's still straight, Mama. He's been straight for about a year or more."

Mama said, "Yeah, and I remember when Danny use to stand right out there on that corner, on 145th Street and Eighth Avenue. He'd be so doped up, looked like he was standin' on his feet sleepin'. Looked like his head would hit the ground and come back up. Pimp ain't never been that bad. He might get doped up and go to sleep, but he ain't never been so bad that he would sit out there on the stoop and just nod and nod half the day and half the night. He ain't never caught those fits like Danny use to have out there, jumpin' up and down in the middle of the street and stoppin' traffic."

I said, "Yeah, Mama, Pimp ain't never been that bad. Maybe there's a chance of him making it."

She said, "Yeah, you know, I feel for sure that he's gon make it this time, because that boy has really got his mind made up. He knows all the trouble he's done caused his family, and he says that he's in love with this little girl on 143rd Street. Maybe he'll want to get married or somethin'."

I just said, "Yeah, Mama. Maybe this time. I'll try and help him too." I knew that this was what she wanted to hear. I watched her as I said it. She looked hopeful, as if to say, "Everybody's not against me, and everybody's not beatin' on me." It was as if what Dad said didn't matter.

Dad said, "Yeah, you and your mama, go on; y'all believe all that bullshit. Hear? And when that boy go out here and get himself killed, it ain't gon be nobody to blame but you and your mama. Y'all killin' that boy. Y'all killin' that boy by listenin' to all that bullshit he's talkin', and he's been talkin' for so long, instead of tellin' that boy that he's just got to stop messin' with that damn dope, and throwin' him out on his own, and makin' him see that he got to stop messin' with it. Y'all just keep him around here and keep listenin' to all that bullshit. He ain't no baby no more, you know. I want y'all to know that."

I didn't say anything. I just kept looking at Mama. I couldn't say anything to Dad, because his argument was too strong. As a matter of fact, it was my argument too. It was just impossible for me to say anything against it. Mama kept looking at me as if she wanted me to tell him he was wrong, but I couldn't do that. I didn't believe he was wrong.

I went down to Bellevue the following Sunday. Pimp said, "Sonny, it's only gonna take me a little while, man, to kick this thing, because it's in my mind now."

I looked at him, and the cat looked serious. But I wasn't sure whether he was serious but wouldn't be able to do it or whether the seriousness was also an indication of new-found strength. I said, "Pimp, what are you doing? I mean, what do you plan to do? What's in your mind for the future, when you get out of here?"

"Well, Sonny, I want to put some time in school, man, and finish out my high school so I can get that diploma."

"Yeah, man, that's good." This was something that I had been telling Pimp for a long time now, to go back to high school and finish up. He only had one more year to go. I felt that he was telling me this now because he knew that this was what I wanted to hear. He was just giving me back all the stuff that I had tried to give him to straighten him up.

He looked at me and said, "Sonny, you don't believe me, huh? You don't think I'm ready to make it? I guess that's natural, man, because you've been in my corner a long time, and I blew, all those times. It's natural for you not to believe me now."

"Pimp, I'd like to believe you, but I can't do it, baby, I just can't do it any more. But I'll tell you something. I believe you can do it. I think if you want to do it, it doesn't mean a damn thing who doesn't believe you. If you are going to do it, you're going to go on and do it, regardless. It's the same way with your usin' your drugs. Shit, if you're going to do it, man, you just go on and do it. It doesn't mean a fuckin' thing what I say or what anybody else says. Man, when you get out of here, I'll know what you're going to do by what I see."

He said, "Yeah, Sonny, I'm glad you're takin' it that way, man."

About five weeks later, Pimp was released from Bellevue. His arm was clear. He didn't have his spike track any more. He started working.

About a month after he got out, he was still clean. He still had his job, and he started going to evening high school. Things were looking pretty good. He had a nice girl, and they were talking about getting married after he got his diploma and could get a decent job.

Everybody was pleased, especially Mama. Every time I saw her, I'd ask about Pimp, and she would say with pride, "Oh, he's doin' fine," with that "I told you so" in her voice.

I felt happy for her and happy that my little brother was showing so much strength. He was kicking his habit. He'd been on stuff about eighteen months, and he was kicking it and staying in the neighborhood. I felt that Pimp was out of the woods now. After he'd been going to school for a month and a half, he started talking that college talk. I said, "Wow, that's damn nice! It's wonderful!" When I heard that, I was certain that he was out of the woods.

We didn't hang out in the same crowd. Pimp was younger than I was, and he was still trying to prove a lot of things to himself. Most of the cats I hung out with were older than me. They were guys in their thirties, and I had known them for years and years. Some of them had sort of raised me, in the streets. Pimp wasn't quite ready for this. I knew he had an inferiority complex about being young and not knowing certain things. I suppose that was half the reason he took to drugs.

I'd just see him occasionally. Sometimes, we'd go to a bar together. If I saw him hanging out with cats I knew were weak, who might be using drugs sooner or later, I'd run it down to him. I'd tell him, "Pimp, so-and-so is a dangerous companion."

Once I did this. I told him about hanging out with a cat on 144th Street. He was a young boy, and I didn't know him from way back. He'd only lived uptown for a couple of years. He was about Pimp's age. I told Pimp about hanging out with him, and Pimp said, "Damn, Sonny, man, this sounds almost as bad as Mama and Dad. They don't say that shit to you. They see you talking to Reno and Danny Rogers, and everybody knows Danny is the main man in drugs, and Reno is gonna be in jail in three months at most, but nobody says anything, man. But they all treat me like a little kid. It's somethin' that keeps fuckin' with me. As a matter of fact, I'm thinking about pullin' out of there, Sonny. I got to get out, because I can't stand that kid thing any more. This hurts me, man. Now you come and run it down to me too."

I knew Pimp was right, but at the same time I felt that he was just using this as an excuse to get away from what I was telling him. But it was a damn good defense, and I couldn't get through it. I said, "Yeah, Pimp, I'm sorry, man. I guess we all just worry about you too much, man."

He hit me playfully and said, "Yeah, the baby's grown up, now."

I just walked, and I didn't mention it to him any more. I felt kind of bad.

I was walking down East Twenty-third Street one day, and I met an old friend, a person who used to be a counselor up at Wiltwyck. He left in 1949. I hadn't seen him in about ten years. He said he was coming from Children's Court, on Twenty-second Street. He was going to lunch, and I was just coming from lunch. I'd had lunch with a girl who worked down there.

He said, "Why don't you join me for a cup of coffee?"

"Sure, Lou." Lou was always a warm, friendly person.

We went to a small delicatessen and talked. He had lunch, so I did most of the talking. He asked me what I'd been doing. I told him that I wasn't doing anything. I had been working part-time. Now I wasn't working at all. I was just collecting unemployment insurance.

He said, "That sounds good," just jokingly. "What have you been doing schoolwise?"

I said, "I quit school when I was about sixteen. I went back and got a diploma in evening high school. I finished that last year."

"You have a high-school diploma?"

"Yeah, man, I thought about going to college for a long time. I was just thinking about it, disregarding the fact that it takes money to go."

"Look, have you ever heard of the Reverend James, at the Metropolitan Community Methodist Church?"

"No, man, I haven't heard too much about any churches."

Lou said, "Well, we have a council of committees who are interested in sending Harlem students to school."

"Yeah? It sounds good, but I don't belong to any church. I'm kind of leery about churches, and I'm kind of leery about preachers too."

"Well, that's only because you haven't met this preacher. You know, Claude, there's a difference between ministers and preachers."

"Yeah, Lou, so I've heard. One's got a degree, and the other hasn't."

"There's a little more to it than that. This one is a minister."

"Lou, anyone who wears a turned-around collar, they make me kind of skeptical."

"Why?"

"Well, I always thought this was something to distract people from the continual hard-on that these guys always had."

Lou laughed.

I said, "Yeah, man, I've never met any preachers that didn't have a long cunt collar."

"Oh, Claude, you sound as though you've no faith in people. And after all you've been through!"

"Yeah, man, all that I've been through has shown me what people are, and just how much faith you can have in them."

"No, Claude, I want you to meet this man." He started telling me something about Reverend James. Lou said that Reverend James was not only a unique person but a patron saint for the community around 126th Street and Madison Avenue. He told me how this guy sacrificed himself and gave most of his salary away to people who were suffering. He made the guy sound almost like a black Jesus.

"Lou, are you sure you've really peeped this cat? This guy sounds more dangerous than any of the other preachers I've known."

"Yeah, Claude, I know it's hard to believe that such a person exists."

"No, man, it's just hard to believe that such a person exists in Harlem. I've been here all my life, and I never met anybody like that, man—and a preacher too."

"Claude, I keep telling you that the man is a minister, and I wish you'd stop calling him a preacher."

"You mean to tell me, the man is a colored minister, and he resents being called a preacher?"

"No, it's not that he resents being called a preacher. It's just that I don't like the way that you've described that preacher clique. You make it sound like it's something somewhat disgraceful, a preacher."

"Okay, man, this minister, how old is the cat?"

"Oh, I imagine Reverend James is about forty-five, something like that. He's a very energetic man. He has a heart of gold, and he has a love for people that I've seldom seen anywhere."

"Lou, do you know Ernst Papanek? He was at Wiltwyck."

"Oh, yeah, I know Mr. Papanek."

"Well, man, this cat's got the greatest love for people I've ever seen in anybody. He's been through a whole lot of stuff, in Germany, with the Nazis, and all this kind of business. Nothing has taken it out of him. He maintains this love throughout everything. He's impressed me more than anybody I've ever met as a person who has a great amount of love for his fellow man."

"Well, I don't know, Claude. I don't know Mr. Papanek that well, but I wish you would come by and meet this man."

"Yeah, Lou, I'm kind of curious about this guy. I want to see this preacher, just to see what he looks like."

He said, "I keep telling you, he's a minister, not a preacher."

"Well, the minister. I want to see this minister. All right?"

"Yeah, and, Claude, I wish you wouldn't refer to him as a preacher when you're talking to him. This guy is something else."

"Oh, yeah? You're getting into this slang thing in Harlem, huh, Lou?"

"The 'something else'? All the boys say this." We had a big laugh. Lou worked as a probation officer in Juvenile Court, and I told him that maybe the boys were having a greater influence on him than he was on them.

I had made an appointment to go around to the church on 126th Street and Madison Avenue and meet Lou's patron saint. I don't know what I expected, but I went to the church that night. Lou introduced me to the minister, Reverend James.

He wasn't what I had expected. He was about medium height, a gaunt man with a very serious-looking face. At the same time, it looked like a kind face, as if the seriousness was not something that was intentional. It seemed as though his face had been made serious by the life he had lived, all the things he had seen. He looked like somebody who might really know things.

I sat down and talked to him. I didn't know that anybody with such a gigantic intellect existed in Harlem. When I first met him, I wanted to talk for hours to the guy. I could have gone on and on, and this man would still have been able to talk. Somehow I had the feeling that talking to him that night was more profitable than sitting in the library and reading for weeks. He seemed to know so many things. I hadn't met too many ministers. I'd met a lot of preachers, and the preachers were phonies. They were guys hollering about God and spouting all this nonsensical holiness.

I had expected something like this. This was my idea of the colored preacher. But he wasn't like that, far from it. We sat there for a long time, and he never said anything about God. This sort of puzzled me. I didn't think there was a colored preacher who could sit and talk for more than three hours without saying anything about God. But this man was doing it. It seemed as though there was far more to the man than I could see in that visit. But that one visit was enough. I knew I wanted to talk to him again.

He knew a hell of a lot about politics. He could run down the Civil War, shot for shot. It was just astonishing. We talked about things in the Harlem community. I expected him to look down on the Harlem community with an attitude that was partially one of disgust, partially one of sacred disapproval. But he didn't. He looked at the Harlem community somewhat analytically. More than that, he showed a sympathy for junkies that most of the people didn't have.

As a matter of fact, Reverend James seemed to know a lot about street life that I never expected any minister to know. It's not something that you read in the papers or that sort of thing. He just knew people. He understood human nature, and he knew the kind of people who became involved in street life. When he talked about them, he talked about them as people, not as things, fallen souls, or that sort of nonsense. He seemed to be a person, somebody who really knew what was going on. As a matter of fact, at first I suspected him of being an ex-hustler or something like that; but after talking to him, I knew that this couldn't be the case.

Before I realized it, he had me listening to him without any doubts and without any skepticism. I wanted to ask him something about drug addicts, but I didn't want him to suspect that it was about anyone related to me. I hesitated to say anything. I wasn't close enough to him yet.

After a while, I started coming by to see Reverend James just about every other day. I used to like to sit and talk to him. I'd listen to him for hours and hours, and he never got boring. The man knew so much.

As time went on, he kept telling me about school, and why I should want to go to school, this sort of thing. But now I had a bigger problem, and I wasn't too set on going to school, not right away. As a matter of fact, I figured I'd need at least a year, perhaps not to solve the problem, but merely to figure out what I should do about it. So one day, I happened to mention to Reverend James that I had a younger brother named Pimp and that I wanted to do something for him. I told him that Pimp had had some trouble in Harlem, and I was afraid to leave him here all by himself, out in the woods.

He said, "Well, what kind of trouble are you afraid of?"

"Well, he might get involved in some of the vices."

"What vices? Like drug addiction?"

"Yeah, that's a possible one, the most probable one, I suppose."

"Has he gotten involved in it?"

For some reason, I didn't want to tell him. But I didn't see any point in lying to him. I said, "He's had a few small bouts with it."

Reverend James smiled and said, "Yeah, those small bouts are frequent in our community." He started telling me that a person must have a strong attitude toward himself and toward life in order not to become engulfed in the vice of our community. He'd said something about a strong spiritual attitude.

I said, "Slow down a minute, Reverend James. I haven't done much thinking about this spiritual thing, and I haven't done too much thinking about this religious thing either."

"You haven't done too much thinking."

I looked at him for a while. I said, "Yeah, that's a possibility also."

He said, "Now, your brother, I would imagine that he has done less thinking than you. All youngsters in Harlem are confused in their thinking. Their thinking is influenced by their environment, by external values—not their own, but the values of the community, the people around them."

"Yeah, that's true."

"They form their attitudes on the basis of these things. If one boy doesn't want to use drugs, but everybody else is using drugs, he's going to feel as if he's somewhat left out."

"Well, yeah. I've heard all this before."

He told me a little more about drugs and the attitudes toward them. It made Pimp sound so weak to me, it made him sound almost hopelessly lost. I said to myself, I never thought about it this way. It's an attitude in the community. It's fostered by the community. It's the thing to do. I'd been somewhat aware of it, but I'd never given it too much consideration. Aloud I said, "But, look, I came up in the same community and through the same thing."

He said, "Yeah, I'm still wondering about you. It's something of an oddity. You came up in Harlem, and from what I've heard, you've had a pretty reckless life, far from dull. It seems as though you've been undaunted by all these experiences, and I'm wondering why. You seem to be a pretty intelligent young man, and you can be strongly impressed by some things. That's going to take a little time to figure out, but in the meantime, let's get on with the problem of your brother. Look, why don't you bring him around and introduce me to him?"

"Oh, that's fine. But I couldn't introduce you to him as a minister or as somebody that's going to help him."

"No. What does he do?"

I told him that Pimp was going to school and that he was working. I said I thought there was no problem that he would go back on drugs now, but I didn't feel as though I could leave the city without being certain that he was out of the woods and on his way.

Reverend James said, "Well, you've been here all this time. Has your presence here prevented him from getting on drugs?"

I didn't answer that question. I said, "I couldn't go and leave him. That's all. I couldn't do that."

Reverend James said, "Okay, bring him around when you get a chance."

I promised him that I would.

The next time I saw Pimp, he told me that he had stopped going to school.

"Why, man? I thought you went for it."

He said, "Yeah, but I didn't like what they were teaching me, man. They didn't give me the courses that I wanted to take."

"You could always change."

"Yeah, but I messed around in these for eight weeks. I just got tired of that typing and all that kind of stuff."

"Uh-huh. Well, so what are you gonna do now?"

"I'm gonna wait until the next term starts, then I'm going back."

"Okay." I felt a little bad about it, but I knew that I couldn't force anything on him. I didn't mention Reverend James.

About a week later, I went uptown to see the folks. I said, "How's Pimp?"

Mama said, "He's eatin' a lot of sweets."

It was a big blow; it sort of knocked me down. It didn't really frighten me; it just made me very tired. I was depressed. It knocked all the heart out of me, all the fight. All I could do was say, "Well, it doesn't mean that he's usin' stuff, Mama, just because he eats a lot of sweets."

Mama wouldn't look up. She was doing one of the neighborhood kids' hair. She said, "No. No, it doesn't really mean that."

I could hear in her voice that she knew that it was more than just the sweets thing. I said, "You find any works around?"

"No, I didn't find anything."

"Well, that's not so bad, Mama. I'll talk to him and let you know if it's for real. Did he come home from work yet?"

Mama didn't say anything for a while. I waited, and I knew before she answered. I knew because she waited so long. She said, "He didn't go to work."

Then I got nervous. I said, "Mama, has he still got his job?"

"I don't know. He just said he was feelin' bad and wasn't goin' in today."

"Well, Mama, where is he?"

"Oh, he said he was going around Ellen's house. I don't know. Sonny Boy, I don't know where that boy is. I don't know what he's doin'. I don't know nothin' no more. I just don't know. Sometimes I think I'm better off not knowin'. I don't want to know nothin' no more. I don't want to be hurt no more. I don't want to be havin' your daddy tellin' me about I'm a big fool and about 'I knew it all the time.' I don't want to know nothin'."

I said, "Yeah, well, I got to find him." I jumped up and ran out of the house. I was frantic. I just had to find Pimp. I felt as though he was just getting started again, and if I could find him in time, maybe I could save him. Maybe I could do something. Maybe I could stop him.

As soon as I got on the street, I spotted him. He was coming up to the stoop. He was hanging out with some boy from 143rd Street by the name of Joe Norris. I asked him, "Pimp, where you goin', baby?"

He said, "Hey, Sonny. How you doin'?"

I could see he was high and trying to fight it. I said, "Look here, Pimp, why don't you go on upstairs, man?"

He said, "For what?"

"Because you look tired, man. Why don't you go on upstairs and lay down and take it easy?"

Joe Norris said, "Hey, Sonny, how you doin'?"

For some reason or other, I just wanted to hit him. I didn't say anything to him. I couldn't remember the last time I'd been in a fight in the streets, but I wanted to hit him. I knew I had to put my hands on something, so I grabbed Pimp.

This was how it was with me and the anger thing. It would start building up, and I would think that I had control over it. Then, at the height of this "control," I'd just lash out at somebody. I grabbed Pimp by the arm and said, "Come on. Let's go upstairs, man, 'cause I want to talk to you anyway." I went on toward the stoop.

Pimp said, "Yeah, Sonny, I wanted to talk to you too. I need some money, man. I blew my job."

I said, "Yeah, yeah, I figured as much. Come on."

This Joe Norris came up behind us. He said, "Look Pimp, when are you . . ." and I hit him before he got out the rest of what he was saying.

I had Pimp by the arm, and I was trying to take him away from this guy, or perhaps from the street, from all that, and this cat was pushing it. He was pushing it, and I felt as though he was pushing me. I had told him, not in so many words, but when I just didn't say hello to him, when I took Pimp away from him, I was telling him, "Get the fuck out of here, nigger." This was what it amounted to. Still, he didn't get the message. Before I realized it, I had hit him.

He was lying down, looking up as if to say, "Sonny, what the hell is wrong with you?" I started to stomp him, kick him in the face.

Some people were coming out. A preacher who lived in the next house and had known me for a long time came out. Ever since I was a little boy, in my nicer moments, I would run errands for him and his wife. I don't know if he'd seen me hit Joe Norris and knock him down, but as I raised my foot over his face, I heard the voice of Reverend Caldwell. He said, "Hey, Sonny Boy, how you doin'?" as if he didn't realize what I was about to do.

At that point, I realized that I wasn't really angry with Joe Norris. I was angry with Pimp, and I was trying to put it on somebody else, the way Mama would do. I put my foot down, and I said, "I'm sorry, Joe."

He got up and moved away from me. I guess he figured, This cat's crazy, or something like that.

When I turned around, Reverend Caldwell was right behind me. He put his hand on my arm and said, "Sonny Boy, I hope you ain't havin' any trouble out here with none of these people. Look, they can't bother you. You've shown this Eighth Avenue what you can do. Don't let none of those young hoodlums out there get on your nerves or bother you, because they can't do a thing to you. You're on your own and out of it."

I just didn't want to hear it at that time, but I still had a lot of respect for him. I said, "Yeah, thanks a lot, Reverend Caldwell." I said, "Come on, Pimp." I guess Reverend Caldwell thought that I was being a little rude, but at that time I just didn't care. I told Pimp to go on, and I sat down on the stairs in the hall.

I felt bad. I had to pull myself together. I didn't know what had happened. Maybe I was losing out. I hadn't felt this bad in a long time. I used to feel this way about every other day in my childhood. As a matter of fact, it seemed as though the last time I had felt this way it was the time I jumped up, ran out of the house, and asked Turk and Bucky to go with me to steal some sheets.

I started thinking about what had happened the last time I had really gotten violent, what had provoked it. I remember I was in a cafeteria down on Eighth Street and St. Mark's Place. I had taken Judy in there to get something to eat. We were waiting, and I had the tray. I used to come in there all the time by myself. It was a Jewish cafeteria, and the counterman was Jewish too. He used to always smile at me and act friendly.

I came there this time with Judy. We had one tray. We were making our selections together. I had asked her what she wanted. The counterman looked at me scornfully. I said hello to him, because we had always acted friendly toward each other. He just seemed to resent me all of a sudden.

I thought about it, and I realized that it was my being with Judy. To me, he was saying, "I thought you were a good colored boy; you knew your place." He could smile at me as long as he thought I was a good colored boy who knew his place. Once I started acting like a no-good colored boy, or a colored man, he stopped smiling.

After a while, he just turned his back to us. I asked him for something. I didn't know his name, so I just said, "Hey, mister, we would like a cup of fruit salad."

He just never said anything, and he kept his back to us. Two other people came in. They asked him for something. He turned around and served them. I got mad, but I thought, Maybe I'm getting all pissed off about nothing.

Somebody else came in, and he served him too. Then I knew that he was just doing this to spite us, to spite me. He was saying, "Look, you can't come in here and bring that white girl in here and get any service." I felt myself getting hot all over.

Judy grabbed my arm and said, "Come on, Claude, let's go."

I said, "No, wait, Judy. I've got to at least say something. If I go out of here now, I might want to come back and fight him."

She said, "Come on, Claude. It's not that important. Let's forget it. As a matter of fact, they've got crummy food in here anyway. Let's go on Fourteenth Street."

I said, "Wait a minute. Wait a minute. It's okay." They had those heavy plastic trays there. Just when I thought I had control, I threw the tray across the counter and just missed his head. It hit a price sign in back, up over the grill, and it fell down.

It frightened the hell out of the guy. He said, "Hey, call the police! This guy's goin' crazy!"

Judy kept pulling on me. She said, "Come on, Claude. Please, let's go, please, please." We left.

I was sitting on the stairs at my mother's, and I was thinking, Damn, I thought I had grown out of all that sort of thing. I thought I had grown out of hitting anybody in the street. I thought I had grown out of not being able to control my anger. I thought I had grown out of putting the blame on somebody else. I guess I hadn't.

I just sat there for a while. A wino came in. He was talking to himself. He had a bottle of cheap wine, Two Star Port or something like that. He got halfway behind the stairs and started drinking his wine. He made a loud sound, "Ummm!" and he wiped his lips.

I just happened to look at him, and it sort of snapped me out of it. I just realized that he was there and that he seemed to be having so much fun with that wine.

He said, "Hey, buddy, you want some wine?"

I said, "I don't want no fuckin' wine. What's wrong with you?"

"Okay, okay, partner, I didn't mean no harm."

"Look, man, I didn't mean that. I'm sorry. I want some wine, man. Shit, I'm sorry. Give me some wine!"

"Okay, here. Don't take it all, now."

I smiled at the thought of taking all his wine. I hesitated for a long time about putting the bottle up to my mouth, because I had a lot of fears about the germs these cats must carry. But I just went on. I thought, Fuck it, I'm gon drink some wine. I'm gon get with the people again, all the people. I turned it up, drank some wine, and said, "Here, thanks a lot, buddy." I gave him a quarter. I said, "Here's something toward the next one."

He said, "Look, I got twenty cents. I'll go get another one right now, and we could kill it."

"No, no, thanks. You go on and get it, and you kill it."

"Thanks a lot." The cat wanted to talk all kinds of stuff about how somebody had cheated him out of some money and how this other guy, who he thought was his buddy, would hide his wine when he got some. He said he wasn't like that. He would share his wine with anybody. He said, "Like, I come in here and offer you a drink."

I said, "Yeah, yeah, you seem like a generous guy."

"Well, I do that to anybody, especially to all the guys I know around there in the backyard."

"Yeah, you go on. You get another bottle. Have some fun; have a drink for me."

"Yeah, okay, buddy, thanks a whole lot."

I went on upstairs. That wine was burning me up; I never thought it was that strong.

Pimp was sitting in the living room playing some funky jazz records. I went in, and I said, "Pimp, I want you to meet somebody."

"Who's that, Sonny?"

"It's a guy named Reverend James."

He said, "A reverend, man? How'd you get to know any reverend?"

"The cat's a minister, man."

"He's a what?"

"He's a minister."

"A real minister, Sonny? He ain't jivin', is he?"

"No, man. He's a minister."

He said, "Man, I don't know about that. I don't know what you're puttin' down, but I don't believe that it's straight up, Sonny, probably another one of those games. I remember when Billy Graham had his convention down there at Madison Square Garden, and you and Reno went down there with shopping bags, collecting money, and all that kind of shit. If this cat is a real preacher, he better beware, 'cause I know you got somethin' on the fire now."

I said, "No, man. This is straight up."

"Square business, Sonny? You mean he's a real preacher? How do you know him, man? Where do you know him from, and what you doin' with him?"

"I'm not doin' anything with that cat. I'm just talking to him. He's got a church, and he's on a council that's gonna send me to school. I'm trying to get him interested in sending you to school too."

"To college, man?"

"Yeah, man, to college."

"Damn, Sonny, that shit would be real nice. I mean real nice, baby," and he went into a nod.

I said, "Pimp, I want you to come and talk to this cat."

"This is not that other preacher you were tellin' me about? He hasn't got anything to do with that cat, has he?"

"No, this isn't Norman Eddie. He's in the same parish, the East Harlem Protestant Parish. He has this church on 126th Street and Madison Avenue, the Metropolitan Community Methodist Church."

"Oh, yeah. Yeah, I passed that church a few times. Man, what kind of preacher is he? Has this cat really got somethin' on the ball?"

"Man, you wouldn't believe it. You've got to meet the guy."

"Okay, I'll go down there and meet him sometime, but I got to get some money, Sonny."

"Look, let's go down and meet him tonight."

"I got somethin' to do tonight."

"We could go and meet this guy about seven o'clock, and you could do it afterwards."

"Yeah, okay, Sonny, I guess I could do it. But first I have to get some money."

"Uh-uh, Pimp, you got to be straight when you go to see him."

"Man, I can't even get a high?"

"No, man, not even a little high."

"Sonny, I'm just dabblin' now, man, lightly."

"Yeah, Pimp, I know." I couldn' get mad at him any more, because it was something that I'd seen before, time and time again. I'd known that there were strong cats, great cats, who were strung out for a long time. Pimp had never been strung out but for so long. As a matter of fact, he'd never really been strung out. He'd always had someplace to go until Dad put him out, and that wasn't for long. Carole and Margie would keep giving him money. He was their brother, and they loved him. They couldn't see him as a drug addict. They just had to give to him, whether it was going to hurt him in the long run or not. They couldn't stand to see him in pain.

That night we went to see Reverend James. Most of the time, I just listened. Pimp seemed interested in Reverend James, but I think he looked on him as a preacher, and a preacher was just a preacher. They couldn't be but so hip or know but so much about life. Pimp was going to try to outsmart him at every turn, in everything he said.

Reverend James had started telling Pimp about a minister at another church, the Church of the Master. He said this minister had done a lot of work with young drug addicts and users. He said he'd like Pimp to meet him. I was really surprised when Pimp agreed. I didn't expect this.

After we'd been there for about an hour and a half, Reverend James wrote down an address, gave it to Pimp, and said he could go there about 9 A.M. the next day. Pimp said he would.

After we left Reverend James' office, Pimp said that he would go by and see the minister at this Church of the Master the next day. He said, "I liked that cat, man."

"Yeah, Reverend James is a pretty hip guy for a minister."

"Yeah, man. He surprised me with a lot of the stuff he knew."

"Yeah, he's a surprise to most people."

"Yeah, I'm going by tomorrow to see this cat that he told me about, at the Church of the Master, but I want to see this cat again and talk to him. He's got a good mind."

I sort of smiled when Pimp said that, because I knew he didn't really know how good a mind Reverend James had yet. I said, "Yeah, man, I think so too."

Pimp went to see the minister at the Church of the Master, and he got him into something. Pimp wasn't strung out. I don't think he had to have any drugs at this stage of the game. He was just dabbling. He would use it when he wanted to get high. He didn't have to use it if he didn't want to. The minister made arrangements to get Pimp into Metropolitan Hospital, where they had just opened up a new ward. A whole floor was devoted to treating young addicts. Pimp said he was all for it.

He started saying that he was sorry about not continuing in school. Reverend James had told him about a school for people just like him, in North Carolina, that could probably do him a lot of good.

Pimp thought that his whole problem was not being able to get away from Harlem. He said, "Man, this place is . . . it just ruins me, Sonny. I feel like I'm being smothered to death sometimes. If it weren't for you, I guess I could've spent my whole life here and never been downtown, except for the trips that you take in grade school."

I said, "Yeah."

"Or when you get out and start going to work and take the subway downtown."

"Yeah, Pimp, but that all depends on the person, man. Downtown isn't going anywhere. You could go there anytime you want."

He said, "My whole life has revolved around Harlem, man, uptown. I think if I could get out of here, I could see somethin', man, and see somethin' different, see some other kind of life. Shit, I don't know anything, man.

I wanted to go in the service last year, and Mama started talking all that crazy shit about, 'Boy, you'll go in there and you'll get yourself killed. You ain't got no business in nobody's Army.' You know how that is, Sonny. It was, man . . . it was hard. She had to sign for me then. I was only seventeen. She wouldn't let me go. I guess she still sees me as sort of like a second baby. What is it that the old folks called it? The yellin' baby?"

I said, "Yeah, the yellin' baby." We both laughed.

"Yeah, Sonny, I'm gonna make some plans to cut this whole thing loose. As a matter of fact, I think I'll cut Ellen loose too, man."

"Why? She seems to be a nice girl."

"Yeah, but look at it like this, Sonny, I haven't seen any other women. I haven't seen any other girl outside of Harlem. Man, it would be a drag for me to come up in this place, spend my whole life here, get married here, and never go anywhere. That would be a damn shame, Sonny.

"We got this little thing goin'; she's a nice girl and all that, but I'd feel buried right here, man, if I was to go and do somethin' like that. I come up here, and raise all my kids here, and we'd become some hillbillies, man, or some farmers, the people from the woods. We'd be big-city backwoods people, you know, that don't know nothin' about people, even if they lived on the East Side, in the Bronx, or if they lived out in Brooklyn. That's as far as we would go. Sonny, I get scared when I think of that shit."

I couldn't say anything, but I was moved because I never thought that Pimp did that much thinking about this sort of thing. It made me feel good to know that he did and that he had some good thoughts about it. I felt that this was a sign of maturity. I said, "You know, Pimp, I think you're gonna do everything that you want to do, man. I think you can do anything you want to do. There's only one thing that can stop you, and that's shit."

He said, "Yeah, Sonny, I've been thinking about that too, and to tell you the truth, man, I don't know where it is, man. I don't know just where I am with usin' stuff. I don't think that I'm really dependent on it, but if I stay here in Harlem, I know I'm gonna have somethin', man. And right now stuff gives more peace than anything, Sonny, than anything in the world. I couldn't go to church and pray or any kind of shit like that. I couldn't go to bed with the finest chick. There was nothing else that could do anything for me that stuff does for me, man."

He said, "I think if I could get out of here, man . . . I think it's this place, all of it's dead. There's just nothing happenin', man. If you grow up in all this shit, when you get nineteen, there's just nothing else to do. You're through, man. There's just nothin' happening. You've got to find some kind of excitement, something different, or you've just got to keep yourself blind . . . I mean wasted, man, to take all this damn monotony. Boredom. Day in and day out, man, no place to go but the same damn place, nobody to see but the same old faces you've been seeing all your life. That shit can really get on your nerves. You don't know. You have to get away from it somehow. Stuff was the thing for me. This is the only thing that lets me get away.

"Sonny, you know what? I'm gonna go into this new thing, man. They're suppose to have a six-week program in the Metropolitan Hospital that's dynamic, man, really dynamic. I'm gonna go in and see what's happening. And when I come out, I don't want to be hanging around here for any time. I want to get on the train, man, and shoot right down South and get in school, man, start doin' somethin' with my life."

I said, "Yeah, like, it sounds good, Pimp. It sounds damn good. You don't know how good it makes me feel to hear you talkin' like that."

"Yeah, Sonny, I feel as though my mind is clearer, man, than it's been in a long time. For the first time in ages, I'm sayin' the stuff that's really been on my mind."

Pimp went into Metropolitan Hospital for six weeks. He came out looking good. I stayed in his corner while he was in there. I sent him money. When he came out, everybody was happy. Mama was excited over how fat he was.

He came out around April or May, and he got a job. We were planning on sending him down South. Reverend James had selected the perfect school for him. He was all set.

In July, he was working in a hospital. They found out why he had been in Metropolitan, and they fired him. After that, Pimp was hanging around the street most of the time, but he still wasn't dabbling, or so I thought.

When August rolled around, Pimp was supposed to go down South. I was supposed to give him two hundred dollars, which was half of his first term's tuition. I was downtown, and I called Sunday night, the day before he was to leave, and asked Mama if Pimp was there. She said he wasn't. I told her, "When he comes in, tell him to meet me at the bank Monday morning."

Mama said Pimp hadn't been around. He hadn't been home the night before, and she hadn't seen him since early Saturday evening. I said, "He didn't start dabblin' again, did he?" Mama said no, not that she knew of. So

I said, "Look, there's nothing to worry about; as long as he's straight, he's gonna be home. As long as he's not dabblin', there's no problem."

Mama said she wished that she could believe there was no problem. I said, "Why? He's probably shackin' up with some chick. There's nothin' to worry about."

Mama said, "Ellen's been calling him since Saturday evening, and she's called him all day today. She said she hasn't seen him either."

I said, "Look, Mama, he'll probably be home. There's nothing to worry about. Damn, he's a young man, and he'll be all right."

She said, "Yeah, well, I sure hope so, but that ain't like Pimp. That boy, he never stay out all day Sunday and miss his Sunday meal."

"Oh, Mama, come on. He's just growin' up. Maybe he found somebody who could cook better than you."

I tried to make a joke out of it, but Mama was a little bothered. She wasn't in a mood for jokes. She just said, "Yeah, I hope so," and she said it in a sort of frightened way.

"I tell you what, Mama. Just tell him to meet me there tomorrow. I know he'll be back. And I'll call first. Hear?" I felt pretty certain that Pimp would be home that night.

The next morning, I got up and went to the bank. I'd forgotten to call Mama. Instead, I just went to the bank. I'd told Mama to tell Pimp to meet me at nine o'clock. After I'd been there for fifteen minutes, I decided to call Mama to find out whether Pimp was on his way, because the train was supposed to leave at ten-thirty.

I called up, and Mama answered the phone. I said, "Hey, Mama, what happened? Didn't Pimp show up?"

"Lord, child, I ain't seen that boy since he left outta here Saturday evening."

"Oh, hell, he can't be messin' up now. It's too late."

She said, "I hope he ain't, but I got some bad feelings. I been sittin' here lookin' out the window, all day yesterday and all night last night. Lord, I sure don't know where that boy could be, but I sure hope ain't nothin' happened to him."

"Look, Mama, who was he with when he left?"

"He wasn't with nobody. He just went out by himself. The last time I saw him, he was goin' down the avenue by himself."

I jumped on the subway and went uptown. I started going around to all the different dope dens. I started asking all the junkies around there if they'd seen Pimp. Nobody had seen him. Nobody had seen him since Saturday.

I got kind of scared. I went everyplace I could think of where he might possibly be. I even went to the police station, and they didn't know anything. I called the city morgue, and they didn't have anybody by that name. I called hospitals, and they hadn't taken in anybody by that name over the weekend. It seemed like he had just disappeared.

I didn't know what to do. I gave up the idea of his going away to school that morning. This was just out of the question, and I knew this. I hated to tell Mama that I hadn't found him, but eventually she'd have to know. I just kept looking, even though I knew I wasn't going to find him. I didn't know anyplace else to look.

After about twelve o'clock, I felt as though I had to go back and tell Mama something. I came in and said, "Mama, did you hear from him?"

She had looked hopeful when I walked in, but my question just crushed all her hope. She said, "No, I ain't heard nothin'. You couldn't find him?"

"No, Mama, I couldn't find him. But I found out something."

"What?"

"I found out he's not in the morgue, and he's not in the hospital, and he's not in jail."

"Yeah, well, that ain't nothin', because he could be someplace dead, in some backyard, and nobody'd know about it."

"Yeah, Mama, but he don't have to be. Look, Mama, I'm gonna look for him again, and I'll check with you before I go to work. If you don't know anything, I'll just go to work, and I'll look for him after I get off. I'll start looking some more."

I got off that night, and instead of going home, I went uptown and stopped in a bar. I started playing around with a girl friend of Margie's. She asked me if I wanted a drink, and I said, "No, baby, I'm not in the mood for a drink."

She said, "Did you hear about Pimp?"

I got scared. The phrase just echoed through my head, Oh, Lord, and I started trembling. I said, "Look, Cecilia, I'll take that drink now."

She said, "Okay, Sonny, what you gonna have?" She called the barmaid.

I said, "Bourbon. Give me hundred-proof bourbon, straight."

I just dumped it down; I didn't want to taste it. I just wanted a bracer for whatever was to come.

Cecilia got very serious, almost sad. She said, "Oh, well, Sonny, there's . . . Look, I don't think I ought to tell you anyway. Sonny, are you going up to your mother's?"

I said, "Yeah."

She said, "She knows it, and she probably knows more about it than I do. So she'll tell you."

I said, "Look, girl, would you stop playin' with me, and tell me what's on your mind! I don't want to hear that bullshit!"

"Sonny, I'm sorry. I'm sorry I said anything about it."

"Well, you did. Now go on and tell me."

"Okay, if that's the way you want it. Pimp is in jail."

I looked at her, and I could feel myself stop shaking. My body was vibrating, but it was calming down, it was steadying. I grabbed her and held on to her.

She said, "Wow, man, take it easy, will you?"

I guess I was crushing her. I just felt good. More than anything, I needed something to hold on to, and she was the nearest thing.

She said, "Sonny, you better get a hold of yourself, dear. I go with Marty, you know." Marty was the bartender, a big cat, more like a bouncer than a bartender.

"Yeah, well, I hope Marty's understanding," and I laughed.

She said, "You don't seem too upset about it, you know."

"Cecilia, it's not the worst thing that can happen, baby. Look, I'll see you around."

"Sonny, I'm sorry I had to tell you, but I thought you knew."

"That's okay, Cecilia. Look, I'll see you around, baby. Thanks a lot. Take it easy."

I ran across the street, but before I could get upstairs, I saw Louis Howard, Ray, and another old friend Mickey. Mickey was Turk's brother and a friend of Pimp's. Mickey, Lou, and Ray came up to me. Ray had been a counselor up at Wiltwyck. I suppose everybody knew how I felt about Pimp, everybody in the neighborhood anyway. They'd sort of watched me raise him, sort of pull him up by his bootstraps, on the streets. As I came across Eighth Avenue, these three guys were looking at me as though there'd been a wake.

Mickey said, "Sonny, did you hear about Pimp?"

I said, "I heard he was in jail. Cecilia told me. But I don't know what for."

Mickey said, "I called up to find out about him. We were all looking for him, all day. I went around on Seventh Avenue manhandling some junkies."

I said, "Yeah, thanks, baby. I asked them politely, and I couldn't get anything out of them."

Mickey was a pretty big cat. He was almost as big as Turk, and he was known all around the neighborhood for the way he could hit. He'd found out by putting the arm on some junkies. He said, "This junkie told me to call up police headquarters in Brooklyn. I called up, and I asked about Pimp. They said, 'Yeah, we got somebody here by that name.' They said he was arrested Saturday night."

I said, "Did you find out what the charge was, man?"

"Yeah, Sonny, it's an A.R., baby."

I said, "Oh, shit!" I couldn't believe that, because Pimp didn't even have a gun.

Mickey said, "I don't know, Sonny, maybe he was with somebody. I don't know what happened. Maybe he was just an accomplice. All they would tell me was when you could come and see him and that he was going to be arraigned next Monday at the Brooklyn Court of General Sessions."

I said, "Damn, man. That's terrible!"

Lou said, "Don't take it too hard, Claude. You tried."

"Yeah, Lou, but I'm not finished trying yet."

Ray said, "Claude, it just might turn out for the best yet."

I said, "Ray, do you know what that means, man? That means that he's got a sheet on him. He's got a sheet for the rest of his life. Pimp is nineteen."

"Yeah, well, it's not the worst thing that could happen."

I said, "Yeah, he could've been killed. That's a cheerful thought."

I guess everybody saw that I wasn't in a good mood. They started saying, "Well, I'll see you, Claude. Try not to take it too hard."

I went on upstairs and told Mama what I'd heard. She said they had already told her about it.

I got to see Pimp about two days later. It was a frightening place. I couldn't even see his face. It was screened and dark. I was wondering if the cops had beat him. But I couldn't see anything. We were talking through a sort of transmitter.

I said, "Damn, man, you really got yourself into some shit, you know."

He said, "Yeah, well, you know how that is, man. Like you always say, maybe it was in the cards."

I said, "Yeah, man, maybe it was in the cards."

"Shit, Sonny, I don't feel too bad about it, man, and I hope you don't, because, well, hell, everybody's got to pay some dues someday, and I guess it's my time to pay."

"Look, nigger, you ain't in no position to be gettin' so fuckin' philosophical right now. Do you understand the predicament you're in? Pimp, you can get seven to ten years for armed robbery, man."

He said, "Yeah, they might do it. Shit, it's not that bad."

"Look, man, I'm gonna put up bail for you and get you out."

"No, don't do it, Sonny. Save your money. You know why I pulled that sting?"

"Stuff, man?"

"That's right, Sonny. I had to get me some stuff."

"You really did it? I was hopin' that you didn't do it."

"Yeah, I did it, man. I just had to have some money, and I knew if I started askin' anybody for some money, like you or Mama or Carole or Margie, they would've started gettin' worried. They would've known that I was back on stuff, and they would've started worryin' about it. I didn't want to put them through anything, man. I didn't want to put anybody through anything."

"Yeah, well, you really puttin' us through some shit now."

He said, "I didn't expect it to go this way. I'm sorry. I don't want you to spend any money on me to try and get me out on bail. I'm just gonna walk with this. I'm gon face up to it. If I go to court and the bench man throws a dime on me, I'll walk with that too, Sonny. Shit, this is New York. I'll make parole in three years."

I said, "Pimp, the thing is not the parole. You know why I'm spendin' so much money on you, nigger? I wanted to keep you out of jail. I wanted to keep you out of jail before you got a sheet on you."

"Yeah, I understood that, Sonny, and I appreciated it, but this is my life. I've never really gotten into the street life. Nothin' has ever happened to me—until now."

I said, "Yeah, too much is happenin' to you now. You're wasted."

He said, "That's okay, Sonny. It's my life. I don't think you ever realized that it's my life, to waste, to do whatever I want."

"Yeah, Pimp, it looks like you wasted it now. I hope that's what you wanted to do."

He said, "Yeah. Did you see Ellen?"

"No, man. I didn't see anybody."

"She's pregnant, Sonny."

I said, "Yeah, man, that's a beautiful fuckin' situation you're in. Your girl's pregnant, and you're facing an armed robbery bid. Damn. That's just about beautiful."

"Damn, Sonny, I'm surprised at you. You're gettin' to be a worrier in your old age. All the shit you been through and you're all up in the sky like this. I mean, all up on the ceiling, man, over a little thing like this."

"I don't know, Pimp. Shit, I guess I shouldn't worry about it if you're taking it so lightly, huh?"

"Yeah, man. Fuck it, Sonny. Whichever way it comes, man. . . . You heard about the nigger woman and the white woman?"

"Yeah, I heard a lot of things about both of them, but I don't know which thing you're referring to."

"You know the thing about when the white woman brings a male child into the world, she can look at him, smile, and say, 'Son, someday, you may be President.' Sonny, they tell me that he's got one chance in eighty million that he'll be President."

"Yeah, Pimp, that's about right."

"But even if he misses it, Sonny, there's a good chance that he won't be too far from President."

I said, "Uh-huh."

He said, "When a nigger woman brings a male child in the world, she looks at him, shakes her head, and says, 'Oh, my son, forgive me for what I've done.'"

"Damn, Pimp, you sure seem to be not too worried about it."

"The way I look at it, Sonny, it's too late for worryin' now."

"Yeah, well, maybe you've got a point there."

"Like you always say, Sonny, c'est la vie, man. That's the way it went. I guess we all couldn't make it."

"No, Pimp, I guess we couldn't."

I was pissed off, but this just wasn't a time for scolding him.

I saw Pimp a few more times after that. I suppose it didn't go too bad with him. I felt that something had been gained in all of it, that he'd gotten something. I liked, most of all, the way he took it: "This is my bed; I made it myself, and I'll lie in it."

Most people said Pimp was lucky. I guess he was. He only got one to five years. Mama said that Pimp was better off. He couldn't use any drugs up there, and now she knew where he was. In a funny sort of way, maybe he was better off, and maybe everybody was better off.

I made up my mind that I was going to go to school. I didn't know where or what school or what I was going to study, but I knew that I had to go to school somewhere, and it couldn't be in New York.

I tried talking to Tony. Tony had gotten his diploma. He'd graduated from Washington Irving Evening High too. I don't know what happened to him, but he started dabbling. Tony became more and more frustrated. He tried working, but he said he just couldn't get along with these white folks who were running the world. He would quit one job right after another, mess around uptown, and start dabbling more and more and more. He never got hooked. He was a sort of now-and-then drug user. When he was feeling bad or something was bothering him, he would start using drugs. If nothing was bothering him, he just wouldn't use drugs.

I told Tony I was going to try to get ready to go to school in February. Tony said, "Yeah, Sonny, that's damn nice, man."

I told him I could cut him into some people who would aid him in going to school if he wanted to go. He said he'd like to meet them. Anytime I wanted to cut him into them, he'd be ready. I didn't live near Tony any more. He was still living in the Village, and I was living up on Ninetieth Street.

I told him to meet me uptown the next Friday night. I was going to take him to meet Reverend James. I'd told him a lot about Reverend James, and he had said, "Man, he sounds like a powerful cat. I'd like to meet him."

I had been working a heavy tour at the post office, ten to twelve hours a night. I came home that Thursday at about three o'clock in the morning. I'd put in some overtime. When I got in the house, I was real tired. As soon as I hit the bed, the phone rang. Mama was on the other end.

I said, "Hi, Mama. How you doin'?" I got kind of leery, her calling me up so early in the morning. I started joking with her. I said, "Little girl, aren't you ashamed of yourself, bein' up so early in the mornin'? Aren't you sleepy?"

She said, "Boy, I been tryin' to get you all night."

"Well, I work, Mama, you know that."

"Oh, I thought you got off twelve o'clock."

"I'm puttin' in some overtime."

She said, "Oh, well, that's good. Sonny Boy . . ." She stammered and stuttered, "Oh . . . uh . . ." She paused.

I said, "What, Mama?"

She just blurted it out, as if she had to spit it out as fast as she could because she didn't know how else to say it. She said, "Sonny Boy, Tony is dead."

It hit me just like a bullet. I was stunned. I just couldn't say anything for a long time. I think Mama knew the effect it would have on me, because she didn't say anything. The phone was dead for a long time.

I said, "Mama . . ."

"Uh-huh?"

"Did you see him dead?"

"Sonny Boy, everybody on Eighth Avenue knows he's dead. I was over sittin' with his mother tonight, tryin' to get her to relax. The poor woman's almost out of her mind."

"Mama, I'll be uptown. . . . I'll be uptown."

They had the lights on when I got there. Carole and Margie were there. They were all talking about Tony being dead. I just couldn't believe this. I sat there for a long time, and they kept saying it over and over.

Somebody said, "Yeah, he's dead."

And Carole would say, "I guess he is."

I said, "Mama, where? How did they find him? How do you know he's dead? How did he die? Damn, Mama, Tony was only twenty-three or twenty-four."

Mama said, "Well, Sonny Boy, they found him in the backyard."

I said, "They found him in the backyard how?"

"Dead."

"An O.D., Mama?"

She said, "Yeah, I guess so. He died from that dope."

"I don't believe that, Mama, not Tony, because Tony knew what he was doin'. He wouldn't have gotten strung out. He knew how to dabble in drugs. I don't believe he died from any O.D."

Then Carole said, "They say he had a lot of bruises on his face, like somebody'd been hittin' him with somethin' or somebody'd kicked him."

I said, "No, not Tony . . ." I just sat there thinking about it, thinking about wanting to take Tony down to see Reverend James this very evening, thinking about all we'd come through together, and thinking about all the dreams that Tony had had.

Everybody stayed silent, as though they were respecting my thoughts. I got up and said, not to anyone in particular, just to all of them, anybody who happened to be there, "You know, nobody should be so surprised now, because Tony was dyin' for a long time."

Mama said, "What you mean he was dyin' for a long time?"

"Mama, some people look like they're in the best of health. When they start dying, it takes them years and years. I once knew a Japanese guy. He use to work with me. He told me that, in Japan, they don't believe that people die of old age or a natural death. They believe that they just get tired-a livin', Mama. When they start feelin' useless, they just close their eyes. I think Tony was beginnin' to feel as though he wasn't doin' anything, Mama, and he was kind of closin' his eyes for a long time. You know, tryin' to fight that useless feelin'. I don't think he died all of a sudden. Young people don't die that easy, Mama."

18

I haven't lived in New York for nearly four years now, but from time to time I still go back to Harlem to see if the streets are the same, to see if I recognize any of the faces of the junkies along Eighth Avenue, to see if I can recognize any of the slang terms that they're using. It seems as though the changes now are even faster than before.

Sometimes I walk along the street and look at the luxury apartment houses they are building in Harlem and wonder who lives there, what kind of people.

I recall once having met an elderly white man who said he had lived in Harlem around the turn of the century. He told me that he remembered Harlem when the Alhambra Theatre, on 126th Street, was a vaudeville theater. I thought that was really something, because the Alhambra Theatre was far from being a vaudeville theater in my lifetime. My strongest memory of the Alhambra Theatre was standing outside pouring some buttermilk down Danny once when he had taken an O.D. I could never imagine it having once been a vaudeville theater. Then, there are so many things about Harlem that I could never imagine.

I could never imagine the Black Muslims starting riots on 125th Street, but they tell me that they've done it. I could never imagine Alley Bush being in jail accused of murder, but they tell me that he's there.

There are so many things about Harlem that have changed, and they don't seem possible for Harlem. I suppose no one who has ever lived in a Harlem of the world could ever imagine that it could change so drastically and yet maintain so much of its old misery.

Not too long ago, some junkies broke into my folks' house and stabbed my mother. I panicked. When I heard about it, it seemed as though I just forgot everything else in the world. All I knew was that something had to be done about it. Exactly what, I didn't know.

I remember walking the streets, night after night, for nearly two weeks. All night long, I just walked the streets and looked in dope dens and other places where junkies hung out. I remember meeting Rock, who was usually in jail, down on 129th Street. It was surprising to see him so changed, so clean and still so young looking and talking the way he was talking. I told him that I was looking for a junkie named Skippy.

Rock said, "Yeah, I heard about it, Sonny. Just about everybody's heard about it, but, man, I didn't know it was you and your moms."

"Yeah, Rock, I wish it wasn't."

"Yeah, well, Sonny, I hope you're not ready to do anything crazy, man."

"Crazy like what, Rock?"

"Well, you know, Sonny, I've been out on these streets about nine months, man. The one thing I've noticed is that Harlem's changed. Man, it's changed a hell of a lot."

"How do you mean that, Rock?"

"You remember when we were comin' up, man, if a cat fucked with you, you could get your piece and go looking for him. And if he heard that you were lookin' for him, he'd get his piece and start looking for you too."

"Yeah, Rock, I remember."

"Well, man, the shit ain't like that no more, Sonny. It's just not the way it was when we were comin' up."

I looked at him, and I said, "Yeah, I sort of had that feeling." I knew that Rock was going to offer some advice and that I was going to listen. Rock was street-wise. He knew about hurting people and even about killing people. I wasn't sure that that was what I wanted to do, but at the same time, I wasn't sure that it wasn't what I wanted to do. So I listened to him.

Rock went on. He said, "Yeah, if a cat hears you're gunnin' for him now, man, these niggers'll run to the police. You know?"

I said, "Yeah."

"Sonny, if you've got anything on you, baby, your best bet would be to get rid of it in a hurry, because, for one thing, just about everybody in Harlem knows you're lookin' for the nigger."

"Yeah, that's probably true, Rock."

"And another thing, Sonny. You ain't got no business on these streets gunnin' for somebody, huntin' somebody down. Look here, why don't you just let me find him?"

"Rock, you know better than that."

"I'll probably run across the cat anyway."

"What makes you think that you'll do that?"

"I see quite a few junkies, Sonny. Eventually, they all come lookin' for me."

"No wonder you're so clean."

"Yeah, baby, that's the way it is." Then he said, "You can't give up the hunt, huh, Sonny?"

"No, Rock, I can't do it."

"Look, if you can't do that, why don't you just let me come along?"

"No, Rock, thanks for the offer, but I can't do that either." I just wasn't sure that I wanted somebody like Rock along with me, somebody as cold as him. I knew I wanted to hurt this cat when I found him, but I didn't know just how badly I wanted to hurt him. I knew that there was no controlling Rock. I guess I just never forgot the way that boy flew off the roof on 147th Street, or that gang fight on 148th Street. I told him that it was something I felt I had to do by myself.

Rock said, "Okay, Sonny, I can halfway understand that. But, look here, why don't you let me give you a little advice on it?"

"Sure, Rock, maybe you can tell me where to find him?"

"I wish I could. If I could, Sonny, you wouldn't have to find him."

"Yeah, well, thanks anyway."

"Sonny, look, whatever you've got on you, why don't you put it down and just take this roll of pennies from me and do whatever you're gon do with that?"

"With a roll of pennies?"

He said, "You could do a whole lot with a roll of pennies, man."

I sort of laughed at this.

"Look, Sonny, this is not the Harlem that we grew up in."

I said, "Yeah, man, I had that suspicion a few times."

"Sonny, I'm not jokin'. You've got to face it, man. You can't be doin' that old kind of shit no more. What you got to do today if a nigger mistreats you is catch him, break his hands, break his legs, or something like that. That's what you got to do."

"I think you're right there, Rock, I really think you're right."

"Well, if you really think so, man, let me come with you, just to cool you. I think you ought to have somebody with you, somebody whose moms is not involved in it."

I said, "Yeah, Rock, I wish I could, man, but I just can't do it. You know?"

"Yeah, man, I know, but, anyway, good luck."

I never saw Rock again after that. He got busted again, and he was a three-time loser.

I never found Skippy either. The police found him. That was surprising, that the police would really find somebody—that they'd really look for somebody for two weeks—for having hurt somebody else in Harlem. I guess Harlem was changing.

Every time I see Danny, he makes me want to look back into the past and wonder if it was real, if it all happened. The last time I saw Danny, it was on 125th Street. I bumped into him, and we stopped and talked for a while. He had two little kids with him, a boy about three and a girl about four or five. I asked him whose kids they were. I thought they were his niece and nephew or something. He said, "Mine, man."

I said, "Damn." It didn't seem real. I said, "Has it been that long?"

"Yeah, Sonny, it's been that long. I'm really in that father role now, man. I take the kids to church on Sunday, even. Why don't you come and join us sometime, man?"

It almost frightened me. It seemed like the world was changing too much for me. I said, "Look, Danny, I'd feel real out of place in church, man, even still. But, look, the next time you go to church, man, you say a prayer for me."

"Yeah, Sonny, we all will, man. My moms keeps tellin' me that it was all an answer to her prayer. Every time I take the kids by and we have dinner there or she comes by my house for dinner on Sunday, she says grace, man. She comes up out of it with a little smile on her face, looks at the family, and says a little, 'Thank you, Lord.' I don't know. I use to think it was crazy at one time, Sonny, but now, man, I'll tell you the truth, I really don't know."

"Yeah, Danny, I don't know either. Something's happened to people and things. Life seems to have changed."

"Yeah, Sonny, I guess maybe it's for the good, man."

I looked at Danny's little boy, and I said, "What'd you say his name was, Danny?"

"His name is Melvin, man."

"I wonder if he'll play hookey when he gets to school?"

Danny said, "Hell, he better not, 'cause I'll beat his ass and take him to school every mornin' and wait right there for him."

"Yeah, Danny, I bet you will. I bet you know the value of school, more so than most people."

Danny and I talked about people who had come up in the neighborhood. It seemed as though most of the cats that we'd come up with just hadn't made it. Almost everybody was dead or in jail. But I got the feeling that the worst was over for our generation. The plague wave had come, and we were in its path. It just swept through, and then it was gone. It took a lot of people with it.

Danny asked me what had become of people I knew, "those young boys you use to hang out with," meaning Bucky and Mac and Tito and Alley Bush and Dunny. I told him that most of them had gone the same way, that they were in jail, the last I'd heard of them. Mac had settled down, but his brother Bucky was crazy and was still acting up. I'd heard he was doing five years for stealing a car.

Danny said, "Yeah, he always was a kind of crazy cat."

"Yeah, maybe he was."

"I read about Turk, man, in the paper. He's doin' good, making the entire neighborhood proud of him."

"Turk is number two in line for the heavyweight crown, man," I said.

He said, "Yeah, could you imagine that, man? I look around, man, and I wonder if I was there. I see cats now, man, who are strung out, and they were strung out when I was strung out. It looks like they're gonna still be strung out for a long time to come."

"Yeah, maybe they're paying, Danny; maybe they're paying for some of the shit that you and I got away without payin' for."

"Sonny, I hope not, man. I felt as though I had done my sufferin'; I felt as though I had done enough sufferin' for me and for all the sins of all my ancestors. You know?"

"Yeah, Danny, sometimes I felt as though you'd done it too, like you'd suffered for everybody in the world."

Danny laughed and said, "Man, it wasn't that bad. Look here, Sonny, why don't you come by sometime, man?" He gave me his address and his phone number.

"Yeah, Danny, I'll do that."

"My moms always asks about you, man. She asks me if you've been saved yet."

I laughed. "Danny, tell her I've been saved, but I don't think it was by the Lord."

"Sonny, how's Pimp?"

"Pimp's changin', man. Or at least I think he is. The cat finished high school in the joint, got a diploma, and he's talkin' some good stuff. He writes a lot of poetry in the joint."

Danny smiled. "Yeah, man. I know how that is. The joint could make a cat deep sometimes, sometimes it'll make him real deep." We laughed.

I said, "Yeah, Mama says he'll be a real fine young man when he comes out, provided he doesn't become a faggot."

Danny laughed and said, "You know, Sonny, I think, man, with most cats, that stuff is all right in the joint."

"What stuff?"

"You know. Taking other outlets, deviating from normalcy. As a matter of fact, that's a normal way of life in there."

I said, "There's no real fear, man. She wouldn't say anything about it if she thought it were true."

"Yeah, I'd like to see that nigger. I remember the time when I talked to him about drugs and about drug life and about the stuff he'd have to go through. He only seemed fascinated by it, Sonny. It didn't frighten him. I knew, man, I knew that he was gonna be all right."

"How do you mean you knew he was going to be all right?"

"Because he understood it. I was certain that he understood everything that I was telling him, and at the same time, he had to do it on his own. There was somethin' in his eyes that kept tellin' me, 'Shit, if that's the way I'm gonna have to suffer and if that's what's waitin' for me, I'm just gonna go on and meet it.' Pimp was a game little cat, Sonny, and somebody like that's got to make it, man. Those are the cats who always do."

"Yeah, Danny, I hope you're right."

I haven't seen Danny lately, but I've seen so many other people in Harlem. Most of the junkies around there now are young cats; they're younger than Danny and younger than me. I wish I could get out in Harlem in a truck with a loudspeaker on it, like the politicians do around election time, and just tell the story of Danny to some of the cats out there on the streets nodding and scratching—and maybe tell the story about Turk, the stuff he came through, and the achievements he made despite it all.

I'd like to show them that despite everything that Harlem did to our generation, I think it gave something to a few. It gave them a strength that couldn't be obtained anywhere else.

The last time I walked up 145th Street, I remembered the little boy and the dog with the black spot over his eye, and the boy standing in front of me and saying, "I want to be like you." I thought, Well, maybe now I wouldn't be so embarrassed about it all. But I thought that there were a lot of guys around there who would have been a better example, guys like Turk and Danny. There were a few cats who'd made it pretty big.

It was unbelievable to think about Tony being dead, having died before he'd had a chance to realize the things he was struggling for. He had tried so hard. It was unfair of life not to hold on to him a little longer.

Every time I visit Greenwich Village and pass by the old place where we used to hang out—where we hid from Harlem during the uncertain period—I remember that there was somebody else who had wanted to make it too. I always have the feeling that I have to make it for both of us. I remember the times when we got high and walked around the streets in Harlem and planned to save the neighborhood one day. It was really some dream.

It seemed to me that somebody or something else had also had a dream, somebody or something else that I hadn't even been aware of. This dream was there, and slowly but surely, it was coming true. Somebody had had a dream that all Harlem would be completely changed in about ten years.

It seemed as though most of the old tenements have gone. I can hardly recognize Lenox Avenue any more. A whole section of Lenox Avenue where there used to be a lot of drug dens—from 132nd Street to 135th Street—is gone. Now they've got big apartment houses. Only now does it seem to be becoming more of everybody's Harlem.

Al Betts was talking about moving back to Harlem. He said they had some fabulous houses in Harlem now, and this was where his heart was anyway. He'd always wanted to live there, but he couldn't get a decent apartment. Now that it was possible to live there respectably, he felt that he could go back there and really be happy.

I told Al Betts I could hardly wait to get back myself.

The last time I saw St. John, he was still deeply involved in the Coptic. He asked me, "How are you?" in Amharic. I knew what he said, but I couldn't answer him. I felt slightly embarrassed. He looked at me and smiled. "Yeah, Sonny, everybody forgets the word."

I said, "Yeah, I don't know it. I forgot it, St. John." I asked St. John how was

Father Ford. He told me that Father Ford was dead. I said, "I never would've believed it, because he seemed to be a person who was perpetually young and would never grow old. He looked like the perennial young man."

St. John said, "He didn't just die, man. They killed him."

I said, "Who killed him?"

"Those white people killed him, man, for tellin' the truth."

"Oh, did they find out who did it?"

"No, man. He was working at this place. You know how Father was. He'd tell the truth anywhere he was. He was workin' around all those white people. One day they just found him dead, man, down in this boiler room. They said he must've slipped and fell, hit his head on somethin'. But I know better, Sonny. I know Father Ford wasn't the slippin' kind. You know? It would've taken far more than a hit on the head to take all the life out of that man. He was filled with life."

"Yeah, St. John, but so was Christ."

"Sonny, I hope you don't believe that. Christ is still down there in Ethiopia, still filled with life."

"Yeah, I forget sometimes, St. John."

"Yeah, everybody's been forgettin', Sonny, but it won't be long before we'll all know. Sonny, until you come back in the fold, peace, brother."

"Yeah, peace, St. John."

The last time I saw Reno was on the streets in mid-Manhattan about four years ago. Reno looked much older. Maybe it was the hard life. He was walking fast, looking nowhere, and seeing everything. So I knew he had to be jostling, still.

He acted as though he hadn't seen me. I waited for a while to see if he was in the middle of a trick. After I watched him walk down the street for a half a block, I caught up with him and spoke to him. He turned around, almost too fast, when I said, "Hey, Reno."

He said, "Hey, Sonny, how you doin'?" But he was kind of cold.

"Oh, I'm doin' fine, man."

"Yeah, I haven't seen you around lately, man. I've been asking about you, and nobody seems to know where you cut out to."

"Well, I left town, man."

"Yeah, I heard. Is there anything to that rumor, man, about you goin' to school?"

"Yeah, Reno, it's something different, something to do."

Reno threw up both hands, as if to say, "Wow, what a change!" He sort of backed away from me. Then he smiled and said, "Sonny, I always knew you had somethin' like that in you, man. I'm kind of glad that you went on and did it."

"So am I, Reno, because I felt as though I wasn't goin' anyplace in Harlem. I wasn't doin' anything."

"Yeah, that's understandable, Sonny."

I said, "What are you doin' for yourself?"

"Well, you see where I'm at, Sonny. It's the same old thing with me, man. I guess I'm too old to ever change my game, you know?"

"Man, why don't you stop talkin' that nonsense, Reno. I always figured you for a cat who would go places and do things, a whole lot of things."

"Yeah, Sonny, maybe I could go to college, huh? Yeah, but what would I do there, man, but screw all the fine young bitches they got there until they threw me out or somethin'?"

"Yeah, I'll bet." I'd always felt that Reno really had something on the ball. But this is the way it was. He'd resigned himself to the jostling life a long time ago. I had the feeling that he resented me for not resigning myself to a life of petty crime.

He asked me, "Sonny, what you doin', man?"

"I told you, man, knockin' about in school."

"Yeah, but what you studyin', man? You must be into somethin' down there."

"I haven't made up my mind yet what I'm gonna get into."

"Well, do me one favor, man."

"What's that?"

"Now, baby, don't go down there and come back the Man. That'd be some real wicked shit. All the stuff we been through together, if you became the Man and busted me or any of the cats around the neighborhood, that shit would really hurt, man."

"Yeah, I guess it would, Reno." I laughed. I said, "Yeah, imagine me becoming the Man. Even I wouldn't know how to take it."

"That's good. That's good, man. You want to get high, Sonny? I'm not doin' anything now."

"I thought you were takin' care of business."

"Man, shit, that can wait. There's a lot of time for business. I don't see you every day. Who knows? I may need you for somethin' one day. You go down there and you become a big-time lawyer, big-time doctor, big-time teacher, big-time anything. Just don't become a big-time preacher, Sonny. I just can't use you if you go and do somethin' like that."

"I think that's another thing you won't have to worry about, Reno."

"Come on, Sonny, let's get high."

"No, Reno, I don't get high any more."

"Damn, man. They really turned you around at that place, huh?"

"I stopped gettin' high before I went down there, man."

"Oh, yeah, that's right, I remember. You want a drink, man?"

I felt sort of compelled to take it because it was a second offer, a second attempt by Reno to maintain the old friendship. Reno and I went into one of the bars on Forty-third Street and had a couple of drinks. I could tell that the liquor didn't agree with him.

He started telling me about how he wished he had gotten out of Harlem. I said, "Yeah, there are other things to see, but as far as education goes, I don't think anyplace offers a greater one than the Harlem streets, man, right here." I told him I had found out since I had been in school that the things that were most educational were those I'd learned outside the classroom.

He said, "Yeah, Sonny, I can dig that, man. I learned a whole lot of shit out here. The hippest cats I've met, man, were the cats who just came up in the streets. But we still don't make it to college. I'm kind of puzzled at that stuff you did. I still don't know what's behind it, but knowing that it's you, baby, it's got to be all right. It's got to be somethin' to it."

"I wish I could throw some light on it, Reno, but I'm not sure what it's all about myself. I just looked up one day and found me in this groove. That's how it's been with me all the time, Reno. I have admired you from way back, man, because of all the stuff you showed me, not only the stuff you knew, but the way you just made decisions, man, on a snap, and said, 'If I hit, I'll make it. And if I miss, fuck it.'

"Reno, I remember the first time you took me downtown to cut me into the Murphy. I asked you, I said, 'Look here, man, tell me just what happens.' Then you started runnin' it down to me. You said, 'It's simple, Sonny, really. If everything goes off like we plan, we'll each have a good two hundred dollars in our pockets by the time we come back uptown. And if it doesn't go off like we plan, we'll probably be in jail. It's as simple as that.' Reno, that was one of the first times in my life that I didn't mind goin' to jail, that I felt I was ready to go to jail. I admired you for bein' able to assume that attitude, man. I was certain that the things you'd done in street life had given it to you. I saw it as a maturity, man, that I strived for a long time after that."

He said, "Oh, man, come on. Don't bullshit me, Sonny."

"No, man, I'm not stuffin'."

"That's funny, but, believe it or not, Sonny, I've been to college, man; I've been there too. Only, I've been to a different college."

"I'm not readin' you yet, baby."

"Yeah, Sonny. The time I did in Woodburn, the times I did on the Rock, that was college, man. Believe me, it was college. I did four years in Woodburn. And I guess I've done a total of about two years on the Rock in about the last six years. Every time I went there, I learned a little more. When I go to jail now, Sonny, I live, man. I'm right at home. That's the good part about it. If you look at it, Sonny, a cat like me is just cut out to be in jail.

"It never could hurt me, 'cause I never had what the good folks call a home and all that kind of shit to begin with. So when I went to jail, the first time I went away, when I went to Warwick, I made my own home. It was all right. Shit, I learned how to live. Now when I go back to the joint, anywhere I go, I know some people. If I go to any of the jails in New York, or if I go to a slam in Jersey, even, I still run into a lot of cats I know. It's almost like a family."

I said, "Yeah, Reno, it's good that a cat can be so happy in jail. I guess all it takes to be happy in anything is knowin' how to walk with your lot, whatever it is, in life."

Reno put out his hand for me to give him five, and I slapped it. "Sonny, you want another drink?"

"No, man, I'm movin', Reno. I've got to be someplace."

"Yeah, well, me too. I got to get ready for somethin', get ready to get me some money, or either get ready to do some time."

I tapped him on the shoulder and said, "Good luck, Reno."

"Later, baby. I'll see you around."

I had the feeling that Reno had managed to become one of the happiest people in Harlem. I felt very close to Reno. People used to say that friends were "as thick as thieves." Maybe I had a thief's affinity for him. He had taught me a lot.

Reno was somebody right from the streets. I think he took to me because he saw me as somebody from the streets, somebody who hated to see the sun go down on Eighth Avenue, who would run up on Amsterdam Avenue, follow the sun down the hill, across Broadway, to the Drive and the Hudson River, and then would wait for the sun to come back. I guess Reno thought he'd found somebody who was destined to be in the streets of Harlem for the rest of his life.

I felt as though I had let him down. I was saying, "Look, man, we aren't destined. You just bullshitted yourself and messed all up." But I guess he hadn't, really. He'd just made his choice, and I'd made mine.

As a child, I remember being morbidly afraid. It was a fear that was like a fever that never let up. Sometimes it became so intense that it would just swallow you. At other times, it just kept you shaking. But it was always there. I suppose, in Harlem, even now, the fear is still there.

When I first moved away from the folks, it seemed as though I was moving deeper into the Harlem life that I had wanted to become a part of and farther away from what Mama and Dad wanted me to become a part of. I think, as time went on, they both became aware that the down-home life had kind of had its day. But they didn't know just what was to follow, so how could they tell me?

I didn't realize it until after I had gotten out, but there were other cats in Harlem who were afraid too. They were afraid of getting out of Harlem; they were afraid to go away from their parents. There were some cats who would stay at home; they wouldn't work; they wouldn't do anything. I didn't see how they could do it, but they seemed to manage. They just didn't feel anything about it, but it was pretty evident that they were afraid of not being able to turn to their parents when things got rough. And they were afraid of getting out there and not being able to make it.

When I moved up on Hamilton Terrace, I suppose I still had my fears, but it was something. It was a move away from fear, toward challenges, toward the positive anger that I think every young man should have. All the time before, I thought I was angry. I guess I was, but the anger was stifled. It was an impotent anger because it was stifled by fear. I was more afraid than I was angry. There were many times when I wondered if Rock would have hurt anybody if he hadn't been in Harlem . . . or if Johnny Wilkes would have been so mean if he hadn't been in Harlem. I was afraid of what Harlem could bring out in a person. When I decided to move, I was trying to get away from the fear.

Everybody I knew in Harlem seemed to have some kind of dream. I didn't have any dreams, not really. I didn't have any dreams for hitting the number. I didn't have any dreams for getting a big car or a fine wardrobe. I bought expensive clothes because it was a fad. It was the thing to do, just to show that you had money. I wanted to be a part of what was going on, and this was what was going on.

I didn't have any dreams of becoming anything. All I knew for certain was that I had my fears. I suppose just about everybody else knew the same thing. They had their dreams, though, and I guess that's what they had over me. As time went by, I was sorry for the people whose dreams were never realized.

When Butch was alive, sometimes I would go uptown to see him. He'd be sick. He'd be really messed up. I'd give him some drugs, and then he'd be more messed up than before. He wouldn't be sick, but I couldn't talk to him, I couldn't reach him. He'd be just sitting on a stoop nodding. Sometimes he'd be slobbering over himself.

I used to remember Butch's dream. Around 1950, he used to dream of becoming the best thief in Harlem. It wasn't a big dream. To him, it was a big dream, but I don't suppose too many people would have seen it as that. Still, I felt sorry for him because it was his dream. I suppose the first time he put the spike in his arm every dream he'd ever had was thrown out the window. Sometimes I wanted to shout at him or snatch him by the throat and say, "Butch, what about your dream?" But there were so many dreams that were lost for a little bit of duji.

I remember Reno used to say that all he wanted was two bars in Harlem and two Cadillacs. It sounded like something that was all right to me. I used to envy Reno for his dream.

When he first told me, I thought to myself, Wow, if I could just want two bars and two Cadillacs. I was hoping all the time that he'd make it. Once I asked him, "Reno, what's the two Cadillacs for, man? You can only drive one at a time."

He said, "One I'm gon get for my woman."

I said, "Oh, then the other one'll be hers."

"No, man, you can't expect but so much out of a bitch, not any bitch, I don't care how good she is."

"Uh-huh. So what?"

Reno said, "Every time a bitch fucks up, I'm gonna just cut her loose and get another one. Every time I get a new bitch, the other Cadillac's gon be hers. You dig it?"

"Yeah, I dig it. It sounds like a pretty hip life."

"I don't know, man, but that's what I want to do, Sonny."

"Yeah, Reno, I guess that's all that matters, that a cat does what he wants to do."

I used to feel that I belonged on the Harlem streets and that, regardless of what I did, nobody had any business to take me off the streets.

I remember when I ran away from shelters, places that they sent me to, here in the city. I never ran away with the thought in mind of coming home. I always ran away to get back to the streets. I always thought of Harlem as home, but I never thought of Harlem as being in the house. To me, home was the streets. I suppose there were many people who felt that. If home was so miserable, the street was the place to be. I wonder if mine was really so miserable, or if it was that there was so much happening out in the street that it made home seem such a dull and dismal place.

When I was very young—about five years old, maybe younger—I would always be sitting out on the stoop. I remember Mama telling me and Carole to sit on the stoop and not to move away from in front of the door. Even when it was time to go up and Carole would be pulling on me to come upstairs and eat, I never wanted to go, because there was so much out there in that street.

You might see somebody get cut or killed. I could go out in the street for an afternoon, and I would see so much that, when I came in the house, I'd be talking and talking for what seemed like hours. Dad would say, "Boy, why don't you stop that lyin'? You know you didn' see all that. You know you didn't see nobody do that." But I knew I had.

Manchild in the Promised Land

For Discussion

1. To what does the promised land in the book's title refer?

2. When Claude is admitted into Bellevue Hospital's psychiatric division as a child, he is comforted by the fact that he will be away from his father for a few weeks. How would you characterize Claude's relationship with his father? How does it compare to Claude's relationship with his mother?

3. How do Claude's parents explain his misbehavior as a youth? Why does his mother think someone caused it by "working roots" on him or that he was "born with the devil in him" (page 12)?

4. How does the shell game that Claude's father plays with him before he leaves home for reform school at Wiltwyck enable Claude to see his father in a different light? What does Claude's father understand about his son?

5. How does Claude's early friendship with K.B. at Wiltwyck bear fruit later in life when he is enrolled at Warwick?

6. How does the arrival of Ernst Papanek, the new director of Wiltwyck, forever alter the course of Claude's life? Discuss his influence on Claude and the other inhabitants of Wiltwyck.

7. How does the court award that Claude receives for his bus injury raise his awareness of social injustice? What roles do race and class play in Claude's experiences of inequality?

8. Discuss Claude's first use of horse (heroin). Why does this experience change his feelings about using drugs?

9. Consider the examples of masculinity in Claude's young life: his father; Ernst Papanek, the director at Wiltwyck; Johnny, the drug dealer in his building. How do these men shape Claude's sense of self? To what extent does he model his own behavior after them?

10. Discuss the hopelessness that Claude feels about his future on the street. What opportunities are available to him if he remains in Harlem?

11. Describe the culture at reform schools like Wiltwyck and Warwick. How effective are these schools?

12. At Warwick, Claude encounters music and literature, seemingly for the first time. Why are these discoveries so significant to him then? How do they have an impact on him as an adult?

13. Claude's parents are migrant farmers from South Carolina who move to Harlem to seek a better life. To what extent are Claude's early conflicts with his parents grounded in the differences that arise from their rural and urban backgrounds?

14. How does Claude's determination not to see jail time, or to get "a sheet," propel his move from Harlem to Greenwich Village?

15. Describe the role religion plays in Claude's life. To what extent does he believe in God?

16. How do Claude's feelings about Harlem change as he applies himself to his job at the watch repair shop, working out at the gym, and practicing piano day and night?

17. Discuss how Claude feels as he watches his younger brother, Pimp, get swept up in petty crime and drug abuse.

18. Why do Claude's parents encourage him and Pimp to get jobs rather than stay in school? What does this reveal about their dreams for their children?

19. Discuss Claude's casual encounter in Harlem with a little boy walking his dog who tells him, "I want to be like you" (page 278). Why does this experience resonate so powerfully for Claude?

20. Discuss Claude's friendship with Judy Strumph. Claude writes of Judy: "[S]he was the best thing that had ever happened to me." How does his relationship with Judy differ from his prior romantic attachments?

21. How does Claude make sense of his decision to choose education over life on the street in Harlem? How does he explain it to Reno—his old friend from the neighborhood—and to himself?

22. Discuss the rise of the Coptic faith and the Nation of Islam in Harlem in the 1950s. How does this affect Claude Brown?

23. What themes of friendship does *Manchild in the Promised Land* explore? How do the bonds of friendship that Claude establishes in Harlem and in Greenwich Village factor into his childhood and into his development as an adult?

24. Discuss the attitudes about race in *Manchild in the Promised Land*. How does Claude Brown experience race as a resident of Harlem? How does he experience race in other places?

25. If *Manchild in the Promised Land* had been written as a novel inspired by Claude Brown's childhood, rather than one that is almost a memoir, how might its impact on readers have differed?

26. Of the many episodes from Claude Brown's life described in *Manchild in the Promised Land*, which do you feel were most instrumental in helping him escape the life that awaited him if he remained in Harlem?

Guide prepared by Julie Cooper, a graduate of Harvard University, Oxford University, and the University of Washington.